Modern American Drama: Playwriting in the 1930s

DECADES OF MODERN AMERICAN DRAMA: PLAYWRITING FROM THE 1930s TO 2009

Modern American Drama: Playwriting in the 1930s
by Anne Fletcher

Modern American Drama: Playwriting in the 1940s
by Felicia Hardison Londré

Modern American Drama: Playwriting in the 1950s
by Susan C. W. Abbotson

Modern American Drama: Playwriting in the 1960s
by Mike Sell

Modern American Drama: Playwriting in the 1970s
by Mike Vanden Heuvel

Modern American Drama: Playwriting in the 1980s
by Sandra G. Shannon

Modern American Drama: Playwriting in the 1990s
by Cheryl Black and Sharon Friedman

Modern American Drama: Playwriting 2000–2009
by Julia Listengarten and Cindy Rosenthal

Modern American Drama: Playwriting in the 1930s

Voices, Documents, New Interpretations

Anne Fletcher

Series Editors: Brenda Murphy and Julia Listengarten

methuen | drama
LONDON • NEW YORK • OXFORD • NEW DELHI • SYDNEY

METHUEN DRAMA
Bloomsbury Publishing Plc
50 Bedford Square, London, WC1B 3DP, UK
1385 Broadway, New York, NY 10018, USA
29 Earlsfort Terrace, Dublin 2, Ireland

BLOOMSBURY, METHUEN DRAMA and the Methuen Drama logo
are trademarks of Bloomsbury Publishing Plc

First published in Great Britain 2018
Paperback edition first published 2021

Copyright © Anne Fletcher and contributors, 2018

Anne Fletcher has asserted her right under the Copyright,
Designs and Patents Act, 1988, to be identified as author of this work.

For legal purposes the Acknowledgements on p. ix constitute
an extension of this copyright page.

Cover design: Louise Dugdale
Cover image © Bastos/Adobe Stock

All rights reserved. No part of this publication may be reproduced or
transmitted in any form or by any means, electronic or mechanical,
including photocopying, recording, or any information storage or retrieval
system, without prior permission in writing from the publishers.

Bloomsbury Publishing Plc does not have any control over, or responsibility for,
any third-party websites referred to or in this book. All internet addresses given
in this book were correct at the time of going to press. The author and publisher
regret any inconvenience caused if addresses have changed or sites have
ceased to exist, but can accept no responsibility for any such changes.

A catalogue record for this book is available from the British Library.

A catalog record for this book is available from the Library of Congress.

ISBN: HB: 978-1-4725-7187-8
PB: 978-1-3502-1548-1
ePDF: 978-1-3501-5360-8
eBook: 978-1-3501-5359-2
Pack: 978-1-4725-7264-6

Series: Decades of American Drama: Playwriting from the 1930s to 2009

Typeset by Fakenham Prepress Solutions, Fakenham, Norfolk NR21 8NN

To find out more about our authors and books visit
www.bloomsbury.com and sign up for our newsletters.

CONTENTS

Acknowledgements ix
Biographical Note and Notes on Contributors x
General Preface Julia Listengarten and Brenda Murphy xii

1 Introduction to the 1930s *Anne Fletcher* 1
   Life in the 1930s 1
   The Great Depression and the New Deal 4
   Domestic life 6
   Education 8
   Sports and recreation 10
   Science and technology 11
   Labour and the working class 13
   Arts and culture 14
      Literature 16
      Poetry 19
      Painting 20
      Photography 21
      Architecture and design 21
      Music 22
      Dance 23
      Media 24
      Radio 25
      Film 26

2 American Theatre in the 1930s *Anne Fletcher* 29
   Before the Crash 29

After the economic collapse: The 1930s 31
Labour(ing) drama: The production companies, the
  playwrights and the plays 37
Not a success story for John Howard Lawson 49
Poetry and politics: Maxwell Anderson 58
No time for comedy? 61
Hokum: High and low 67
The mythic, the surreal and the sublime: William Saroyan's
  My Heart's in the Highlands and *The Time of Your Life* 77

3   Gertrude Stein: *Four Saints in Three Acts*
    (written in 1927, published in 1932), *Doctor
    Faustus Lights the Lights* (1938), *Listen To Me*
    (1936) *Laura Schultz* 81

Early life 83
Early writing 86
Approaching the play 88
Conversation pieces and landscape plays 91
Identity and fame 93
The war and after the war 96
How many saints are there in it?: *Four Saints in Three
  Acts* 99
Gertrude Stein and Thornton Wilder 106
And the dog says thank you: *Doctor Faustus Lights the
  Lights* 108
Important productions of *Doctor Faustus Lights the
  Lights* 112
Nobody has met anyone: *Listen To Me* 114
The impact and legacy of Gertrude Stein on theatre and
  performance 118
Gertrude Stein onstage 119

4 Langston Hughes: *Mulatto* (1935), *The Mule Bone* (1930) (with Zora Neale Hurston), *Little Ham* (1936) Adrienne Macki 121

Mulatto 127
The Mule Bone: A Comedy of Negro Life 133
Little Ham 139
Conclusion 142

5 Clifford Odets: *Waiting for Lefty* (1935), *Awake and Sing!* (1935), *Paradise Lost* (1935), *Golden Boy* (1937), *Rocket to the Moon* (1938), *Night Music* (1940) Christopher J. Herr 145

Waiting for Lefty 153
Awake and Sing! 157
Paradise Lost 161
Golden Boy 164
Rocket to the Moon and *Night Music* 167

6 Lillian Hellman: *The Children's Hour* (1934), *Days to Come* (1936), *The Little Foxes* (1939) Anne Fletcher 171

The Children's Hour 177
Maybe too well-made 179
Days to Come 183
The Little Foxes 186
The plays today 191

Afterword Anne Fletcher 195

Gertrude Stein – 'What is the answer?' 201
Langston Hughes – 'I, too, am America' 205
Clifford Odets – 'The last sixteen wasted years' 207
Lillian Hellman – 'No secrets about her feelings' 212

Documents 219

Excerpts from the Gertrude Stein Symposium at New York University (2001) 219

Langston Hughes, 'The Negro Artist and the Racial Mountain' (1926) 221

'Langston Hughes Proposes an Oath to End All Oaths for Americans' (1951) 226

Excerpts from Clifford Odets's HUAC testimony (1952) 228

Draft of Lillian Hellman's letter to HUAC, written in the form of a public statement, to be issued in the event Hellman refused to testify (1952) 234

Workers' theatre: Excerpts from Mordecai Gorelik, 'Theatre is a Weapon' (1934) 236

Notes 243
Bibliography 277
Index 291

ACKNOWLEDGEMENTS

I would like to thank series editors Brenda Murphy and Julia Listengarten for offering me this opportunity to expand my ongoing exploration of American theatre of the 1930s. Brenda – whose work I have always greatly admired – was remarkably available to me throughout the process of compiling this volume. The fine scholarship of Adrienne Macki, Chris Herr and Laura Schultz in each of their chapters adds continuity to the work. I would also like to thank Mark Dudgeon and his staff for their patience and confidence in our work.

BIOGRAPHICAL NOTE AND NOTES ON CONTRIBUTORS

Anne Fletcher is Professor of Theatre at Southern Illinois University Carbondale. She is the author of *Rediscovering Mordecai Gorelik: Scene Design and the American Theatre* (2009), and co-author (with Scott R. Irelan and Julie Felise Dubiner) of *The Process of Dramaturgy: A Handbook* (2010) and (with Scott R. Irelan) *Experiencing Theatre* (2015). Fletcher's work has appeared in assorted journals, and she has contributed book chapters on 1930s theatre and American labour drama in particular, but also on American scene design, Thornton Wilder and Lillian Hellman.

Christopher J. Herr is Professor and Chair of the Department of Theatre & Dance at Missouri State University. He is the author of *Clifford Odets and American Political Theatre* (2003). Herr's further work on Odets, as well as on American political drama, interwar theatre and satire, has been published in various collections.

Adrienne Macki is Associate Professor of Theatre History/Criticism/Literature and Faculty Affiliate in the Institute for African American Studies at the University of Connecticut, where she specializes in black drama and performance, early twentieth-century American drama and gender/performance. Macki is the author of *Harlem's Theatres: A Staging Ground for Community, Class, and Contradiction, 1923–1939* (2015) and has published several articles and chapters on African-American theatre.

Laura Luise Schultz is Associate Professor in Theatre and Performance Studies in the Department of Arts and Cultural Studies at the University of Copenhagen. Her dissertation was on Gertrude Stein's plays, and she is the co-editor of *Gertrude Stein in Europe: Reconfigurations Across Media, Disciplines, and Traditions* (2015).

GENERAL PREFACE

Decades of Modern American Drama: Playwriting from the 1930s to 2009 is a series of eight volumes about American theatre and drama, each focusing on a particular decade during the period between 1930 and 2010. It begins with the 1930s, the decade when Eugene O'Neill was awarded the Nobel Prize for Literature and American theatre came of age. This is followed by the decade of the country's most acclaimed theatre, when O'Neill, Tennessee Williams and Arthur Miller were writing their most distinguished work and a theatrical idiom known as 'the American style' was seen in theatres throughout the world. Its place in the world repertoire established, American playwriting has taken many turns since 1950.

The aim of this series of volumes is to focus attention on individual playwrights or collaborative teams who together reflect the variety and range of American drama during the 80-year period it covers. In each volume, contributing experts offer detailed critical essays on four playwrights or collaborators and the significant work they produced during the decade. The essays on playwrights are presented in a rich interpretive context, which provides a contemporary perspective on both the theatre and American life and culture during the decade. The careers of the playwrights before and after the decade are summarized as well, and a section of documents, including interviews, manuscripts, reviews, brief essays and other items, sheds further light on the playwrights and their plays.

The process of choosing such a limited number of playwrights to represent the American theatre of this period has been a difficult but revealing one. In selecting them, the series editors and volume authors have been guided by several principles: highlighting the most significant playwrights, in terms both historical and aesthetic, who contributed at least two interesting and important plays during the decade; providing a wide-ranging view of the decade's theatre, including both Broadway and alternative venues; examining many historical trends in playwriting and theatrical production during the decade; and reflecting the theatre's diversity in gender and ethnicity, both across the decade and across the period as a whole. In some decades, the choices are obvious. It is hard to argue with O'Neill, Williams, Miller and Wilder in the 1940s. Other decades required a good deal of thought and discussion. Readers will inevitably regret that favourite playwrights are left out. We can only respond that we regret it too, but we believe that the playwrights who are included reflect a representative sample of the best and most interesting American playwriting during the period.

While each of the books has the same fundamental elements – an overview of life and culture during the decade, an overview of the decade's theatre and drama, the four essays on the playwrights, a section of documents, an Afterword bringing the playwrights' careers up to date, and a Bibliography of works both on the individual playwrights and on the decade in general – there are differences among the books depending on each individual volume author's decisions about how to represent and treat the decade. The various formats chosen by the volume authors for the overview essays, the wide variety of playwrights, from the canonical to the contemporary avant-garde, and the varied perspectives of the contributors' essays make for very different individual volumes. Each of the volumes stands on its own as a history of theatre in the decade and a critical study of the four individual playwrights or collaborative teams included. Taken together, however, the eight volumes offer a broadly representative critical and historical treatment of 80 years of American theatre and drama that is both accessible to a student first encountering the subject and informative and provocative for a seasoned expert.

Brenda Murphy (Board of Trustees Distinguished Professor Emeritus, University of Connecticut, USA)
Julia Listengarten (Professor of Theatre at the University of Central Florida, USA)
Series Editors

1

Introduction to the 1930s

Anne Fletcher

Life in the 1930s

The American lived experience belied the homogeneity with which the Great Depression era is generally viewed. While historians and lay people alike find convenience in contrast as an organizing principle – rich versus poor, left versus right, etcetera – the decade of the 1930s reveals itself as both dichotomous and diverse.

Contrasts, coincidences and incongruities abound in the areas of domestic life, education, consumerism, popular entertainment, art, culture, virtually every aspect of daily life. On the one hand, pastimes like the Sunday drive (car ownership was surprisingly widespread then), listening to the radio and going to the movies transcend social class and offer a classless experience, a 'level playing field'. On the other hand, soup kitchens in major cities and the black rollers (moving topsoil), black rain comprised of water and dust, and dustbowls in the Midwest illustrate how very differently life was experienced across the country. In *Franklin D. Roosevelt and the New Deal*, historian William H. Leuchtenberg speaks of 'the savage irony of want amidst plenty' that characterized the Depression, with breadlines assembled in agricultural America beneath full silos.[1]

The 'roaring' twenties concluded[2] and the decade of the 1930s opened in the wake of the Stock Market Crash in October 1929; at its close, the United States found itself poised to enter the Second World War. Between autumn 1929 and spring 1933, more than 5,000 banks failed, crippling the American banking system, and some 600,000 homeowners faced foreclosure, half of all home mortgages technically in default.[3] With the building industry at a grinding halt, construction at a standstill, workers in lumber and steel, carpenters, plumbers, electricians – all connected with the industry – faced unemployment. National income fell by 50 per cent.[4] Some 10–15 million people, between one-fifth to one-fourth of the US population, were unemployed by 1933.[5] The numbers of unemployed workers skyrocketed to almost 50 per cent in industrial centres like Chicago and Detroit.[6] In rural America, agricultural income fell by 50 per cent, and farm owners abandoned their properties in favour of sharecropping and tenant farming.[7] Others, like the Joad family in John Steinbeck's *The Grapes of Wrath*, piled their worldly possessions into their automobiles and drove west to California in hope of better prospects there.

Despite this dire picture, the unemployed actually remained in the minority, and two-thirds of Midwestern farmers maintained their homesteads. The unemployment crisis consisted more of drastic cutbacks in hours, reductions from full-time to part-time employment, wage reductions and temporary lay-offs, a socio-economic situation repeated to a lesser degree following the 2008 US banking crisis.[8]

Surprisingly, despite horrific living conditions, overall life expectancy in the United States in the 1930s actually rose.[9] As might be expected, however, the fortunes of black Americans were bleak: death from tuberculosis, a major killer of the decade, and infant mortality rates were twice as great for African-Americans in New York City as for whites.[10] Black workers' wages fell precipitously. Strangely, a racist radio programme, *Amos 'n' Andy*, gained in popularity, providing Louisiana governor, senator and presidential candidate Huey Long with his epithet, the Kingfish.

The lower and middle class were hit hardest – not only minority workers, but the extremes in age, young and old.[11] Those between sixteen and twenty-five years old, and those over 60 faced lay-offs and cutbacks first.[12] Widowhood presented economic challenges, as the elderly – especially women – were less employable and often remained reliant on children and other family members for financial support, at least until the social security system was established.

The results – and debate – of social reform like the initiation of social security legislation in 1935, under Franklin Delano Roosevelt, whose presidency dominated the decade, resonate today. Likewise, the political monikers of 'left' versus 'right' continue to characterize American political contests. Immigration issues and the idea of deporting Mexican-Americans were as much a source of contention then as in the twenty-first century.[13] At the same time, Communist Party leader Earl Browder's mid-decade slogan 'Communism is Twentieth-Century Americanism' was evoked alternatively by both those who supported social service programmes and those who did not.

Notions of patriotism and citizenship were variously defined: radical writers and artists used their work (and their constitutional rights) to question and critique the world in which they lived, both materially and ideologically. In 1932, a group of leftist writers including Malcolm Cowley, Langston Hughes and Edmund Wilson published a manifesto that supported the Communist presidential candidate William Z. Foster, *Culture in Crisis*. To some degree, the Communist Party offered literati and working class alike a feeling of solidarity, and societies like the John Reed Clubs provided a voice for writers and artists. While the left found itself somewhat invigorated, as Peter Conn points out in *The American 1930s: A Literary History*, 'to see the thirties exclusively as "the red decade" is to reduce a complex palette to a monotone [*sic*]'.[14]

A year-by-year perusal of current events reveals ironies such as congressional approval of the national anthem (March 1931) in the very same month as the erroneous arrest of the 'Scottsboro Boys'. Just before Franklin Delano Roosevelt's first election in 1932, destitute First World War veterans seeking their bonuses were gassed and bayoneted in the nation's capital. Adolf Hitler was installed as Germany's chancellor (January 1933) within months of FDR's inauguration as US president (March 1933), and the signing of the Rome–Berlin Axis agreement (October 1936) coincided with FDR's re-election (November 1936). W. E. B. Du Bois's groundbreaking study, *Black Reconstruction* (1935), found itself sandwiched between Ruth Benedict's seminal *Patterns of Culture* (1934) and Arna Bontemps's *Black Thunder* (1936). Dale Carnegie's famous self-help guide *How to Win Friends and Influence People* was also published in 1936.

The decade of the 1930s was ironically a time of celebratory fairs and expositions. Chicago boasted the 1933–4 World's Fair, or the Century of Progress, with its 'crystal house' and house of tomorrow. Audiences were wowed by the German airship *Graf Zeppelin*'s fly-by. The Chicago Museum of Science and Industry first opened at the Century of Progress Exposition. The California–Pacific International Exposition took place in 1935, the Great Lakes Exposition in Cleveland in 1936, as well as the Texas Centennial Exposition in Dallas in the same year. The 1939 New York World's Fair was not alone as on the West Coast, in San Diego, the Golden Gate International Exposition was mounted in the same year. By far the largest and most impressive, the New York World's Fair symbolically rose like a phoenix (its foundation was Flushing, New York's ash-dump) and exhibited an optimism and 'can do' American spirit. Like all world's fairs, the one at the decade's close pointed to the future – in many ways to the real lived experience of future attendees at the extraordinary 1964 World's Fair, also mounted in New York City. Designer Norman Bel Geddes's 1939 main exhibit, *Futurama*, predicted a nation of vast highways (begun under President Eisenhower later, although never 'automated' as Geddes suggested they might someday be) and suburban sprawl, an American fact of life after the Korean War.

And so, as perhaps with any decade, the 1930s may be viewed as pointing to the future at the same time looking to the past, with both nostalgia and disdain. And, as with any era, the decade of the Great Depression offers valuable lessons for the future.

The Great Depression and the New Deal

The 'New Day' promised by President Herbert Hoover in his 1928 campaign for the presidency was not to be. The Stock Market crashed on 24 October 1929, ending almost a decade of exceptional economic growth, speculation and spending. Many factors contributed to the collapse of the US economy, among them overuse of credit, lack of regulations on Wall Street, a slow-down in industrial production, a decrease in credit for farmers (additionally across the Depression, overproduction of produce) and, perhaps most important, the disproportionate distribution of wealth. The nation's richest 3 per cent held one-third of the country's purse, a phenomenon that would become, in the 2010s, the 'One Per Cent'.

In his acceptance speech at the Democratic National Convention in 1932, Franklin Delano Roosevelt pledged to the American people a 'new deal'. This catchphrase would become symbolic of a host of federal programmes executed under his administration to combat the effects of the Great Depression on the unemployed and working poor. After a campaign in which the future president appeared at times to 'waffle' regarding potential solutions to the nation's socio-economic crisis, by 1933, when he took office, armed with an inner circle of experts from a variety of fields (his 'Brain Trust'), FDR was ready to take action. The '3 R's' – Relief, Recovery and Reform – became his mantra.

During his first 100 days in office, fifteen crucial bills were passed (following a four-day bank 'holiday'), effecting:

- the establishment of the FDIC (the Federal Deposit Insurance Commission that guaranteed individual savings);
- the Federal Securities Act that regulated the Stock Market;
- the first Agricultural Adjustment Act that provided farmers with relief by paying them to produce less; the National Industrial Recovery Act that attempted to stimulate the economy by raising prices was later ruled unconstitutional;
- the Civilian Conservation Corps (discussed below under 'Education');
- the Tennessee Valley Authority that addressed electrical power in the South;
- the Federal Emergency Relief Act that provided direct relief to the unemployed, replaced in 1935 by the Works Progress Administration (renamed the Works Projects Administration in 1939), an umbrella agency under which were housed many programmes that provided employment for literally millions of Americans in a wide range of fields from construction to the arts.

Some historians divide the New Deal era into two phases: the first from 1933 to 1934, and the second and more controversial from 1935 to 1938. In essence this is because, during the first phase, relief was badly needed and any change for the positive was welcomed;

but as time passed, FDR's executive orders and strong control of the government were questioned as overbearing. From FDR's presidency to the present, the United States' two major political parties have continued to represent two ends of an economic spectrum of spending, divided as to the degree to which the government should influence US citizens' daily lives. Regardless of pro- or anti-feelings about it – then or now – the New Deal had a profound effect on life in the 1930s that reverberates in the twenty-first century.

Domestic life

Surprisingly, despite the failed economy, many American families continued to own automobiles in the 1930s, and domestic life in general may be characterized by convenience, streamlining and efficiency. Electric refrigerators and washing machines were widely owned, due in part to manufacturers' reduction to 'Depression' pricing and instalment plans (that, of course, portended the prospect of repossession).

Family life responded to the nation's economic crisis with an increase in separation and divorce rates, shrinkage in the size of the American family, and couples postponing marriage[15] (like Sid and Flo in Clifford Odets's play *Waiting for Lefty*). With the increase in unemployment for males, women entered the workforce, leaving their husbands feeling ashamed. Whether 'stay at home moms' or single women in the marketplace, wives, mothers, single men and women alike struggled to stretch their dollars.

Saving both time and money was crucial in everyday life in the 1930s. Ready-to-wear clothing and even 'pre-fab' garments that required only the stitching of seams and hems became popular. Over the course of the decade, print dresses made of synthetic fabrics whose patterns might mask stains became the craze for women. Sears, Roebuck and Company offered a variety of choices in their 'Hooverette' (named after previous president, Herbert Hoover, whom many blamed the Great Depression) line of inexpensive, reversible, wrap-around dresses.[16]

Like ready-to-wear clothing, ready-to-eat or 'fast food' today – obtainable at central locations – became popular during the Depression. The King Kullen Market, possibly the nation's first supermarket, opened in Jamaica, New York, in 1930, and the Cincinnati-based Big Bear Super Market, the first to use the term 'supermarket' in its advertising, opened in 1933. The Safeway chain began converting its small stores into larger ones, and the Kroger chain emerged in 1933.[17] The most famous of the chain restaurants of the 1930s was Howard Johnson's, which began franchising, but others arose, some of which remain active today, including Toddle House, Krystal, White Castle, A&W Root Beer and Dairy Queen.[18]

Commercial desserts and fancy pastries may have been among the first products struck from shopping lists by the cost conscious consumer, but America's sweet tooth was not deterred by the Depression. Because sugar was relatively inexpensive, bread with a little butter and sugar became a treat, as did roasted crackers with a touch of butter.

Among products that made their premiere in the 1930s were the ubiquitous (and less than nutritious) Hostess Twinkie (1931) and numerous candy bars including Snickers, the Heath Bar, Mars, 5th Avenue, Nestlé's Crunch and Hershey's Krackel. Frito corn chips (1932), Nabisco Ritz Crackers (1934) and Lay's potato chips (1939) were all popular as well.[19] 'Junk food', then as now, presented itself as an inexpensive and filling alternative to a nutritionally sound diet. So, even in terms of diet and food, the 1930s offer seemingly odd contrasts.

While many, especially in rural America, canned and otherwise preserved foodstuffs, 'making do', others, in country and city alike, took advantage of new products, like Bisquick (1931), for their baking needs, or consumed processed WonderBread. Hormel's Second World War staple, Spam, actually premiered in 1937, as did Ragu spaghetti sauce and Kraft macaroni and cheese.[20] In addition to the preceding convenience foods, advertisements from the 1930s display Campbell's and Van Camp's Pork and Beans, Campbell's and Heinz soups, Royal pudding, Cream of Wheat, 3-Minute Oats, All-Bran Cereal, various manufactured canned fruits and vegetables, the popular Gerber processed baby foods, and other products that promoted reduced 'prep' time. With its less expensive supermarket freezer case and widely distributed *20-Minute Meals* pamphlet cookbooks, Birds Eye popularized frozen foods.[21] In advertising, a fictitious Betty Crocker (created in 1921) took on a life of her own, blossoming in the 1930s on the radio and acquiring her familiar smiling face in 1936, the same year the Jolly Green Giant made his debut.[22]

American dinner table settings consisted of Depression (or 'tank') glass place settings, sold for as little as two dollars for a service for four; Fiesta Ware, at a cost of approximately $11 for a 24-piece place setting, produced in five colours in 1936; Salem china; or at the close of the decade, Russel Wright.[23] In another strange Depression-era twist, *Brides* magazine was founded in 1934, and preparations for weddings (while there were fewer) included registries and prompted the selection of formal place setting patterns, crystal and cutlery by manufacturers such as Noritake, International Silver, Cambridge or Fostoria.[24]

In urban centres, some people were literally starving, rummaging in trashcans for rations or making the legendary lunch counter tomato soup from hot water and ketchup. An the other extreme, those who began the decade as wealthy seemed to glide through the Depression with little to no changes in lifestyle. In fact, the upper class elite flaunted their wealth, as exhibited by extraordinary debutante balls such as Barbara Hutton's (grand-daughter of the Woolworth store founder) 'coming out' party, at a reported cost of $60,000, in 1933. The upper crust and movie stars frequented elegant establishments like the Stork Club and the El Morocco, the stuff of movies for the less well-to-do. The Waldorf-Astoria Hotel opened in 1931, at a reputed cost of $43 million.[25] With this flagrant display, it appeared that the wealthiest of Americans (as in the twenty-first century with talk of the One Per Cent) might actually have resented federally-funded social service programmes intended to offer a 'leg up' to the poor and disenfranchised. Perhaps, despite the headlines, they were simply unaware.

Education

In their 1930s volume of the *American Popular Culture through History* series, William A. and Nancy K. Young assert that the Depression 'changed perceptions about being young in the United States'.[26] Prior to the 1930s, because they often entered the workforce so early, young people in their teenage years were viewed more as adults. The paucity of jobs in the decade forced young people out of the workforce, causing them to remain in school longer and precipitating the creation of more organized activities for this age group. 'Teenager', a term formerly restricted to wealthy high school students, began to be used in reference to young people of all classes during the Depression.[27] And, teenagers became the target market for products and social activities.

In major cities, dues-paying (generally 30 cents per week) youth gathered for hours on end in 'cellar clubs' adapted from previously existing buildings. The clubs were often outfitted with radios, ping-pong tables and pianos, and young people found a safe haven where they could amuse themselves and visit with each other. One Brooklyn block allegedly sported forty such establishments. Naturally, aggregates of youth in one place pointed to 'gangs', but an equal number of cellar clubs accomplished their intention of providing a place for young people to congregate during hard times.[28] Sometimes young men (cellar clubs were predominantly peopled by men) assisted in outfitting the establishments with dance floors, rest rooms for the girls who attended, or other niceties. Some clubs distinguished themselves as photography laboratories or automotive workshops.[29]

Government assistance programmes were created for at-risk youth, a tradition that has continued into the twenty-first century. Established in 1933, a New Deal programme, the Civilian Conservation Corps (originally titled the Civil Corps Reforestation Youth Rehabilitation Movement), focused on unmarried, unemployed male youth aged seventeen to twenty-seven. At its height, the CCC boasted 3 million young men, offering room and board and a monthly salary of $30 in exchange for manual labour[30] related to the nation's forests, irrigation and other outdoor public works projects. Nicknamed the 'tree army', the CCC built more than 800 parks and planted more than 3 billion trees.[31] Beautifully crafted structures, like the still-operational Giant City Lodge in the Shawnee National Forest, Makanda, Illinois, pay tribute to the CCC's success even today.

In 1935, another agency, the National Youth Administration, was established under the auspices of the Works Progress Administration (WPA). Slightly different from the CCC, this organization was created to offer useful work for young people on relief. The NYA offered two specific programmes: the student work programme for youths in school (lower grades, high school, college and even graduate school), and out-of-school employment for unemployed youth aged sixteen to twenty-four.[32]

These programmes served as the progenitors for many others, some of which remain in existence today. Additionally, non-government sponsored activities for youth, such as the Boy Scouts and Girl Scouts of America, flourished during the Depression.

Sports and recreation

The United States was a nation in search of heroes in the 1930s, and the sports arena did not disappoint.

At the start of the decade, the All-American sport, baseball, was already in its heyday, with the legendary Babe Ruth's salary rising to $80,000 (more than the president's).[33] Lou Gehrig was popular, and Joe DiMaggio was a baseball hero by mid-decade. Attending a live game was affordable, games were broadcast on the radio, statistics were readily available in newspapers, and collecting baseball cards was a hobby for youth. Lights were added to the fields in 1935, increasing after-work attendance.[34] It is hard to imagine life without the NBA (National Basketball Association) or Monday Night Football, but these team sports were in their infancy then.

Surprisingly, although there was some talk of doing so, the Olympics were not suspended during the 1930s (they were, subsequently, across the years of the Second World War). Held in Lake Placid, New York, the 1932 Olympics were the first winter Olympics held in the United States; the summer Olympics that year were hosted by Los Angeles. In both events, the United States earned more medals than any other country, in some measure proving the American attitude of 'stick-to-it-a-tive-ness'.

The 1936 Olympics proved contentious as they were hosted in Berlin, with Hitler in power and many predicting war. Hitler attempted to ban Jewish athletes from competing but recanted in the face of a boycott by the majority of participating countries. Nevertheless, the games were wielded as a Nazi tool and the country 'promoted an image of a new, strong, and united Germany'.[35] Black American athlete Jesse Owens emerged as an even bigger track and field star at these Olympics than he was at home, breaking three records and winning four gold medals. Germany out-medalled all the other countries, with the United States ending second.

The tale of race horse Seabiscuit – an equine Horatio Alger story

– befits the spirit of the 1930s. The horse appeared lazy and recalcitrant, an unlikely candidate for the Race Horse of the Year Award he earned in 1938. Once paired with Canadian jockey Red Pollard, who understood the horse's personality, Seabiscuit exhibited the speed for which he would become known. When Pollard was injured riding another thoroughbred, jockey George Woolf took the saddle for Seabiscuit's triumph over legendary War Admiral at Pimlico in November 1938. The horse suffered an injury in a subsequent race, so he and Pollard recovered together, reunited for the 'Match of the Century' with War Admiral, in which Seabiscuit trounced the other champion. Seabiscuit's story has been depicted three times in films, one starring Depression screen sweetheart Shirley Temple.[36]

Difficult economic times demanded inexpensive forms of sports and recreation. The radio proved a gathering place for the family; for example, boxing matches aired on the radio on Friday evenings (and heavyweight boxer Joe Louis's twelve-year reign as champion began in 1937). Families literally made music together, gathering around pianos for sing-alongs. The American flyer wagon (Radio Flyer) debuted in 1930.[37]

Ping-pong, Pick-Up Sticks, Marbles, Jacks, Monopoly, Sorry!, Scrabble, Contract bridge[38] and jigsaw puzzles (reaching a sales peak of 10 million per week in 1933)[39] were all popular. Of course, Mickey Mouse was all the rage, and for those who could afford one, there was the ever-popular wristwatch with his image. The 1930s continued the '-athon' craze, with talking marathons, piano playing marathons, kissathons, rockathons (in rocking chairs) and dance-athons. June Havoc (née Hovick) of *Gypsy* fame (as Gypsy Rose Lee's sister) holds the dance marathon record of 3,600 hours, established in 1934.[40]

Unfortunately, as in any time of stress, gambling on sports events took its toll on some. At the other extreme, those of wealth continued with tennis, golf, horseriding and their other more expensive sports and recreational activities.

Science and technology

Advances in American science and technology continued in spite of the Depression, and this area, too, offers diversity and debate

– debate over a future 'in which humanity would either be free of routine labour or become a slave of machinery'.[41] In his 1938 *The Culture of Cities* (revised and reissued in 1961 as the National Book Award-winning *The City in History*), public intellectual Lewis Mumford advocated a balance between the mechanized and the ecological worlds. Sadly, his prescient thoughts on urban and cultural renewal would be silenced by the Second World War.

The trope of speed, streamlining and efficiency characterized scientific progress and industrial development in the 1930s every bit as much as it revealed itself in other aspects of daily life and of the arts. The decade saw inventions as varied as the parking meter,[42] the zippo lighter,[43] Alka-Seltzer,[44] the beer can[45] and the photocopier.[46]

Seminal advances were made in the field of medicine, many of which remain useful in treatments today. The pathologies of both Cushing[47] and Crohn[48] syndromes (each named for the physician who identified the conditions) were determined in 1931. The first yellow fever vaccine was developed in 1932 at the Rockefeller Foundation's Yellow Fever Laboratories, the dangerous undertaking executed by Wilbur A. Sawyer, Wray Lloyd and S. F. Kitchen.[49] Sodium thiopental (aka pentothal, or 'truth serum'), the first intravenous anaesthetic, was created at the Abbott Laboratories in 1934.[50] The 1934 Nobel Prize in Physiology or Medicine was conferred jointly on George R. Minot, William P. Murphy and George H. Whipple for their discovery of liver therapy to combat anaemia. Defibrillation was used successfully on a dog (1933).[51] In 1939, John H. Lawrence treated a cancer patient with beams of energized neutrons from a particle accelerator.[52] Chemist C. C. King first isolated Vitamin C,[53] and Vitamin E was first isolated in a pure form by Gladys Anderson Emerson, with Herbert M. Evans, director of the University of California, Berkeley's Institute of Experimental Biology.[54]

On a bleaker note, a shameful American medical study, the Tuskagee Syphilis Experiment, was initiated in 1932 and continued in various phases for 40 years. The premise of the study – to ascertain the effects of untreated syphilis on black men in the rural South – was noteworthy, and participants were compensated with free medical treatment, meals, transportation and burial insurance. The insidious aspect of the study is that after penicillin was found to combat the disease in the 1940s, participants were not informed, and their disease was allowed to go untreated.[55]

In physics, Ernest Lawrence invented the cyclotron,[56] popularly known as the *atom smasher*, and Carl David Anderson discovered the positron, or positively charged electron, in 1932, for which he won the Nobel Prize in Physics. The related field of astronomy burgeoned, with the discovery of the planet Pluto (stripped later of planet status) in 1930; the nation's first planetarium, the Adler, in Chicago, opened the same year. In 1933, a shortwave radio hiss was determined to emanate from the Milky Way, marking the beginning of radio astronomy;[57] and 1935 saw the openings of both the Hayden Planetarium in New York City and the Griffith Observatory in Los Angeles. In 1939, the man who would later be famous as the 'Father of the Atom Bomb', J. Robert Oppenheimer (with George Volkoff), calculated the structure of neutron stars[58] and (with Hartland Snyder) ascertained the existence of what would come to be called 'black holes'.[59]

Pre-dating by three decades the quintessential line about plastics in the film *The Graduate*, the man-made substance was 'tagged as the savior of the new age'.[60] Although it was known that plastic could never be reduced to its former components, biodegradability would not become a national concern for many years. Fibreglass was invented in 1932–3, as material for thermal building insulation.[61] Early in 1935, while working at the DuPont Experimental Station, American chemist Gérard Berchet (under the direction of Wallace Carothers) developed the synthetic polymer nylon,[62] which was finally introduced to the public at large at the 1939 World's Fair. In a happy accident (1938), also at DuPont, polytetrafluoroethylene, or Teflon, was discovered.[63]

Labour and the working class

In some ways, the overall prosperity of the 1920s contributed to a downward turn in the American labour movement; prices of goods were fairly stable, and, except for coal mining and farming, most industries flourished – temporarily. Union membership declined, and, as a result, the American Federation of Labor's strength weakened. Management associated unionism with communism, opposed to the all-American spirit of individualism, and applied 'Red Scare' tactics, coercing workers into signing 'yellow-dog' contracts whereby they pledged not to join a union. The National Association of Manufacturers adhered to the 'American Plan', refusing to negotiate with unions. The court system proved less supportive of workers across the 1920s, and corporations sought more injunctions against potential strikes than ever before. Although organized labour made some gains earlier in terms of working conditions, in the late 1920s, 'speed-ups' or 'stretch outs' forced workers, especially in the textile and mining industries, to work longer hours for less pay, often under unsafe conditions. Strike after strike broke out across all areas of industry, from longshoremen, to coal miners, to textile workers and those in the automotive industry, and continued throughout the 1930s. In the middle of the decade a faction of workers broke away from the American Federation of Labour (AFL), forming the Congress of Industrial Organizations (CIO); the two organizations later amalgamated to become the AFL-CIO.[64] The Depression simply 'sealed the deal' for American labour, pitching millions of workers into unemployment and abject poverty. The second flurry of New Deal programming, with the National Labor Relations Act (the Wagner Act, 1935), assured labourers the right to unionize and to strike if necessary. The Fair Labor Standards Act (1938) set maximum and minimum wages for most workers.

Arts and culture

Perhaps nowhere is the diversity of the 1930s more apparent than in the arts. Again, the temptation to view arts and culture through a bifurcated lens is great because of the tendency among practitioners to gravitate to political extremes, to participate in political and social advocacy, or, on the other hand, to seemingly avoid pressing issues of the day. In actuality, writers and artists of the decade, whether overtly political or not, as in any era, responded to and reflected the tenor of their time, across a wide stylistic spectrum. Unique perhaps to the Depression era are the degrees to which the arts and culture were used as tools for social change both within the Works Progress Administration and in the private sector.

Arts projects produced across the nation as part of the WPA provided employment for unemployed artists and espoused the 'rhetoric of the people'.[65] Although the National Endowment for the Arts was founded in 1965 (in the age of President Lyndon Johnson's 'Great Society'), it pales in comparison to the federal arts programmes of the Depression. Historian David Eldridge recounts New Deal data regarding the arts:

> 168 symphony orchestras, thirty-five choral groups and thirty chamber ensembles formed by the Federal Music Project. Thirty million people attended shows put on by the Federal Theatre Companies in forty cities in twenty-two states, The Federal Writers Project produced 1,200 publications ... Five thousand artists were employed by the Federal Art Project to produce 108,000 easel paintings, 17,700 sculptures and 11,200 print designs ... 400 murals and 6,800 easel works were created in five months by the Public Works of Art project, and another 1,200 murals commissioned by the US Treasury's Section of Painting and Sculpture. There were also 77,000 photographs taken for the historical section of the farm Security Administration.[66]

The WPA literally brought art into the streets and created a more democratized notion of it. Arts accessibility is evidenced by the Federal Theatre Project's (see *American Culture in the 1930s*, 2008) remarkable 30 million overall attendance.[67]

Stylistically, literature and all of the arts (including architecture and film) exhibit *Modernism* on the move. Emanating from late nineteenth century thought and persisting well into the twentieth century, Modernism is characterized by its embrace of the subconscious, multiple perspectives and fragmentation, expressed in literature via stream-of-consciousness writing and/or polyvocality. Modernist tactics abound in this period, but often, regardless of the artist's socio-economic standing, they are projected from a proletarian perspective, with a political slant. Hints of and even direct influences on styles of the 1960s are displayed in the 1930s, and perhaps the only profound delineation between Modernism of the 1930s and *Post*modernism much later is the centring of Depression-era art in the present, while often self-referential. Postmodern art, on the other hand, overtly signals or critiques the past.

Literature

Prose, drama and poetry in the 1930s offer a cornucopia of form and style. Some authors, like John Dos Passos and Langston Hughes, for example, produced work across genres. Dalton Trumbo, John Howard Lawson and others of the later infamous Hollywood Ten wrote fiction and drama in the 1930s, turning to work as scriptwriters later.

In the non-fiction arena, works like Frederick Lewis Allen's *Only Yesterday: An Informal Study of the 1920s* (1931) and Malcolm Cowley's *Exile's Return* (1934) chronicle the transition from the 1920s into the 1930s. Constance Rourke's *American Humor: A Study of the National Character* (1931) offered an early formal study of American folk culture – before popular entertainment was an area of inquiry – and, in the same year, James Truslow Adams's history, *The Epic of America*, in which he references 'the American Dream' – a dream already unattainable by most US citizens – was published.

The American Guide Series, a New Deal project, sought to create a written record of the past and present of each state and several individual cities in the United States. Completed in over fifty volumes, the series totals over 31,000 pages. The guidebooks' authors, however, came from varying degrees of experience, and the works exhibit different tones, some of the Southern volumes exhibiting benevolence toward slavery, for example.[68]

Documentary pieces, although not particularly popular among the general reading public, emerged as writers took to the road in some number, practising immersion among the working-class impoverished, drawing on their observations to pen ethnographic studies, often published in journals, like Edmund Wilson's articles in *New Republic*. In 1936, James Agee and Wallace Evans, commissioned by *Fortune* magazine, conducted such a study, *Let Us Now Praise Famous Men* (1941), a work decades later recognized as a classic of the documentary form. At the same time as Agee and Evans's travels, *Fortune* dispatched reporters to Rochester, New York, where they found the city's dwellers experiencing a more comfortable existence, thus exhibiting the heterogeneity of life in the decade.[69] Similarly, Charles Morrow Wilson's travelogue *Roots of America* paints a pastoral picture of rugged, rural life in the 1930s. Journalist Lorena Hickok, famous as First Lady

Eleanor Roosevelt's closest female friend (and perhaps lover), travelled across the country, chronicling Depression conditions and reporting back to Washington on her findings. Literary documentaries include Theodore Dreiser's *Tragic America* (1931), Edmund Wilson's *American Jitters* (1932) and Sherwood Anderson's *Puzzled America* (1935), and, in the realm of fact-based fiction, Erskine Caldwell's Georgia sharecropper story, *Tobacco Road* (1932), Grace Lumpkin's tale of textile workers, *To Make My Bread* (1932), and John Steinbeck's exploration of Mexican California in *Tortilla Flat* (1933), an apple pickers' strike in *In Dubious Battle* (1936) and, of course, *The Grapes of Wrath* (1939).

'Quasi-autobiographies', reflecting their authors' socio-political slants, include Mike Gold's *Jews Without Money* (1930), Edward Dahlberg's *The Bottom Dogs* (1930) and Jack Conroy's *The Disinherited* (1933). Gold advocated a form and style he deemed 'proletarian realism'. The epithet 'social realism' would be coined only in retrospect.

Others approached the lived experience of Americans deeply affected by the economics of the day – like Nathanael West's 'tetralogy of disillusionment'[70] (*The Dream Life of Balso Snell*, 1931; *Miss Lonelyhearts*, 1933; *A Cool Million*, 1934; and *The Day of the Locust*, 1939). West turned American myth on its end, presenting the dream of success as an empty shell. John Dos Passos also subverted and attacked the American democratic myth, commenting on what he saw as a tragic disparity between the American dream and the reality of the times.

Costume novels, particularly those focused on wars, comprised a large segment of the fiction market. Some, like *Guns Along the Mohawk* by George D. Edmonds, took the Revolutionary War for inspiration. Others looked to the French and Indian War, as in Kenneth Roberts's *Northwest Passage*, the 1940 film version of which starred Spencer Tracy. Margaret Mitchell's ever-popular but arguably racist 1936 *Gone With the Wind* turned, of course, to the Civil War. For subject matter, authors also returned to legendary figures like Pocahontas or Abraham Lincoln (a constant across the decades of the twentieth century).

'Women's novels' (some categorize *Gone With the Wind* among them) gained in popularity – *Back Street* by Fannie Hurst (first adapted as a film in 1932, and subsequently in 1941 and 1961) and Rachel Field's *All This and Heaven Too* (filmed in 1940) are examples of this subgenre.

Eldridge claims that half the bestselling novels of the decade were detective novels by Erle Stanley Gardner, John Dickson Carr, Rex Stout, Ellory Queen and others, with the 'hard-boiled' style of Dashiell Hammett[71] (*Maltese Falcon*, 1930) and his Sam Spade character continuing to intrigue readers across the decades. Like *The Maltese Falcon*, Hammett's *The Thin Man* (1934, originally published in *Redbook*) was adapted for film, and in the 1950s, for television, a medium that popularized Gardner's Perry Mason as well.

The Nancy Drew detective series, targeting adolescent girls, debuted in 1930, and the juvenile reading series the Hardy Boys continued to grow in popularity since its inception in 1927. Laura Ingalls Wilder's decade-long romance with her Midwestern upbringing expressed in novels for young people began in 1932, with the famous (much later serialized for television) *The Little House on the Prairie* reaching the general public in 1935.

Perhaps because of its low cost, pleasure reading, a solo activity, became more popular across the Depression. Book-of-the-Month Club sales grew, and in 1939, late in the decade, Pocket Books, reprints of bestsellers and classics, became available for 25 cents a copy.[72]

The 1930s was, indeed, one of the great eras of the American novel, as represented by the works of John Steinbeck, William Faulkner, Zora Neal Hurston, Pearl S. Buck and others. Buck's Pulitzer Prize-winning *The Good Earth* (1931) constituted the first of her trilogy (followed by *Sons*, 1932, and *A House Divided*, 1935) dealing with life in a Chinese village.

By the mid-1930s, especially after a 1935 riot, the Harlem Renaissance (the blossoming of 'Negro' art in New York in the 1920s) was over. Many of the black literati, like James Weldon Johnson and W. E. B. Du Bois, left Harlem, often taking teaching positions at colleges.[73] Despite this diaspora, dialogue continued among black intellectuals about systemic racism and assimilation. The decade opens with some works that continue to perpetuate negative racial stereotypes, but by mid-decade in *Mules and Men* (1935), anthropologist/writer Zora Neal Hurston details black 'folklore' to scrutinize representations of race and gender in black life, and, in her best-known work, *Their Eyes Were Watching*

God (1937), she clearly challenges racial uplift ideology by representing southern blacks without filter, rather than, as was common, presenting their behaviour as imitative of white culture.[74] Like many in the Depression, black writer Richard Wright sought solutions to racism and economic depravity in Marxism, and the decade turns with his *Native Son* (1940) and a character who finds identity only through violence.

As this brief overview of prose of the 1930s indicates, 'authors were pulled in various directions at once: political radicalism vs escapism; literary modernism and theatricalism vs realism; region vs nature; man vs nature; and nostalgia vs hope for the future'.[75]

Poetry

Poetry's contribution in terms of literary criticism in the 1930s may be seen as the roots of New Criticism, with its emphasis on 'close reading' of the text itself (apart from the author's biography), explored in the seminal *Understanding Poetry* (1938) by Cleanth Brooks and Robert Penn Warren.

Like many of the novelists, the careers of several poets represented in the 1930s, including T. S. Elliot and, perhaps the United States' most famous poet, Robert Frost, span decades of American literature. As with virtually all aspects of life in the Great Depression, variety and diversity were *de rigueur* in the realm of poetry. Many poets directly attended to the historical moment in their verse, some more overt than others in their politicization. Wallace Stevens, Stephen Vincent Benét, Hart Crane, e. e. cummings, Marianne Moore, Muriel Rukeyser, Archibald MacLeish and Langston Hughes are among the most notable, with MacLeish and Hughes crossing into the realm of dramatic literature as well.

Known for his communist sympathies and socialist practices, Langston Hughes's poetry, in particular, resounds with radicalism and even revolution. Additionally, like Zora Neale Hurston's novels, his poetry takes to task assimilation and was criticized for its representation of black life. Among his poems of protest is 'Advertisement for the Waldorf Astoria', first published in the communist organ *New Masses* in December 1931, which mocks the lavish hotel's marketing of its opening. *Scottsboro Limited:*

Four Poems and a Play in Verse (1932) captured the historical moment immediately following the wrongful conviction of nine black youths for rape (the Scottsboro case would limp on for decades before the boys were vindicated). In 'Waiting on Roosevelt' (1934), Hughes versifies a string of disappointments with the president's inaction.

Muriel Rukeyser's massive 'The Book of the Dead' (1938) illustrates what might be dubbed 'high' Modernism in its use of montage, drawing on the Egyptian *Book of the Dead* for inspiration. Rukeyser deploys congressional transcript, dialogues from personal interviews she conducted in the wake of the 1927 Hawk's Nest Tunnel disaster, in which black miners working without proper gear contracted silicosis, and polyvocality to illustrate the virtual invisibility of these workers and their families in the face of racist and capitalist practices.[76] Still more left-wing poets, like Alfred Hayes ('In a Coffee Pot' and 'Joe Hill'), Kenneth Fearing and Joy Davidman, represented the disenfranchised in their works of the 1930s.

Painting

The Depression virtually annihilated the art market, in both the private-owner and museum sectors. Nevertheless, visual artists continued their practice. A great discrepancy is displayed in aesthetics between Regionalists like Thomas Hart Benton and the bleaker urban and social realists like Edward Hopper and Charles Sheeler who reached prominence as the Second World War approached. Regionalism 'employed themes of national identity using land as a carrier of meaning', depicting nostalgia for the past, mythologizing and elevation of the commonplace, 'giving it heroic status'.[77] As with the other art areas, visual artists sometimes turned to historical subjects to comment, as with Grant Wood's *Daughters of the Revolution* (1932)[78] and Thomas Hart Benton's imposing *A Social History of Indiana* (1933), in which he critiqued the past, incorporating images, for example, of the Ku Klux Klan and of a trapper offering alcohol to a Native American.[79]

Mural art, especially because of the WPA's sponsorship of it, flourished in the 1930s. Mexican muralists like Diego Rivera, Jose Orozco and David Siqueiros exerted influence in the United

States.[80] The debacle of Rivera's commission to create murals in the Rockefeller Center ranks high in the annals of American art history and is immortalized in Mark Blitzstein's musical *The Cradle Will Rock*, particularly in the 1999 Tim Robbins film version. Several artists who went on to fame, like Abstract Expressionists Jackson Pollack, William de Kooning, Mark Rothko and Arshile Gorky, began their careers as part of the Federal Art Project that employed over 1,100 artists in its muralism division.

As in other genres, visual art often depicted daily life and conflict in the Depression, with pieces like Edward Laning's *Unlawful Assembly, Union Square* (1931); Jacob Burck's ironically titled *The Lord Provides* (1933), depicting a policeman with a baton as he arrests a striking woman; William Gropper's *Miners* (1935); and Philip Evergood's *American Tragedy* (1937), depicting the bloodbath that was Chicago at Republic Steel on Memorial Day of that year.

Photography

Although well known today, at the time, the most widely looked at photographs of the Depression were not Dorothea Lange's iconic *Migrant Mother* (1936) with its Madonna imagery, or *The White Angel Breadline*, or Arthur Rothstein's *Fleeing from a Dust Storm*, or Margaret Bourke-White's *You Have Seen Their Faces*, or those included by Wallace Evans in *Let Us Now Praise Famous Men* (1941), but, rather, the film star shots taken of actors like Joan Crawford, Norma Shearer, Greta Garbo and so on by George Hurrell, Ernest Bacharach, Lazlo Willinger and Clarence Sinclair Bull.[81] Stars of stage were photographed by Carl Van Vechten. Ansel Adams remained dedicated to art photography in the 1930s,[82] but other photographers, like Lange, Ben Shahn, Marion Post, Rothstein and Bourke-White, moved by the sights of the Depression, were literally drawn to the streets and to rural America for photographic inspiration.

Architecture and design

Architectural conflict in style characterized the 1930s, illustrating the shift from art deco and Modernism to streamline modern. The popularity of streamline modern paralleled the focus on economy and efficiency displayed in most aspects of daily life. At the same time, the neo-classic Jefferson Memorial's groundbreaking occurred in 1939, and the faces of Mount Rushmore, memorializing four US presidents, were initially carved between 1934 and 1939.

The decade opened with the completion of the Chrysler (1930) and Empire State (1931) buildings in New York City. Young aptly notes the correspondence between their completion and the onset of the Great Depression, as well as their reflection of the marked shift in architectural style: 'iconic as they are, both buildings are relics, art deco masterpieces erected in a period that was in the process of rejecting that very style'.[83]

Recognized in 1991 by the American Institute of Architects as the greatest American architect of all time, Frank Lloyd Wright's mid-career work epitomizes the sleek 1930s. Designed as private residences, Graycliff, Fallingwater and Taliesin West in Arizona represent his mature organic style in which a modern, often block building is blended with landscape. Known later for the geodesic dome that dominated his career, Buckminster Fuller spent the 1930s as an engineer, in research and development. He pioneered mass-produced kitchens and bathrooms at Pierce Foundation & American Radiator Standard Manufacturing, created three Dymaxion cars and served as the Science and Technology Consultant for *Fortune* magazine from 1938 to 1940.[84]

Stage designers entered the field of industrial design, and Norman Bel Geddes's 1932 book, *Horizons*, addressed the notion of streamlining in the areas of transportation, housing and the accoutrements of daily life, like appliances. Bel Geddes's student, Henry Dreyfuss, is credited with the creation of the cradle telephone and the look that continued to define it into the 1950s. Sears, Roebuck commissioned Raymond Loewy to design a streamlined refrigerator in 1935. Other notable designers include Cedric Gibbons, Walter Dorwin Teague and the prolific Russel Wright.[85]

Music

Duke Ellington's 'It Don't Mean a Thing (If It Ain't Got That Swing)' sums up the swing craze of the decade, in both music and dance. Listening music was comprised of mostly romantic love songs, like Cole Porter's 'Night and Day', Richard Rodgers and Lorenz Hart's 1934 'Blue Moon' and Irving Berlin's 'Cheek to Cheek' (1935). This was the Golden Age of songwriters: Porter, Rodgers and Hart, Berlin, Hoagy Carmichael, Johnny Mercer, Dorothy Fields and more.[86] In contrast, songs depicting the plight of the Depression, like 'Brother, Can You Spare a Dime?' (1932), by Jay Gormey and Yip Harburg, and Herman Hupfeld's 'Are You Makin' Any Money?' (1933) were also popular, but mostly with a niche audience. 'Life is Just a Bowl of Cherries' appeared earlier in the decade, in the topical *George White's Scandals of 1931*. Protest songs, such as balladeer Woodie Guthrie's 'So Long, It's Been Good to Know Ya', typified the 'Dust Bowl Ballad' genre.[87]

Despite the popularity of musicians of colour like Duke Ellington, and the appropriation of black musical style by white musicians, racism was a problem seldom overtly depicted in the industry until Billie Holliday sang 'Strange Fruit', with its focus on lynchings. But the song would remained banned from the airways for another decade and a half.

Both the disc jockey and the jukebox became popular in the decade. Approximately 150,000 jukeboxes were manufactured by Wurlitzer, Seeburg and other companies between 1933 and 1937. Typically each held fifty records (singles), and by 1939 60 per cent of all popular recordings were included on them.[88]

Dance

Dance displays the same dichotomies and diversity as other disciplines and activities across the 1930s. Modern dancer/choreographer Martha Graham burst upon the scene at the same time that Fred Astaire and Ginger Rogers glided across the screen and George Balanchine reinvigorated American ballet.

Graham's style, with its emphasis on the body's contraction and release, with angular movements, was not only unique, but particularly suited to the country and to the time. In her 1937 essay, 'A Platform for the American Dance', Graham alludes to this propriety. Her mid-decade piece, 'Chronicle', takes fascism as its subject and was choreographed in the same year, 1936, that Graham refused Hitler's invitation to perform at the International Arts Festival.[89]

Swing dominated popular dance, but in addition to traditional ballroom dances like the waltz and fox trot, variations of swing, such as the Lindy (named for Charles Lindbergh) and the Carolina Shag, were popular, especially at dance competitions.

Media

The media – print, radio, film – each played a major role in popular culture of the 1930s. Magazines – popular, pulp and political – faired surprisingly well: by 1938 over 1,200 weeklies and approximately 2,000 monthlies were in publication.[90] Low purchase cost undoubtedly contributed to this success (as it did with movie-going). Likewise, newspaper circulation rose across the decade, but in reality by only 3 per cent as the nation's population dropped.[91]

Pulp magazines – originally named because of their inexpensive paper, but by this time bearing connotations of cheap and tawdry – were in their glory in the 1930s. The 'pulps' displayed an array of subgenres, including 'spicy', detective, fantasy, science fiction, western, romance and horror.[92] With lurid covers, pulps were unique in the magazine world as they published almost exclusively fiction (no art); and reputable, even famous, writers offered their work. The most famous detective pulp, *Black Mask*, serialized Dashiell Hammett's *The Maltese Falcon* at the beginning of the decade. Isaac Asimov published a short story in the *Amazing Stories* in 1938.[93]

Many magazines popular during the 1930s continue to circulate today (among them *Ladies Home Journal*, *Good Housekeeping*, *Cosmopolitan*, *Vogue* and *Time*). *Fortune*, with its in-depth articles and financial review, was founded in 1930; both *Newsweek* and *U.S. News & World Report* began publication in 1933; *Life* magazine was launched in 1936, with Bourke-White contributing the first cover. Among others created across the decade were *Family Circle*, *Newsweek*, *Esquire*, *Popular Photography* and *Glamour*.[94] Then, as now, America displayed a diverse reading audience.

Well-known comic strips from the 1930s include *Little Orphan Annie*, *Popeye*, *Dick Tracy*, *Bringing Up Father*, *The Gumps*, *Blondie*, *Moon Mullins*, *Joe Palooka*, *Li'l Abner*, *Tillie the Toiler*, *Superman*, *The Secret Life of Walter Mitty* and more. Most, as indicated by this list, were comic, and, while the serials might allude to current events, they were intended as light-hearted. Several comics, like *Little Orphan Annie*, *Popeye*, *Li'l Abner* and *Superman*, were later reimagined in other media. Several others continued to experience extremely long runs, up to four decades. A mid-decade marketing brainstorm – packaging 'best of's' comics in pamphlet form – resulted in the creation of the comic book.[95]

Radio

The 1930s represented the golden age of radio. The radio 'linked rural and urban America together in a common listening experience'.[96] At its peak, radio reached an audience of some 40 million, between 7.00 and 7.15 pm on week nights[97] – ironically one-third of the nation, the equivalent of the 'one-third of the nation ill-housed, ill-clad, ill-nourished' of FDR's second inaugural address. By decade's close, approximately 28 million households and millions of automobiles boasted radios. 'For most Americans, radio was considered a necessity, along with food and shelter.'[98] Social workers reported that the poorest of families would sacrifice essentials like furniture for their radio.[99]

Radio in the 1930s exhibited a wide array of genres: variety shows, soap operas, situation comedies, classical music, popular music, detective stories, westerns, shows created from popular comic strips, and news (although not broadcast with regularity until mid-decade). When radio producers realized how 'up to the minute' reporting could be, a newspaper–radio war ensued, with the print media crying 'foul', ultimately to no avail.

Two broadcasts in particular, one an event in real time, the other a drama, best illustrate the power that radio achieved in the 1930s. Herb Morrison's shout, 'It burst into flames!', and his continuing broadcast of the *Hindenberg* disaster of 6 May 1937 demonstrated live-action news reporting as never before. Fact and fiction coalesced in the listening public's panic at Orson Welles's Halloween 1938 Mercury Theatre Broadcast of *War of the Worlds* in which the 45 minutes or so of material were read as a news report, mistaken by many as real.

Manufacturers soon realized the potential of radio advertising, and the notion of the 'sponsor' was born – hence, the phrase 'soap opera' for dramatic serial programming. In fact, many radio programmes incorporated their sponsors' names in their titles: *Fleischmann's Yeast Radio Hour* (later the *Royal Gelatin Radio Hour*), *The Kraft Music Hall*, *The Pepsodent Program*, *The Lucky Strike Program* and others.

FDR's 'Fireside Chats' ushered in an era of unprecedented presidential media coverage, as shortly after his first election Roosevelt and his First Lady recognized the potential of radio to reach the American public. Radio personalities included singers Rudy Vallee, on whose variety show the husband and wife comedy duo George Burns and Gracie Allen first appeared, and Eddie Cantor, and comedians such as Jack Benny and Fred Allen. Another couple (less enduring perhaps), Jim and Marion Jordan, starred in *Fibber Magee and Molly*, the prototypical radio situation comedy.[100] Benny Goodman and Glenn Miller's 'big bands' were aired on the radio, and Arturo Toscanini conducted the NBC Symphony Orchestra. Father Charles E. Coughlin's controversial radio sermons paved the way for 'televangelism'. *The Shadow*, which premiered in 1937, with its famous lines, 'Who knows what evil lurks in the hearts of men? The Shadow knows', was one of America's most popular series.

In the radio version of *Amos 'n' Andy* (later a television series with black actors), the main characters were voiced by white actors from the minstrelsy tradition. Some black audiences responded favourably to the programme; the white actors were actually honoured by Chicago's prime black newspaper, *The Defender*,[101] but others recognized the ugly stereotyping that the programme perpetuated.

Film

Although film exhibited varied styles, the genre was united by its tendency 'to portray contemporary societies thrown into chaos, whether because of the emergence of gangsters, the presence of zany characters like Groucho Marx, or the arrival in New York of King Kong'.[102] In retrospect, film critics often acknowledge underground monsters depicted in 1930s films as thinly veiled codings of race and class. Gangster films included classics like *The Public Enemy* (1931) and *Scarface* (1932). The decade was immediately preceded by the Marx Brothers' screwball comedy *Cocoanuts* (1929), followed by *Duck Soup* in 1933. *Dracula* and *Frankenstein* appeared in 1931, *King Kong* in 1933. Audience escapism presented itself in differing ways, ranging from Shirley Temple's break-out film *Bright Eyes* (1934) to the dance extravaganzas of Busby Berkeley (*42nd Street*, *The Gold Diggers of 1933* and so on). *The Wizard of Oz*, a now-classic parable of optimism in the face of adversity starring Judy Garland, closed the decade with its famous burst of colour.

As in the other arts and other areas of culture, some films took as their topics the unemployed and discontented of the Depression, including *Fugitive from a Chain Gang* (1932), *Heroes for Sale* (1933) and *Dust Be My Destiny* (1939). Other socio-economic issues addressed in films include banking collapse in *American Madness* (1932); collectivism in *Our Daily Bread* (1934); labour strikes in *Black Fury* (1935); eviction in *Moving Day* (1936); juvenile delinquency in *Dead End* (1937); and lynchings in *They Won't Forget* (1937). Government corruption was depicted in *Washington Merry-Go-Round* (1932), *Washington Masquerade* (1935) and *Mr. Smith Goes to Washington* (1939), directed by the prolific Frank Capra. Even some sunny Shirley Temple movies referenced the Depression: in *Stand Up and Cheer* (1934), FDR appoints a Secretary for Amusement, and in *Just Around the Corner* (1938), Temple's film father loses his job.

Films like *Black Fury*, despite their romanticized depiction of the working class,[103] encouraged documentary filmmakers in the 1930s. The communist-organized Film and Photo League (FPL), founded in 1930, produced low-budget newsreels that were distributed to unions. The Spanish Civil War prompted the Ernest Hemingway/Lillian Hellman project, *The Spanish Earth* (1937), and Frontier Films produced *United Action* in 1939, created by the United Auto Workers themselves. By the mid-to-end of the decade, leftist playwrights like John Howard Lawson and Clifford Odets worked as screenwriters, with Lawson creating, for example, Warner Brothers' *Blockade*, starring Henry Fonda as a peasant.[104]

Movies about newspaper reporters, including *The Front Page* (1931) and *His Girl Friday* (1940), rounded out the decade. B-movie westerns were popular, as well as the 'singing cowboy' films of Gene Autry, Hopalong Cassidy and Roy Rogers. The popularity of Charles Lindbergh and Amelia Earhart prompted more than twenty-five commercial films centred on aviation.[105]

In 1930, the weekly movie-going public equalled three-quarters of the nation's population in number, and *All Quiet on the Western Front* was the nation's box-office hit movie.[106] That year, in response to the dipping economy, admission prices dropped, and by 1933, neighbourhood houses generally charged only a dime, larger venues maybe 25 cents. Programme formatting changed to accommodate the sagging economy, and the double feature emerged – the showing of two full-length feature films (generally one of higher production value than the other 'B' film), with the addition of a cartoon, a newsreel and sometimes a weekly serial episode. Other audience attractions included 'dish nights', when the popular Depression glass was raffled off, 'bank nights' (drawings for cash prizes) or bingo with prizes.[107] As another enticement for audiences, concessions were added, and eating in the theatre became acceptable behaviour. The nation's first drive-in cinemas made their appearance in 1933.[108]

Like live theatre long before, film bore a licentiousness according to the taste of some critics. Calls for censorship resulted in the 1930 Hollywood Production Code, not the first such code. Around 1934–5, after some producers pushed boundaries, the Code was enforced, so from then on, for three decades, every film produced or exhibited in the United States was scrutinized by the office of Joseph Breen, the head of the Production Code Administration.

Issues of censorship recall other ethical dilemmas, and while we leave life in the 1930s at this point, many of the artists and practitioners discussed here and in the next chapter would be subjected to a different kind of scrutiny and prosecution in the decades to come.

2

American Theatre in the 1930s

Anne Fletcher

Before the Crash

'Wall Street, It's the Rise and Fall Street'[1]

The 1929 Wall Street Crash changed the face of the American theatre in both the number of Broadway productions that could feasibly be mounted and the kind of dramas produced. The 'boom' to 'bust' economic downturn affected both aesthetics and audience.

Before the Depression, drama demonstrated not only a continuation of traditional fare (e.g. 'boy meets girl' comedies), but highly experimental theatre as well. During and shortly after the First World War, theatre practitioners, like playwrights John Howard Lawson and John Dos Passos, visited Europe's stages and cabarets, returning to offer the American theatre a European avant-garde aesthetic. Arguably their company, the New Playwrights Theatre, the last of those discussed here to be formed,[2] was the most daring of the decade as its repertoire exhibited the most innovative dramatic forms and styles of production, beyond even the New Stagecraft popularized in this country by designer Robert Edmond Jones. Pre-Crash, the New Playwrights' brand of expressionism – and even surrealism – and their overall production style that Lawson called 'The New Showmanship' – often incorporating popular entertainment idioms – were met with critical disdain. It would take a depression to bring the working-class concerns and left-wing ideology the New Playwrights espoused to the stage. And it would be workers themselves, not 'do-gooders' from the privileged class, who would come to influence the changing face of performance, performance as protest in particular. Perhaps for the first time in American theatre history, in the 1930s, the working and immigrant class truly emerged as active audience members and performers as well.

The most noted experimental theatre of the teens and twenties, the Provincetown Players (early artistic home of Eugene O'Neill and Susan Glaspell) and two others, the Washington Square Players (which evolved into the Theatre Guild) and the Neighborhood Players, negotiated a delicate balance between the avant-garde and the traditional by including some of each in their repertoires. They brought to the stage an Americanized, humanized expressionism, one suited to a capitalist economy and a democratic political system, and perhaps more suited to its audience.[3]

Participants in each of these companies – not only playwrights, but actors, directors and designers – continued to work in the 1930s and beyond. The most significant contributions of these companies to later American theatre are perhaps their non-realistic styles of production, particularly the staccato rhythm indicative of expressionism; a focus on ethnic diversity in play selection; and community-based production methods. While these characteristics sometimes appear across the drama of the 1930s, as discussed in this book, the economic pattern of the era, followed by the Second World War, prevented their robust revival until much later, when socio-political conditions and economic strength would allow, once again, for aesthetic experimentation.

Periods of prosperity, leisure and disposable income offer time (and money) that fosters exploration, challenges to the norm, and development of new and exciting styles. Moments of crisis demand artistic response: a mirroring of, a protest against or, often through comedy, a deliberate diversion from current concerns – hence the overtly (and sometimes subtly subversive) socio-political features of Depression-era dramas. Dramatists and producers of the 1930s reflected and responded to the tenor of their time in varied ways. In this decade, theatre simultaneously mirrored, protested against and sometimes attempted to avoid the crisis that constituted its historical moment.

After the economic collapse: The 1930s

As with life in the decade writ large, theatre of the 1930s is, then, both dichotomous and diverse. The binary framework alluded to in the last chapter with reference to popular culture is frequently adopted in discussion of the dramatic literature of the time (as in 'left' versus 'right' or 'high brow' versus 'low brow'). This bifurcated vision is the most common lens through which plays and productions of the era are viewed. However, this sort of categorizing is troublesome and often reductionist as it limits our capacity to appreciate nuances that the plays (and their authors) present.

With the understanding that classifications of some sorts are essential in organizing a discussion of the theatre of the 1930s, this chapter embraces theatrical and literary diversity.[4] It takes as its conceptual framework the broad (and generally accepted) view, alluded to above, of theatre as responsive to and/or reflective of its time. For each play and production in its own way – from Marc Connelly's *Green Pastures*, winner of the 1930 Pulitzer Prize for Drama, to Susan Glaspell's *Alison's House*, which took the prize in 1931, all the way to Robert E. Sherwood's renewed patriotism and turn to a beloved political icon with *Abe Lincoln in Illinois* (1939 Pulitzer Prize) – illustrates or offers commentary on various facets of the Depression era. Viewing the dramatic literature of the period in this way allows us to observe sometimes unexpected similarities within the array of theatrical offerings that crossed the stage.

As the works of the four major playwrights featured in this book confirm, the decade's drama exhibits great range in theme, form and content. These playwrights elucidate the diversity and complexity of their time from both historical and aesthetic perspectives; at the same time, collectively and individually, they offer a wide assortment of styles. Indeed, through their contributions to drama of the 1930s, Lillian Hellman, Langston Hughes, Clifford Odets and Gertrude Stein may be viewed as a microcosm of the dramatic literature as a whole, and of artistic and socio-political engagement of the period. But the decade offers even more in terms of dramaturgical diversity.

In this chapter, we step back for a more 'macro' look at theatre of the decade, an overview of how theatre – both broadly construed and with regard to individual playwrights – interacted with the material and socio-economic conditions of the time.

Options for tracking this interaction abound, and historians have approached dramatic literature of the decade from multiple perspectives, all useful. With over 1,500 plays premiering in New York City from 1930 to 1939,[5] critics are hard pressed to uncover a 'one size fits all' critical structure for analysing them. Adding non-Broadway plays, productions and alternative performances to the discussion further intensifies the conundrum.

In an attempt to reflect the wide assortment of drama in the 1930s, and in fairness to those playwrights and other practitioners who figured prominently at the time but have subsequently fallen into obscurity, this chapter will cover non-canonical playwrights – those no longer anthologized and examined only in special topics classes, often purely at the graduate level. It will also include and attempt to offer new insights into some 'old chestnuts' of the dramatic canon, like Kaufman and Hart's *You Can't Take it With You* and *The Man Who Came to Dinner*, that have been fodder for community theatre, and dismissed as simple and superficial 'senior class plays'.

A season-by-season approach to examining the plays – even positioning them alongside politics as the Great Depression deepened, political posturing predominated inside and outside the arts, the Popular Front prevailed and the United States moved towards war – is baffling. For example, how could Zoë Akins's *The Old Maid* garner the Pulitzer Prize in 1935, the same year Clifford Odets's penultimate labour drama *Waiting for Lefty*, his poignant social drama *Awake and Sing!* and Lillian Hellman's play dealing with taboo subject matter, *The Children's Hour*, were produced?

Several scholars – namely, for the purposes of this chapter, Sam Smiley,[6] Susan Duffy[7] and, to a degree, Christopher Herr[8] – argue for analysing plays of the decade from the standpoints of their authors' levels of (political) commitment and the works' efficacy regarding social change. These theatre historians recognize that so-called labour drama or political theatre plays to a particular pre-defined audience of the like-minded; it does little in the way of changing people's minds. Instead, it may be said to 'preach to the choir'. These critics focus, then, on the playwrights' rhetoric: Smiley looks at the plays' abilities to depict, exhort, accuse or censure;[9] Duffy looks at their degrees of epideictic (praise or blame) rhetoric. Herr, having acknowledged the first two modes of analysis, groups (political) plays according to recurring central topics in the pieces: oppression of minorities and marginalized groups; anti-war; anti-capitalism; labour; social justice; anti-fascism; and pro-American intervention.[10] In so doing, Smiley and Duffy point to the plays' social arguments, and Herr adds a thematic organizational framework to their foundational work, thus avoiding an 'us' (workers/labourers) versus 'them' (wealthy capitalists/bosses) approach. His mission in his chapter is to capture the essence and purpose of political drama of the decade.

In discussing drama of the 1930s, one cannot escape the age-old argument over whether drama's purpose is to delight or to educate. Data on lengths of runs, degrees of critical acclaim, and attendance, not surprisingly, reveal that the key to a play's success before, during and after the Depression seems to depend upon a balance of entertainment and edification.

As Herr mentions in 'American Political Drama, 1910–45',[11] notions of the *social*, the *political* and the *socio-political* tend to blur, with only illusory definitions of these concepts emerging. Nonetheless, these words are used by the majority of critics and historians, so they warrant some explication here.

Social drama may address politically timely issues, but it tends to do so without becoming mired in time or culture-bound in its implementation of period-specific turns of phrase or concepts (think late nineteenth century Henrik Ibsen, or Arthur Miller in the 1940s, for examples). *Political* drama is frequently more topical and/or site-specific (think Aristophanes). Often, but not always, political dramas adopt a form other than realism. They may be polyvocal; characters may be stereotypical, even caricatures (a 'big boss' with a cigar, a capitalist wearing a dollar sign); and the pieces may resemble the German theorist/playwright Bertolt Brecht's work in their implementation of alienation or aesthetic distancing, third-person commentary and use of supporting data or statistics in the forms of placards or slides. As a result of any or all of these characteristics, political, polemical drama is less likely than social drama to stand the test of time and meet with production in later eras. That said, social drama is not without reference to political or economic concerns. It simply exhibits a lighter touch and more often than not is cast in a realistic form. However, even the most serious-minded or tragic social dramas seldom cross the line from realism to pure naturalism (in the sense of the style as conceived of by Emile Zola in the nineteenth century).

Although social comedies certainly exist, in general, to borrow a phrase from C. W. E. Bigsby with reference to Robert Sherwood's *Idiot's Delight*, the most successful social dramas are 'moral melodramas'.[12] Several of the plays discussed in this chapter will fall into this category; they might also be categorized as *socialist realism*, a phrase not used in the 1930s but coined retrospectively with regard to plays of the time. Several of them display a Marxist ideology and conclude with the martyrdom of a central character and/or a cry for action.

Especially during the 1930s, there was considerable overlapping among theatre practitioners, including playwrights, as they moved from company to company, sometimes working with the same actors, directors or designers in different venues, often participating in leftist producing companies like the Theatre of Action, Theatre Collective or Theatre Union at the same time as working with the established Theatre Guild or America's preeminent home of social drama from 1931 to 1940, the Group Theatre. Five noted playwrights (Maxwell Anderson, S. N. Behrman, Sidney Howard, Elmer Rice and Robert Sherwood), dissatisfied with Broadway producing conditions, banded together in 1938 to form their own producing agency for Broadway shows, the Playwrights Producing Company, Inc. Due to the economic conditions of the Depression, a workers' theatre movement burgeoned in the 1930s, with more than 400 companies in existence by mid-decade, and labour concerns infiltrated the subject matter of drama across the boards, from tragic pieces to drawing room comedies, manifesting to some extent in virtually every form in between. As a result, individuals and theatrical producing agencies influenced one another as theatrical forms, styles and even missions cross-pollinated, with the social, political and socio-political ever present.

Playwrights cut across genre lines in their works, sometimes suiting new forms to content, with plays displaying ideological changes or shifting political perspectives as their writing and the decade itself unfolded. Robert Sherwood, for example, moved from political critique in his dramas of the first part of the decade to support of the United States' entry into the Second World War. While he did not write labour drama per se, William Saroyan was so incensed with the economic machinations of American capitalism that he refused the monetary award associated with his Pulitzer Prize for *The Time of Your Life* in 1939. Elmer Rice's career spanned a full half-century (1914, *On Trial* to *Court of Last Resort*, 1965), and he deployed forms and styles that ranged from expressionism and near naturalism in the 1920s to writing in a realistic vein with melodramatic overtones in the 1930s, concluding his work in the decade with fantasy in *American Landscape* (1938). Rice's *oeuvre* illustrates a writer in search of a form and style commensurate with his changing times. Playwright John Howard Lawson's stylistic experiments point to political hair-splitting in terms of dramatic criticism across the decade. Often criticized by the mainstream as too 'left' and attacked by Marxists as uncommitted, Lawson waffled in form, style and subject matter, caving in to rewrites projected on him by Group Theatre leader Harold Clurman, joining the Communist Party USA and abandoning playwriting for screenwriting. He became the first President of the Screenwriters Guild, facing indictment and a prison sentence for his testimony before the House Un-American Activities Committee (HUAC). Lawson's playwriting career ended in the late 1930s when he committed himself fully to political engagement and fighting for workers' rights.

Like Saroyan in his refusal, and Lawson with his newfound political allegiance, other playwrights of the 1930s exhibited perhaps unprecedented personal principles. Elmer Rice resigned from his position with the Federal Theatre Project when he faced government censorship over the never-staged production *Ethiopia*.

During these turbulent times, like everything in life, the drama was often conflicted, confused, at times sending at best mixed and (more often) contradictory messages regarding, for example, race, gender and class. The decade saw progress in the depiction of African-Americans, progress initiated earlier by Langston Hughes and Zora Neale Hurston, but simultaneously the drama often (unintentionally) promoted gross racial stereotypes in many of the plays produced. Black servants populate the dramas of Lillian Hellman and the high comedies of S. N. Behrman, and a black maid and her boyfriend figure in the action of Kaufman and Hart's *You Can't Take it With You*. At the same time, the Theatre Union, when mounting Paul Peters's *Stevedore*, insisted that local restaurants and other establishments near their theatre accept the patronage of black actors lest the company publicly boycott them. The company also paid their black actors standard union wages. Yet, the play itself, in its depiction of life surrounding a New Orleans wharf, included stereotypical black dialect.

Female characters were treated with varying degrees of agency; generally speaking, although female leads might be featured, playwrights demurred to the traditional 'madonna/whore' or 'mistress/wife' dichotomies decried by feminists decades later. The 1930s exhibited a paucity of female playwrights produced on Broadway. It would be decades, as well, before an alleged gay or lesbian character might, if not 'live happily ever after', at least dwell on some level comparable to a heterosexual of the same economic class. For example, in Hellman's notorious *The Children's Hour*, which addresses veiled homosexuality, one of the protagonists commits suicide, and the other breaks off her engagement.

Perhaps, given the indulgences of those in the top percentage of income mentioned in the previous chapter, and the dreadful living conditions of so many of the unemployed and working poor across the decade, in drama, class may be considered the most accurately depicted (if, at times exaggerated) of the categories examined here. Hallie Flanagan and Margaret Ellen Clifford's 1931 *Can You Hear Their Voices? A Play of Our Time*, based on the short story 'Can You Make Out Their Voices' by Whittaker Chambers and first produced at Vassar College's Experimental Theater, epitomizes the portrayal of class conflict with its juxtaposition of desperate family scenes from Dust Bowl Arkansas with a Washington senator's daughter's debutante ball. Agit-prop (agitation and propaganda)[13] scenes alternate with the domestic drama. The piece exhibits the style of pure workers' theatre like the German Prolet-Bühne and local union performances, at the same time anticipating the polyvocality, calls for 'Strike!' and mosaic structure of *Waiting for Lefty* as well as the use of news stories, placards, slides and so on of the Federal Theatre's Living Newspapers.

Of course, outright polemics lacked general appeal and agit-prop pieces were not accepted Broadway fare. The plays that reached the general populous were those that combined recognizable realism in dialogue and décor and characters with whom the audience might empathize. Playwrights dedicated to social justice, the workers' plight or even communism as a panacea to the era's economic demise quickly learned that couching their messages in compassionately created characters and peppering their plays with emotional peaks and valleys, adding a strong climax, would best serve their cause. Nonetheless, because the Depression permeated the decade's worldview and undergirded its drama, this chapter continues with a section on labour drama and workers' theatre.

Labour(ing) drama: The production companies, the playwrights and the plays

The 'ing' is added to the title above for a number of reasons: 1) due to critics' analyses of the workers' theatres' output as heavy handed or laborious; 2) because of the early companies' creation by actual workers whose lived experience was authentic and depicted honestly in their dramas, rather than by more experienced professional theatre practitioners; 3) since these companies focused on creating productions *by* and *for* the working class, often against great financial and politically risky odds; and, 4) because of the workers' theatre's unflinching homage to those who toiled daily in manual labour positions, vital to the nation's lifeblood and economy. Early labour drama and production in the decade sprang from workers' theatres like the German Prolet-Bühne, founded by John Bonn in the United States circa 1925 and the Workers Laboratory Theatre (WLT), established in 1929; the drama paralleled but seemed not to intersect with theatrical work at progressive labour colleges like Brookwood.[14]

The Theatre Collective arose from the Workers Laboratory Theatre (WLT) in 1932, and employed several Group Theatre participants, among them designer Mordecai Gorelik and actress Virginia Farmer who ran their school. These professionals often volunteered their time, pro bono or at reduced wages, because they believed in the workers' causes. They always worked for the Theatre Collective at a far lower pay scale than that to which they were accustomed, even if they were card carrying union members. Other Group Theatre members who migrated further to the left to work with the Theatre Collective's studio included Morris Carnovsky, Cheryl Crawford, Sanford Meisner, Clifford Odets and Lee Strasberg. However, the Theatre Collective was founded by workers Hiram and Jake Shapiro and maintained the working-class spirit from which it first sprang. The Theatre

Collective is important in a study of 1930s labour drama, not for its repertory, which is scant and difficult to uncover,[15] nor because the company engaged the participation of noteworthy and knowledgeable theatre practitioners, but, rather, because it portrayed the real-life drama of strikes and protest against management 'monkey business' as they called it in the day, and as it deliberately crossed the line from agit-prop toward what Ira A. Levine calls, in *Left Wing Dramatic Theory*, 'revolutionary realism'. Only fairly recently, in pieces like Daniel Opler's 'Monkey Business in Union Square: A Cultural Analysis of the Klein-Ohrbach Strikes of 1934–5',[16] have historians grappled with the sociological implications of strikes and protests, and their dramatic representations in their time. The examination of site-specific productions, like many labour dramas, often ignored by theatre historians because of their ephemeral nature, has habitually been left to the work of Performance Studies scholars.

The WLT eventually changed its name to the Theatre of Action (1935), a 'shock troupe' for which later famous director Elia Kazan mounted the first production, *The Young Go First*, based on co-author Arthur Vogel's experience with the Civilian Conservation Corps discussed in the previous chapter. The company's change in name, surprisingly because it maintained its extreme leftist philosophy (as the word 'action' indicates), signalled its departure from agit-prop and a distinct move to the realm of revolutionary realism. The play's plot concerns male youths who meet in the course of their participation in the CCC, but they revolt, reflecting the extreme left's suspicion that the CCC was in actuality a military training ground. Embedded in the script's realistic structure is a polyvocal moment in which the boys chant together, reminiscent of agit-prop conventions. In order to effect ensemble acting of the first order, Theatre of Action actors spent weeks under the tutelage of Group Theatre (discussed below) members, and, by and large, the press recognized the company's sound work.[17] It is of note that the Group Theatre acquired new, young actors from the Theatre Collective and from the workers' theatre movement, among them Julie (John) Garfield and Nicholas Ray – a fact Group Theatre director Harold Clurman seems to have conveniently forgotten. Members of the Theatre of Action's advisory council also included Moss Hart, Clifford Odets and Lee Strasberg.[18]

The Prolet-Bühne (who produced, among other polemic pieces, a mass recitation, *Scottsboro*) and WLT staunchly adhered to agit-prop techniques whereas the other companies were more imitative of traditional dramaturgy and production values. Several of the companies (or their members) were covertly or overtly associated with the Communist Party USA (CP-USA). Curiously, political allegiance did not seem to determine styles of production or production values, but, rather, those choices appear to have been purely aesthetic and in keeping with global ideological swings across the decade. For example, the Theatre Collective – maybe owing to its relatively late development – was associated with the CP-USA, but its dramaturgy was typically social realism. Members of the Group Theatre were later revealed to have been party members, but the company's plays were realistic as well, and social rather than political in content.

The Prolet-Bühne and the WLT joined forces in publishing *Workers Theatre*, at first a modest mimeographed pamphlet of sorts, then a more polished periodical. Participants in the workers' theatre movement were serious about imparting political points of view (in this case communist, with a hammer and sickle as *Workers Theatre*'s logo) as well as proffering practical production tips for working on a low budget or constructing mobile scenery.[19] The communist organ, the *Daily Worker*, routinely included pieces on theatre and reviews, as did *New Masses*. *New Theatre*, while decidedly 'to the left', but not allegedly communist or Marxist, focused on contemporary theatre and later film, with more of an emphasis on the drama's form and style than on its politics; *Theatre Arts Monthly* chronicled current theatrical production and theory as well. Mordecai Gorelik's seminal *Theatre Arts Monthly* article, 'Theatre is a Weapon',[20] offers an overview of Marxist production mid-decade (excerpted in the 'Documents' chapter). In it, purposefully deploying a class-conscious Marxist vocabulary with words like 'exploitation' and 'bondage', Gorelik sets apart the true workers' theatre from more characteristically bourgeoisie endeavours. He also discusses the playwright's place in society, criticizing Eugene O'Neill, Philip Barry and others for their penchant for the abstract at the expense, he thought, of action. His focus on the unemployment of theatre practitioners predates the creation of the Federal Theatre Project (discussed later). Across the decade, critical debate about the nature and purpose of drama as it relates to politics persisted in a war of words between mainstream critics and newspapers and those decidedly to the left.

The Theatre Collective offered regularly scheduled 'Workers Theatre Nights' with featured speakers. Theatre Union board members attended union meetings across the city, and the company offered symposia connected with each production. The workers' theatres all maintained an allegiance to the working class as well as a desire to improve the quality of their productions without losing their political clout.

The Theatre Union (1932) developed independently of the more unabashedly workers' theatre (read agit-prop or union) companies, created from a confluence of influences that stemmed from a variety of sources and inspirations including writers and editors of leading liberal or radical publications like Edmund Wilson of the *New Republic*, *New Masses* editor Michael Gold (née Irwin Granich), labour journalist Manuel Gomez (née Charles Shipman) and the company's prime mover, would-be playwright and writer on labour relations and the steel industry, Charles Rumford Walker. Members of the Theatre Union Executive Board included political writers Harbor Allen and Liston Oak and film writers like later-blacklisted Albert Maltz. The company practised board diversification decades before it became a phrase. The Theatre Union proclaimed itself to be America's first professional leftist theatre and sought to produce plays of high quality (literary and visual). The company differentiated itself from other Broadway theatres, reaching its working-class audience by offering the lowest ticket price scale in New York, by providing free tickets to the unemployed, and through its unique audience development techniques. Of all the producing organizations discussed here, the Theatre Union most determinedly embodies the inclusiveness of the Popular Front mentality at its best, attending to issues of class, race, gender and the inalienable right to question and protest, both onstage and off.

During its four-year existence, the Theatre Union produced eight works significant for their political impact, exemplifying socialist realism underpinned with American idealism, Brecht's epic theatre, and experiments in 'performance ethnography' (the creation of dramatic texts based in part on first-hand, ethnographic research). The company's repertory consisted of five American plays – George Sklar and Albert Maltz's *Peace on Earth* (1934);

Paul Peters (aka *New Masses*' Harbor Allen) and George Sklar's *Stevedore* (1934); Albert Maltz's *Black Pit* (1935); Albert Bein's *Let Freedom Ring* (1935); and John Howard Lawson's *Marching Song* (1937) – interspersed with three European pieces of like theme: *Sailors of Catarro* (1934–5) by Friedrich Wolf; Brecht's *The Mother* (1935); and Victor Wolfson's *Bitter Stream* (1936), which addresses fascism in Italy.

Peace on Earth concerns a pacifist college professor; *Stevedore* illustrates the plight of black dockworkers; *Black Pit* dramatizes strife within the coal mining industry and features the character of a 'scab'. *Let Freedom Ring* is based on Grace Lumpkin's novel *To Make My Bread*, in turn inspired by the 1929 Gastonia textile strike, and John Howard Lawson's *Marching Song* conflates several autoworker strikes and is set in an abandoned automobile wheel factory.

Peace on Earth, with the subtitle *An Anti-War Play*, by Albert Maltz and George Sklar, was the Theatre Union's inaugural production. The fledgling group, which operated collectively under a system of direct democracy of sorts that included a vetting of all scripts and suggested revisions by committee, struggled mightily to keep this production afloat. They succeeded in doing so due in large measure to the heroic efforts of pioneer arts administrators Margaret Larkin, Sylvia Reagan and Martha Dreiblatt, assisted by Zelda Dorfman – women working on audience development and marketing behind the scenes throughout the company's tenure.

Classmates and friends as undergraduates at Yale, besides their college theatrical endeavours, playwrights Maltz and Sklar collaborated earlier on *Merry-Go-Round* (1932), an exposé of political corruption in New York City. *Peace on Earth* set the tone for the Theatre Union's subsequent plays and productions, but it differed from their other offerings in that the protagonist was a middle-class college professor (the others are workers), and the style of production (the script as written, as well) employed kaleidoscopic expressionistic devices.

The story is that of a pacifist academic who, convinced by his union advocate friend, moves toward activism, attends a strike meeting and participates in peaceful protest. He is framed for a murder of someone at a demonstration, then jailed and ultimately wrongly executed. Of particular note, dramaturgically, is the subversion of American myths, exhibited by a mock Boston Tea

Party, reading of the Declaration of Independence, recitation of the Gettysburg Address, quotation of the First Amendment and a rendition of 'My Country 'Tis of Thee, Sweet Land of Liberty' – each juxtaposed with moments of flagrant abuses of individual liberties in the play's action.

With Peters and Sklar's *Stevedore*, the Theatre Union hit its stride. This production constituted the beginning of a series of plays dealing with the plight of American workers, gleaned from the playwrights' ethnographic research. Appreciated for its social content and its fast-paced action, framed by a melodramatic structure, *Stevedore* received considerable critical praise, from both the mainstream and Marxist presses, and ran for 175 performances. Theatre historian Ilka Saal dubs *Stevedore* 'the most successful proletarian melodrama on the New Deal stage'.[21] Peters's crafting of the play was preceded and informed by his ten months working with an all-black crew on a wharf in New Orleans (*Stevedore*'s setting). His attitude toward racism (and the 'Black and White Unite and Fight' credo of the Communist Party USA) was intensified by the Scottsboro case, which he covered, publishing a pamphlet entitled 'Eight Who Lie in the Death House' for the express purpose of raising funds for the defence of the 'Scottsboro boys'.[22] Prior to rehearsals, director Michael Blankfort also visited New Orleans docks to film the longshoremen's activities.

Stevedore's script illustrates Marxist doctrine in both content and form, as it not only advocates workers' rights and a classless and integrated society, but its protagonist is martyred, dying in a *pietà* pose. In the play's final moments, one character, Blacksnake, emits a battle cry, 'Come on, let's give it to 'em!'[23] Then a female character joins the fray, felling the 'villain'[24] just as reinforcements of 'good guys' are heard in the distance. The combination of black and white union activists, winning this fight with their opposition, points to a potentially brighter future for all.[25]

Black Pit and *Let Freedom Ring*, each dealing with glaring worker–management conflicts and abuse of labourers, were both produced by the Theatre Union in 1935, at the apex of Popular Front sentiments. Set in a coal mining community in West Virginia (based on real-life troubled Harlan County sites), *Black Pit*, another social realist melodrama grounded in the playwright's field work (Maltz lived in mining camps for four months, chronicling his experiences and stories he heard), focuses on Eastern European immigrant workers and includes the character of a 'scab'. Again, the protagonist is martyred, but this time he is forced into exile (although in the film version, *Black Fury*, the story is reinterpreted as a romance that ends happily). Like *Stevedore*, *Black Pit* was praised for its *scène à faire*, its evocative environmental authenticity.

Albert Bein's *Let Freedom Ring* depicts the 1929 Gastonia, North Carolina, textile strikes during which union activist and balladeer Ella Mae Wiggins was assassinated. *Let Freedom Ring*'s ethnographic credibility begins with that of the original novel's author, Grace Lumpkin. Southerner, Communist Party member and Theatre Union supporter, the author was present at the 1929 Loray Mill strike in Gastonia, upon which the novel draws. Theatre Union secretary Margaret Larkin was there as well.

Not only did Larkin write about labour conditions in the South in *The North American Review*, but she interviewed activist songwriter Ella Mae Wiggins and went on to champion her work after the worker/singer's murder. Wiggins's martyrdom in the name of the workers' cause – and her continued life through the popularity of her songs – added pathos to *Let Freedom Ring* before it reached the stage. Larkin's subsequent writing in relationship to *Let Freedom Ring* included data on millworker wages, statistics from the North Carolina State Bureau of Health on 'miller's plague', from which the character Emma in the play dies. The first published version of the script offers an Introduction by labour organizer/poet Don West, who was also involved in the Gastonia strike, reprinted from the 18 November 1935 *Daily Worker*.

The play details the implications of 'speed-ups' or 'stretch outs' (more work for the same or less pay) for the textile workers as well as the deplorable conditions under which those labourers lucky enough to remain employed lived. In addition to the life of the Carolina 'lint heads', it illustrates conflicts faced by 'mountain folk' whose poverty and inability to any longer draw sustenance from their land forced them to descend to textile villages in search of work. Again, *Let Freedom Live* presents the labourers' perspectives, advocating union activism and workers' rights. The play is an indictment of the textile industry, with the fictional McClure family standing for the masses of struggling millworkers. Marxist in thought, the play projects a theme of class against class; the protagonist is martyred, and his brother awakens to take up the cause.

With its explicit reference to the Angelo Herndon case, the Supreme Court and the US Constitution, the Theatre Union's last play, John Howard Lawson's *Marching Song* (1937), forecasts the future (of racial unrest and possible progress and of the dilemmas of democracy and capitalism in the late twentieth century). Lawson brought to his writing political commitment enriched by his experiences meeting the 'Scottsboro Boys' and returning to the South as part of a delegation representing, among other alliances, the Herndon Defense League.[26]

Fifty different nationalities are represented in the play's fictional automotive plant. Characters directly involved in stage action include Irish, (Southern) black, Italian, Jewish and Nordic. While their working-class status, solidarity, unionism and belief in the strength of numbers align these disparate groups, their relationships, assumptions and prejudices are expressed as extraordinarily complex.

As with other Theatre Union plays and productions, focus lies on the worker, on the hope for a democracy that would one day be efficacious for all and on the playwright's valiant attempt to depict race and ethnicity responsibly and devoid of stereotype. In *Marching Song*, Lawson appears to have consciously deployed racial and ethnic biases by including them as character and plot points.

The play's last scene takes us through the branding, torture and death of union leader Bill Anderson to a march on the street, complete with tear gas, to the city-wide blackout created by electric workers in support of their automotive brothers. The character of Lucky, who orchestrated the power outage, concludes the play with a battle cry when, leaning out of a second-storey window of the plant, he shouts, 'We stopped the power 'cause it's us that made it! ... We put a saddle on the lightning like you saddle a mule! ... You hear me, you multitude, power is people!'[27]

Marching Song constituted the Theatre Union's 'swan song'. An expensive piece to mount, it broke the company's bank. Forced into dire financial straits before the production, it took additional fundraisers and private donations to conclude as little in the red (no pun intended) as it did. The company was compelled to increase ticket prices slightly. As a result of company malaise, the production did not receive the blast of publicity releases and unique marketing strategies from which earlier shows had benefitted; little effort was made to procure block bookings and group sales. There had been a company reorganization – a shake-up in fact, too convoluted to detail here – in part precipitated by an ideological schism surrounding board members' attitudes toward Russia. Interest in the Theatre Union on the part of founding members was waning, and many of them turned to other endeavours, literary or political. Sadly, the collective spirit of the Theatre Union was broken well before the depletion of its coffers. A socially engaged artistic collaborative faltered not merely because of financial exigencies, but due, in part, to its adoption of a professional theatre business model.

The Federal Theatre Project was the United States' only government-supported theatrical company – ever. To many, the notion of the federal government financially supporting the arts is still anathema, somehow standing in marked contrast to the American modus operandus, capitalism. To many, free enterprise, the pursuit of the 'American Dream' and rugged individualism seem antithetical to government subsidy for anything, let alone the arts. Nevertheless, with funding initiated by an Act of Congress on 21 January 1935, Harry Hopkins, director of the Works Progress Administration, quickly planned for the FTP's implementation. With Hallie Flanagan, Hopkins's Grinnell College classmate, head of Vassar College's Experimental Theatre, at its helm, this agency would blend art and social service as it offered work to unemployed theatre practitioners across the country. Flanagan's task loomed large, probably greater than she imagined. She would find herself in constant conflict with Congress as she attempted to execute her charge to offer the American public the 'free, adult, uncensored' theatrical fare Hopkins promised, and to put across her own agenda, that of creating a federation of theatres across the land – one that would serve the dual purposes of art as entertainment and as instruction.

Much has been written on the FTP; the agency has been virtually mythologized. Most important to the time and space allotted here is to convey the diversity of participants and of programming the FTP presented and to emphasize the enormity of its geographic stretch, far beyond New York City, on which much of the scholarly work on the company has focused. The FTP reached across the country to an active unit in Seattle, Washington, for example, and other units in the Deep South. The FTP reflected multiple races and ethnicities, with a number of black units and Jewish units, and productions in a variety of languages including Yiddish, French, Russian, Italian, Spanish and German. Programming included not only traditionally scripted plays (classics, contemporary and new plays), but circus, puppetry, children's theatre, musicals, vaudeville, dance projects and more.

The FTP generated a new genre, the Living Newspaper, which ingeniously blended news stories, data, excerpts from court transcripts, iconic American documents and other projected images with scripted dialogue, often ominously magnified through a loudspeaker or recited repeatedly, with moments heightened through the use of actors in tableaux.

Material was selected and arranged in the Living Newspapers to create what might be termed empathetic documentaries, or 'social allegories',[28] that mixed presentational and representational styles. Scripts were generally structured in several short titled scenes (typically 20 or more), and characters were most often presented as types, with epithets for names, as in earlier expressionism and workers' theatre dramas. A team of researchers, led by an experienced playwright, collectively crafted the scripts, in a setting akin to that of a newsroom, with writers, editors and other staff. Full-length examples of note are *Triple-A Plowed Under* (1936), *Power* (1937), *Injunction Granted* (1938) and *One-Third of a Nation* (1938).

Since all of the Living Newspapers, and other FTP productions regardless of dramatic form, grappled with current events and social issues, an element of risk was involved. Despite Hopkins's vow to create uncensored theatre, in their mere subject matter, FTP Living Newspapers habitually faced governmental objections. In fact, the FTP's first production, *Ethiopia*, was cancelled, ostensibly because it depicted living heads of state onstage.

Triple-A Plowed Under took on the Supreme Court's recent ruling that FDR's New Deal Agricultural Act was unconstitutional. Famous for its gigantic projection of the United States Constitution as one of its backdrops, the piece included excerpts from a speech by Communist leader Earl Browder and a quotation from Secretary of Agriculture Henry Wallace. The piece advocated that farmers and labourers unite in protest against the US Supreme Court's decision, a concept easily compared to one promoted by the Communist Party USA. As with the other Living Newspapers, it can be argued that, rather than promoting a particular political agenda *Triple-A Plowed Under* projected myriad perspectives, exercising the inalienable right of free speech, the American way.

Taking as its subject government-supplied utilities, namely support of the Tennessee Valley Authority, *Power* opened simultaneously at several cities across the nation. As the nation was poised waiting for a decision from the Supreme Court concerning a lower court injunction on the TVA, the piece ended with a huge question mark projected on the stage. Pitting the 'little man' in New York City against the wealthy property-owner and focused on housing and the rapid development of slums across the country, *One-Third of a Nation* critiques the Housing Act of 1937 that did little to alleviate current problems or offer affordable housing. *Injunction Granted* lampooned big business and tycoons, recommending that unions join the CIO.

Ultimately the FTP, after many battles with Congress, lost its funding in 1939. At congressional hearings, Hallie Flanagan held her own under accusations of communism and behaviour by representatives that recalls the inane actions of characters in Maxwell Anderson's *Both Your Houses*. A line of questioning that asked Flanagan about Christopher Marlowe's current political affiliation summarizes the theatrical literacy of some government officials.

As with the other art agencies discussed in 'Life in the Decade', the FTP employed renowned theatre artists and others who would go on to great acclaim. One of these theatrical luminaries was a young Orson Welles (of later *Citizen Kane* fame), who directed the FTP's sparkling version of *Macbeth* with an all-black cast, often referred to as the 'Voodoo *Macbeth*' because of its Haitian setting. Welles also directed the legendary FTP production of Mark Blitzstein's political musical, *The Cradle Will Rock*, famous for the manner in which, barred from performance in its original theatre, it was staged elsewhere, with union-member actors singing their roles from the audience. Welles and John Houseman would form the Mercury Theatre in 1937.

The most prominent of the decade's theatre companies was without doubt the Group Theatre (1930–41), the brainchild of director Harold Clurman and managed by a triumvirate that included, with him, Cheryl Crawford and Lee Strasburg. The Group was consistently lauded for its acting prowess and high production value standards, which together supported its mission to dramatize the conditions of their time. The company's repertory consisted of social rather than political plays, a source of some members' frustration. Nonetheless, those who participated, the more politically to the left, even communist, considered membership in the prestigious company a privilege and looked back at their time with the Group fondly. The Group Theatre truly 'altered the course of American theater forever'.[29]

Plays produced by the Group, during its decade-plus existence, included the following: Paul Green's *The House of Connelly* (1931); Paul and Claire Sifton's *1931–*, in the same year; *Night Over Taos* by Maxwell Anderson, in 1932; *The Big Night* by Dawn Powell (1933); John Howard Lawson's *Success Story* (1932–3) and *Gentlewoman* (1934); Sidney Kingsley's *Men in White* (1934); *Golden Eagle Guy* by Melvin Levy (1934–5); Nellise Child's *Weep for the Virgins* (1935); *The Case of Clyde Griffiths* (1936), written by Erwin Piscator and Lena Goldschmidt, adapted from Theodore Dreiser's book *An American Tragedy*; Paul Green's *Johnny Johnson*, with music by Kurt Weill (1936–7); *Casey Jones* (1938) and *Thunder Rock* (1939) by Robert Ardrey; Irwin Shaw's *The Gentle People* (1939) and *Retreat to Pleasure* (1940–41); and, for an extremely limited run, William Saroyan's *My Heart's in the Highlands* (1939). But it was Clifford Odets's approximately half-dozen plays for the company that precipitated the young playwright's meteoric rise to fame and positioned him as the Group Theatre's 'cash cow', forever indebted to the producers for giving him his start, and ever loyal, often sending money back to New York in support of the Group after he became a Hollywood screenwriter (see Christopher Herr's chapter on the playwright in this book).

Initially a minor actor with the Group, Odets penned his strike play *Waiting for Lefty* (1935) as a part of one of the New Theatre Nights, where it was performed to great acclaim, then picked up by the Group. *Lefty* was quickly followed by *Awake and Sing!* in the same year, Odets's first full-length play to debut with the Group. To varying degrees of critical and popular success, Odets contributed to the company, in rapid fire succession, *Till the Day I Die* (1935), *Paradise Lost* (1935–6), *Golden Boy* (1937–8), *Rocket to the Moon* (1938–9) and, finally, *Night Music* (1940). In fact, time and time again, the Group Theatre returned to Odets's work with a remounting of *Waiting for Lefty* (1935–6) and subsequent productions of *Awake and Sing!* (later in 1935, and again in 1939).

The discussion of Group Theatre plays that follows focuses on those that reflect some of the company's strengths and struggles; it is by no means exhaustive.[30] In some instances, for organizational purposes, plays produced by the Group Theatre have been included in other sections in the chapter.

While the Siftons' *1931–* captures the socio-economic import of its historical moment, it is a piece whose form straddles a dramaturgical fence between the experimental style of the late 1920s (exemplified by the New Playwrights Theatre with whom the Siftons worked) and the realism that would be *de rigueur* by mid-decade. The script follows the demise of a Depression Era 'Everyman' named Adam. Constructed in fourteen episodes interspersed with ten interludes, in ways reminiscent of the choral odes of Greek tragedy, its plot combines the story of Adam's romance, postponed marriage and poignant but brief chance encounter with his ex-fiancée with his initial firing, pursuit of work, collapse in a work line and sudden commitment to a communist protest. The piece concludes with the offstage sound of police machine-gun fire that seals the protagonist's fate. The play, then, employs an episodic structure and expressionistic effects supported by an empathetic and identifiable depiction of the human condition. Despite a talented and committed cast and Lee Strasberg's insightful direction, supported by Mordecai Gorelik's inspired industrial-style set, *1931–* appealed to neither the usual theatre-going public nor to critics of the time. When the Group lowered ticket prices, the production did, however, capture a new audience of workers who packed the balcony. Later, *Waiting for Lefty* would employ the episodic structure and humanity the Siftons sought, and the Federal Theatre Project's Living Newspapers would more nearly perfect the style.

Not a success story for John Howard Lawson

John Howard Lawson's playwriting struggle is well covered in Jonathan Chambers's study, *Messiah of the New Technique: John Howard Lawson, Communism, and American Theatre 1923–1937*, but, insofar as it relates to the Group Theatre (and beyond), it warrants inclusion here. While *Success Story* achieved a respectable 121-performance run, *Gentlewoman* survived only twelve performances, and it is worth noting that Lawson's *The Pure in Heart*, mounted by the Theatre Guild, opened at almost exactly the same time as the latter and abruptly closed. Nonetheless, as Chambers so eloquently argues, Lawson's career represents not that of a failed playwright but, rather, the story of a writer/political activist caught in (and representative of) the aesthetic and socio-political turmoil of his time – and a citizen-writer who, in Chambers's words, affected the 'direction, shape, and scope of American theatre between the world wars'.[31] In addition, John Howard Lawson's experience with the Group Theatre, especially in terms of the ways in which he acquiesced to demands of the company's management, reveals the underbelly of this producing agency that is so often lauded by critics and historians.

As produced, *Success Story* – the rags-to-riches tale of the character Sol Ginsberg's movement from impetuous, sincere and radical youth to ruthless capitalist – is cast in a realist form, with a melodramatic bent. Mordecai Gorelik's towering glass-infused Modernist set accentuated the trappings of wealth acquired through corporate greed. An array of characters from varying classes crosses the stage, all, while markedly indicative of their station in Depression days, drawn by Lawson with humanity. Group Theatre actors including Luther and Stella Adler and Franchot Tone played their roles with energy and emotional commitment.

While it is impossible to ascertain the degree of more long-standing artistic or political acclaim *Success Story* might have achieved as Lawson originally wrote the play, the changes to which he succumbed (and those he fought or ignored) are important as they constitute a chronicling, through his art, of the writer's deepening political activism and his ponderings on playwriting that would be manifested in his publication of the widely used *Theory and Technique of Playwriting* in 1936, a text in which he discusses the relationship between political commitment and writing, offering advice on theory as it relates to play structure. This book was utilized in playwriting programmes across the United States for decades and is still referenced today. Although Lawson had not yet joined the Communist Party in 1932, he was scrutinizing its theories, and some of them are admittedly borne out in *Success Story*.

Two significant changes to the script, foisted on Lawson by Harold Clurman, concern the character of Sarah (Sol's long-suffering, 'stand by her man' childhood sweetheart, who shoots him in the end) and the play's concluding scene. Clurman insisted that Sarah was muddled and that Lawson should recraft the character to reflect a definite point of view. Lawson vehemently disagreed, stating in a manifesto he presented to the Group that her responses were emotional and did not emanate from an ideological perspective.[32] Lawson did not view *Success Story* as a revolutionary piece; instead, he was 'convinced that the communism mentioned in the play is simply a cultural backdrop for Sol and Sarah, to which she clings and on which he turns his back'.[33] The other change promoted by Clurman concerned the final moments of the play: the Group sought some ray of hope at the end. Ironically, so did the communist press, for a different reason. *Success Story* was panned by the *Daily Worker*, for example, as 'an apologia for the bourgeois society', one in which 'the audience is asked to weep over the sexual problems of a finance-capitalist swindler'.[34] To the communist press, the play lacked leftist commitment.

John Howard Lawson's turmoil over *Success Story*, briefly outlined here, is important not merely as it pertains to this particular playwright, but, more significantly, as it reflects the aesthetic dilemma of the day. Every one of the American playwrights of the 1930s – perhaps more than in any other decade – was faced with the questions, 'To what degree should art display politics?' and 'How topical should a piece of dramatic literature be?'.

Like *Success Story*, *Gentlewoman* was first drafted by Lawson a few years earlier, and so maintained vestigial elements from the playwright's past ventures and ideological reflections: in Lawson's words, as cited by Chambers, this play, too, 'demonstrated the war within myself'.[35]

Set in a stylish drawing room, the epitome of wealth and power, yet not a 'drawing room comedy' in the S. N. Behrman vein, *Gentlewoman*'s dramaturgy is problematic at best. Yet one is drawn to the predicament of the characters: Gwyn Ballantine, the cool, classy widow of a prominent businessman; and her newfound love, Rudy Flannigan, a brash, young radical who recalls John Howard Lawson himself. The two take an apartment together but discover that their world ideologies are inherently and drastically opposed. Despite her best efforts, Gwyn cannot free herself from the bondage of the upper class, lavishing Rudy with extravagances like fresh flowers and steaks, which they can little afford, as Gwyn was left penniless by her husband. In *Gentlewoman*, as well, Lawson offers topical references and a communist perspective only fleetingly, as a backdrop to the action. Again, due to his lack of personal political commitment at this time in his life, the playwright, a seeming 'people pleaser', fails to satisfy either the mainstream press or that to the left. Lawson thought that his message was clear – that commitment (to the party) and revolution would bring one honour, but neither script nor production came close to toeing the party line. The inclusion of a few Depression details and even Gwyn's final speech about walking 'towards a red horizon' were not sufficient in providing a clear, never mind potent, political point of view. The character of Rudy is filled with self-doubt, and actor Lloyd Nolan, who played the role, overemphasized the character's debauchery. Stella Adler, as Gwyn, played the part with such emotional sincerity that the character became ennobled, losing the keen capitalistic nature with which Lawson had sought to imbue her. Lee Strasberg was troubled with Lawson's fluctuating form and content, and the designer was at a loss as to how he might complement the script. Having found relative success earlier in his career (the Theatre Guild's 1925 production of *Processional*, for example) and a home in the experimental theatre of the 1920s with the New Playwrights, clearly Lawson grappled with social realism in the 1930s.

The closing of *Gentlewoman* marked a turbulent time for the Group: denied full membership in the company, designer Mordecai Gorelik walked away from it for three full years; actors complained that they deserved more decision-making power; and the company was without a script. Nonetheless, the Group's processes in mounting their first few plays, including Lawson's, hinted at its very best work to come.

Men in White by Sidney Kingsley, the Group's next production, remains underrated and excluded from the accepted dramatic canon. Arguably the first 'hospital drama', the play was awarded the Pulitzer Prize in 1934. The plot centres on the dilemma of a young doctor who impregnates a young nurse and then must operate and try to save her life after she secretly gets an abortion. The play's climax is during the operating room scene, choreographed like a classical ballet by director Lee Strasburg.

At times with earlier productions, Strasberg's now legendary 'adjustments' or, in acting parlance, substitutions whereby actors are offered alternative realities or given circumstances in which to play particular moments to gain depth and reality, had succeeded in heightening actors' performances. In *Men in White*, the young director further tested his technique. After taking the cast to visit hospitals and inviting physicians to lecture to the company, he staged the operating scene as a ritual, attending to each second of action. The result was the effect of an actual operating room in action, when, in reality, every movement had been rehearsed to music, with great precision. Designer Gorelik adding 'up lighting' engineered with a simple desk lamp, and the set was comprised of movable screens that afforded quick changes in location, but gave the illusion of a hospital. The production lifted a script that was written with detailed stage directions, in an almost naturalistic style, to a minimalist yet believable level. *Men in White* exhibited the Group processes at their most highly crafted to date, and the production was the hit the company needed, propelling it to the forefront of the American theatre.

Mid-decade brought the Group Theatre's greatest successes with productions of the plays of Clifford Odets, interspersed with some ignominious scripts, now almost entirely lost to the annals of theatre history. These included *Golden Eagle Guy* by labour activist/writer Melvin Levy (1934–5), whose only other play appears to have been the seven-performance flop *A House in the Country*, a piece about a San Francisco magnate that included the character of an actress set just prior to the Civil War; Nellise Child's *Weep for the Virgins* (1935), a bitter comedy focused on three sisters' rags-to-riches dream of stardom, described by Don Wilmeth and Millie Barranger as 'an impossible mess' on all counts;[36] *The Case of Clyde Griffiths* (1936), a reworking of the murder trial novel, adapted as a docudrama by Erwin Piscator and Lena Goldschmidt; and Paul Green's *Johnny Johnson*, with music by Kurt Weill (1936–7), inspired by *The Soldier Schweick*.

As the decade closed, the Group mounted *Casey Jones* (1938) and *Thunder Rock* (1939) by Robert Ardrey. The first piece, although inspired by the folk hero railroad man, is a 1930s Oedipal tale of hubris in which the protagonist's failing eyesight and misjudgement cause a train wreck. This production marked Elia Kazan's directorial debut. *Thunder Rock* is set in a lighthouse, with a reporter turned lighthouse keeper as protagonist. The character has concocted a fantasy life based on the passenger list from a sunken ship, but, in the end, he leaves the lighthouse to re-engage with life ashore – Ardrey's metaphor for a non-isolationist rally. Both plays deal with the idea of an increasingly mechanized society, and they won more kudos for Mordecai Gorelik's stage designs than for their scripts. Both the train engine and lighthouse were massive in scale and stylization. The same was true with Irwin Shaw's *The Gentle People* (1939), in which the designer employed abstract projections as the protagonist wandered through a dream.

Even with their less successful productions, the Group's work was laudable, for the company provided opportunities for up-and-coming playwrights and was willing to experiment stylistically beyond its characteristic realistic portrayal of everyday life and concerns in the 1930s. Although it lasted until 1941, the Group's collective spirit waned as the decade of the 1930s closed. Financial duress contributed to quibbling and downright 'bad blood' among members, and several succumbed to the lure of capitalist Hollywood.

The Group Theatre did much to advance the quality and style of the American theatre. Noted for its passionate and well-crafted ensemble acting, the company spawned a number of famous acting studios that promulgated variations on the Method, the company's unique adaptation of Constantin Stanislavsky's System. Actors came to state with pride their adherence to Adler (Stella), Sanford Meisner or Lee Strasberg, for example. Elia Kazan moved on to great acclaim as a film director and infamy, according to many, for his 'naming names' at the later HUAC hearings.

Founded in 1938, the Playwrights Producing Company, Inc. was the brainchild of Robert E. Sherwood, his effort to wrestle agency away from Broadway producers and to mount his own scripts and those of others. An unprecedented collaboration among creative artists/writers, the company survived for twenty-two years. Purely an artistic endeavour, in which the five playwrights sought financial and moral support (and forthright, honest criticism) from each other, as well as artistic freedom unfettered by typical Broadway constraints, political allegiances were absent from this company's mission.

During the last two years of the decade, the Playwrights Producing Company mounted five productions: Sherwood's *Abe Lincoln in Illinois* (1938); *Knickerbocker Holiday* (1938, book and lyrics by Maxwell Anderson, music by Kurt Weill, who would become a company member later); Elmer Rice's *American Landscape* (1938); S. N. Behrman's *No Time for Comedy* (1939); and *Key Largo*, also penned by Maxwell Anderson (1939). The company's one unmitigated flop in this first year was Rice's *American Landscape*, a strange fantasy play in which historical characters mingle with a contemporary Connecticut family as the father contemplates selling his shoe company to big business.

The group's fifth member, playwright Sydney Howard, who met with acclaim for *They Knew What They Wanted* and *The Silver Cord* in the mid-1920s, died tragically before any of his plays were successfully produced by the company (despite substantial rewriting by Sherwood, Howard's *Madam, Will You Walk* closed in out-of-town try-outs in 1939). Howard won the Academy Award posthumously in 1939 for his film adaptation of *Gone With the Wind*. Robert Ardrey (*Casey Jones* and *Thunder Rock*) was selected by the other company playwrights as recipient of the first playwriting award given by the company in Howard's name.

Robert Sherwood won three Pulitzer Prizes for drama in the 1930s: the first in 1932 for *Reunion in Vienna*, the second in 1936 for *Idiot's Delight* and the third for *Abe Lincoln in Illinois* in 1939. As the Playwrights Producing Company, Inc.'s attorney and Sherwood's friend, John Wharton notes in *Life Among the Playwrights* no one knew, in 1938, that he would win two more Pulitzer Prizes for drama, and one for non-fiction, for *Roosevelt and Hopkins: An Intimate History* (1948). Sherwood's plays of the 1930s are best discussed here, although not all of them were produced by the Playwrights Company since it was not formed until 1938.

Reunion in Vienna, set in the play's title city, is a romantic comedy about deposed royalty that starred Alfred Lunt and Lynn Fontane. At the urging of her husband, who hopes a reunion with his wife's former lover will cure her longing for this bygone relationship, Eléna Krug travels to Vienna where she is reunited with Prince Rudolf Maximilian Von Hapsburg, now a taxi driver but a member of *the* Hapsburgs who have gathered here in Vienna. Their love is rekindled, but ultimately they depart, returning to their normal lives. In this play, cast as comedy, Sherwood's underlying messages have to do with the contrast between new (rational) world order and the romanticism of the past.

In contrast, *The Petrified Forest* (1935) takes as its location the American West (the stone forest of Arizona) and offers an extended metaphor for the Depression, expressing, as Miller and Frazer phrase it, 'the playwright's concern for ordinary people in an America gone awry'.[37] The play's protagonist, a faded intellectual, encounters an idealistic young woman at a truck stop, the Black Mesa Bar-B-Q. She fantasizes about travelling to France, and in his desire to see her dream come true, he determines to leave her the money required for the trip. To accomplish this, when a raid takes place on the premises, Adam Squier persuades a gangster-type to shoot him. This simple plot summary does little justice to the beautifully lyrical drama, illustrative of Robert Sherwood at his most contemplative. A host of 'outsider' characters, average 'Joe's' and representatives of various social classes people the play, and Sherwood's inclusion of the iconic Billy the Kid forecasts William Saroyan's more fully developed mythologizing of America in *The Time of Your Life*.

Idiot's Delight, like *Reunion in Vienna*, is set in Europe, at a chalet in the former Austria, and illustrates Sherwood's skill at using comedy to portray serious issues like the realities of war. Overshadowed by his later work, *Abe Lincoln in Illinois*, this delightful piece showcases the playwright's versatility in terms of both genre and style. It also serves to express Sherwood's increasing anguish over global concerns as the decade progressed, corroborated in his diaries, personal writings and in prefaces to his plays. In the play, a phony Russian countess encounters the American icon of the vaudeville performer. The rest of the cast of characters is comprised of a motley crew, including a distributor of poisonous gas, a honeymoon couple, fascist soldiers and a soon-to-be executed revolutionary, among others. Sherwood's juxtaposition of an Italian air base (unseen in the playing) with the chalet increases the portentousness of war; no one is permitted to cross European borders, no trains are allowed to depart, stranding the cast of characters in the chalet. The curtain rings down on the old trouper and the 'countess' singing 'Onward Christian Soldiers' at the piano, sipping champagne, as bombs fall.

Abe Lincoln in Illinois, best known of Robert Sherwood's plays, perhaps eclipses all the others in the volume of dramatic criticism written on it. By the time it was produced in 1938, frightening conditions in Europe loomed large, and the playwright's anti-war stance changed as he saw the necessity of supporting efforts against the Third Reich. During the Second World War, he served as a speechwriter for Franklin Delano Roosevelt and oversaw the radio broadcasts he dubbed Voice of America. A homage to the United States' Civil War president, *Abe Lincoln in Illinois* illustrates Sherwood's pro-America outlook. In his 2006 dissertation, Scott R. Irelan encapsulates the effect this play produced on its readership and theatre-going public and ways in which Sherwood's depiction of Abraham Lincoln reflects his attitude toward FDR and toward the country he so deeply loved – a country, having just faced the ravages of the Great Depression, now poised for war:

> In no other Lincoln Legend drama of the day or since were the concerns of the playwright, his subjectivity as a United States citizen, and the politics of a sitting president so keenly woven together. Words and phrases such as 'birthright,' 'Union,' 'freedom,' 'sovereignty,' 'enslavement,' 'bondage,' 'strike,' 'brotherhood,' 'the Almighty,' 'rebellion,' 'equality,' 'doctrine,' and many, many more pervade Lincoln's utterances with the same attitude, intent, and force summoned by FDR during his Fireside Chats and public appearances.[38]

The twelve-scene play depicts Lincoln's early life, including his romances with not only Mary Todd, but his first love, Ann Routledge, and its action concludes with Lincoln's final speech in Illinois as he prepares to depart for Washington, DC.

The piece has been the subject of much discussion, but despite the book's rather homey and conversational tone, Wharton's 1974 *Life Among the Playwrights*, hardly a piece of traditional dramatic criticism, offers some seldom addressed and noteworthy insights into the production process. One concerns scene designer Jo Mielzener, already a well-respected Broadway designer and later known for his beautifully executed and thematically appropriate use of the scrim, particularly in works by Tennessee Williams. Thinking it would facilitate rapid scene changes, Mielzener suggested the use of a scrim in *Abe Lincoln*. Unfortunately, at a pre-production run through, light leaked so that stage hands madly moving scenery became visible to the audience, prompting unwanted snickers from them. Another of Wharton's anecdotes concerns a conversation he had with Sherwood about the Mary Todd scenes in the play. A persistent rewriter and playwright who sought suggestions and remained carefully attuned to audience responses, Sherwood was troubled by them and was in the process of attempting to craft lines that might add interest. Wharton recalls one such line, to be uttered by Todd: 'We'll be in the nation's capital, think of it, Abe, we'll be able to meet all the famous people of all sorts, artists, musicians – [*Pause*] – we'll be able to go to the theatre!'. Sherwood abandoned the joke.[39] Scrim removed and bad joke omitted, *Abe Lincoln in Illinois* opened to great success in out-of-town try-outs and then on Broadway.

Life Among the Playwrights includes correspondence of the Playwrights Producing Company members, a raft of personal recollections, and details about the company's experiences that present a composite of the group at work across two decades, revealing the successful collaborative process of an independent producing organization, albeit one that elected to further no collective socio-political agenda, proving, perhaps, that a simple mission unaffected by the temporality of politics may contribute to a company's longevity.

Poetry and politics: Maxwell Anderson

Initially known as a prose writer of dramas (the gritty, photo-realistic war play, *What Price Glory*, 1924, with Laurence Stallings; *Gods of the Lightning*, with Harold Hickerson, inspired by the Sacco–Vanzetti case that he would revisit in verse seven years later, 1928), playwright Maxwell Anderson is most discussed for his valiant revival of poetic and historical drama (*Elizabeth the Queen*, 1930, and *Mary of Scotland*, 1933). He not only used English characters and events from America's past (as in *Valley Forge*, 1934) to illuminate present conditions, but he also employed verse in his depiction of the more recent (1920) Sacco–Vanzetti case, with *Winterset* (1935), which Brenda Murphy praises as an American classic[40] and Jordan Y. Miller and Winifred L. Frazer uphold as illustrating 'the classic concept of tragedy'[41] most clearly of all Anderson's verse plays. *High Tor* (1937) differs from the other poetic dramas in that it combines verse and fantasy, with a plot that concerns controversy over-quarrying the Palisades in New York and Rip Van Winkle-inspired ghosts of Dutch sailors on the Hudson River. Written in blank verse, *Key Largo* (1939) offers the Spanish Civil War as backdrop. Its action moves from Spain to present-day Key Largo, Florida, where the protagonist, who walked away from battle, makes atonement by giving his life to save another's.

In his verse dramas, Anderson often critiqued the socio-political forces at work in his time by historicizing the past to reflect issues and attitudes from the contemporary world. His playwriting in the 1930s was prolific, and his career continued across the 1940s (*Anne of a Thousand Days*, for example) and 1950s, with *The Bad Seed* (1955), into the early 1970s (with the book and lyrics for *Lost in the Stars*, 1972, for example).

Because he adhered to no single political ideology, Anderson has been labelled as an *anarchist* by critics on multiple occasions. With regard to the playwright, however, the word anarchist has been left undefined and seems an ambivalent term at best, especially as descriptor for a student of history like Anderson. More recent studies by Fonzie D. Geary II – his 2011 dissertation, 'Social Critiques in Three Prose Plays by Maxwell Anderson: *Saturday's Children, Both Your Houses,* and *The Star-Wagon*', followed by two spin-off articles – offer new insights on the playwright's prose plays, his philosophies and his social commentary. Because of Geary's new interpretations, and because the subject matter of the verse plays is often somewhat self-explanatory, Anderson's prose piece *Both Your Houses* represents the playwright here.

Anderson was disappointed when production of *Both Your Houses* was delayed, as it was intended to critique the Hoover administration and failed to be presented before FDR took office. Nonetheless, this 'send up' of the United States government, with its dysfunctional House of Representatives, garnered Anderson the 1933 Pulitzer Prize. Not only, through satire, does the play offer critical commentary on graft and stonewalling in the United States government of the time, but it reflects Anderson's firm grounding in American political philosophy. In *Both Your Houses*, Anderson dramatizes the age-old debate about government's size and scope (the threat of 'big' government) in the United States, adding a depiction of the agrarian trope, à la historian Frederick Jackson Turner and the 'Yankee' character that became a staple of the American stage as early as the late eighteenth century, with Royall Tyler's *The Contrast*.

In his article 'A Plague on Both Your Houses: Mr. Anderson Goes to Washington', Geary draws comparisons between issues in the play and US politics in the twenty-first century,[42] especially with the preposterous – Geary dubs them 'absurd'[43] – efforts on the parts of Congressmen to add 'pork' or special interests for their districts to the bill on which they are to vote. Period allusions in the play reverberate to the present day, recalling, in addition to those mentioned by Geary, the infamous 'bridge to nowhere' that plagued 2008 vice presidential candidate Sarah Palin, and the congressional gridlock during the Obama administration that produced newfound reverence for 'old time politicians' like Lyndon Johnson and Tip O'Neill, who worked behind the scenes to 'cut deals', 'crossing the aisle' to facilitate the passing of bipartisan legislation. Rather than stultifying contemporary understanding of the play, the way topical allusions limit more polemical pieces, in *Both Your Houses* these details are deftly handled, with just the right amount of specificity to maintain audience/reader interest, and as a result, the play remains timeless.

Maxwell Anderson, unlike many political playwrights of the decade – and arguably because of his chameleon nature, since dramaturgically speaking Anderson is not necessarily rightfully labelled entirely 'political' – offers no ideological solution to the pressing socio-economic issues of the Depression. Although Geary notes that 'his lack of a specific remedy not only sets him apart from his contemporaries, but was actually an asset to the message of the play',[44] he also mentions the farmer/Congressman protagonist's martyrdom (political not literal death), so we might, metaphorically, contemplate a tentative Marxist interpretation of the play.

Geary's subtitle, 'Mr. Anderson Goes to Washington', references the 1939 film *Mr. Smith Goes to Washington*, starring Jimmy Stewart; and the play itself, written before the film, forecasts a genre of plays and films about idealistic young men confronted by the duplicitous behaviour of professional politicians with their eyes on re-election rather than focused on the common good.

Plays about government abound in the decade of the 1930s, many of them award-winning, including not only those discussed in more or less detail throughout this chapter, but the musicals *Of Thee I Sing* (book by George S. Kaufman and Morrie Ryskind, music and lyrics by George and Ira Gershwin) and its sequel *I'd*

Rather Be Right (book by Moss Hart and George S. Kaufman, lyrics by Lorenz Hart, and music by Richard Rodgers).

No time for comedy?

For this section on comedy of the 1930s, the title of S. N. Behrman's 1939 *No Time for Comedy* offers a thematic framework. It is for this reason that this end-of-the-decade play is the first of Behrman's works discussed here.

The meta-theatrical piece takes as its subject a playwright who specializes in comedies in which his wife plays the starring roles. He has encountered a 'dry' period and has acquired another woman as his muse. The playwright character, Gay, determines that the late 1930s is no time for writing comedy and, with the Spanish Civil War as a backdrop, he attempts to write a ponderous and somewhat political play, dealing with death and immortality. *No Time for Comedy* is a piece in which Behrman's characteristic glistening repartee is characteristically underscored by a serious dilemma: the writer's moral obligation to engage in the world in which he lives. Complications arise as Philo, the taciturn husband of Gay's inspiration, becomes infatuated with Linda, the playwright's wife. Gay writes the play, but he cannot craft a final act, so he sends it to his wife to read. At the same time, he plans on leaving her for Amanda, his newfound inspiration. His actress/wife, having realized that she is not always supportive and that her husband is deeply sensitive, suggests he write another play altogether, one that focuses on a man's choice between a woman who functions as 'builder-upper' (Amanda, the muse) and one who serves as 'breaker-downer' (Linda, the wife). The play concludes with Gay cradling the telephone when Mandy calls, looking to his wife for assistance in deciding what to do next, how to respond and who to choose:

(*He implores Linda, he beseeches her, hoarsely*) What – What shall I say – What –?

Linda (*Looks up at him*) You ought to know – you've got to write it – (*Straightens his necktie*) it's the curtain for your last act, isn't it?

> (*Gay recognizes the wisdom of this: that there is nothing to be done; that he must face it ... He prepares to speak ... No words come from his parched lips... It is in the eternity of his inarticulateness, the Curtain swiftly comes down.*)[45]

The character of Gay Easterbrook, then, in his indecision, may be seen to stand for all playwrights of the decade, determining their styles, thematic concerns, conflicts and content, writing in the midst of a devastating national economy and impending world conflict. The playwright's dilemma in the 1930s is, in this way, depicted by Behrman in *No Time for Comedy* as it expresses the lived experience for many of the period's playwrights.

A writer of 'high' or 'drawing room' comedy, with a spate of successful plays across the 1930s (his playwriting career spanned from the late 1920s through the 1960s, with a posthumous adaptation as late as 1979), Behrman used comic form to capture the socio-political moment. The settings for his plays were the dwellings of the upper crust, the characters' dialogue casual and witty, yet proletarian issues were embedded in both his characters and plotlines. He was a popular playwright with the Theatre Guild, a New York producing company, established in 1918 for the purpose of mounting non-commercial American and foreign plays. By the 1930s, however, the Guild was considered traditional by many. Behrman became part of the Playwrights Producing Company, Inc., who mounted *No Time for Comedy*, in an effort to achieve more agency with regard to productions of his works.

The socio-economic conditions of the 1930s could not be ignored, even by writers of comedy. For S. N. Behrman and other comic playwrights, questions arose concerning precisely to what degree, and exactly how, to address the day's dilemmas. Target audience also constituted a major factor in determining the manner in which politics and economics might manifest in their plays. Behrman – and Kaufman, considered next in this chapter – played to the traditional, Broadway audience, inclined toward the wealthy in composition. Yet, employing the drawing room, or even it may be said 'comedy of manners', style, allowed Behrman to poke fun at and even critique his own theatre-going public.

Across the decade he developed a rather formulaic approach to his craft, with recognizable character types, settings and plot lines. At the same time, as the 1930s progressed, his plays became imbued with more seriousness of purpose. Characteristics of the playwright's works included meandering plots (his plays were situation driven, 'anecdotal'[46] rather than propelled by character); repartee for the sake of amusing conversation rather than in the service of plot progression; fairly large casts; and, typically, variations on an 'independent woman' character type around whom the story revolved, with the other characters responding to her and dependent upon her decisions. Behrman also takes as his subject matter money, marriage issues and the generation gap, often combining the latter with conflicting political or economic views. It might be said that, for the most part, one may have attended a Behrman play not seeking surprise, but, rather, intrigued by how the playwright would work out the details of a particular piece.

In *Brief Moment* (1931), Behrman addresses the ennui of the upper class with the dilettante Rod Deane and his acerbic and corpulent sidekick, Sig. As Sig summarizes early in the play, 'Nowadays I go in for languor.'[47] Deane meets and marries a social-climbing nightclub jazz singer, Abby, who proves to be a self-proclaimed mimic of social graces, mannerisms and vocabulary, hosting endless parties filled with aspiring celebrities. Rod calls a (temporary) halt to his wife's emotional games when it becomes apparent that she is dallying with her former lover, Cass, a pretty-boy polo player. The couple separates, and, for 'a brief moment' (four weeks offstage time), it appears that Rod may have reflected and even matured a little, or at least to have turned his attention outward, no longer focusing on himself. He contemplates a trip to Russia, 'like John Reed'.[48] However, the play ends with the couple back in each other's arms, the world no better or worse for these characters' existence. Despite some Depression details and his introduction of what may have been his first overtly Marxist character in the person of minor character, film director Sergei Voloschyn, Behrman offers no ideological solutions to national or global problems. Although his characters are intriguing, and the play holds one's attention, the 'pay off' is dissatisfying, which may have been Behrman's point.

In Behrman's *Biography* (1932), we meet artist Marion Froude, the independent woman who has lived her life, with its financial highs and lows, basically as she pleased. She has been asked to write a serialized version of her biography for a tabloid. Her life story may affect the potential senatorial bid (and impending marriage) of her first love, Leander ('Bunny') Nolan. She is supported in her writing endeavour by acquisitions editor Richard Kurt, one of the playwright's many youthful radical characters. The future senator's hypocritical future father-in-law threatens a libel suit and hints at a financial pay-off (capitalism at its most insidious), while Kurt, as a matter of principle, risks his job at the periodical to see the biography's publication through. Ultimately, in a Hedda Gabler-like gesture, Froude burns the manuscript, but, unlike Ibsen's character, and in keeping with the spirit of comic resolution, she breaks with Kurt, her most recent affair, and travels on after receiving word that her portraiture painting is wanted in Hollywood. Froude's romantic gesture of destroying the manuscript arises from her desire to simply get along, to avoid 'scenes' as she calls all disagreement, and is met with the younger Kurt's derision, ' – as they grow older – people become tolerant! Things amuse them. I hate you and I hate your tolerance. I always did.'[49] Despite her somewhat bohemian existence that stands in contrast to the playwright's life, Froude serves as Behrman's *raissonneur* of sorts; her tempered responses, tolerance and desire for a middle ground somewhere between radicalism and conservatism is characteristic of Behrman himself and appears in characters across his corpus of plays. As in *No Time for Comedy*, we see the conflict between two philosophies, one conciliatory and one stridently socio-political, but without the meta-theatrical layering.

Unlike the other Behrman plays discussed here, *Rain from Heaven* (1934) is set abroad, at an English country estate. Nonetheless, it offers keen commentary on the United States at the time. The play boasts a large cast of characters, ranging in socio-political tenor from penniless German refugee philosopher to conservative capitalist. Rand Eldridge, an innocent arctic explorer, based loosely on Charles Lindbergh, is in love with Lady Lael Wyngate, the woman around whom the plot revolves. His older brother, Hobart, evolved from the Orrin Kinnicott character in *Biography* – a blustering bulldog of a man, the ultra-conservative – has arrived in England to meet with a British newspaper mogul about creating an anti-communist youth organization. A young would-be musician, love-interest for the elder Eldridge's daughter; a German pamphleteer, recently escaped from a concentration camp; a music critic (based on Alfred Kerr); and a Russian refugee, freeloading off the all-too-kind Lady Wyngate, round out the cast. Mrs Hobart Eldridge also appears to serve as the gender foil to her husband. Imbued with the confusion of a 'bedroom farce', *Rain from Heaven* adopts a more serious tone, with Behrman's depiction of the dilemma of Jewishness and anti-Semitism in the 1930s, and with its treatment of fascism. In his treatment of serious social problems, as with *Biography* and *End of Summer*, Behrman deploys comic structure and carefully created banter to address global issues, again advocating peace and tolerance, through the character of Lael Wyngate.

In *End of Summer* (1936), Behrman again focuses on the wealthy, with characters spouting self-congratulatory bon mots. However, this play is painted with a heavy brush; while twists of plot offer the reader/viewer temporary 'red herrings', the story's end is ultimately predictable. Paula Frothingham, a wealthy young woman with a delicate, ornamental mother and sensible father (her parents are estranged from one another yet cordial), loves a young radical. In a manner almost imitative of Chekhov, Behrman offers in the mother, Leonie, a woman who admits that she has based her entire life on being loved. In the play she dallies with Boris, a Russian aristocrat who pretends to be writing a book, and with Dr Rice, a charlatan Freudian psychologist who practises on virtually everyone. We are to assume there have been other similar men in the past. Leonie's life has been defined by 'helping' people, as she puts it, and, when she feels she can no longer be of assistance, she dismisses them. Boris's place is quickly usurped by the doctor.

A generation 'gap' is apparent between the young radical, Will, and his friend, Dennis, and the older characters. Like most of Behrman's works, the play contrasts the mid-1930s disenfranchised, unemployed (although college-educated), politically engaged youth with those of inherited wealth and privilege. To this end, Behrman includes both topical allusions and humour. For example, the mother innocently quips, 'Why can't radicals be chic?' and goes on to describe a photograph of Karl Marx she observed to support her point.[50] From Dennis we hear, 'When we're in New York doing nothing, we belong to the most respectable vested group going! The unemployed. As such we have status, position, authority. But if we stay here doing nothing – what are we? Low-down parasites.'[51] And, Dr Kenneth Rice, who has no use for the boys and prides himself on being a self-made man, exclaims, 'I detest those young firebrands whose incandescence will be extinguished by the first job! I detest radicals who lounge around in country-houses.'[52] Dennis and Will keep count of the number of job rejections they receive, as badges of honour. Dennis picks up some pay writing for pulp magazines, and, since graduating four months ago, Will has earned a total of $11 (writing book reviews for the *New York Times* and the *New Masses*). The two young men remain remarkably cheerful and somewhat self-aware: 'When I was in college, my interest in the "movement" – was really impersonal. I imagined myself giving my energies to the poor and downtrodden in my spare time. I didn't believe I'd be one of the poor and downtrodden myself.'[53]

Each of the characters in *End of Summer* – even Paula, who uses her feminine wiles to expose Dr Rice's true character – takes advantage of others. In the play's concluding scene, Dennis is depicted charming Leonie, plotting to gain her financial support for the radical magazine he hopes to found. Will, on the other hand, realizes his friend has persuaded him to take advantage of his fiancée's wealth, so he breaks off with Paula; but, for once in her life, Leonie offers her daughter some sound advice, and Paula runs after Will, allowing the requisite reconciliation between the lovers inherent in comedy.

With its passing of the seasons, *End of Summer* suggests that social change is overdue, but as with his other works, Behrman recommends as solution to current problems what Kenneth T. Reed repeatedly refers to in his study of the playwright as *via media* – mediation, a middle ground or a humanistic approach to conflict, not revolution. All told, while S. N. Behrman incorporates details of the Depression in his plays, he presents himself as an ideological liberal, removed from the radical leanings of other more militant playwrights of his day.

Overall, while entertaining, *End of Summer* waffles between presenting itself as the political piece Behrman may have wanted it to be and the high comedy for which the playwright remains renowned. As a result of its hybrid form and its sometimes meandering dialogue – for, like George Bernard Shaw, Behrman sought solutions in discussion – the play, to some extent, falls flat. In *End of Summer*, the Depression does not seem very distressing. Perhaps this is due to Behrman's choice of comic form, and, maybe it is through his depiction of the unemployed as 'frat boys' with social flair that he has missed the mark. In his discussion of Behrman's comic craft, 'S. N. Behrman: The Quandary of the Comic Spirit', Charles Kaplan interrogates the playwright's 'union between powerful social consciousness and the nonsatiric [sic] comic instinct'. He finds, understandably, that the results are 'somewhat unsatisfactory' and 'sometimes confused'. But, Kaplan deduces from the playwright's work at large that, 'In this confusion he [Behrman] merely reflects the larger confusions of our day.'[54]

S. N. Behrman's popularity in the 1930s is evidenced by the lengths of runs his comedies achieved on Broadway: *Brief Moment*, 129 performances; *Biography*, 267 in its initial run and another sixteen in a subsequent 1934 production; *Rain from Heaven*, 99; *End of Summer*, 153; and, *No Time for Comedy* (1939), 185. As with the dramas of the period, it is worth mentioning that the page lengths and running times of Behrman's plays are substantial to say the least by twenty-first-century standards. It is hard to imagine a modern audience remaining actively engaged for the 232-page *Brief Moment*, the almost 100-page *Biography* or even the 90-page *End of Summer*.

Hokum: High and low

In contrast to Behrman, George S. Kaufman (often with collaborator Moss Hart) managed to retain the light, laugh-out-loud characteristics of comedy, at the same time addressing the temper of his time. Kaufman's are the comedies of the 1930s that remain most produced decades later, but often for the wrong reasons. As with Thornton Wilder's *Our Town* (addressed in the next volume to this series), his plays are underestimated as simple to mount and as sure-fire box-office success for school and community productions. Often attention is not paid to the subtlety and satire of Kaufman's dialogue, and his biting social commentary, specific to the period, is frequently overlooked.

Like musical theatre, comedy can offer its audiences escape from the doldrums of their everyday lives. George S. Kaufman's plays provide distraction, but they accomplish much more. Kaufman's longevity as a playwright and director serves as testimony to his indomitable comic spirit, and to his talent; in every season from

1921 to 1958 he worked on the Broadway stage as either writer or director. Unlike Behrman, who maintained the conventions of 'high' comedy, Kaufman – no matter with whom he collaborated – not only skilfully manipulated satire, but pushed his wise-cracking, screwball comedies into the realm of farce. Farce in general is highly tolerant of transgressive behaviour, and tends to depict human beings as vain, irrational, hypocritical, even infantile. In that respect, farce is a natural companion to satire, poking fun at politicians, the wealthy and so on.

Kaufman is attributed with having quipped, of the failed first production of *Strike Up the Band*, that 'Satire is what closes on Saturday night.'[55] In his *New York Times* article 'No, Mr. Kaufman, Satire Lives on, if It's Yours', Charles Isherwood combats the playwright's tongue-in-cheek comment on the fleeting topicality of comedy: 'the durability of Kaufman's immortal aperçu about satire belies the idea that what's funny today is stale, quaint or curious tomorrow. So does a surprising amount of Kaufman's theatrical writing.'[56] Kaufman's critiques of characters and problems that can be said to have only increased in American society has remained relevant across the years since his plays were first produced. Isherwood rightfully argues that the playwright and his collaborators tapped into the idea that 'pop culture and the manufacturing of pop culture was fast becoming one of America's primary obsessions ... the culture of celebrity, that would eventually evolve into an entertainment universe in itself'.[57] Isherwood cites numerous examples from stage, screen and television – some well-respected comedies, others the stuff of reality television – as the potential offspring of George S. Kaufman's work.

Often, across the decade of the 1930s, with *Once in a Lifetime* (1930, with long-time collaborator Moss Hart); *Dinner at Eight* (1932, written in collaboration with novelist Edna Ferber); *Merrily We Roll Along* (1934); *Stage Door* (1936, with Ferber); and *The Man Who Came to Dinner* (1939, with Hart), Kaufman coyly critiqued show business, his very livelihood. The play that continues to possess the most traction, however, is *You Can't Take it With You*, Kaufman's true Depression comedy, written with Hart, and winner of the 1937 Pulitzer Prize. We need only look to the 2015 Broadway revival starring acclaimed actor James Earl Jones and featuring Elizabeth Ashley as Countess Olga to recognize the play's unique durability and suitability to changing times.

Less satirical than their other plays, Kaufman and Hart's *Once in a Lifetime*, with its three principal characters who sell their act to move to Hollywood, looks back to Vaudeville, and forward to the Golden Age of film. The play captures the moment when 'talkies' emerged and silent screen actors were desperate to adapt, or forced to leave the industry altogether if they could not master speaking pleasingly. Having just seen *The Jazz Singer*, the member/manager of the team in the play hatches a plot to open an elocution school at a major film studio. By chance, on their train west, the team encounters gossip columnist character Helen Hobart (based on Louella Parsons), who was previously acquainted with the female member of the act, May Daniels. She is easily convinced of the efficacy of their brainstorm. Hobart will provide the trio with an introduction to a studio head, and the plot is off and running. The Hollywood that Kaufman and Hart portray constitutes the perfect balance between 'over the top' excess to the point of absurdity and underlying recognizable truths. Rumours are rampant; every waiter and cigarette girl wants to be a star; settings are beyond lavish. At the same time, critical commentary on the studio system manifests throughout the piece, including the frustration and waste involved in the studio's employment of a stable of nameless, faceless playwrights as scriptwriters and other practices. Kaufman himself played the cameo role of Lawrence Vail, who endlessly waits for his appointment with Mr Glogauer, an appointment that the studio head never keeps. Studio employees – the protagonist trio included – are hired and fired on a whim, and the dumbest of the three, who has fallen in love with an equally brainless young actress he met on the train (trailed by her stage mother), is promoted to run studio production almost by accident (he is just as abruptly fired and again reinstated). Hare-brained ideas result in critical acclaim, the dim-witted aspiring actress becomes a star, juvenile and ingénue, after complications, reconcile. The topsy-turvy world that the playwrights fashioned rights itself in the end, but only after the controlled chaos that constitutes comedy at its best.

Dinner at Eight (1932) satirizes the upper class at a fashionable supper, reflecting their petty personal problems (and the more serious notion that those of great wealth may have built their lives on money, status and power that the Depression threatened) in a way that astute ticket-purchasers might recognize themselves, but, if not, could still experience an enjoyable evening at the theatre.

The play's single location exemplifies a technique employed often by Kaufman, and also recognizable as a facet of murder mysteries, whereby characters are geographically contained or trapped so that emphasis can remain on plot, character and dialogue.[58] Based on the notion of complications and misunderstandings that arise from a love triangle, multiplied by the number of couples involved, comedy emanates from conversation and subtext as characters listen and respond to one another. *Dinner at Eight*'s popularity resulted in its release as a film just two years after its Broadway premier, starring Billie Burke, Jean Harlow, Wallace Beery, both John and Lionel Barrymore (the former as desperate fading movie star) and featuring Marie Dressler. *Merrily We Roll Along* (1934) is memorable for the way in which its authors play with time, structuring a plot that moves backwards from 1934 to 1916, and because it served as the impetus for Stephen Sondheim's troubled musical version in 1981.

The more poignant play, although still a comedy, *Stage Door* (1936) takes as its focus the struggles of young actresses who reside at a New York City hotel for women (based on the one where co-author Edna Ferber's niece lived). One character's failed theatrical career prompts her suicide and another succumbs to the seduction of the film industry and moves to Hollywood. The ingénue, Terry Randall, the plucky Midwestern girl who travelled to the big city with stars in her eyes, succeeds and captures the lead in a legitimate production – but only after she becomes involved with two contrasting men: a fiery, radical playwright, Keith Burgess, modelled on Clifford Odets, who leaves for Hollywood; and a genteel film producer who returns to Broadway. As with many of Kaufman's plays, several characters are based on living legends, personalities from theatre, Hollywood and/or society who are larger than life and easily mimicked. In the case of *Stage Door*, however, character construction takes the form more of homage, for MGM producer Irving Thalberg, on whom the David Kingsley character is based, had only recently died. In his creation of this role, George Kaufman paid public tribute to a man for whom he felt great respect. With its constant depiction of the 'vampire-like' lure of Hollywood, *Stage Door* may be seen as a 'valentine to the legitimate stage'.[59] This play, too, rapidly met the screen in 1937, but with a text so altered – without the entire indictment of the film industry – that Kaufman is said to have retorted that it should have been retitled *Screen Door*.[60]

You Can't Take it With You (1937) offered its weary, Depression-era audience precisely 'what the doctor ordered', the morale boost America needed, a return to the 'American icons of rugged individualism, Yankee ingenuity, and freedom of choice'.[61]

The fictional head of the Sycamore household depicted in the play, Grandpa (Martin Vanderhof), serves as the living embodiment of conscientious objection and peaceful social protest. According to the play's backstory, he was on his way to his office one day when it struck him that he was perpetually worried, often about circumstances beyond his control, and as he came to the realization that he was chronically unhappy, he simply quit. He has neither worked nor paid the Internal Revenue Service for thirty-five years. No longer a part of the workforce, nor a participant in government subsidies for the unemployed, he now has time to explore reading and other interests and hobbies, and he takes full advantage of his home's proximity to Columbia University. His entire family has followed suit, pursuing a delightful range of endeavours from studying ballet to writing, or painting, or playing the xylophone, or even pursuing herpetology, the accoutrements for which (including the family's snake) remain strewn across the living room – or, in the case of Grandpa's son-in-law's explosives, the basement. As in many Kaufman plays, the author's stage directions provide amusement for his readers: the Sycamore residence is described by the playwright as 'a house where you can do what you like, and no questions asked'.[62] Into this welcoming home tromps an unexpected cast of characters from daughter Essie's eccentric Russian ballet instructor and his friend, allegedly a former grand duchess, to the perennial guest, Mr De Pinna, who works to create fireworks with Paul Sycamore and whose portrait in Roman garb was previously painted by Penelope Sycamore when she was intrigued by the brush. In earlier offstage action, an ice man arrived only to be adopted by the family and stay until he died, at which time the group realized they had never learned his name, so they assigned him Grandpa's – a lucky break for Vanderhof later in the play when we learn that, since he is recorded as dead, he no longer owes back taxes! At the same time, the Sycamores respect the right and desire of others to engage in traditional work, as Grandpa says, 'There's always people who like to work.'[63] One member of the immediate family, the play's ingénue, Alice, does indeed have an office job.

'Normal' family life for the Sycamores is established in the opening scene, then Alice declares that, despite her best efforts, her new beau, the boss's son, will be calling for her at home. This information sets up the play's conceit, the collision course that will follow as the stodgy Kirbys encounter the raucous, happy-go-lucky Sycamores, and calamity ensues. In the end, with Grandpa's set speech about the freedom time has afforded him and his admonition to the elder Kirby about his wealth that 'you can't take it with you', and, after a temporary break-up, the young couple is reunited, the plot resolves in the tradition of comedy.

But *You Can't Take it With You* offers more than laughs; this comedy is truly reflective of the time in which it was written, the New Deal days with their corresponding debate over the efforts of the US government to pull the country out of the Great Depression. Kaufman and Hart weave allusions to contemporary issues into character, plot line and dialogue. Paul reads his son-in-law Ed's copy of Trotsky's writing in the bathroom, and the black maid's boyfriend, Donald, finds his routine interrupted by waiting in line to obtain his relief money. Surprisingly witty and well informed, Donald comments in discussion with Grandpa about Columbia's commencement, 'You want to listen to a good speech you go up and hear Father Divine.'[64] When he sees Penelope Sycamore appear in her artist attire, complete with smock and beret, he comments, 'I didn't know you was working for the WPA.'[65]

Not only is the play peppered with these characteristic allusions, but its entire premise is founded on inherently American ideals, specifically one's right to choose one's profession and/or path in life. Admittedly, the Sycamore household shows no visible sign of financial support, save Alice's job, and perhaps Paul's yearly sale of fireworks. Mr Kirby's accusation that Grandpa's philosophy is 'downright Communism'[66] might be received differently in a didactic drama or overtly political play, but in reading or viewing *You Can't Take It With You*, one suspends disbelief and acquiesces to the conventions of comedy, at the same time, possibly (re)learning a thing or two.

Critically acclaimed, popular with the public (running for 739 performances) and released as a feature film in 1942, *The Man Who Came to Dinner* (1939) might surpass *You Can't Take it With You* in its scope for revival or regional and community performance but for casting the difficult central role of Sheridan Whiteside, founded on the real-life critic and playwrights' friend, Alexander Wollcott, who, while he did not originate it, eventually played the part. In seeking a vehicle for the theatre critic/radio personality, Kaufman and Hart drew inspiration from Moss Hart's experience when Wollcott paid an unexpected visit to the playwright's Bucks County home, terrorizing Hart's staff and generally taking over the house. *The Man Who Came to Dinner*, indeed, is dedicated to Wollcott, and the text bears the inscription, 'To Alexander Wollcott, for reasons that are nobody's business.'

As Miller and Frazer note, this wild satirical farce, once dubbed 'a comedy of bad manners', is indeed what is frequently referred to as a 'roast' or merciless, verbal skewering of a particular person, generally a celebrity, all in the name of good fun.[67] A romantic plot – the newborn love of Whiteside's loyal secretary, Maggie, for newspaperman (and aspiring playwright) Bert Jefferson, writer for the local paper in the small Ohio town in which the protagonist finds himself stranded because of an unhappy encounter with an ice patch – provides the dramaturgical excuse for the non-stop antics that surround the play's central character. This play, like Kaufman's others, involves a large cast of characters. In the case of *The Man Who Came to Dinner*, Kaufman's habitual practice of incorporating a household guest or guests into his plays is even more pronounced.

With this piece, not only do the playwrights confine their action to one locale, but they prohibit their protagonist from leaving his wheelchair, even when he learns that through a mix-up in X-rays he was misdiagnosed and can actually walk. The farcical humour, then, derives in part from the entrances, exits and characters' interactions with Whiteside, including the arrival of packages, since the play is also sentimentally set at Christmas. These sometimes anthropomorphized items include among others a Mummy case and in-the-flesh penguins, all gifts from Whiteside's famous friends. In this way, through their implementation of comic entrances, exits and even brief appearances of characters followed by Whiteside's abrupt dismissal of them, Kaufman and Hart substitute people and props for the ubiquitous farce set comprised of doors. While doors offer opportunities for hiding, changing clothes, eavesdropping and so on that increase the pace and confusion of the action, people (and objects) can function in the same way in the farcical satires of Kaufman and Hart. The madcap pace of *The Man Who Came to Dinner* becomes accentuated through their implementation.

Once again, in this play Kaufman and Hart 'send up' show business. The stereotypical siren actress manifests itself in the character of Lorraine Sheldon, loosely based on Gertrude Lawrence; Beverly Carlton was modelled on Noël Coward; the madcap Banjo is based on Harpo Marx, and dialogue references his brothers, with their names changed to 'Waccko' and 'Sloppo'.

Like *You Can't Take it With You*, but to a lesser degree, *The Man Who Came to Dinner* includes period-specific references as part of its backdrop. Whiteside's host, Ernest Stanley, is a wealthy factory owner whose daughter's love for a union organizer, encouraged by Whiteside, provides the play with class stratification and ideological difference. 'Mr. Stanley behaves as though it were all a big plot – John L. Lewis sent me here just to marry his daughter,'[68] comments the young man. Stanley's son Richard runs away to pursue his photography career, and in his comments on the young man's works, Whiteside references Depression photographer Margaret Bourke-White.[69] But, by and large, the cultural landscape of *The Man Who Came to Dinner* is painted in broader strokes, for good reasons and to a successful end. By de-emphasizing yet at the same time acknowledging pressing problems of the day, and in creating the quintessential curmudgeon Sheridan Whiteside, who, Scrooge-like, softens in the Christmas spirit, Kaufman and Hart reaffirmed the American spirit and offered their public a much-needed opportunity to laugh.

The last of the 'big three'[70] comic playwrights of the era, Philip Barry, occupies far less space here than S. N. Behrman and George S. Kaufman, for a number of reasons. Although Miller and Frazer credit his plays of the 1930s (*The Animal Kingdom*, 1932, and *The Philadelphia Story*, 1939) as sealing the playwright's lasting fame as a writer of comedy, it seems perhaps that by this time this writer's 'ship may have already sailed', or perhaps it was merely dry-docked for a time, for his works served as the basis for popular revivals in the 1970s and 1980s.

Barry's first Broadway play was produced in 1923 and, while eight crossed the Great White Way during the 1930s (*Hotel Universe*, 1930; *Tomorrow and Tomorrow*, 1931; *The Animal Kingdom*, 1932; *The Joyous Season*, 1934; *Bright Star*, 1935; *Spring Dance*, 1936; *Here Come the Clowns*, 1938; and *The Philadelphia Story*, 1939), the average length of run for these plays, 127.75, is due almost exclusively to the success of *The*

Philadelphia Story (417 performances), which starred Katharine Hepburn in both the stage and screen versions, at the close of the decade and beginning of the next. All told, their forms and content are incongruous with concerns of the decade. While Barry masterfully executed the polish demanded of 'high' comedy, his lack of recognition of working-class issues and his failure to acknowledge critical given circumstances of the day prohibit him from but brief mention here. Talented and technically skilful, Barry did not reflect or mirror the issues of his day that have been the focus of this chapter.

More important to the present study is an often misinterpreted piece – and the play that inspired use of the word *hokum* in the title for this section – Jack Kirkland's 1934 adaptation of Erskine Caldwell's novel by the same name, *Tobacco Road*. This play ran on Broadway for an astounding eight years (3,182 performances), as of 2014 still the second-longest non-musical play on Broadway. Considered by many as downright distasteful, *Tobacco Road* sits at the opposite end of the spectrum from Philip Barry's works.

The script is scrambled with a smattering of styles – comedy, farce, tragedy, pseudo-documentary or, perhaps, photorealism. Shockingly blunt in its depiction of the hard scrapple life of a Georgia 'cracker' family, the Lesters, *Tobacco Road* brought infidelity, domestic abuse, duplicity, death, debauchery and deprivation to the stage. The mother, having borne seventeen children, announces that her favourite, Pearl, is the product of an affair. Pearl refuses to allow her husband to touch her, and he, in turn, fondles one of her sisters in plain view. Jeeter Lester, the father, attempts to force Pearl to return to her husband's bed in order to cut a deal with his son-in-law that will avoid foreclosure on the property. When Pearl runs, Dude, who has proven himself unfit behind the wheel across the action of the play, runs over his own mother. 'Grandmother Lester' is physically and mentally abused by the rest of the family.

While *New York Times* critic Brooks Atkinson turned largely to the novel in his review of the play, acknowledging its seeming discomfort on the stage, he praised the material:

> Although 'Tobacco Road' reels across the stage like a drunken stranger to the theatre, it has spasmodic moments of merciless power when truth is flung into your face with all the slime that

truth contains ... Mr. Caldwell's grossness cannot be dismissed as morbidity and gratuitous indecency. It is the blunt truth of the characters he is describing, and it leaves a malevolent glow of poetry above the rudeness.[71]

It has been suggested that the original cast of *Tobacco Road* ran away with their comic portrayal of the piece as time went on, something that is difficult to ascertain retrospectively. Preston Lane, director of the Triad Theater's (North Carolina) 2007 revival of the piece, alludes to this idea: 'The production that had inspired no less than Theodore Dreiser to encourage the Pulitzer Prize committee to honor *Tobacco Road* ... became a tourist attraction that was played for laughs.'[72]

Without a successful crop in years, lacking food, fuel or funds, the Lester family has clearly reached a point of desperation and despondency; yet, at times, their existence is touched by levity. There are comic elements in the script; for example, the scene in which Lester family members try to reach a window in order to observe Dude's conjugal sex. There are other moments when the humour is the sort that emanates from discomfort, even, as Mark Fearnow points out, from grotesquery, such as the onstage depiction of a character with the disfigurement of a cleft lip. Fearnow alludes to *Tobacco Road*'s 'doubleness' and to contemplating the authors' (Caldwell and Kirkwood) own statements on the play's genre as viewing a 'delicate dance'.[73]

Denigrated when it first appeared as unfit fodder for the stage, and banned in Chicago and Detroit, although, surprisingly, not in Boston, one of the problems in evaluating the play in the 1930s may have stemmed precisely from its lack of clear-cut genre. For then, unlike today, dramatic literature was still categorized by formal genre. *Tobacco Road* suffered from its hybridity. As Mel Gussow so aptly explains, echoing Lane, in his discussion of the play's 1984 revival at the Long Wharf Theatre, the original production was created within the context of a theatrical milieu not yet inhabited by the likes of Sam Shepard. Leah D. Franks addresses the play's relevance in the 1980s as well, in her mainly negative review of the Arena Repertory Theatre's 1985 revival:

[T]he dissolute, ignorant and spiritually defeated Lester family is still very much a part of our society, and the script retains its shock value for what it tells us about the underbelly of humanity. The setting may be rural Georgia, but the people, the poverty and the state of mind it describes can be found almost anywhere.[74]

With its use of the n-word and other socially deplorable actions in the play, *Tobacco Road* is admittedly problematic, but the play should not be dismissed as a hillbilly comedy.

The mythic, the surreal and the sublime: William Saroyan's *My Heart's in the Highlands* and *The Time of Your Life*

Hybridity and humanity are two hallmarks of William Saroyan's work. The plays represented here both reached the stage at the end of the decade, in 1939. The Group Theatre offered the grateful playwright their sponsorship for a limited run of his short, experimental piece, *My Heart's in the Highlands*. The 1939 published version of the text includes not only a Preface by Group Theatre director Harold Clurman followed by an Introduction by the playwright, but Saroyan bravely allowed reviews of the play – positive and negative – to be published as well. As Clurman attempts to explain and as the reviews attest, *My Heart's in the Highlands* was confounding in its simplicity. As Clurman comments, 'The play does not proceed from logic but from emotional truth.'[75] In his deployment of direct language, 'the simplest that Americans can speak – true poetry',[76] Saroyan relies on his audience's sensory response and, perhaps, sense memory, taking what might have later been called a phenomenological path.

Several critics of the original production discuss the play as 'surreal', their commentaries testimony to the fact that, again, in the 1930s dramatic literature was categorized by genre, and that, at this time, a clear definition of surrealism had yet to be derived. The play, whose story focuses on a poet/father and his son, who, were it not for the boy's ingenuity in flattering the local grocer, would likely starve, and two visits from an old man, who has run away, is unabashedly non-realistic. Like the proverbial Pied Piper, the old man magically plays 'My Heart's in the Highlands' on his bugle, and neighbours arrive bearing offerings of food. After he is recaptured by his keepers, the old man returns once more, for a final time, plays his song and then dies after delivering a recitation from *King Lear*. As Clurman intimated, the piece is not plot-driven, and its composite effect is acknowledged by a few astute critics, among them John Anderson of the *New York Journal-American* and the *New York Post*'s John Mason Brown. Anderson suggests that the play be taken 'all in one piece ... as a parable of beauty – the unearthly longing of people for a place that the heart knows'.[77] Brown describes the piece as conveying 'that world of unprecise meanings ... not the one to which humdrum Broadway often leads us ... there can be more to seeing than believing, that seeing can mean feeling, too, even when you do not understand exactly what you have seen', concluding that the play 'moved' him more than most productions of late.[78] Audience members openly sobbed at *My Heart's in the Highlands*, the way that Edward Albee's much later and equally mysterious and mythic *The Goat, or Who is Sylvia?* would elicit a similar response.[79] William Saroyan would make his mark shortly, with his next play of mixed form, *The Time of Your Life*, his full-length Pulitzer Prize-winning drama.

In the manner of Anton Chekhov, in this play Saroyan craftily 'combines the detachment of comedy with the engagement of tragedy',[80] employing American myth in the name of critiquing American capitalism, at the same time questioning the American Dream. The drama ultimately reflects the regeneration implicit in comic structure, at the same time exhibiting some of the spiritual malaise and sense of futility exhibited by avant-garde playwrights Saroyan would later champion.[81] *The Time of Your Life* defies plot summary, as this piece is really a series of character studies, a mosaic of vignettes that all coalesce in the end.

Set in a honky-tonk saloon, managed by Joe, the bartender, who secretly has money and is quietly making atonement for having acquired it on the backs of others, the play is populated by outsiders or misfits, not unlike those at the truck stop in Sherwood's earlier *The Petrified Forest*, even reminiscent of Eugene O'Neill's deployment of the bar convention in *The Iceman Cometh*, coincidentally penned in the same year as *The Time of Your Life*, but neither produced nor published for almost another decade. Utilizing the convention of the bar allows Saroyan to offer a microcosm of the world, one that he can exploit for the purpose of exploring the business of 'being' *versus* 'doing' and in which he can explore core values in life.

The Time of Your Life is simultaneously touching, tinged with (sometimes heartbreaking) comedy, tragic, patriotic and pacifistic. This pre-Second World War drama presents Saroyan's subversion of American myth with a Kit Carson character as a sort of deus ex machina, and its action culminates with American flags bursting from a pinball machine. The playwright brings us to the point of tears when the Tennessee Williams-like character of Kitty Duval relates her dream of marrying a doctor, and allows us to laugh aloud as a character proposes on the telephone, only to learn that he has dialled a wrong number. William Saroyan's play rings out the decade of the 1930s with all the diversity and confusion that the United States experienced across the Great Depression.

3

Gertrude Stein: *Four Saints in Three Acts* (written in 1927, published in 1932), *Doctor Faustus Lights the Lights* (1938), *Listen To Me* (1936)

Laura Schultz

> When I see a thing it is not a play for me because the minute I see it it ceases to be a play for me, but when I write something that somebody else can see then it is a play for me.
>
> Gertrude Stein, *Everybody's Autobiography*, 199

When Gertrude Stein arrived in New York in 1934 after thirty years in Europe, an electric billboard on Times Square announced, 'Gertrude Stein has arrived.' Stein was sixty years old and had just published her first bestseller, *The Autobiography of Alice B. Toklas*, the year before. This tongue-in-cheek autobiography is told in the voice of her lifelong companion, Alice Toklas. *The Autobiography of Alice B. Toklas* is full of entertaining anecdotes about all the famous artists and writers who passed through Stein's Parisian salon – Henri Matisse, Pablo Picasso, Ernest Hemingway and other luminaries from the world of art and literature. Naturally, with all its juicy anecdotes and gossip from Paris, the book was designed to reach a broader audience than Stein's highly experimental books would normally do. Somehow her experimental books, like the 900-page Modernist novel *The Making of Americans*, or the collection of cubist prose poems *Tender Buttons*, never seemed quite as attractive or accessible to a broader audience.

All the more surprisingly, Stein's sudden rise to stardom continued with the unlikely success of her avant-garde opera *Four Saints in Three Acts*, which opened in 1934 with music by prominent American composer Virgil Thomson, an all-black cast of gospel singers from Harlem and cellophane set designs by Modernist artist Florine Stettheimer. The opera opened in February in Hartford, Connecticut, but soon moved on to Broadway and eventually to Chicago, where Stein herself saw it in November 1934, having arrived from Europe to enjoy and reinforce her newfound fame with a lecture tour across America. Stein proved to be a generous and engaging celebrity, accepting invitations from universities across the country and meeting stars and notabilities from Eleanor Roosevelt to Charlie Chaplin, before going back to France in May 1935 – never to return to the States again.

At first glance, the success of an avant-garde opera like *Four Saints in Three Acts* may seem extremely unlikely. In his book *Prepare For Saints – Gertrude Stein, Virgil Thomson and the Mainstreaming of American Modernism*, Steven Watson explains how completely unprepared the American audience must have been for the experience of Stein and Thomson's work:

> The libretto told no coherent story, the staging and costumes were deeply eccentric, and most of the lines made no apparent sense. The cellophane set, brilliantly lit to evoke a sky hung with rock crystal, defied comparison to anything the audience had ever seen. The music was too naïve, too simple, and too American for an opera.[1]

As Watson explores in his book, the success of *Four Saints in Three Acts*, as unlikely as it may seem, was by no means a chance event but the result of careful planning and unceasing commitment, especially on the part of composer Virgil Thomson.

No other play of Gertrude Stein's would see a similar large-scale production during her lifetime, and yet it makes complete sense to list Stein among the major American playwrights of the 1930s. Stein's impact on modern theatre came with a certain delay – in fact, it was mainly Postmodern and post-dramatic theatre that she influenced – and her influence came about through her texts and words. Stein was never a theatre practitioner, but her plays and her lecture 'Plays' do not simply deconstruct conventions of *written* drama. They always question basic assumptions about theatrical performance as well, and for that very reason they have seemed difficult or even impossible to stage. But as German playwright Heiner Müller declared, a playwright should always write plays that are 'unstageable for the theatre as it is'.[2] Müller wanted the dramatist to challenge the existing vocabulary of the theatre and force it to develop new means of expression. Stein's plays have certainly proved a challenge to theatre as it is. Her famous concept of the *landscape play* breaks with all conventions of classical drama, with its time-bound plot-development and causal chronology, in favour of visual and spatial patterns of composition where movements do not lead to dramatic actions, but compose ever-changing patterns, like the slight, continuous changes in a landscape where time is layered in space. Stein's landscape plays may seem difficult if not impossible to stage, yet they have inspired generations of theatre artists to develop new scenic and dramaturgical approaches. Paradoxically, what Stein's plays and lectures inspired later stage directors to do would eventually lead to a new understanding of how her own highly experimental plays might be brought to the stage.

Gertrude Stein, in other words, is a unique figure in modern drama and literature. It took her almost a century to enter literary and theatre histories on equal terms with her Modernist peers and become truly recognized for her own work – while at the same time her influence on generations of artists across the visual arts, literature, performance and music is indisputable, as is her fame as an American icon.

Early life

Gertrude Stein was born in Allegheny, Pennsylvania, in 1874 and died in France in 1946. Her early childhood was spent partly in Europe, in Vienna and Paris, before the family went back to the United States in 1879, staying with her mother's relatives in Baltimore before finally settling in Oakland, California.

Stein herself made a point of her being the youngest of five siblings: 'One should always be the youngest member of the family. It saves you a lot of bother [as] everybody takes care of you.'[3] Not only was Gertrude the youngest of the Stein siblings, she was also very close to her brother, Leo, two years older. She turned that relationship into a general advantage too:

> It is better if you are the youngest girl in a family to have a brother two years older, because that makes everything a pleasure to you, you go everywhere and do everything while he does it all for you and with you which is a pleasant way to have everything happen to you, sometimes accidents happen to you but after all it is very easy not to have them hurt you and anyway it altogether is a pleasant excitement for you. Anyway as I say my brother and I were always together.[4]

Losing both their parents at a young age, in 1892, Gertrude, Leo and their sister Bertha moved to Baltimore to live with their mother's family. While Gertrude Stein is famous for her repetitious style, often consisting of endless modulations and variations of a very limited vocabulary, she nevertheless relates that she learned from her time in Baltimore that there is actually no such thing as repetition. Instead there is *insistence*, which means simply the slight changes in emphasis and phrasing that keep words lively and writing fresh: 'if it is alive it is never saying anything in the same way because emphasis can never be the same'.[5] Stein said she learned the difference between repetition and insistence from living with her 'eleven little aunts' in Baltimore:

> If they had to know anything and anybody does they naturally had to say and hear it often, anybody does, and as there were ten and eleven of them they did have to say and hear said whatever was said and any one not hearing what it was they said had to come in to hear what had been said. That inevitably made everything said often.[6]

One can just imagine how every time a new aunt enters, any story told must be repeated, until finally there are no more different nuances to be emphasized or new meanings to emerge, and therefore no longer any interest in the story.

When Leo went to Harvard in 1892, Gertrude soon followed and enrolled at the Harvard Annex (later Radcliffe College) in 1893, where she studied with some of the most outstanding American philosophers at the time: George Santayana, Josiah Royce, Hugo Münsterberg and William James. Gertrude Stein was a gifted student, and especially her mentor William James would influence her later writing. James's notion of 'stream of consciousness' – the idea that human consciousness is in constant change in its perception of a similarly shifting, moving world – would become the guiding principle for all her writing. Taking his advice to go to medical school in order to pursue her interest in consciousness and psychology, Stein moved on to Johns Hopkins University. At first she continued her success, conducting research on the development of the human embryo brain, but she never cared much for clinical work. After an unhappy love affair with another woman, and failing several exams, Stein left Johns Hopkins without graduating, and by 1903 she was settling in Paris with Leo for a new life as a writer and art collector. Soon after, their elder brother Michael Stein followed with his wife, Sarah, and his son, Allan.

The Steins would come to play an important role in the formation of modern art. Buying paintings by young upcoming artists like Matisse and Picasso – and by the elder hero of these young artists, Paul Cézanne – the Steins soon gained a name among artists. Gertrude and Leo began to open their studio on Saturday nights, since everybody wanted to see their collection of works by Modernist artists, whose pictures were not yet on display in museums or other public spaces. In the winter of 1905–6, Gertrude Stein modelled for Picasso, who was painting her portrait. The extremely well educated Stein shared with Picasso her knowledge of recent developments in science and philosophy. Probably this exchange of ideas influenced Picasso's conception of art and perception. Be that as it may, Picasso's famous portrait of Gertrude Stein is generally seen as one of the first steps in a development that would lead him to the famous painting *Les Demoiselles d'Avignon* (1907), and ultimately towards cubism.

In 1907, Gertrude Stein met Alice B. Toklas, and a lifelong relationship began. Alice soon became the most important person in Gertrude's life, gradually supplanting Leo, who, claiming the role as the family's genius for himself, could not bring himself to support his sister's writing. Alice, on the other hand, soon became Gertrude's first reader, secretary, and eventually cook, housekeeper and designated wife. Alice moved in with Gertrude and Leo at 27 rue de Fleurus in 1910. In 1914, Leo left for Italy. The two siblings divided their art collection between them and never spoke to each other again. Gertrude Stein and Alice Toklas continued the Saturday salons.

Early writing

Gertrude Stein began seriously writing around the time she left college and settled in Europe. Her first mature work, a collection of three short stories called simply *Three Lives*, was written in 1905–6 and published in 1909. It was inspired by Flaubert's *Trois Contes*, as well as by Cézanne's *Portrait of Madame Cézanne*, which Gertrude and Leo had acquired in 1905. The stories depict three working-class women who share Stein's own issues of not fitting in – sexually and socially – with dominant society. What is truly innovative in *Three Lives* is the style and technique with which Stein, through minute modulations and permutations of a limited vocabulary, manages to fuse the voices of the characters and the voice of the narrator into one movement.

This ambition of fusing different layers of a text into one composition is a crucial aspect of Stein's poetics that would later lead her to challenge basic principles of conventional drama, for example the distinction between dialogue and stage directions.

Another significant point in *Three Lives* is the inspiration from painting. Stein would soon begin to apply painterly genre designations to her writing – portrait, still life, landscape – as a means to renew literature by approaching it from the perspective of a different medium. Later she would even claim that a writer should always write with his eyes, while a painter should paint with his ears.

During this early period, Stein was also writing her great American novel, *The Making of Americans*. The 900-page work was begun in 1903 and finished in 1911, but not published in its full length until 1925. The novel began as a family chronicle based on Stein's own family, but eventually developed into the quasi-scientific project of describing 'every one who ever is or was or will be living'.[7] In *The Making of Americans*, Stein's scientific interest in psychology and character, and her philosophical interest in time, developed into an original artistic voice and project.

But it was neither the novel nor the short story that would come to be Stein's most original choice of genre. Rather, her signature genre would become a most unconventional literary genre, the *portrait*. From 1910 to the end of her life, Stein wrote more than a hundred portraits of friends and acquaintances. Stein herself describes in *The Autobiography of Alice B. Toklas* how she wrote her first portrait, *Ada*, as a portrait of Alice Toklas and immediately went into the kitchen to make Alice read it, while the food was getting cold on the plate. Soon followed portraits of the painters Matisse and Picasso, and of the dancer Isadora Duncan, the poet Guillaume Apollinaire, the author and photographer Carl Van Vechten and many, many more.

These portraits are not conventional descriptions of the life and psychological character of the person portrayed. Rather, they are concentrated efforts to capture 'the rhythm of anybody's personality'[8] with a relatively limited vocabulary, which she varies in rhythmic permutations and modulations, like here in her portrait of the dancer Isadora Duncan, *Orta Or One Dancing*:

> Even if one was one she might be like some other one. She was like one and then was like another one and then was like another one and then was like another one and then was one who was one having been one and being one who was one then, one being like some.[9]

Clearly, for Stein, identity is in no way a fixed or static condition, but changing according to shifting relations and positions, just like the movements of a dancer in space. This concept of identity as ever changing would eventually lead Stein to a deconstruction of the idea of coherent characters in her plays.

Stein's portraits of dancers, along with her portrait of the word *Play* from around the same time (1911–12), demonstrate how she combines her interest in movement as a quality of living and writing with a sense of the playfulness of words and language.[10] In that respect, these portraits already point towards her interest in playwriting. What Stein explores in these texts is actually what we could call the *performative* aspects of language – the fact that words do not merely represent an already existing reality, but that they actively participate in the creation of this reality. Words can play, and when they play, they change their own meaning and thus the way we understand the world around us. This quality is at the heart of all playwriting: the idea that words on a page can actually create actions on a stage. Words do not simply represent a pre-existing world; they also actively affect and shape our understanding of the world and as such create new realities.[11]

Approaching the play

Around 1912–13, Stein's writing style changed dramatically. In a small collection of prose poems called *Tender Buttons*, written in 1912 and published in 1914, Stein turned her interest from character to objects, and instead of the repetitious style, we see a more collage-like combination of words that do not immediately seem to fit together or constitute meaningful sentences. Stein herself referred to *Tender Buttons* as *literary still lifes*, and claimed that they were her attempt at 'including looking': that is, they were her concentrated examination of the visual, material world. *Tender Buttons* consists of three sections, labelled *Objects*, *Food* and *Rooms*. The first two parts consist of small pieces of text labelled with the names of everyday objects or food like 'A BOX', 'A SELTZER BOTTLE', 'CHICKEN' or 'RHUBARB' and so on. These titles are followed by completely abstract texts whose relation to the title object is not always obvious. The last part, *Rooms*, perhaps quite logically, consists of one long text, since rooms are not separate entities the way we think of objects.

Like in a cubist painting, Stein so to speak breaks with linear perspective and causal logic in *Tender Buttons*. She plays with several, and incongruous, levels of representation in the same piece or even in the same sentence, cutting up sentences and bringing together pieces of text that do not fit, either syntactically or semantically. Elements from different layers of language and reality collide in the same piece, objects are presented from several angles at the same time, and so on. Here is an example of the small cubist word-collages of *Tender Buttons*:

A PURSE

A purse was not green, it was not straw color, it was hardly seen and it has a use a long use and the chain, the chain was never missing, it was not misplaced, it showed that it was open, that is all that it showed.[12]

This is actually one of the more straightforward texts of *Tender Buttons*. It could be read as a painting, a description of a purse as seen from a specific angle, in a certain light, which determine what is seen of it – the chain and the opening – and how the colour appears due to effects of light and shadow. Many of the other poems are more difficult to relate to their title, but what is definitely sure is that the reader *will* try to relate title and poem – and it is precisely this creative, or performative, use of language that Stein explores: the inevitable interplay between words in a text, and how new meanings inevitably emerge when words are put next to each other on a page.

Around this time, Stein was also experimenting with group portraits, and these two new interests of hers – attempting to catch the visual world and creating portraits of more than one person at a time – eventually led Stein to write her first play, *What Happened. A Five Act Play*, in 1913. According to Stein's anecdotal account in both *The Autobiography of Alice B. Toklas* and the lecture 'Plays' from 1934, the immediate occasion was a dinner party celebrating the birthday of the painter Harry Phelan Gibb.[13] As Ulla Dydo points out in her introduction to the play, the title is tautological, a rhetorical question: What happened (at the theatre)? – A play.[14] The play is written in the collage style of *Tender Buttons*, and although it is divided into five acts, there is no plot, no clear distinction between dialogue and stage direction, no character names. There are, however, as Dydo points out, words that evoke an atmosphere of voices mingling, creating a 'din of superimposed or simultaneous utterances', a play of puns and new combinations of words and idioms.[15] 'Length what is length when silence is so windowful' is one line from the play, where 'windowful' simultaneously echoes the word 'wonderful' and suggests an occupation with the visual world.[16]

Stein would continue to write plays for the rest of her life, and she would write about writing plays in her lectures and autobiographies, most notably of course in the lecture called plainly 'Plays'. Here is her own account of why she began writing plays:

> I came to think that since each one is that one and that there are a number of them each one being that one, the only way to express this thing each one being that one and there being a number of them knowing each other was in a play.[17]

Stein's emphasis on interrelations is interesting because she also claims in this lecture that she was never interested in stories, but rather in 'the essence of what happened'.[18] Stein is not interested in dramatic action, but she is occupied with *movement*, the movement of consciousness, the lively changes in a person's character, and the performative exchange between different persons, and between stage and audience. These early plays display Stein's interest in the performative aspects of life and language.

In addition to completing portraits of dancers like Isadora Duncan and La Argentina, Stein even wrote a portrait of the word 'play'. In the manuscript of her portrait *One Carl Van Vechten*, written shortly after *What Happened,* she plays with the subtitles 'almost a play' and 'A kind of play'.[19] In *The Autobiography of Alice B. Toklas*, she claims that the setting for this portrait of Van Vechten was the scandalous second performance of Russian composer Igor Stravinsky's ballet *Le Sacre du Printemps*, which she, fictitiously, stages as her first encounter with Carl Van Vechten.[20]

In other words, Stein's approach to playwriting was thoroughly prepared and well considered. It was the necessary result of a gradual approach towards the performativity of language, and her way of approaching playwriting was to question all conventions of the drama and the well-made play. Or rather, it was a genuine, basic questioning of what really, essentially, constitutes a play; and this would be her critically-naive approach throughout all her playwriting.

Conversation pieces and landscape plays

During the first part of the First World War, Stein and Toklas spent time in England and on Mallorca, but by the summer of 1916 they returned to France. Gertrude Stein bought a Ford car and learned to drive, and for the rest of the war, the two women drove supplies to hospitals for the American Fund for French Wounded. The car was named Auntie after Stein's Aunt Pauline 'who always behaved admirably in emergencies and behaved fairly well most times if she was properly flattered'.[21]

Especially during the first part of the war, Stein wrote many plays, known either as her 'Mallorcan plays' or her 'conversation pieces'.[22] The language of these plays is not as dense and concentrated as either the early repetitive style or the cubist style of *Tender Buttons* and the very first plays. Rather, these Mallorcan plays seem to be made up of pieces of conversation. One can imagine Stein and Toklas in Mallorca, sitting out the war among people of different nationalities, hearing everywhere around them different languages and modes of discourse – from tourist chitter chatter to real anxieties caused by the war. Stein is combining or recomposing these ready-made phrases of spoken words. Seminal pieces of this period are *Ladies' Voices*, *Mexico* and *Counting Her Dresses. A Play*, all published in 1922 in the collection *Geography and Plays*. Here is Act Two from *Ladies' Voices*:

> Honest to God Miss Williams I don't mean to say that I was older.
> But you were.
> Yes I was. I do not excuse myself. I feel that there is no reason for passing an archduke.
> You like the word.
> You know very well that they all call it their house.
> As Christ was to Lazarus so was the founder of the hill to Mahon.
> You really mean it.
> I do.[23]

What we hear seems to be snatches of different conversations – of different ladies' voices – on different themes: bits of tourist information about location (Mahon) combined with everyday phrases ('Honest to God'; 'You really mean it') and personal worries ('I do not excuse myself'). They do not suggest any coherent action or concrete setting, but they do suggest an atmosphere and climate of waiting and temporary pastimes.

The play was becoming an increasingly important genre in Stein's work, and in the 1920s she coined her seminal concept of the *landscape play*, her singularly most important contribution to Western theatre. It was also around this time that the saints entered her plays, and, in fact, for Stein, the saints and the landscape were one and the same. As she says herself about *Four Saints in Three Acts*, 'all these saints together made my landscape'.[24]

In 1922, Stein published her seminal volume *Geography and Plays*, which contained portraits, plays and other pieces written between 1908 and 1920. At the same time, Stein and Toklas opened a new chapter in their life together, when they began spending their summers in southern France. In August 1922, the couple went to Saint-Rémy in Provence and actually stayed there the whole winter until March 1923.[25]

The stay in Saint-Remy was a very happy and productive period. Stein and Toklas explored the countryside, and many places in France are of course named after saints: Saint-Remy, Saint-Etienne, Saint-Benoit and plenty more. So the saints literally make up the country's landscape as names of different places, cities, villages, monasteries, sites and sights.

As the title of one of her plays from 1922, *Saints and Singing*, indicates, this period was also a period full of music and melody. Stein's saints are associated with nuns, with prayer and with hymns, with praising the joy of life.[26]

Dramaturgically, the basic idea of the landscape play is that it is not concerned with plot development and drama. The problem with theatre, according to Stein, is that the audience members' emotions are always either ahead or behind the action on stage. The audience becomes distracted by their very physical presence in the theatre – by the noise and presence of the other spectators, their knowledge of the actors and so on – and thus removed from the fictional action onstage. Instead of the linear dramaturgy of plot-based drama, Stein imagined theatre as a landscape, a space filled with movement and change, but without reference to a fictitious storyline with which the audience would have to keep pace. As she explains about *Four Saints in Three Acts*, 'it made a landscape and the movement in it was like a movement in and out with which anybody looking on can keep in time'.²⁷

The problem that Stein raises here is in fact the same that French theatre visionary Antonin Artaud, also in the 1930s, criticized as the doubleness of the theatre, always troubled by the dichotomies between presence and representation, between real time and real space on the one hand and the time and space of the plot on the other.

Stein's concept of the landscape play in many respects anticipates performance art and theatre of the 1960s and 1970s, with its rejection of representation in favour of an insistence on visual imagery and physical presence. And significantly, artists from that period, like John Cage, Richard Foreman, Robert Wilson and others, would turn to Stein for inspiration.

Identity and fame

During the 1920s, the clientele attending Stein's salon changed slightly. The old crowd of painters and visual artists was dispersed after the war, and with Stein's growing reputation, she was now instead approached by young American poets. Many of them had joined the war in Europe and suffered from that experience. It was Gertrude Stein who famously dubbed them 'the lost generation'.

When he copied excerpts of Stein's family chronicle *The Making of Americans* in order to have them published in Ford Madox Ford's magazine *The Transatlantic Review*, Ernest Hemingway, for one, learned something from Stein about condensation, about keeping a vocabulary simple, and about suggestion. Another new friend of the 1920s was the composer Virgil Thomson, who would be the main force in actually bringing her plays to the stage. For although Gertrude Stein was well known among artists and writers, she had never had a play performed, and had published very few books: the already mentioned short stories *Three Lives* (published 1909), the cubist prose poems *Tender Buttons* (published 1914) and the collection of shorter portraits and plays, *Geography and Plays* (published 1922). The bulk of her work remained unpublished.

In the early 1930s, Stein and Toklas therefore ventured into the publishing business with their label Plain Edition, eventually publishing five volumes between 1930 and 1933, including *Operas and Plays* in 1932. It seems that Stein went through an exceptionally prolific period of playwriting from 1930 to 1932, probably inspired by the prospect of publishing a full volume of plays. According to Ulla Dydo, she wrote 21 plays in less than three years.[28] The plays from this period are full of names and references to historical or biographical figures from Stein's own life; in fact, Dydo labels the period from 1930 to 1931 'History'. For example, Stein writes three plays, which are labelled as 'historic drama' in their titles.[29] But the references never comprise what we would consider a conventional 'history play'. Rather, as Jane Palatini Bowers states in *'They Watch Me as They Watch This': Gertrude Stein's Metadrama*,

> Stein will have her fun with us, calling dramas in which temporal continuity is distorted 'historic,' invoking memory and sequence in the titles of three plays where nothing continues from one to the other except character names.[30]

Even if Bowers is right that Stein is playing with our ideas of history and historical drama, we should probably not reduce her genre marks to a merely ironic gesture. Rather, we should take Stein's interest in, and even wrestling with, concepts of history during this period seriously. Stein's notion of history is in no way a linear, time-based conception. She is clearly reflecting on her own career and prospects of fame and large-scale publication, and while doing so, she is continuing her search for a different way of rendering time as composition, which was a consistent goal of her general poetics all along, and a prevalent motive for her deconstruction of the conventional drama and the well-made play.

The idea of transforming the time-bound art of drama into a spatial composition is a primary aim of Stein's playwriting poetics, and in *Four Saints in Three Acts* she is clearly playing with the concept of history, merging different historical periods on stage, bringing saints who never met in life together onstage, and of course, as Bowers rightly points out, exploding or dispersing our sense of action from a cohesive, linear plot culminating at a certain point in time, to seemingly idle or futile movements in space, not leading anywhere, not leading to any peripety or catharsis, but gradually and kaleidoscopically transmuting the spatial composition.

In 1933 with *The Autobiography of Alice B. Toklas*, fame finally reached Gertrude Stein, immediately throwing her into an identity crisis and writer's block. Stein, who had always craved publicity, now feared that she had compromised herself by subjecting in *The Autobiography* to what she referred to as 'audience writing' as opposed to her real, experimental writing. The writer's block luckily turned out to be a brief, if unpleasant, experience. In fact, the 1930s would be a most prolific decade for Gertrude Stein, in part because she managed to turn her existential troubles with, and critique of, identity into writing. After all, Stein had always been occupied with 'the rhythm of anybody's personality' in order to get beyond a mere description of superficial or anecdotal identity traits in her portraits.

After *The Autobiography of Alice B. Toklas*, Stein would write several autobiographies, although none of them became as successful as the first one: *Everybody's Autobiography* (1936), *Paris France* (1938) and *Wars I Have Seen* (1944). More importantly, in the 1930s, the combination of her new autobiographical writing, her engagement in identity issues and her lecture tour led her to produce new poetological writings, an amazing cluster of interrelated texts in different genres that share thematic issues on writing and identity. Plays are an integral part of these texts, and usually the play is either employed or discussed when performative aspects of language are involved.

The short play *Identity A Poem* (1935) demonstrates how integral the play was to Stein's poetological writings on what she called her *literary thinking*. Compiled from little plays that she wrote as part of her volume *The Geographical History of America, Or, The Relation of Human Nature to the Human Mind* (written 1935), the play *Identity A Poem* was first produced in 1936 as a puppet play by Donald Vestal, a young puppeteer whom Stein had met in Chicago, and for whom she actually stitched it together. One can understand already from the first line why Stein thought it suitable for a puppet play: 'I am I because my little dog knows me. The figure wanders on alone.'[31]

The figure and the little dog bring together a childlike simplicity that is shared between philosophy and children's books.[32] The little dog even refers to a Mother Goose poem, called 'The old woman and the peddler', and the point is, ironically, that in the poem, the little dog does *not* recognize the old woman. The opening line of the play thus demonstrates how precarious identity is in its dependence on recognition by the other. The question of identity and recognition is in no way an innocent question in Stein's writing, but rather an existential one: it asserts the loneliness of the human figure.

The cluster of interrelated texts engaging with issues of identity includes not only lectures and poetological texts, but also novels and longer plays. While writing *Ida A Novel* (finished 1940), Stein made a detour to playwriting with the libretto *Doctor Faustus Lights the Lights* (1938). And in 1936, in the play *Listen To Me*, she considered questions also discussed in the children's book *The World Is Round* (1938): the paradox of how to reconcile the fact that 'the world is all covered with people' with the human experience of isolation and loneliness in the midst of our search for love and companionship. The tightly woven cluster of texts on identity demonstrates how central the play is to Stein's aesthetics.

The war and after the war

During the 1930s, Europe was increasingly moving from democracy towards totalitarian dictatorships. Not only in Germany, but also in Italy and Spain, fascist regimes gained power, and by autumn 1939, war was a fact. In May–June 1940, Germany occupied northern France, including Paris. Stein and Toklas were forced to sit out the war in the countryside, first in their beloved house at Bilignin, and later in the small village of Culoz. The Second World War was in no way as heroic for Stein as the First World War had been. It is a wonder that she survived, as a Jew, a lesbian and an American citizen. It was probably only due to a combination of protection from the local authorities in Bilignin and Culoz, and the powerful protection from her close friend Bernard Faÿ, who after the war was convicted as a collaborator responsible for the persecution of hundreds of freemasons. But the anti-Semite Bernard Faÿ also saved the lives of Stein and Toklas, and he even managed to save Stein's collection of modern art from the Gestapo. In return,

Toklas later helped finance his escape from prison where he had been sentenced to hard labour for life.

Even though they survived, the war was tough on Stein and Toklas. Food was scarce, and from 1942, when the so-called 'free zone' of Vichy France was also occupied, they were literally cut off from any contact with the rest of the world, especially the US. Their situation was extremely precarious, even if they did not fully realize it – or only realized it too late, when there was no longer any way out. In *The Letters of Gertrude Stein and Thornton Wilder*, Edward Burns and Ulla Dydo give a sober and factual account of Stein's life during these years.

In recent years, a critique of Stein's activities and especially her reactionary political views in support of Marshal Pétain and his Vichy government has been voiced. There is probably no doubt that Stein's judgement of the political situation in Europe was flawed, but for us today to criticize whatever she did to survive is probably even more ignorant. What we need to understand when trying to evaluate Stein's movements, actions and sympathies during the Second World War is that Pétain was actually a French war hero from the First World War, while the conservative Catholic Bernard Faÿ was one of her closest friends at the time, whose views of course influenced her understanding of the political situation. Still, he was in no way her only friend. Birgit Van Puymbroeck in her article 'Triangular Politics: Stein, Bernard Faÿ, and Elisabeth de Gramont' has explored the triangular relationship between Stein, Faÿ and the left-wing duchess Elisabeth de Gramont. Van Puymbroeck's analysis demonstrates that friendships, even around 1930, were not necessarily formed according to political views.

The political situation, furthermore, was in no way static or stable, and it was not easy to get a clear picture of it. In times of war, truthful information is first to vanish. During the war, Stein definitely did not have the same knowledge of the Holocaust that we have today. She knew about deportations of French citizens to work in German factories, but she could hardly have known the scale of the exterminations of Jews and other unwanted groups like freemasons, communists, the disabled and other persecuted groups.

Immediately after the Second World War, Stein published her last autobiography, *Wars I Have Seen*, as well as her book on American GIs in France, *Brewsie and Willie*. Written during the occupation, *Wars I Have Seen* makes a very mixed reading experience.

Obviously, in times of war, and especially in an occupied country, information and communication are lost first. In *Wars I Have Seen*, we follow Stein and Toklas's everyday and not very glamorous fight for survival, but also the dangers of misinformation and misinterpretations that flourish among people, the mistrust among neighbours, the superstitions that arise, the uncertainties about the fates of detained or deserted young men and so on.

The book was the material for a so-called *staged concert* by German director and composer Heiner Goebbels in 2007. Goebbels has produced several pieces based on Stein's work, most prominently the amazing visual opera *Hashirigaki* from 2000 based on excerpts from Stein's *The Making of Americans* and music by the Beach Boys. For Goebbels, the fascination of Stein's writing is that you can always follow the movements of her thoughts in her writing. About *Wars I Have Seen*, Goebbels said that its peculiar mixture of fear and repression, of personal defence mechanisms and political distance, provides a rare image of precisely how mixed and contradictory the emotions of anyone living through a war must be. *Wars I Have Seen* is full of anecdotes, but none of them are compatible with one another, as personal experience collides with naive or rigid, even outrageous, political statements. The different voices or modes of narration do not seem to fit together. So the way she does *not* state something or states the same thing again and again instead of something else actually becomes a way of rendering the condition of war, where you can never talk about the essential, about what really matters.[33]

After the war, Stein also wrote two plays, which seem at first sight very different. The play *In Savoy; or, Yes Is For a Very Young Man* is Stein's most straightforward realist play. It presents a French family with their American friend living through the Second World War and the German occupation, which almost tears the family apart due to their divergent sympathies. Stein tries to render the difficulties of doing the right thing during occupation, while at the same time presenting the French people as heroic in their endurance of the hardships and precariousness of wartime. Produced in March 1946 at the Pasadena Playhouse, it is one of her few plays that saw a full-scale production during Stein's lifetime.

Stein's last play, the libretto *The Mother of Us All* (1946), belongs to her most important playtexts. While the title is clearly meant to connote Stein's own position among Modernist artists and writers, on the narrative level the play is about the famous suffragette Susan B. Anthony and her fight for women's right to vote. The libretto brings together characters from different periods of American history, personal friends of Stein and public figures, as well as purely fictional characters. The libretto was written as part of a new collaboration with Virgil Thomson, and the opera opened in 1947 at Columbia University. By that time, Stein herself had passed away, and due to the analogies between Stein's and Susan B. Anthony's lives – they both became American icons, both had a female life companion and so on – the opera has been seen as Stein's last legacy and attempt to ensure her own name and position. However, the final note is one of doubt: at the end of the opera, the ghost of Susan B. Anthony appears at the revelation of a statue of herself and critically discusses the value of her lifelong struggle and achievement. *The Mother of Us All* is one of the most performed works by Gertrude Stein, and especially the 1967 Walker Art Center and the 1976 Santa Fe Opera productions with costumes and set design by Robert Indiana have been much acclaimed.[34]

How many saints are there in it?: *Four Saints in Three Acts*

Four Saints in Three Acts is an opera, and more so since it is *An Opera to Be Sung*, as the subtitle makes clear with the same kind of tautological emphasis that the title of her first play from 1913, *What Happened. A Five Act Play*, already demonstrated. A play is what happens at the theatre, as Ulla Dydo points out in her introduction to the play.[35] Similarly, an opera is to be sung. But the subtitle may not be mere affectation, since the main 'plot' of the libretto, if we can speak of a plot at all, is the (artist's) effort to actually make the saints sing. Large parts of the text are meditations on how to narrate, how to tell about the saints, how to put them on stage – literally make them arrive on stage – where to place the saints on stage, how to make them move about and in what scenographic setting, and finally, how to make them raise their voices in prayers or hymns, in short, how and what they should sing.

It is important to note that Stein's original text differs significantly from Thomson's score and Maurice Grosser's scenario. One reason for this is that Thomson had to make a stageworthy version of Stein's text, which deconstructs so many of the usual theatrical conventions. First of all, the title *Four Saints in Three Acts* is misleading. There are dozens of saints in the play, many of which are only mentioned once or a few times. Many of the saints do not figure – or only figure – in the list of dramatis personae, which itself only turns up on the fifth page of the text.[36] The list almost compiles the saints into two choruses, since it is organized into two groups of ten female and eleven male saints. An additional complication is that more often than not each character's name is mentioned again with each of their new lines, implying that they could either be the same or a different character. For example, one could assume that a different Saint Therese was introduced for each new line in the following excerpt:

> **Saint Therese** How many saints are there in it.
> **Saint Therese** There are very many many saints in it.
> **Saint Therese** There are as many saints as there are in it.
> **Saint Therese** How many saints are there in it.
> **Saint Therese** There are there are there are saints saints in it.[37]

Due to this excess of saints' names, it is rather difficult to make out exactly how many saints there are in the play. And, the questions 'How many saints are there in it?' and 'How many acts are there in it?' are repeated throughout the play, along with similar questions like, 'How many saints can sit around?',[38] 'How many saints can be ...?',[39] 'How many windows are there in it?'[40] and 'How many nails are there in it?'[41] and so on.

It is even more difficult to determine precisely how many *acts* there are in the play. There are at least four acts mentioned, not three, but it is quite impossible to be sure, since the exact number of acts is made incalculable, and the structure confused by Stein's technique of repetition, which is also applied to the larger structures of the work, when she inserts several acts and scenes with the same number, or divides one act into several parts. For example, there is an 'Act I' after the list of characters on the fifth page of the play, which is followed by a section called 'Repeat First Act' and after that a section called 'Enact end of an act' followed by 'Act

Two' followed by 'Act One' followed by an 'Act II' and so on. In between these acts, the *scenes* seem to follow an irregular system of their own, with several scenes given the same number within each of the acts. Some of the scenes are even personalized and seem to have lines to say:

> Scene eight. To Wait.
> Scene one. And begun.
> Scene two. To and to.
> Scene three. Happily be.
> Scene Four. Attached or.
> Scene Five. Sent to derive.
> Scene Six. Let it mix.
> Scene Seven. Attached eleven.
> Scene Eight. To wait.[42]

As Jane Palatini Bowers remarks, 'The only certainty regarding the number of acts in the play is that which is obvious at the end: 'Last Act. / Which is a fact.'[43]

Due to all these literary devices for the deconstruction of dramatic reason, the play text must have seemed impossible to stage as it is. In addition came musically as well as theatrically motivated changes. Large parts of Stein's text are not aligned to any specific characters or speakers.[44] Thomson distributed most of these lines as dialogue among different characters, some of which are only mentioned briefly or play minor roles in Stein's original text. Thomson introduced not one, but two choruses, and further, in order to make the text stageworthy, he introduced two narrators, the Commère and the Compère. These two figures are very active. They introduce the dramatis personae at the end of the prologue,[45] and often they announce shifting scenes and acts, like 'Act two' or 'Scene five'. They also sing more substantial parts of the text, like the stage direction – or weather report – at the beginning of Act I: 'Saint Therese in a storm at Avila there can be rain and warm snow and warm that is the water is warm the river is not warm the sun is not warm and if to stay to cry.'[46] Finally, Thomson changed the main character's name from Saint Therese to Saint Teresa, which was easier to sing, and divided the character into two singers, Saint Teresa I and Saint Teresa II.

The play centres on Spanish sixteenth-century saints, especially Teresa of Avila, who in Stein's play is called Saint Therese, and in Thomson's score Saint Teresa. The other main character is Saint Ignatius of Loyola, and the two saints are in many respects contrasted with each other.

Stein's saints are not psychological characters but rather figures in a composition – a (theatrical) landscape, a piece of scenery. Historically, Teresa and Ignatius were part of the Spanish history of Catholic orders and the Spanish landscape of monasteries during the Counter-Reformation. Both of them were also very material and concrete parts of Stein's own urban landscape, since the character of Saint Therese was inspired by a picture of a young girl turned into a nun that Stein saw in a shop window, while Saint Ignatius was inspired by a tall figure in a group of porcelain figurines in another shop window. Stein tells the story of these very mundane inspirations for the saints in her lecture 'Plays', but their sources also enter the playtext of *Four Saints* itself:

> Saint Ignatius could be in porcelain actually.[47]
> Saint Therese could be photographed having been dressed like a lady and then they taking out her head changed it to a nun and a nun a saint and a saint so.[48]

All the saints are, of course, historical figures brought together in Stein's play where they display different characteristics, evident in their movements and language. While Therese is described as seated, Ignatius is standing:

> Saint Ignatius could be in porcelain actually while he was young and standing.
> Saint Therese could not be young and standing she could be sitting.
> Saint Ignatius could be in porcelain actually actually in porcelain standing.
> Saint Therese could be admittedly could be in moving seating. Saint Therese could be in moving sitting.
> Saint Therese could be.
> Saint Ignatius could be.
> Saint Ignatius could be in porcelain actually in porcelain standing.[49]

Her language is plain and made up of simple, everyday words; his is latinized and complicated, often with numbers and calculations in it:

> Saint Ignatius. Foundationally marvellously aboundingly illimitably with it as a circumstance. Fundamentally and saints fundamentally and saints and fundamentally and saints.[50]

> Saint Therese. Like and it might be as likely it might be very likely that it would be amounting to once in a while as in a way it could be what was meant by that at once. There is a difference between at most at once.[51]

Ulla Dydo has demonstrated how the libretto literally grows out of Stein's writing of a different text, 'Regular Regularly In Narrative', which, as the title suggests, is a study of narrative, that is, a completely different genre and type of text from 'an opera to be sung'. In the manuscript notebook, the two texts are merely separated by two heavy lines.[52] It is as though the essay on narrative continues into the opera. And, *Four Saints* actually begins as a meditation on narrative. After an initial evocation that might be a love song to Alice Toklas as well as to Saint Therese – 'To know to know to love her so' – variations on the lines 'Four saints prepare for saints' and 'In narrative prepare for saints' alternate, until suddenly the tone shifts with the line 'What happened to-day, a narrative.'[53]

Here follows what could be the beginning of a perfectly straightforward story: 'We had intended if it were a pleasant day to go to the country it was a very beautiful day and we carried out our intention.'[54] Since this is a Stein text, the story does not continue in a straightforward way. Instead, shifting motives are introduced, patterns of words and phrases that seem to circle around the issues of beginning the opera, setting the stage and bringing the saints on stage, in short, simply making the saints be present. Questions of the scenery merge with questions related to introducing and placing the figures in the landscape:

> He came and said he was hurrying hurrying and hurrying to remain he said he said finally to be ...[55]

> Imagine four benches separately.
> One in the sun.

> Two in the sun.
> Three in the sun.
> One not in the sun.
> Not one not in the sun.
> Not one.
> Four benches used four benches used separately.
> Four benches used separately.
> That makes it be makes it not be at the time.[56]
>
> To mount it up.
> Up hill.
> Four saints are never three.
> Three saints are never four.
> Four saints are never left altogether.
> Three saints are never idle.
> Four saints are leave it to me.
> Three saints when this you see.
> Begin three saints.
> Begin four saints.
> Two and two saints.
> One and three saints.
> In place.
> ...
>
> The difference between saints forget me nots and mountains have to have to have to at a time.[57]

What we literally follow here is the process of composition. Virgil Thomson claimed that the motif of the opera was 'the working artist's life', which Bowers corrects to 'the artist at work'.[58] According to Bowers, we are following the writer's mind during the writing process, and this is what Stein tries to stage, in an effort to reach her theatre audience as immediately as she wanted to reach her readers, and thus as unmediated by theatrical means as possible.

This means that composition itself becomes a performance event:

> Like Saint Therese, who is half in and half out, the performance itself is suspended in a kind of limbo. It consists entirely of

preparation, beginning with the narrative which prepares for the play, followed by a play which prepares for a performance, and ending with the only fact, which is the last act.[59]

Bowers suggests that Stein's landscape plays should really be called *lang*-scapes, since it is the composition of the language or text that is at the centre of Stein's playwriting.

While Bowers's analysis of how the process of composition is at the centre of the play is both precise and convincing, the play is not anti-theatrical, as she suggests. On the contrary, an acute awareness of the theatrical and scenic challenges of staging and visualization is at stake. It is precisely because Stein does *not* want the performance to be completely reduced to and subordinated to the literary text that her plays are so open and inconclusive. In the epigraph that begins this chapter Stein states:

When I see a thing it is not a play for me because the minute I see it it ceases to be a play for me, but when I write something that somebody else can see then it is a play for me.[60]

Here Stein makes clear that she is a playwright who sets the stage director free. She writes playtexts that are open for other artists to visualize. The conditionals and tentative and contradictory suggestions, of course, mirror Stein's own process of composition, but they also open the text for different possibilities of staging and *mise-en-scène*. The crucial thing to understand is that Stein never conceived of performance as an illustration of the playtext, but as a work in its own right. The production can never and *should never* be an imitation of the playtext. Accordingly, a playtext by Stein suggests images, names, motifs and textual material for a performance that might be actualized in a number of ways in performance, but it seldom dictates exactly which parts of the text should be spoken, or sung by whom, or visualized in the set design. Stein was not disinterested in the theatre, but she wanted to create a new kind of theatre, where text and movement, sight and sound would fuse into one complex and fluctuating composition. She challenged the hierarchy among the different elements and means of expression in conventional drama, where everything else has to support and illustrate a dominant plot dictated by the dramatic text. In dramatic theatre, characters, dialogue and setting, as well as light, sound and music, all serve the *dramatic* unfolding of the plot. Stein was not interested in plot and gave equal weight to the different elements of the dramatic text and the theatrical performance. In fact, her plays are non-dramatic. In the words of Polish-German theatre professor Andrzej Wirth,

> The time of a landscape play is not 'dramatic,' but identical with the observer's time ... The experience of a landscape play does not lie in the expectation of some sort of resolution, but rather in the act of watching it unfold: 'Gradually wait.'[61]

In performance, the images and poetic patterns of the text may be rendered as choreographic patterns of movement, as everyday actions, as visual images, as song or sound, music, dialogue, spoken or recorded text and so on.

Even if Thomson and Grosser did feel they had to make changes to the text in order to make it stageable, the 1934 production in itself proved that it was completely possible to perform Stein's poetic landscape plays. Judging from the documentation – film clips, photos and reviews – the final performance was a marvellous experience with its cellophane decorations by Florine Stettheimer, and the carefully choreographed cast of black gospel singers.

Gertrude Stein and Thornton Wilder

One of the most important results of Stein's American lecture tour was her friendship with Thornton Wilder. They met in November 1934 in Chicago and immediately became friends. Wilder persuaded the president of the University of Chicago, his friend Robert Maynard Hutchinson, to invite Stein to come back and do a lecture series with a master class on the theme of *Narration* in March 1935.[62]

Wilder was a shining young talent in American literature, Pulitzer Prize-winner and of a prominent Chicago family. He was well acquainted with Modernist writers like Ernest Hemingway and F. Scott Fitzgerald, even if he had only read Stein's *The Autobiography of Alice B. Toklas* and a bit of *The Making of Americans* when they met.[63] And then he was famous. As Dydo and Burns emphasize in their introduction to *The Letters of Gertrude Stein and Thornton Wilder*, Wilder had already at a young age experienced the fame that Stein finally achieved so late in life, and this gave their relationship a kind of intimacy of mutual respect and understanding. It was probably inevitable that they should develop a warm friendship.

More importantly, there is no doubt that they affected each other's work profoundly. An obvious point in common is demonstrated by Wilder's use of the Stage Manager in *Our Town*, which seems clearly inspired from the Commère and Compère that Virgil Thomson inserted into *Four Saints in Three Acts* in order to turn Stein's text into a stageable libretto. While Wilder did not merely imitate Stein in his unique development of the Stage Manager, his use of this figure challenges some of the same dramatic conventions that Stein's narrative elements and general deconstruction of the distinction between dialogue and stage directions also address: the ideal of dramatic presence, the unity of time, place and action, and so on.

It seems clear that Stein and Wilder already shared a dramaturgical sensibility, motivated by an interest in human identity in relation to time and motion, which produced an affinity between the dramaturgical experiments of the avant-garde Modernist and the young upcoming Pulitzer winner. In fact, they both seem to have been determined to renew the drama from within and break with dramatic conventions. In his *Theory of the Modern Drama* from 1956, Peter Szondi develops his thesis of how an epic drama, developed after 1900, challenges the classic Aristotelian ideal of drama. Szondi analyses Wilder's Stage Manager as the prime example of the introduction of 'the epic I' that replaces dramatic action with scenic narrative. One could argue that Wilder indeed unfolds many of the significant traits in Szondi's epic drama, whereas Stein, in a more radical leap, abandons drama altogether and writes truly post-dramatic plays in the sense described by German theatre professors Hans-Thies Lehmann and Andrzej Wirth.[64] Despite these different approaches to dramatic form, there are significant similarities between the formal and thematic interests of the two authors.

Wilder's *The Long Christmas Dinner* from 1931 already exhibited traits that strike a chord in anyone familiar with Stein's plays and poetics. In fact, the idea of demonstrating a family's rise and decline over several generations through the single image of a prolonged Christmas dinner with endlessly repeated lines and recurring actions, thoughts and worries through the years is reminiscent of several of Stein's formal concepts, like the prolonged present, her endless modulations and repetitions of a limited vocabulary of almost identical phrases. Even some of Stein's most persistent themes, like the struggle between social identity and the singular being, are curiously evoked in Wilder's play.

No wonder Stein wished to involve Wilder in her writings on identity of the 1930s.

Dydo and Burns have published Wilder's notes on Stein's *Ida A Novel* and state that Wilder is present in many of Stein's writings that deal with the tangled motives of fame, identity and narration from the last decade of her life. One important piece in this group of texts is the libretto *Doctor Faustus Lights the Lights* from 1938, which Stein wrote while she was wrestling with her novel on fame and identity, *Ida A Novel*. The play treats the same themes and motives and seems to have helped Stein solve the challenges encountered by the material of the novel.

And the dog says thank you: *Doctor Faustus Lights the Lights*

Four Saints in Three Acts made Stein's breakthrough as a writer for the stage, and *The Mother of Us All* was supposed to secure her afterlife on the stage. But, in fact, *Doctor Faustus Lights the Lights* more than any other piece induced Stein's impact on both American and European stage art. Somewhat surprisingly, the theatrical avant-garde embraced Stein's most Gothic and Romantic play, which is also one of her most narrative plays, with plot, characters and dialogue. It has been produced by the Living Theatre, the Judson Poets' Theater, Richard Foreman, Robert Wilson and the Wooster Group. Each of these performances has been an important hallmark in the work of the artists.

Doctor Faustus Lights the Lights is really a libretto, and should have been set to music by Lord Berners, who allegedly declined the job due to a personal depression at the outbreak of the Second World War. Perhaps the Faust theme with its ties to German idealism seemed somewhat inappropriate at the time of international German aggression.

It is, however, significant that Stein turns to the Faust legend at exactly this historical moment, since the myth explores the relations of knowledge, power and sexuality in Western culture, exactly the complex forces at stake in the world at this time. 'It is astonishing that Gertrude Stein, who explored not great themes and figures but words, should have written a Faust,' Ulla Dydo writes in her short introduction to the piece in *A Stein Reader*.[65] In fact, Stein's *Faust* is a humorous and intelligent critique of dominant figures of enlightenment and technological progress in Western thinking, as well as of the biblical conflation of sex and knowledge. *Doctor Faustus Lights the Lights* is a precise analysis of how the gendered access to knowledge and power in Western society is legitimized through myths like those in Faust and Genesis.

In Stein's *Faust*, the female character is the real protagonist. Goethe's self-sacrificing Gretchen is turned into a quite competent character with several simultaneous and shifting identities, as demonstrated by her double double name: Marguerite Ida and Helena Annabel.

The plot is that Faust has sold his soul to the devil, Mephisto, in return for the power to invent the electric light. By the time of the play's action, Faust is quite disappointed with his ever-bright world and longs only for the darkness of hell, where he, unfortunately, cannot go since he sold his soul. Faust lives with his two companions, a little boy and a dog which says 'Thank you' all the time. The play opens with Faust's rage against Mephisto: 'The devil what the devil what do I care if the devil is there.'[66] The scene ends with Faustus kicking Mephisto 'to hell'. After that there is a ballet of electric lights, and the dog and boy appear, while Doctor Faustus sings his song 'Let me Alone' to them.

Meanwhile, Marguerite Ida and Helena Annabel is lost in the wild woods, where she is bitten by what she assumes must be a viper. She is afraid to die from the poisonous bite, but a countrywoman with a sickle tells her to go to Doctor Faustus. Faustus, however, does not want to help her, and whether he is persuaded to cure her is never clear, but in any case Marguerite Ida and Helena Annabel does not die: 'Enough said / You are not dead,' as Faustus concludes.[67] Instead, Marguerite Ida and Helena Annabel gains power over the light – not the artificial electric light, but real natural candlelight. She adorns herself with an artificial viper, and people come from everywhere to see her as she sits with a halo around her. A 'man from over the seas' tries to seduce her with his love song: 'Pretty pretty pretty dear / She is all my love and always here / And I am hers and she is mine / And I lover her all the time.'[68] Marguerite Ida and Helena Annabel confuses the man from over the seas with Doctor Faustus: 'Is it you, Doctor Faustus is it you, tell me man from over the seas are you he.'[69] Despite her distrust, she faints into the arms of the man from over the seas, while Mephistopheles appears behind him. Another innocent, childish couple, a little boy and girl, sing a song addressed to 'Mr. Viper' – who might be the man from over the seas or the viper that bit Marguerite Ida and Helena Annabel (or indeed the snake from Genesis). Their song invokes the heterosexual order of stable gender distinctions and links it to *truth*: 'Mr. Viper think of me. He says you do she says you do and if you do dear Mr. Viper if you do then it is all true he is a boy I am a girl it is all true dear dear Mr. Viper think of me.'[70]

Faust, however, is furious that a woman can have power over the light without even selling her soul. He demands from Mephisto that if Marguerite Ida and Helena Annabel can go to hell, he wants to go too, and Mephisto replies that he must 'Kill something', whereupon Faust makes the viper kill the little boy and dog. Mephisto now turns Faust into a young man again, so that he can seduce Marguerite Ida and Helena Annabel to go to hell with him, but Marguerite Ida and Helena Annabel does not recognize the youthful Faust, and, instead, she faints once more into the arms of the man from over the seas, while Mephisto grumbles that he is always deceived, and Faustus sings 'Leave me alone' while 'he sinks into darkness and it is all dark and the little boy and little girl sing / Please Mr. Viper listen to me he is he and she is she and we are we please Mr. Viper listen to me.'[71]

It is clear that identity, and not the least sexual identity, is a major issue in this play. All figures mirror one another, blend into one another or appear behind one another. They come in couples and appear under several names or in different guises. Furthermore, the question of (sexual) identity is related to the themes of power and knowledge, which are emblematically concretized in the ability to make light, an almost literal interpretation of the idea of knowledge as *insight* and *enlightenment*.

What is amazing is that in this play Stein is at once exposing the dominant norms and discourses of Western society and simultaneously revealing their most deadly dangers and effects, while at the same time suggesting the possibility for change and difference. *Doctor Faustus Lights the Lights* grew out of Stein's work on *Ida A Novel* (1940), her important work dealing with issues of fame and identity. The protagonist of the novel is a twin, and twins or doubles abound in *Doctor Faustus Lights the Lights* as well. Just like the protagonist with her double double name, Marguerite Ida and Helena Annabel, most of the other characters appear under several, slightly different names. Faust appears under the names Faust, Faustus and Doctor Faustus. He is further confused with the man from over the seas. Mephisto is addressed as Mr. Devil and designated as Mephisto or Mephistopheles. Mr. Viper is mentioned only when addressed by the little girl and boy. He might be an incarnation or a name for any one of the other figures, and as such works as a kind of electric current that connects all the figures in the same circuit of interchangeable identities or positions in the play. He is a childish anthropomorphic version of the viper that bites Marguerite Ida and Helena Annabel, and, with his biblical undercurrents, he merges traits of the devil and the seducer in one. Finally, the innocent couples mirror each other: little boy and dog are the apprentices of Doctor Faustus, related to him through a hierarchy of work and knowledge, whereas the little girl and boy represent the innocent, childish approach to gendered, heteronormative sexuality.

In *Doctor Faustus Lights the Lights,* the order of good and evil is turned completely upside down as soon as the female protagonist claims access to the knowledge of the male figures. Instead of sacrificing herself for Faust like Goethe's Gretchen, Marguerite Ida and Helena Annabel literally disentangles the coupling of knowledge, evil and sexual taboo, which Western culture installs through the biblical myth of the snake as both seducer and provider of knowledge. If the Faust myth is about enlightenment and German idealism, Stein's Marguerite Ida and Helena Annabel clearly refuses idealism, instead insisting on natural light and female insight in earthly life rather than life after death, be it in heaven or hell. She is, however, tempted and confused by hetero-normative sexuality in the guise of the man from over the seas – this is the Helen of Troy part of her identity included in her name Helena. Stein does not entertain any naive hopes for saving the world through women's liberation. But she does provide a precise analysis of the cultural condition and how to navigate in a man's world, in a society whose myths serve to control female sexuality and women's access to knowledge in order to secure male power.

Written on the brink of the Second World War, the play has often been construed as a warning against the Faustian powers of technological warfare and male dominance rigidly fossilized into fascist dictatorships and the longing for a strong leader. The end of the play may seem depressing as Faustus sinks into a darkness consuming everything – 'and he sinks into the darkness and it is all dark' – but the libretto is nevertheless a playful rewriting of these founding father myths from a female perspective.[72] It seems to have been necessary for Stein to deconstruct these myths before she could finish her novel on a female character who is completely independent and self-made, that is her novel on fame, identity and female genius, *Ida A Novel*.

Important productions of *Doctor Faustus Lights the Lights*

Doctor Faustus Lights the Lights became something of a signature play for the New York avant-garde in the second half of the twentieth century. The Living Theatre produced the play as the inaugural performance when they opened their Cherry Lane Theatre in 1951. Originally they wanted John Cage to compose the music, but unfortunately Stein's literary executioner, Carl Van Vechten, rejected that choice.[73] Instead, Richard Banks composed the music. In 1979, the Judson Poets' Theater mounted a production directed by Lawrence Kornfeld with music by Al Carmines, and, in 1982, Richard Foreman presented the play at the Freie Volksbühne in Berlin and the Avignon Festival. Ten years later, in 1992, Robert Wilson offered a seminal production of the play at the Hebbel Theater in Berlin. This time the music was by German composer and sound artist Hans Peter Kuhn, who composed a truly original musical work that lives on in its own right. Finally, in 1996, the Wooster Group produced the play under the title *House/Lights*. In their production, Stein's text is mixed onstage with a 1964 sexploitation film by Joseph Mawra called *Olga's House of Shame*. The year 1996 was the 50th anniversary of Stein's death, a year that also saw Robert Wilson's grand production of *Four Saints in Three Acts* at the Houston Grand Opera.

The productions of *Doctor Faustus Lights the* Lights by Robert Wilson and the Wooster Group are particularly interesting, not only because they are the most well documented, but first of all because they use seemingly reverse strategies in their approach to character and dramaturgy.

Robert Wilson literally multiplies and merges the characters onstage, when he makes several actors play the same character at once. The two protagonists, Marguerite Ida and Helena Annabel and Faust, are played by three actors each. All three actors are usually onstage at the same time, but some of these actors take on other roles as well, like the man from over the seas or the little girl and boy. There are two Mephistos, a black and a red one. With several actors playing one character, Wilson, like Stein, can take the action in different directions at the same time, and he can provide the myth-like merging of characters that Stein employs in her play.

Wilson's production featured students from the famous East German Ernst Busch Academy of Dramatic Arts. Many of the students barely spoke English, a fact that added a robot-like quality of *Verfremdung* to the performance. Wilson's minimalist scenography contributes to the depersonalization of the performance. For example, the bite of the viper is illustrated by a rising vertical line of red light, while the three actors playing Marguerite Ida and Helena Annabel hold up their feet in a motionless gesture. This provides a very stylized and cool but still dramatic effect. In several scenes, cords from the light bulbs, combined with the slow, minutely choreographed movements, make the characters appear like string puppets. In Wilson's live puppet show, the characters are but figures in the larger patterns of myths and social forces that govern their lives.

The Wooster Group displayed a seemingly opposite strategy, with each actor playing different characters in several plots of action at one and the same time, grafting Stein's rewriting of the Faust myth onto the porn film by Joseph Mawra, so that each actor is at once playing a character in Stein's play and in the Mawra film. The play and the film are both simultaneously re-enacted onstage in one movement, where live recordings of the actors' movements onstage are projected into the film clips displayed on monitors onstage.

Thus, the mixing of words, action, sound and pictures happens onstage in front of the audience, through a complex interplay between live actions, recorded media and mediated actions. The use of voice masks or voice distortions supports the effect of several characters being layered in one actor's body. The overall result is a stunning montage of shreds and bits from the cultural catalogue of American popular and high culture, tightly woven together to form a vision of what Stein's cluster of cultural myths may look like today: in what guises do we meet these normative mythological patterns in contemporary culture today? The actors' highly skilled interactions with the technology, and the technicians' understanding of the aesthetics of the group, enable director Elizabeth LeCompte to form a dance with technology that is unique among contemporary stage artists, and in its own very literal sense releases Stein's vision of how the conglomerate of sex, power and knowledge fuse in Western achievements of technological skills.

Nobody has met anyone: *Listen To Me*

Like *Doctor Faustus Lights the Lights*, *Listen To Me* from 1936 belongs to a cluster of interrelated texts in different genres from the 1930s dealing with issues of identity, fame and existence. *Listen To Me* counts among Stein's most important plays, due to its radical deconstruction of character, or what Andrzej Wirth has called the 'dissolution of character into discourse'.[74] Sarah Bay-Cheng similarly claims that *Listen To Me* reduces characters 'to total anonymity'.[75]

The unity of character and actor has been one of the basic ideals of drama, especially in its naturalist vein. In *The Death of Character*, theatre scholar Elinor Fuchs traces how this unity has been challenged throughout the twentieth century, with Stein's landscape plays an important contribution to this development. Both Fuchs and Wirth understand Stein's deconstruction of the organic unity of the character as a way to make the theatre modern: 'It was the most radical step to make drama abstract through the dissolution of the figure ...'[76]

German playwright and theatre director Bertolt Brecht is, of course, the modern playwright with whom we most readily associate the breach between actor and character, due to his principle of alienation or *Verfremdung*. In Brecht's theatre, actors may distance themselves from their character and even comment on the character's actions, in order to make space for critical reflection on the part of the audience. But as Wirth remarks, Stein would probably find the political programme of Brecht's Epic Theater aesthetically old-fashioned and insufficiently radical with its dependence on plot and storyline.[77] In Stein's plays, we witness a much more radical dissolution of character as part of what Wirth calls her *critique of dramatic reason*. For Wirth, as for Stein, conventional drama is the paradigm of a logic governed by linear causality that has dominated Western thought throughout the centuries.[78] Stein's critique of drama is an epistemological challenge to this limited model of knowledge and thinking. If *Doctor Faustus Lights the Lights* negotiates the myths that define the relationship between power, sex and knowledge in Western culture, *Listen To Me* reveals the basic rules of language and representation that sanction this dominant logic. In *Listen To Me* the deconstruction of character takes place on the level of language and dialogue rather than plot and action.

Stein's deconstruction of character is part of a fundamental critique of drama as the predominant model for theatrical representation, and *Listen To Me* is one of Stein's most radical plays in this respect. In *Listen To Me*, no individual characters with a dramatic fate or destiny ever manage to manifest themselves out of the overall discourse of the play. Except for Sweet William, who is a genius and is looking for his Lillian, the characters do not have individual names, they are just called First character, Second character and so on. The play begins with the introduction of three characters, and then four characters. These are not identical:

> A chorus of three characters and then a chorus of four characters but the characters that are the three characters are not the same as the characters that are four characters.[79]

This rather ponderous way of introducing the characters turns out to serve the purpose of avoiding the Fifth character. Already on the second page of the play we are told that 'There are never five characters in listen to me.'⁸⁰ This dodge to avoid the Fifth character and even the Fifth act, and so on, continues throughout the play. It causes the characters to be mentioned backwards: 'The last of the seven speaks first' continues with 'the next to the last', 'the third from the last', and so on, so that the Fifth character is never mentioned directly, although 'the fifth one from the end' is mentioned. But since this sentence really signifies the *second* character (from the beginning, that is), direct mention of the Fifth character is still avoided.⁸¹ Act II, Scene V again points out that 'the fifth character does not exist'⁸² and is followed by a second Scene V that consists of only one sentence: 'There is no scene V,' which seems to somehow invalidate the first Scene V.⁸³ Other play-rules are introduced only to be broken. For example, the characters claim that they will speak only in words of one syllable, but this rule is not adhered to either.

Bowers interprets the trouble with the omission of the Fifth character and the monosyllabic words as a conflict between Stein – the writer and authorial voice of the play – and her characters, a conflict over her stage directions and how they should be carried out onstage:

> In *Listen To Me* Stein plays with the fact that her play cannot control the physical world which it creates. There is an inevitable collision between Stein's conception and its projected enactment – a collision that she engineers almost as though she wanted to look at it and think about it.⁸⁴

In Bowers's interpretation it is the complex relationship between the dramatic text and the performance that is addressed in *Listen To Me*. She reads *Listen To Me* as a personification of this interplay, when she identifies the narrative voice with Stein's. But this reading tends to reduce the complexity of Stein's deconstruction of the conventional logic of drama to biographical or personal idiosyncrasies. Wirth seems better to grasp the aesthetic and epistemological implications of the play, when he states:

> *Listen To Me* holds an exceptional position in the dramatic literature of the 1930s because it *explicitly* makes the metalanguage of drama and theatre the subject of discussion by consistently using the system of secondary codes as primary speech codes.⁸⁵

Wirth further relates Stein's discursive deconstruction of character to later artists from the 1960s and 1970s, like German playwright Peter Handke, who is famous for his spoken-word pieces where real dialogue never occurs, and to the physical and visual theatre of artists like Jerzy Grotowski, Robert Wilson, Pina Bausch and others. Wirth understands Stein's challenging of the unity of character and plot as based on a critical analysis of the structure of communication in the drama, *both* as a literary work *and* as a scenic work, rather than a power struggle between the literary and the theatrical layers of drama.

Wirth's analysis further touches upon the existential dimensions of the play. *Listen To Me* is also a love story in which Sweet William, who is a genius, is looking for his Lillian: 'Sweet William had his genius and so he did not look for it. He did look for Lillian and then he had Lillian.'[86] But actually, Lillian seems difficult to grasp: 'Lillian Lillian is not as easily remained or remaining as Sweet William.'[87] Every time the text asserts that Sweet William has his Lillian, it immediately negates this statement. Obviously, this instability of Lillian makes it difficult to tell their love story:

> Now Sweet William had his genius and so he could tell a careful story of how they enjoyed themselves. But he did not have his Lillian, he looked for Lillian and so he could not tell a careful story of how they enjoyed themselves.[88]

In the end, it is doubtful whether they ever meet, which means that Stein's formal questioning of dramatic discourse is simultaneously enacted as an existential challenge. The play centres on the paradox that the Earth is covered with people (like flowers and weed, which Sweet William's name of course refers to), while absence, lack and loneliness still define our relations. Also, war loomed on the horizon in 1936 with German rearmament and the reoccupation of the Rhineland. The inadequacies of conventional structures of communication, and the need to develop new forms of expression, are not just aesthetic concerns but have very real political implications. The play's concluding statement, 'Nobody has met any one', constitutes perhaps the ultimate deconstruction of drama, and as a political situation it poses extreme danger.

However, a more optimistic reading of *Listen To Me* is even as plausible. The trouble with storytelling in *Listen To Me* also relates to time and remembrance: 'To forget is not to remember but to remember is not to forget.'[89] Loss and absence are intimately related to hope and revival. In *Everybody's Autobiography*, Stein sees death as a necessity without which the world would soon be crowded with people, since *the world is round*, as the title of her 1938 children's book on the same theme points out.[90] Bowers reads Stein's verbal pattern of flowers' names, genius, time and death as a somewhat consoling vision of how Stein's own work of genius will live on:

> Like the flower for which he is named, Sweet William's genius will not disappear when its physical incarnation, its flower, dies. It will come again in the next flowering. Sweet William will continue to admire his work because his work will always continue.[91]

The impact and legacy of Gertrude Stein on theatre and performance

It has taken almost a century for Stein to be regarded on equal terms with her Modernist peers in theatre and literature, and her influence seems to have come in seasons. In the 1960s and 1970s, the New York avant-garde in theatre, dance and performance looked to Stein for a model for the non-mimetic and non-dramatic forms of expression they sought to develop. Julian Beck and Judith Malina included Stein plays in the early repertoire of their Living Theatre, and Al Carmines and Lawrence Kornfeld performed several of her plays with the Judson Poets' Theater. Robert Wilson, Richard Foreman and to some extent the Wooster Group were inspired by Stein's deconstruction of drama even before they actually performed any of her plays in the 1980s and 1990s. But the crucial figure is, of course, John Cage, who co-authored a book on Virgil Thomson. As such, Cage is the direct link between the generations of artists with whom Stein herself collaborated and her heirs. Probably no other artist did so much as Cage to open the arts towards each other in the intermediate field we today call performance. Cage used Stein texts for his *Three Songs* (1932–3) as well as his *Living Room Music* (1940), which has as its second movement a spoken setting of the opening lines of Stein's children's book, *The World Is Round*: 'Once upon a time the world was round and you could go on it around and around.'[92] Perhaps one should also mention here Cage's influence on the fluxus movement, since their so-called fluxus scores, where you make music by dripping water into a bucket from the top of a ladder or by releasing a butterfly into the room, share with Gertrude Stein's method of composition the attention to the everyday and ready-made: often she would simply start her compositions from the motif on the cover of the notebook she was writing in.

In the 1980s, with new feminist approaches inspired by post-structuralism, academic research finally developed analytical tools to read Stein's experimental texts. At the same time, in the 1980s and 1990s, her influence on theatre and stage arts travelled across the Atlantic with artists and scholars like Robert Wilson, Richard Foreman and Andrzej Wirth, who in turn influenced new generations of European artists. Today we see Stein's influence both on German post-dramatic theatre artists, from Heiner Goebbels to René Pollesch, and we also see her influence on a British dramatist like Sarah Kane, as well as, of course, on new generations of American artists and playwrights like Suzan-Lori Parks and others.

Gertrude Stein onstage

In addition to Stein's work as a writer and playwright, she is also a public figure, an American icon. She appears as a character in movies and paintings, and even in comic strips and children's books. Similarly, there is also a theatrical tradition for representing Stein herself onstage as a character in productions of her texts. A curious incident of this popularized approach to Gertrude Stein and her legacy is the *Salon de Fleurus* project. It consists of a not too exact reproduction of Stein's studio in rue de Fleurus, with painted reproductions of her famous works of art and furniture loosely in the same old-fashioned style as her actual furniture. From 1992 to 2013 it existed as a salon in an apartment in Manhattan; today it exists as a travelling installation, touring Europe and the US. This strange re-enactment or reinstallation of the space and environment of a writer and art collector allows the audience a performative experience of the myths and narratives, as well as the social structures, that formed our present conception of modern art. As such, it is a literal demonstration of just how radically Gertrude Stein herself inscribed the performative interaction with the audience in the work itself.

4

Langston Hughes: *Mulatto* (1935), *The Mule Bone* (1930) (with Zora Neale Hurston), *Little Ham* (1936)

Adrienne Macki

> The road for the serious black artist ... who would produce a racial art is most certainly rocky and the mountain is high.
> Langston Hughes, 'The Negro Artist and the Racial Mountain', *The Nation*, 23 June 1926, 694

Literary artist Langston Hughes, renowned for his poetry, penned over sixty dramatic works during his prolific career. Hughes's writing spanned multiple genres, from theatre, film, opera, poetry and short fiction to novels, non-fiction, memoirs and books for children. He was a commercial writer, a writer of racial protest and a chronicler of his historic moment. His writing emerged from and gestured to the folk tradition and to the black vernacular. He became one of the most noted leftist writers of the 1930s. His formidable literary achievements and his pioneering groundwork paved the way for dramatists including Amiri Baraka and Lorraine

Hansberry and writers such as Richard Wright and Alice Walker. Hughes should not be singled out merely as a representative black playwright from this era; instead, he warrants inclusion in this book as a significant American playwright recognized for his contributions to commercial and community-based stages. This highly acclaimed writer offers illustrative examples of the racially, socially and politically specific concerns of Depression-era America. In particular, his engagement with the 'red' politics of the period is evident in many of his poems and plays from the 1930s.

This chapter focuses on three representative plays: *Mulatto* (written in 1930 and produced in 1935), *The Mule Bone* (1930) and *Little Ham* (1936); each illuminates how Hughes reflected his historical moment in nuanced ways and endeavoured to project an authentic representation of black culture. That these plays incorporated a black vernacular tradition and sought to destabilize crude representations of black identity from minstrelsy stereotypes to what was termed the 'New Negro' identity in the 1920s through to the early 1930s is also of particular importance. These pieces complicated prevailing sentiments about racial uplift, a popular strategy for racial advancement that emphasized conflicted, limited and paternalistic socio-economic distinctions. Building on historian Kevin Gaines's assertion that during this period the black intelligentsia, professionals and elite 'deemed the promotion of bourgeois morality, patriarchal authority, and a culture of self-improvement ... as necessary to their recognition, enfranchisement, and survival as a class',[1] the following situates Hughes's intervention in this bourgeois ideology in terms of how he deployed character, language and folkways to signify[2] on these conventional expectations through his theatrical representation of class, gender and sexuality.

Hughes, long considered one of the pillars of the New Negro Renaissance or Harlem Renaissance of the 1920s, embodied tensions facing black artists during this era. It is important to clarify that the term 'New Negro' endeavoured to describe an ethos of self-determination and came to signify 'an early twentieth-century trope of black radicalism' in the wake of the Great Migration and blacks' pursuit of power, economic equity and citizenship rights.[3] After the war, several significant New Negro artists (including Hughes, Zora Neale Hurston and Claude McKay) rose up to blaze new paths in art, music, theatre and literature. Theirs was a new proletarian philosophy. Hughes's works responded to and were shaped by virulent debates among race leaders like W. E. B. Du Bois, James Weldon Johnson and Alain Locke about how to best represent the race in the arts and literature.

Born in Joplin, Missouri, in 1902, James Langston Hughes was first raised in Lawrence, Kansas, primarily by his maternal grandmother, Mary Langston. He felt abandoned by his parents, James Hughes and Carrie Langston, who separated when he was a boy. Named for his father and his mother's eminent uncle, John Mercer Langston – the 'first black American to hold office' – the young Hughes's interest in drama was fostered by his mother who loved the theatre and longed to be an actress.[4]

In *The Political Plays of Langston Hughes*, theatre historian Susan Duffy notes a seminal step in Hughes's development as a playwright. She describes the 'Cleveland years, 1916–1920', when Hughes attended classes and workshops at the Karamu House in Cleveland, Ohio, a cultural arts settlement house founded in 1915.[5] He maintained an enduring relationship with the Karamu's theatre troupe, the Gilpin Players, as they produced several of his productions.

Hughes's first play, *The Gold Piece*, a one-act drama for children, was published in 1921. His interest in theatre is also evident in his letters in the early 1920s to Alain Locke and in his acclaimed essay, 'The Negro Artist and the Racial Mountain' (1926). After a short sojourn at the Hedgerow Theatre in 1930 where he worked with Jasper Deeter and observed rehearsals nightly, Hughes completed his first draft of *Mulatto*. Thus began what African-American literature scholar Joseph McLaren describes as the writer's 'most productive period as a dramatist'.[6] Like several of his contemporaries, Hughes turned to social issues. His particular focus illuminated socio-political concerns with race relations, miscegenation, economic inequity and racial injustice. Not surprisingly, most of his plays from the 1930s demonstrate the influence of didactic drama and leftist ideology on his work. While *Mulatto* conformed in some ways to the social realism of the period, *Don't You Want to be Free* (1938), with its episodic structure, use of poetry, music and dance and stylized staging, departed from the era's mainstream aesthetics.

Literature scholar Eric Sundquist observes that 'Hughes's writing of the 1930s was invigorated equally by anti-Americanism and by the scramble for a dollar'.[7] Certainly, Hughes was not immune to the financial realities of his time. During the Depression, African-Americans were frequently 'the last hired and first fired' and routinely endured inordinately worse economic conditions than whites.[8] His work evidences a telling preoccupation with money and highlights the economic disparity endemic to the period.

Though his travels brought him across the United States and abroad, Hughes frequently returned to Harlem; this large, northern neighbourhood in the borough of Manhattan became his home. Its vibrant, urban setting, its music and people often appeared in his writing. Hughes arrived in 1921 to study at Columbia University; however, he spent more time in Harlem than he did at school. As his letters suggest, frequent attendance at the theatre was a regular pastime.

The artist's engagement with the 1931 Scottsboro case signalled his alignment with the left. After nine black boys were accused and wrongly convicted of raping two white girls aboard a train in Alabama, Hughes authored several poems and a one-act verse play, *Scottsboro Limited* (1931), that spotlighted the bias against black men in the US system of capital punishment. Despite refutable evidence, eight of the youths were condemned to death and one was sentenced to life in prison. *Scottsboro Limited*, indicative of the agit-prop tradition (theatre of agitation and propaganda), responded to and raised consciousness about this controversial case that had sparked attention nationally and internationally. The piece offers a view of social transformation through the boys' self-liberation.

Its explicit invocation of communist ideology – from the presence of Red Voices and the waving of a Red flag to the singing of 'The Internationale', the national anthem of the Soviet Union – subjected the play to great scrutiny. In a 1932 letter about creating a publication to raise money to benefit the Scottsboro boys, even Hughes mused, 'Maybe the play is too red to be included.'[9] In the piece, in protest against the death penalty, one of the youths declares:

> Now out of the darkness
> The new Red Negro will come:
> That's me![10]

Using a call-and-response technique, one boy leads the others in a rallying call to stand up against the whip, the lynch rope and the electric chair, which Hughes juxtaposes to suggest how these institutionalized forms of violence against black bodies maintain the social order. A chorus of Red Voices from the audience joins in, as the (communist) workers rise and come forward to the stage linking hands with the black boys. In its mostly bare, minimalistic staging, the boys' stylized movement – from smashing the electric chair to breaking their prison bars – offers a transgressive display of black agency. As American literature scholar Katy Ryan argues, 'Hughes transforms a scene of private execution into a public platform of black-led revolt and remakes prison into a site of physical and spiritual resistance.'[11] That the play hinges on the self-empowerment and uprising of the incarcerated boys makes it especially timely in our contemporary moment with a national outcry against police brutality, the 'racial caste system' in our criminal justice system and the Black Lives Matter movement.[12]

Hughes's 1931 trip to the Soviet Union to work on a film, *Black and White*, also signalled his communist sympathies. Though the film never materialized, his activities, travels and personal interactions were carefully followed by United States government agents. His radical poems (such as 'One More "S" in the U.S.A' and 'Good Morning Revolution'), his publication record with *New Masses* (known as a 'national forum for American Communism'[13]), his involvement with the League of Struggle for Negro Rights, activities with the John Reed Clubs (an association bringing together leftist artists and intellectuals), association with communist and leftist political and literary figures and his service to the American Negro Labor Congress (founded by the Communist Party League) underscore ways in which Hughes aligned himself with the left. Ultimately, he was denounced by the House Un-American Activities Committee (HUAC) and called before Senator Joseph McCarthy's Permanent Subcommittee on Investigations in 1953. Although he later declared that he was not a communist, his red politics and sympathies were well known in the 1930s and 1940s.

While abroad, Hughes attended the first annual Workers' Theaters International Olympiad. His journeys also acquainted him with Russian staging techniques, including Vsevolod Meyerhold's constructivist design and the arena staging at Nikolai Okhlopkov's Krasnya Presnya. Hughes recalled that 'for each production [at the Krasnya Presnya] the entire seating and platform arrangements of the theater were changed, and the whole auditorium was always used as a playing area, front, back and aisles'.[14] Sitting in on rehearsals and talking with Meyerhold and Okhlopkov helped Hughes to realize 'a number of interesting ways of staging plays', which he put to use in *Don't You Want to be Free*.[15] Hughes conceived of this show with an in-the-round staging and an adaptable platform stage that featured two semicircles (signifying an African tom-tom).

Friend and colleague Louise Thompson (later Patterson), a leading communist organizer in Harlem, helped Hughes realize his vision for a people's theatre in Harlem. In a 1988 interview, she recounted how Hughes insisted on constructing a platform stage, a 'round drum' cut in half 'so that it could be used in the round' or adjusted to form two halves as an 'extended platform'.[16] Thompson described how Hughes returned from Spain early in 1938 with a burning desire to create his own theatre and how she set out to help him achieve this goal. From suggesting a way to fuse several of his poems from *A New Song* into a new dramatic piece, to securing 'space and sponsorship' from the International Workers Order (IWO), recruiting players from the IWO's youth group, promoting the organization to outside groups and developing a constitution with guidelines and responsibilities for the leadership, Thompson's assistance was crucial.[17] Among the early members was Robert Earl Jones, father of famed actor James Earl Jones. The group set up shop at the IWO's loft in Harlem, Lodge 691, in a meeting hall above Frank's Restaurant on 125th Street.

Scholar Anne Donlon rightly argues that the founding of the Harlem Suitcase Theatre 'should be viewed as a continuation of Hughes's engagement with the Spanish Civil War, and part of an international antifascist movement'.[18] Immersed in the life-and-death struggles of battle-scarred Spain, Hughes was certainly 'loaded to bear' when he returned to the United States. He quipped to a leftist friend that 'there's nothing left for me except to start a theatre and produce plays. That will be equal to anybody's battle front.'[19] Fighting to sustain a viable theatre occupied Hughes into the late 1930s. In fact, he helped found three community-based theatres: the Harlem Suitcase Theatre (HST), the Skyloft Players in Chicago and the New Negro Theatre in Los Angeles, all of which became vehicles to stage his *Don't You Want to be Free*. While short-lived, these groups emerged as significant examples of a community-based theatre movement, continuing the tradition of activism and artistry pioneered by the Krigwa Players and the Harlem Experimental Theatre in the 1920s and 1930s respectively.[20]

Thompson described HST as 'a social theatre which would concern itself in the main with the working people, oppressed people'.[21] She remarked how it attracted wide audiences, 'people white and black, from Broadway', local friends and colleagues of troupe members, church groups, as well as visitors 'from other countries'.[22] *Don't You Want to be Free* played 135 performances to thousands of spectators, significant for a community-based theatre with limited resources. Included in the audience was communist leader Angelo Herndon, whose case for inciting insurrection made national headlines. His ordeal prompted him to identify parallels between contemporary public practice in America and the play, as he observed how its 'magnificent portrayal of [the] Negro' recalled 'very vividly some of my experiences in the South'.[23] Similarly, critics echoed HST's agenda to 'present a true, clearly defined picture of contemporary life, bringing the Race people up to their true stature in the American scene ... to build a permanent repertory theatre ... from the pay dirt in the rich mine of Race life'.[24]

Mulatto

'I'm hoping it will work up well, but some days the characters will not talk at all – anyhow, I have plenty of excitements besides the conversation: there's a murder, a suicide, and a fight,' wrote Hughes to his friend Carl Van Vechten on Hedgerow Theatre Company's stationary on 25 September 1930.[25] While he describes working diligently on his first full-length play at this commune in Rose Valley, Pennsylvania, Hughes's statement also seemingly anticipates the tumultuous process of the play's opening during which it was dramatically changed and sensationalized by producer/director Martin Jones. Jones often refused to talk with Hughes to address unresolved concerns regarding his unauthorized revisions and withholding of payment of earned royalties to the author. In fact, Hughes faced a series of challenges and acrimonious legal disputes that sharply contrasted with his bucolic experience at the Hedgerow. 'Over-ridden on all sides', balked Hughes, feeling powerless to prevent Jones from radically altering and exploiting his 'poetic tragedy ... into what the producer hoped would be a commercial hit'.[26] Jones, the force behind the sensational Broadway miscegenation drama *White Cargo: A Play of the Primitive* (1925) by Leon Gordon, added sex and violence to *Mulatto*, including the rape of the protagonist's sister.[27] Despite the fact that he had a play on Broadway, due to ongoing battles to receive his royalties, Hughes struggled financially. As literary studies scholar Michele Birnbaum rightly argues, the show's 'production history was a racial debacle' and 'an unwitting example of the very conflicts the play was staging'.[28]

Hughes's work on *Mulatto* began fruitfully at the Hedgerow Theatre. He appreciated observing director Jasper Deeter's rehearsals, receiving feedback on his work-in-progress and watching acclaimed actress Rose McClendon who was in residence that season (and would later perform in the show). Though Deeter complimented the young playwright on his construction of the play and dramatic situations, Hughes laboured with the dialogue as he transitioned from the genre of poetry to drama, and set about to dramatize one of his recurrent thematic concerns.

The play, originally titled 'Cross: A Play of the Deep South', recalled his 1925 poem of the same name. In the poem, Hughes introduced his interrogation of miscegenation and concerns that mixed-race children confronted as they articulated their racial identities. He continued to address this theme in a short story, two plays (*Mulatto* and *Don't You Want to be Free*) and an opera. The play, *Mulatto*, pivots on the tragic relationships between Robert Lewis and his parents, Colonel Tom Norwood and his common-law wife and housekeeper, Cora Lewis. Just as Norwood refuses to acknowledge his son, Robert rejects the system of Jim Crow segregation and working in his father's fields. The play spotlights their crisis and asks whether Robert can overcome his anger, frustration and confusion about his racial identity and survive overlapping systems of oppression in the South. As it draws out these characters and the deeply engrained racial stereotypes of the period, it 'invoke[s] interraciality as a trope for the relationship between race, masculinity, and the nation'.[29]

Running from October 1935 to December 1939 in New York with McClendon as Cora, *Mulatto* was the 'longest-running black-authored play on Broadway' prior to the 1959 production of *A Raisin in the Sun* by Lorraine Hansberry.[30] Its debut received ambivalent reviews. Brooks Atkinson from the *New York Times* praised McClendon, but stated that Hughes 'has little of the dramatic strength of mind that makes it possible for a writer to tell a coherent, driving story in the theatre. His ideas are seldom completely expressed.'[31] His description of the play as 'a moral retribution drama about the misery of a white man plagued by the social misdemeanor of having illegitimate mulatto children' on the grounds that the Colonel is 'killed by a boy so cocky and impudent that he seems more like an ungrateful son than a martyr to race prejudice' signals how white privilege led critics to respond in particular ways.[32]

Owing to the fact that *Mulatto* remains one of Hughes's most recognized plays, its production history warrants further consideration. Though performed nationally and internationally, it met with considerable criticism due to its controversial subject. Barred in Maryland, it was also banned from Philadelphia for more than two years, where a near riot broke out as the production attempted to open there in 1939.[33] Anticipating a positive reception in the otherwise 'staid' city of Boston, a *New York Amsterdam News* press release claimed that *Mulatto*'s opening to a full house in its 1940 premiere at the Copley Theatre offered a 'new experience' for local audiences and that the 'handful of colored Bostonians [who] joined the first nighters ... seemed complete[ly] sold on the production'.[34] However, while the *New York Amsterdam News* expected the show to be a critical success with its 'timely anti-lynch propaganda, and a stark picture of the atrocities borne by Negroes', a *Boston Globe* review described it as a 'tense, descriptive vehicle that offers "different" entertainment'.[35]

Not surprisingly, the production was frequently misunderstood or dismissed by critics. For instance, Charles Collins of the *Chicago Daily Tribune* missed Hughes's social critique, declaring that the character of Robert is 'not intelligent enough to understand the perils of his rebellion against the customs of the environment in which he was born'.[36] This remark substantiates Michele Birnbaum's assertion that the derisive perspectives expressed by white critics 'make clear how radical was Hughes's attempt to restructure the terms by which white largesse is conceived and how fierce the indignation of whites who felt that the hand that fed had been bit'.[37]

On the other hand, Nelson B. Bell of the *Washington Post* wrote favourably of the 1937 production. He found it 'daringly outspoken in its frank discussion of a racial problem of the deep South – but neither blasphemous nor profane'.[38] Similarly, the Capitol Players, in Hartford, Connecticut, enjoyed an extended run with sold-out performances in 1938. A *Hartford Courant* review described the production as 'a fast-moving, tense melodrama that will you hold you fast ... and give you plenty to talk of when you leave'.[39] The play (without Jones's revisions) was finally staged by the Gilpin Players at the Karamu House in 1939.[40]

The play was later adapted as an opera, *The Barrier*, with music by Jan Meyerowitz in 1950. Indicative of its lasting legacy, *Mulatto* received a 1967 revival at the Cooperative Theatre Club with projections highlighting the 1967 Detroit riots to address similarities between race relations in its contemporary moment and in the Old South.[41] Academic institutions such as Howard University and Boston University mounted the show in 1978 and 1979 respectively, and theatres on the east and west coasts continued to stage the play throughout the 1980s. More recently, the Black Repertory Group, a community organization in Berkeley, California, staged *Mulatto* in February 2015.

While some scholars describe Hughes's play in terms of its Brechtian characteristics or highlight its employment of agit-prop, others focus on the universal elements in Aristotelian terms, such as Webster Smalley who comments that it is the young son's 'stubborn, unending pride ... that brings about his downfall and death'.[42] Such views undermine the impact of the institutional racism that Hughes exposes. To unpack the play as a variation on a classical tragedy wherein Robert's fatal mistake stems from his headstrong ways that set him upon a careening path to disaster, oversimplifies the socio-political context and effect of white privilege and systematic racism that work in tandem as his major obstacles. Theatre scholar Harry Elam, Jr and African-American studies scholar Michele Elam rightly argue that *Mulatto* may be 'understood as a cultural intervention specific to the politics of his day rather than an ahistorical meditation on the theme of alienation, and [should be viewed]... as a vehicle for social and sexual critique'.[43] The play emblematizes social injustices at work in the 1930s as Hughes upends the hierarchy of the Jim Crow South with a central character who resists the 'code of "Negro etiquette"' and the limitations of segregated spaces.[44] Hughes's first professionally-produced play demonstrates not only his commitment to the complexities of the tragic mulatto, but also how he used the stage to challenge minstrelsy stereotypes that typically populated commercial theatre. Specifically, while Robert's mother and siblings consciously play a servile part to placate the Colonel (and ensure his patronage in order to send the children to school), the youngest son demands recognition by his father – for his 'rightful blood inheritance' – and insists on full citizenship.[45]

An exchange between Colonel Thomas Norwood and a friend reflects the play's historical moment as it signals the South's preservation of slavery's social order. The friend remarks, 'All this postwar propaganda on the radio about freedom and democracy – why the niggers think it's meant for them! And that Eleanor Roosevelt, she ought to been muzzled. She's driving our niggers crazy – your boy included! Crazy! Talking about civil rights.'[46] References to Senator Theodore Bilbo and Congressman John E. Rankins, two white supremacists from Mississippi, highlight the political tenor of the period. Cora fears that Robert will be punished or killed by a white mob and worries that his defiance will only make things worse for other blacks in their community.

By demonstrating how pursuing higher education does little to equalize the playing field, Robert typifies some of the problems with an ethos of self-help through educational advancement. He is equally frustrated by the lack of support and solidarity from the black community at large and from his family in particular following a highly charged racial confrontation at the post office. The play suggests that challenging white authority, embracing one's racial identity and attempting to trespass against racial barriers are dangerous acts fraught with peril for black Americans. Robert's mother and siblings perform particular racial identities as a means of economic and social survival. Cora attempts to disarm the Colonel in order to protect her children, while unbeknownst to him, Robert's elder sister (who has moved to the North and passes as white) works in an office, not as a cook as the white patriarch has been led to believe.[47] The younger sister, Sallie, older brother William and the mother consciously play the role of dutifully obedient, sycophantic servants who thank the master for his patronage and kindness. William's character suggests the perils of intraracial colourism (he resents the privileges afforded to his lighter-skinned brother), and Sallie carefully resists the Colonel's plan for her as she hopes to effect change by becoming a teacher in their district. Fearful for Robert's safety and for the well-being of other blacks in their household, Cora urges Robert to also play his part and not antagonize the Colonel.

In a dramatic confrontation with his father, Robert refuses to comply with the status quo. Norwood challenges Robert, denying his parentage, insulting the boy's mother and provoking the son to defend the mother's honour. In response to Robert's admission that he does not like the fact that his mother sleeps with Norwood, the Colonel taunts and effectively prompts Robert to take aggressive action, baiting him with the following line: '[W]hat can you do about it?'[48] His retort elicits Robert's transgressive reply, 'I'd like to kill all the white men in the world,'[49] foreshadowing the patricide that follows. According to the stage directions, in the ensuing fight, Robert shifts from *'calmly'* advancing and twisting his arm until the elder man drops his pistol, to laughing derisively in his face and *'hysterically'* strangling his father as he mocks the authority figure and dares him to shoot.[50] The gestures operate in multiple registers, not only suggesting a descent to madness that gives Hughes safe cover to critique the ludicrous situation of black oppression, but also invoking a form of 'critical laughter' to spotlight the insanity of these power dynamics.[51] Clearly, Colonel Tom's inability to protect himself in the face of mortal peril is a stunning reversal of power that revises the expected relationships between fathers and sons, black men and white men. This play, and this moment in particular, richly signifies the black man's experience, specifically his typical lack of agency, experience of powerlessness in protecting his family and desire to avenge the rape of loved ones.[52]

As in other earlier lynching dramas, Cora first assists her son in his attempt to escape; but recognizing that it is futile, she ultimately condones his suicide.[53] Theologian James H. Cone argues that acts like Robert's were 'tantamount to suicide' and 'would incur the full weight of the law and the mob'.[54] Nevertheless, Robert's decision to use the last bullet on himself rather than suffer at the hands of the lynch mob denies the expected narrative of disempowerment for black bodies. It is especially fitting that Cora directs him to go to her room – to her bed 'to rest' – which symbolizes the site of miscegenation that precipitated such a horrific outcome and allows this violent cycle to end.[55]

The Mule Bone: A Comedy of Negro Life

'Brazzle's mule, even in manuscript, has done a mean piece of kicking, and it will probably take all of us several weeks to get unbent again,' wrote Hughes to Carl Van Vechten as he reflected on the tumultuous process of bringing *The Mule Bone: A Comedy of Negro Life* to the stage.[56] Written in 1930 and produced posthumously in 1991, the show sprang from a fraught collaboration with acclaimed Harlem Renaissance writer and folklorist Zora Neale Hurston in an attempt to create an *authentic* folk comedy. They had hoped that their work would appeal to the Dramatists Guild's Theresa Helburn, who had expressed interest in seeing a comedy of black life, but the show became the centre of a convoluted drama that tore apart these one-time friends and alienated Hughes from their patron.[57]

Though the early stages of their collaboration began promisingly in April 1930, the issue of authorship sparked a great divide. Hurston filed for sole copyright in October. On 19 January 1931, Van Vechten wrote that he had received a letter from her explaining that she had begun anew to tell the story of Eatonville, Florida.[58] Meanwhile, while visiting Cleveland, Hughes was blindsided by the fact that the Gilpin Players were working on a production of *Mule Bone* purportedly written by Hurston. In short, the convoluted story of how the draft manuscript found its way to Cleveland is that Hurston shared a copy of the script with Van Vechten, who forwarded it to Barrett Clark from Samuel French & Company, who sent it along to the Gilpin Players.

Dismayed by news that Hurston claimed the piece to be solely hers, Hughes attempted to contact his collaborator to clarify the confusion. In a letter to Van Vechten, Hughes related his phone conversation with Hurston, and explained how the play arrived with 'two first-act endings, and two different third acts – one our collaborated version ... and another evidently her new version'.[59] The director preferred the co-written version, so, she and Hughes sought Hurston's permission to stage the show, but it was slow in coming. Hughes appealed to Van Vechten to speak with Hurston about allowing the Gilpin Players to mount the jointly-written version. To amplify his position, the playwright indicated that he received legal advice that, based on his handwritten notes, 'pages of construction and situations, carbons of the first draft, and the testimony of the stenographer [Louise Thompson] ... Zora can certainly do nothing at all with MULE-BONE without my permission'.[60]

Hughes threatened to sue and offered to take only one-third of the royalties to appease Hurston's claim that *Mule Bone* was more her play (in situation, story and dialogue).[61] In a series of dramatic confrontations and reversals between 20 January 1931 and 3 February 1931, Hurston extended her permission, travelled to Cleveland to support the production, then recanted and cancelled it.[62]

Understanding this contested backstory adds nuance to the drama, which was adapted from Hurston's short story, 'The Bone of Contention'. Hurston's piece, set in her home town, was based on a folktale about two hunters and their dispute over a turkey. *The Mule Bone*, which also employs a black vernacular tradition, borrows heavily from its source with a plot that turns on the competition between two friends, Dave Carter and Jim Weston. Hurston and Hughes adapted the conflict to have the friends fight over the affections of a girl, Daisy Taylor. In Act One, during a physical tussle in the town centre, Weston strikes Carter over the head with the hock-bone of an old mule. The injured party is whisked away to be treated, and Weston is incarcerated, leaving Daisy unescorted. The first scene of the second act illuminates the social context for the play, spotlighting religious clashes in the community and the power dynamics between the founder and mayor of the town, Joe Clarke, and a rival upstart. Act Two, Scene Two includes a biased trial overseen by Clarke. The trial scene showcases the town factions, class rivalries and the tensions between the Methodists and the Baptists. Weston is determined to be guilty and is thrown out of town for two years. The third act, which culminates in the friends' reconciliation, also includes a comic verbal spar to prove who most loves Daisy. In the end, the rival suitors both abandon their love interest, mirroring the image of the lone girl at the end of the first act.

Owing to the fact that Hughes and Hurston quarrelled, the play was neither finished nor staged during their lifetimes. After the Gilpin Players abandoned their efforts, drafts of the play were lost until renowned African-American studies scholar Henry Louis Gates, Jr endeavoured to publish a complete text. Gates brought the piece to the attention of Gregory Mosher, Artistic Director of Lincoln Center Theatre. The show was given a staged reading in 1988, then 'edited and revised by George Houston Bass, Ann Cattaneo, Henry Louis Gates, Jr, Arnold Rampersad, and the director, Michael Schultz', before it was professionally produced in 1991.[63] Bass devised a prologue and epilogue to 'frame' the play, and new music was composed by Taj Mahal to provide the folk music indicated in the script.[64] Perhaps anticipating a backlash against the show, Gates penned a piece for the *New York Times* regarding how the play continued to ignite controversy because of its use of black vernacular. He highlighted ongoing concerns regarding how African-Americans should be portrayed and self-censorship, explaining that 'many black people still seem to believe that the images of themselves projected on television, film and stage must be policed and monitored from within'.[65]

The show opened in February 1991 and closed after 67 performances. Scholar Lynda M. Hill maintains that it represented 'a landmark in American theatre history'.[66] Reviews varied: on one side of the spectrum, the *Christian Science Monitor* applauded its 'exuberance', adding that the show 'occupies a unique place in the history of African-American theater'.[67] In contrast, the *New York Times*'s Frank Rich opined,

> [T]here's something disturbingly disingenuous about the entire production. This 'Mule Bone' is at once so watered down and bloated by various emendations that one can never be entirely sure if Lincoln Center Theater is conscientiously trying to complete and resuscitate a lost, unfinished work or is merely picking its carcass to confer a classy literary pedigree on a broad, often bland quasi-musical seemingly pitched to a contemporary Broadway audience.[68]

However, as Rich asserts, at its best moments – such as when the suitors boast about what they would do to win Daisy's love – it 'succeeds in creating startling, linguistically lush folk comedy that nonetheless reflects the tragic legacy of slavery'.[69]

The above remarks highlight what scholars have identified as the play's crowning achievement – its ability to capture a particular linguistic tradition – which, as Gates notes, was crucial to the authors' vision to develop 'the first real Negro folk-comedy'.[70] The collaborators aspired to create a new dramatic art form deeply steeped in the rhythms, images and polyvocality of the 'black vernacular tradition'.[71] *The Mule Bone* illustrates how they consciously played with what Gates describes as 'verbal "signifying" rituals', word play and a 'ritualized oral discourse'[72] as a way to counter the racist caricatures of the minstrel stage. The play opens with countless examples of this ritualized oral discourse in order to establish tension between the Baptists and Methodists as suggested in the following moment between two men in front of the general store:

> **Walter** Look here, Hambo. Y'all Baptist carry dis close-communion business too far. If a person ain't half drownded in de lake and half et up by alligators, y'all think he ain't baptized, so you can't take communion wid him. Now I reckon you can't even drink lemonade and eat chicken perlow wid us.
> **Hambo** My Lord, boy, youse just *full* of words. Now, in de first place, if this year's picnic was lak de one y'all had last year ... you ain't had no lemonade for us Baptists to turn down. You had a big ole barrel of rain water wid about a pound of sugar in it and one lemon cut up over de top of it.[73]

It sets up how each ridicules the particular customs and pastimes accompanying ritualized (religious) events by suggesting that Baptists are fanatic extremists while Methodists are cheap and cut corners. The phrase '*full* of words' reminds readers and spectators of the pivotal role of language in constructing *Mule Bone*'s representation of local folkways and traditions. Additional ritualized enactments of the town's power struggles between religious groups are echoed in the children's role-playing games and in the elders' games of cards and checkers that set the scene in the first act. Each competition builds on particular rhythms and images to convey the theatricality and conflict in these multiple displays of one-upmanship, such as when Hambo beats the Mayor in a game of checkers and matches his laughing and game playing to a musical scale, singing 'Do, sol, re, me, lo ... three! (*Jumping a third* [checker]) Lo, sol, fa, me, re ... four!'[74]

American literature scholar Carme Manuel insists that the play demonstrates an 'encomium of the linguistic powers of a certain sector of the black collectivity which bursts out [of] class boundaries to emphasize a sense of community'.[75] While its profuse commentary on class and community is evidenced throughout the play, the trial itself spotlights how this event mobilizes the community to gather at the Macedonia Baptist Church for the hearing on Jim's alleged assault on his long-time friend, Dave. Though the mayor, religious leaders and the residents embrace discordant viewpoints, their disagreements are momentarily suspended as opposing factions sing 'Onward Christian Soldiers'[76] (and collectively clamour to testify about the fight). Nevertheless, that the residents act out of bounds (boisterously articulating their concerns regarding a long series of indiscretions and/or injustices, displaying little respect for Mayor Clarke's order and authority) eschews the standards of middle-class respectability and decorum. Mayor Clarke observes that the group sounds like 'a tree full uh blackbirds! Dis ain't no barbecue, nor neither no camp meetin'.[77] Their disavowal of the expected rules of behaviour presents, complicates and destabilizes idealized expectations of the New Negro codes of conduct.

While waiting for the trial to commence, several women engage in verbal skirmishes illustrating another kind of word play. Sister Taylor and Sister Lewis's hurling of insults signify the class tensions between the factions. Their verbal assault nearly descends into a physical attack, repeating the pattern of behaviour that prompted the hearing. As their argument escalates, Sister Lewis declares, 'Well, my house might not be exactly clean, but there's no fly-specks on my *charac*ter! They didn't have to git de sheriff to make Willie marry *me* like they did to make Tony marry *you*.'[78] In response, Sister Taylor assails the character of her rival's daughter, arguing 'Now you sho orter go git de sheriff and a shot gun and make some of dese men marry yo' daughter, Ada.'[79] Sister Taylor suggests that Ada's promiscuity stems from her mother's wanton ways. These barbed attacks add to the scene's satirical humour and amplify the conflicts between the divisive groups.

More importantly, the second act offers several instances in which the women have resisted staid gender roles and have vigorously intervened in the trial. Anthropologist Jennifer Stapleton argues that 'when Joe Clarke declared that the mule bone was a dangerous weapon, he also intimated that the female voice was considered a threat to the social hierarchy and harmony of the town. The reference to the mule's jawbone was associated with the vocalization of the women.'[80] Stapleton adds that Daisy's behaviour was also scrutinized owing to the fact that she 'defied the expectations of a woman's social conduct'.[81]

The third act features a competitive exchange between Jim and Dave to determine who most loves Daisy. Their histrionic professions of devotion constitute an elaborate game of one-upmanship through an elaborate word play relying on comic trumpery and verbal signifying. As Gates argues, the third act's 'courtship ritual, like so much of the verbal "signifying" rituals in which the characters engage throughout the play, are both reflections of historical folk rituals practiced by African Americans as well as their extensions or elaborations'.[82] Dave challenges Jim, 'less we prove which one of us love you do best right now', continuing, 'Jim, how much time would you do on de chain-gang for dis 'oman?'.[83] Jim answers that he would serve 20 years happily. Dave bests him by retorting that he'd '*beg*' the judge for a life sentence, prompting both men to laugh.[84] Dave's reply outmanoeuvres the normally quick-thinking, smooth-talking Jim and seemingly puts him at the front of the race for Daisy's heart, especially when he croons to her, 'Don't you be skeered, baby ... papa kin take keer a you. (*To Jim*) Countin' from de finger (*Suiting the action to the word*) back to de thumb ... start anything I got you some.'[85] But Jim wins out in the end when he says that he'd 'step backwards offa dat aryplane just to walk home wid you'.[86] Daisy is smitten with his response and proposes marriage. Ever practical about housing and money, she also suggests that Jim join her at the white family's estate in Maitland (where she is a domestic) and secure a landscaping job. His rich word play continues as he objects that 'You don't see *me* dragging a whole gang of farming tools into us business, do you?'[87] On the grounds that Jim's willingness to engage in physical labour is limited to lifting his guitar, Daisy cuts her losses and turns to Dave to rekindle that relationship. She probes, 'you wouldn't *talk* to me like Jim did, would you, Dave?' (*emphasis added*),⁸⁸ suggesting a seemingly natural response that nevertheless subtly highlights the importance of 'appropriate', desirable forms of discourse in romantic relationships. When Dave claims that he will carry nothing heavier than his hat, confirming that he's even lazier than his friend, Daisy tells them off. She boasts that she has a 'good job and plenty men *beggin* for yo' chance' (*emphasis added*),⁸⁹ allowing her a semblance of dignity and agency, gesturing to the centrality of discourse in the courtship ritual.

As Carme Manuel maintains, the play utilizes dialect 'not only to transcend the black stereotypes exploited by white literature in minstrel shows and black-faced plays but assertively to depict black experience in the first decades of the twentieth century in America from a hilarious stance and through language that sets its roots in communal knowledge, wisdom, and the capacity of regeneration'.⁹⁰ In this way, Hughes and Hurston yoked humour and dialect to build on verbal tradition as well as to comment on and subvert from within.⁹¹ Yet, as Gates admits, the play reinscribes sexist, patriarchal models in its depiction of spousal abuse, illustrations of physical and verbal violence to control women, and its objectification of Daisy as the love interest. While Daisy's ultimate rejection of both suitors helps her character regain agency, as Gates concludes, the play's representation of women and romantic relationships 'almost never escapes the limitations of the social realities that the vernacular tradition reflects'.⁹² This hegemonic construction of gender and sexuality continues to some extent in Hughes's next play, *Little Ham*, as well.

Little Ham

In January 1936, Hughes mused that he was 'determined to be a playwright in spite of it all. To that end, I've turned out one comedy about the numbers, LITTLE HAM.'⁹³ Hughes also shared his latest work with Van Vechten. Van Vechten replied that, though the *Little Ham*'s plot was weak and lacked 'intensity', he was 'rather fond' of it and felt that 'the comedy would keep an audience in roars. It is real Harlem folkstuff [*sic*].'⁹⁴ In some ways, his praise of the humour and admiration for the 'real Harlem folkstuff' recall the dynamic blend of comedy, signifying and authentic folk ways that Hughes and Hurston strove to capture in *The Mule Bone*. However, while *Mule Bone*'s folk comedy highlighted black culture in the South, *Little Ham* uses humour and signifying to reveal the challenges and consequences of the Great Migration as blacks moved to northern cities. The latter work was particularly illustrative of Hughes's intent to rewrite black comic theatrical conventions while creating a stageworthy vehicle that not only offered audiences an escape but also transformed the genre.[95] For these reasons and more, Hughes's first staged comedy, *Little Ham,* is worthy of study.

McLaren theorizes that *Little Ham* may have emerged as an antidote to the 'grim realities' of the period and as a response to Wallace Thurman and William Jordan Rapp's *Harlem* (1929), a Broadway drama also centred on gambling and complicated romantic relationships.[96] Hughes was broke, fighting for his royalties for *Mulatto* and responding to a family crisis as his mother battled breast cancer. He was determined to develop the genre of comedy, continuing an agenda he set out with the ill-fated *Mule Bone*. African-American literature expert Leslie Catherine Sanders argues that it 'asserts and celebrates a principal cultural mode of communication and self-definition ... it alters the terms of black comic performance by producing it within its own space', namely a shoe shine parlour (that doubles as a local site for gambling), a beauty shop and an upscale dance hall in Harlem.[97] African-American literature scholar Sharyn Emery holds that the show is a 'testament to the project of representation' given the ways in which it reconstructs the genre of screwball comedy into a 'political statement'.[98]

Little Ham engages in the important project of employing comedy to interrogate economic conditions in an urban setting during an era of great change, migration and social mobility. Moreover, it uses this dynamic to complicate ideas about identity, gender roles, sexuality and language that were circulated by black leaders and gained currency with the intellectual elite and black middle class as a way to advance the race. Sanders maintains that the play seeks to 'recuperate comic black speech by setting it in context', enabling the discourse to be 'reclaimed'.[99] Context is critical in facilitating the play's humour. The jokes are '"in-jokes," private rather than public humor – intragroup signifying'.[100] Therefore, this play accomplishes what Hughes and Hurston failed to execute with *Mule Bone* – a folk comedy conceived and produced in *context*.

Complete with physical and verbal sparring, the play hinges on the comic escapades of Little Hamlet Hitchcock Jones, or Little Ham, who is 'promoted' from shoe shiner to numbers agent in an illegal lottery. In this comedy about urban life, economics and gambling in Harlem, Ham's slick word play and sweet talking with the ladies gets him in and out of trouble. He meets his match in Tiny Lee, a strong, independent woman who owns her own hair salon. Described as a large woman who physically dwarfs Little Ham, she demands his fidelity, threatens potential rivals, stands up to anyone who dares to cross her and outmanoeuvres the men in the play. Both Tiny and Little Ham stand to lose and profit in the numbers racket initially overseen by (black) Big Boss LeRoy and taken over by white mobsters who bribe the police to monopolize the underground enterprise.

In March 1936, Hughes reported that the play, produced by the Gilpin Players, opened with 'great success'.[101] Reviewers praised *Little Ham*'s blend of comedy, recognizable characterizations and striking atmosphere. William McDermott of the *Cleveland Plain Dealer* described it as 'flavorous, earthy, highly-individualized ... an unusual experience in the theater'.[102] The production's onstage jazz band helped create the 'active and swarming evening in a Harlem dance hall' deemed by McDermott to be 'unique in the history of the American theater'.[103] Though he felt the play lacked 'dramatic punch', *Variety*'s Glenn Pullen wrote that Hughes captured 'Harlem types with shrewdness and rich humor'.[104] Arthur Spaeth of the *Cleveland News* called it 'a hilarious comedy'.[105] Likewise, the *Amsterdam News* proclaimed that it sketched 'a folk-picture of Harlem life ... rich in character and humor'.[106]

However, this project was not universally well received. A reviewer for the *Gazette* blasted the show and linked *Little Ham* with 'the communist conglomeration of ROT known as Stevedore'.[107] The vast majority of criticism of Hughes's comedies (in general) and this work in particular dismissed it as superficial and failed to see the show's 'implied social critique'.[108] Nevertheless, Hughes maintained that 'there is a serious undertone in LITTLE HAM. There is in all my plays.'[109] Like Georgia Douglas Johnson, Eulalie Spence, Thurman and Rapp, Hughes addressed the significance of playing the numbers, especially for low-income and working-class blacks in urban communities, and 'used it as a vehicle for ruminating about African American identity'.[110] As one reviewer shrewdly declared, 'underlying all that laughter you can hear at the Karamu, there is the terrifying and tragic thread of life where there is no hope',[111] suggesting that laughter in the face of tragedy and terror emerged as a deliberate survival strategy. In *Little Ham*, Hughes plied 'critical laughter'[112] to illuminate the politics of representation while destabilizing the social and cultural norms implicit in the New Negro identity as respectable, upwardly mobile and educated men and women.

Conclusion

> The Negro artist work[s] against an undertow of sharp criticism and misunderstanding from his own group and unintentional bribes from the whites.
> Langston Hughes, 'The Racial Mountain'

As the decade drew to a close, Hughes juggled multiple theatrical projects, overseeing the Harlem Suitcase Theatre, a demanding role that included season planning, the handling of props and dashing off a series of satirical skits that burlesqued stereotypical representations of racial identity. These skits included *Limitations of Life* (parodying *Imitations of Life*, a film about passing), *Little Eva's End or Colonel Tom's Cabin* (a send-up of *Uncle Tom's Cabin*), *Em-Fuehrer Jones* (in response to Eugene O'Neill's *Hairy Ape*) and *Scarlet Sister Barry* (a lampoon of Julia Mood Peterkin's novel, *Scarlet Sister Mary*). In 1938, he also collaborated with Dorothy Peterson on a translation of Lope de Vega's verse drama, *Fuente Ovejuna*, and worked on a translation of Federico Garcia Lorca's *Bodas de Sangre (Blood Wedding)*, a new one-act blues opera called *De Organizer* and *Front Porch*, a full-length drama about the problems of a black urban, middle-class family. Written for the Gilpin Players, it revealed the contradictions and complications of 'intraracial class differences on community solidarity'.[113] In 1939, Hughes worked on a new adaptation of Arna Bontemps and Countee Cullen's *St. Louis Woman* (a dramatization of the former's novel, *God Sends Sunday*) for the Federal Theatre Project. Desperate to break into Hollywood, he also teamed up with

Clarence Muse to work on the screenplay for the film *Way Down South* (1939), a conventional Hollywood musical of the antebellum South that revolved around black stereotypes. Hughes was heavily criticized by his leftist comrades for selling out to racist stereotypes and allowing his name to be associated with the picture. During the Depression, Hughes continually balanced remaining true to his core interests with pursuing financially remunerative projects that covered the rent and living expenses for his immediate family.

Moving into the 1940s, the tone of Hughes's writing shifted to become more anti-fascist and patriotic, including essays such as 'My America' and 'What the Negro Wants'.[114] In Hughes's preface to *Simple Stakes a Claim*, he wrote 'The race problem in America is serious business, but "humor is a weapon, too, of no mean value against one's foes".'[115] Throughout his long career, his dramatic *oeuvre* reflects a range of genres from serious plays to comedies and satires. However, his political views – his advocacy of social justice – remained constant. In 1961, Hughes commented that he was a 'propaganda writer; my main material is the race problem'.[116]

5

Clifford Odets: *Waiting for Lefty* (1935), *Awake and Sing!* (1935), *Paradise Lost* (1935), *Golden Boy* (1937), *Rocket to the Moon* (1938), *Night Music* (1940)

Christopher J. Herr

Over the course of his career, Clifford Odets (1906–63) wrote eleven plays, seven of which were produced in the years between 1935 and 1940. Even though his career as a successful playwright and screenwriter continued for two decades after the 1930s, those plays, produced by the Group Theatre, continue to be the basis for his reputation. Indeed, Odets is perhaps the American playwright most closely identified with the 1930s, largely because he depicts so accurately and poignantly in those plays the ambivalence of American life in a nervous, hopeful and disastrous decade framed by a stock market crash and the beginning of another world war. To make sense of Odets's work in the larger context of the 1930s, it is fruitful to examine three central influences on his work: his second-generation Jewish immigrant background, his leftist political views and, most importantly, his association with the Group Theatre. From these three threads, Odets wove a body of work that depicts in powerful, unique dramatic language the ways in which the 1930s crystallized questions about American consumer capitalism and the common man's place in a culture where success is measured by material possessions, about the anxiety of peace in a period between two world wars, and about the democratic ethos of the American Dream devastated by the economic nightmare of the Great Depression. His career, both in the 1930s and beyond, holds a mirror up to America's mid-century conceptions of itself and finds them failing miserably – not in the democratic ideal of material abundance for all, but in the costs paid by those who seek to achieve that ideal.

Odets was born in 1906, the son of Jewish-American immigrants from Eastern Europe. His mother, Pearl Geisinger Odets, and her sister had emigrated from Romania ten years before, while his father, Lou Odets (born Gorodetsky), had arrived from Russia slightly earlier. Clifford and his family would move between Philadelphia and New York throughout his childhood as his father, a printer, searched for better jobs. The family continued to rise economically, soon establishing themselves as comfortably middle class. Although Odets himself was never particularly religious and his father actively eschewed identification both as a Jew and as an immigrant, speaking only English at home and joining the Masons, Odets also spent a good deal of time with his Yiddish-speaking aunt and uncle in Philadelphia, absorbing in their home Jewish history and culture. Like many of his generation, Odets and his family were caught between two worlds, and his own work depicts characters undergoing the same struggles – first- and second-generation immigrants trying to assimilate into the new world while maintaining some sense of personal identity.

Despite his ambivalence about religious practice, Odets's Jewish background served as the foundation for many of his characters, particularly his first full-length play, *Awake and Sing!* In almost all of his plays there are significant Jewish characters, identifiable more by the language they use than by overtly religious sentiment or action. He mined his experience with his aunt and uncle to forge a new American stage dialect, less formal, earthier and more poetic than what had dominated the stage throughout the 1920s. In doing so, he repeatedly melded Yiddish speech rhythms with leftist politics to give voice to the hopes and fears of an entire generation of Jewish-American immigrants in transition, trying to fit into a new world that itself was in rapid transformation to a culture built on mass production and consumer capitalism. In *Awake and Sing!* – for example, in Bessie Berger's 'I raise a family they should have respect' or Jacob's 'give me for a cent a cigarette' – the Yiddish-inflected English conveys both the Bergers' place in their culture and their desire to fit into their new home. In many ways, especially to immigrants like Alfred Kazin, Odets helped to give dignity to their struggles by turning their common immigrant experience into art:

> Sitting in the Belasco, watching my mother and father and uncles and aunts occupying the stage in *Awake and Sing!* by as much right as if they were Hamlet or King Lear, I understood at last. It was all one, as I had always known. Art and truth and hope could yet come together.[1]

In a larger sense, Odets did not see himself as a spokesperson for just the newly-arrived immigrant, but for all of the downtrodden, those to whom the American Dream, however fleeting, promised safety, material goods and happiness, but to whom it only occasionally delivered what it promised. He speaks of the failures of democracy by couching his critique in an examination of the failures of the marketplace. His plays are filled with ordinary people who struggle to make ends meet: Ralph in *Awake and Sing!* dreams of getting new shoes; Sid and Florrie in *Waiting for Lefty* dream of getting married; Cleo Singer in *Rocket to the Moon* and Steve Takis in *Night Music* dream of escaping the monotony of a life lived under difficult economic conditions; and Joe Bonaparte in *Golden Boy* dreams of finding a way to earn the car that will help him escape. But Odets's sharp-eyed critiques of the flaws in the American Dream do not mean that he discounted that dream altogether. Rather, despite being hailed as the leftist playwright of his generation, he was a fervent believer that democracy – and even consumer capitalism – offered real rewards for its participants and that human progress was made possible through concerted, collective effort that was – and is – still measured in part by material progress: more and better food, better access to consumer goods, safer working conditions. He well knew that one of the means that immigrants used to measure their own assimilation was not their productivity but their consumption, their ability to participate in the marketplace. Like democracy itself, the consumer marketplace was predicated on the ideal of universal participation; the ability of immigrants to purchase the same material goods as non-immigrants helped to bridge the distance between them.

In 1935, when his first plays were produced, Odets was seen as a firebrand of the left, a strident voice demanding the destruction of the old order and the creation of a new one. But a closer examination of the plays shows him as more of a romantic than a revolutionary. His call for change is always tempered by a humanizing sympathy for those caught in the struggle, and for every character who promises radical change there is another who merely wants peace and modest plenty. It is probably accurate to say that Odets's leftist politics were inspired more by Victor Hugo and Walt Whitman than Marx and Engels. As he noted in a 1940 journal entry about *Les Miserables*, '[it was] the most profound art experience I have ever had ... Hugo inspired me, made me aspire; I wanted to be a good and noble man, longed to do heroic deeds with my bare hands, thirsted to be kind to people, particularly the weak and humble and oppressed.'[2] Ironically, after initially being championed as the voice of the literary left, Odets would be criticized in the late 1930s for plays like *Night Music* and *Rocket to the Moon* because they were not sufficiently Marxist in their treatment of social issues.

Early in his career, Odets was radical enough to briefly join the Communist Party in 1935, at a time when party membership was at an all-time high in the United States; he even served as a delegate from the party on an ill-fated fact-finding trip to Cuba. However, he became the theatrical spokesperson for many leftists not because his politics were more radical, but because he more than any other playwright of the period was able to distil the anxieties and hopes of his generation into theatrically compelling language. As theatre critic John Gassner remarked, 'No one gave himself to radical thought stemming from Marxist dialectics as wholeheartedly in the theatre as did Odets, just as no one succeeded in investing cold theory with so much palpitating and tormented flesh.'[3] Unlike a lot of leftist plays of the period, which favour structure and doctrine over character, Odets focuses on the humanity of his characters, recognizing the price that capitalism exacts from its participants, but offering full sympathy for the messy ambivalence that his characters have about the marketplace in which they participate.

In addition to the stamp that Jewish culture and language and leftist politics left on his work, Odets was most profoundly influenced by his connection with the Group Theatre. It was to the Group that he owed his understanding of ensemble acting and his first opportunities to see his work on stage. Founded in the early years of the Depression by Harold Clurman, Cheryl Crawford and Lee Strasberg, the Group became Odets's spiritual and theatrical home until it dissolved in 1941. In forming the Group, Clurman was hoping to address a problem that he believed existed in 1930s American theatre: he argued that even the best theatres operated as mere producing organizations, without a clear aesthetic or goal. They lurched from one production to another, never effectively responding to the needs of their community. In response, Clurman envisioned a new, alternative theatre. He wanted it to produce plays written by American playwrights that addressed significant social issues of the day – even though Clurman himself was not politically radical and remained somewhat sceptical of plays that asserted radical politics. Though the Group was beset by constant tension and financial difficulty, it still can be argued that Clurman was remarkably successful in achieving his vision; over the course of ten years, all of the plays produced by the Group, save one, were written by American playwrights, and by the end of those ten years, the Group's aesthetic – rigorous actor training, meticulous preparation and fluid ensemble performance – was firmly established in the American theatrical world.

The Group was different from the other professional theatres in its resolutely American focus and its insistence upon social relevance; it was also different from the other socially conscious or leftist theatres of the 1930s – the Prolet-Büehne, the Theatre Union and others – in its professionalism and commitment to create artistically important theatre in the United States. Catering to a smaller, more homogeneous audience, those theatres were able to produce strident political dramas without fear of alienating their audiences. However, because of their middle-ground position, the Group was wracked almost from the start by tension between the leftist members of the company, who pushed for more overtly leftist drama, and Clurman and Strasberg, who tried to focus the company on artistic rather than political goals. When Odets's work began to be produced by the Group, he would be caught up in this conflict. His own leftist leanings allied him with the radical actors – he even taught acting classes at the Theatre Union – but as a playwright, he wanted the freedom to write any play he wanted, regardless of political or commercial appeal.

To achieve its goals, the Group sought first to create a permanent company of performers, paid by the season regardless of whether the actor had a role in a particular production. Ultimately, the Group hoped to develop an ensemble of performers, directors and designers – and eventually playwrights – who spoke a common theatrical language, who were steeped in a common system of acting training and who were committed to common political and artistic causes. The Group's aesthetic and goals appealed to many successful actors of the period, a number of whom sacrificed better career opportunities and more money in order to work with the Group, including successful actors such as Franchot Tone, Stella Adler and Morris Carnovsky, and, later, John Garfield. The acting training, based on Lee Strasberg's interpretation of Stanislavski's system, helped to create an ensemble style of performance that was an immediate sensation on Broadway in productions such as Paul Green's *The House of Connolly* and Sidney Kingsley's *Men in White*.

Odets's route to the Group was circuitous. After his plan for attending drama school was rejected by his father, Odets attended high school in New York for two years before dropping out in an attempt to escape ending up in the family business. He drifted around to various part-time jobs, earning some money as a 'rover reciter' at amateur poetry nights and working briefly in radio and at amateur theatres in Greenwich Village. He wrote two one-act radio plays and eventually found work as an actor in a stock company in New Jersey. Finally, in 1931, Odets joined the Group as one of the original members, signing on as an actor even though his stage credits included only several years of summer stock and some small roles in Theatre Guild productions. By most accounts, he was not a strong actor, and he never moved beyond bit roles in Group productions, but Clurman liked Odets and thought he might have potential to do something else. Despite Clurman's confidence, it was not until a few years later that Odets would emerge as a playwright; nevertheless, it is impossible to imagine his work without the influence of those formative early years with the Group. For Odets, being a part of the company and watching Strasberg work was essential to his development as a playwright; it helped him to create a tight-knit ensemble of characters, directly connected to the Group aesthetic, conceived with specific Group actors in mind.

Producing work that addressed social and political issues in 1930s America often led to internal disagreements within the Group about play selection; it also highlighted the peculiar financial position that the company, and individual members within it, faced. Even though the Group was founded as an alternative to commercial theatres, Clurman, Strasberg and Crawford nevertheless chose to showcase the Group's work by directly competing with those theatres. This naturally increased the economic pressure upon them, particularly since they had committed to pay the entire company for the whole season. Given the devastation of Broadway brought about by the Great Depression and the advent of sound film – the number of productions on Broadway dropped 44 per cent between 1928 and 1934[4] – the Group's decision to operate as a Broadway theatre faced both impossibly bad timing and internal contradictions. Indeed, much of the history of the Group can be told by tracing the financial struggles of the company between successful productions. For example, *Men in White* (1933) was a critical success as well as being the first huge box-office success the company had ever had. It allowed the Group to pay debts, raise salaries and secure a new round of plays to produce. But the play's success also fomented discontent among the more radical company members because it was seen as not leftist enough. The small leftist theatres producing more radical content away from Broadway did not have the same financial pressures – but they also did not have the same respect the Group enjoyed. On the other hand, the Group was committed both to Broadway and to producing progressive American plays; it is not surprising that they had a difficult time finding plays that merged the two.

Individual actors faced similar decisions – as would Odets as a playwright in the second half of the decade. As praise for the Group's work grew, Group company members were increasingly in demand from other theatres and from the film industry. Some decided that they were no longer willing to sacrifice their individual careers to the Group ideals and left for Hollywood. Others stayed with the company but demanded more input into the daily operations of the Group. Many of those who stayed, including Odets and Clurman, moved between the Group and Hollywood with varying degrees of enthusiasm, but the economic pressure on the Group continued. By 1935, Odets had achieved success as a playwright – the Group produced four of his plays on Broadway in that year – but this success was fraught almost immediately with complications. As a member of the Group, he was pressured to create socially relevant ensemble dramas that were also box-office successes. In 1938, for example, Clurman wrote to Odets in Hollywood pressuring him to write another play for the Group:

> Of all people *you* Clifford Odets are the nearest to understand or *feel* this American reality ... the reality only half-experienced but nevertheless present for most Americans like us – of whom there are many millions ... Write – write – write – because we need it so much. 'We' is not the Group alone, not the American theatre (pfui! on the American theatre) but our folks, we Americans, we guys who live on University Place, Hester St., Fifth Ave., Central Park West, Santa Monica Blvd., Oshkosh, and Kalamazoo ... for the love of your brothers – *give out!!*[5]

Clurman truly believed that Odets had a profound ability to encapsulate America's internal contradictions in compelling dramatic form, but his letter was also calculated to pressure Odets into producing a play for the Group.

As a result, Odets produced work at times that he felt was unfinished or unpolished but desperately needed by his friends and companions. He commented bitterly later about Clurman's pressure:

> He [Clurman] finally got to think that I was kind of like a cow who dropped a calf, didn't know anything about it. Because this is what happened in the Group Theatre and I was very resentful of it ... They had to have those veal chops on the table. For the next week, or everybody would go hungry. So in a certain way this gifted calf that I'm talking about, that I dropped, was also veal chops for everybody to eat.[6]

Both the Group as a producing organization and Odets as a playwright within the Group faced the same kind of financial pressures and contradictions as the characters in Odets's plays: all three are forced to operate within an economic system that pressures them to sell themselves, to compromise their principles for full participation in that marketplace. Therefore, it is necessary to understand Odets's work in the context of his Group Theatre association as well as the larger context of Depression-era American life.

Waiting for Lefty

> My God, Joe. This world is supposed to be for all of us!
> Edna, *Waiting for Lefty*

Odets's first produced play, *Waiting for Lefty*, was a one-act hastily written for a benefit for the leftist *New Theatre* magazine. Directed by Odets and fellow Group member Art Smith and featuring other Group actors, the play premiered on 6 January 1935 to riotous applause. Clurman remembered the opening night response:

> The first scene of *Lefty* had not played two minutes when a shock of delighted recognition struck the audience. Deep laughter, hot assent, a kind of joyous fervor seemed to sweep the audience toward the stage. The actors no longer performed; they were being carried along as if by an exultancy of communication such as I had never witnessed in the theatre before. Audience and actors had become one ... It was the birth cry of the thirties. Our youth had found its voice.[7]

Clurman is hardly an unbiased observer, but all of the responses indicate that Odets had clearly hit home with his simple play about a taxi strike and its effects on ordinary people.

Structurally and politically, *Waiting for Lefty* is straightforward; much of its immediate success stems from that simplicity. The play is set in a union hall, and during the course of the action, different characters – members of a strike committee – rise to play out their stories while the others watch, so that everyone is both performer and audience. This serves two functions: first, it eliminates the need for all but the simplest props and set pieces, since the individual vignettes are clearly presented as flashbacks, giving the play a stark immediacy. Second, the structure of the play helps to break down the proscenium arch and cue the audience to the expected emotional response. In addition to these structural elements, there is a strong influence on the play from the agitation-propaganda plays (agit-prop) of the early 1930s. Designed to galvanize sympathetic audiences to direct action – usually demanding the release of a political prisoner – those plays ended, as *Lefty* does, with a specific call to action and an audience response. Also, like other agit-prop plays, *Lefty* presents a villain – in this case, the corrupt union boss, Harry Fatt, who opens the play with an insult-laden speech aimed to intimidate a group of taxi drivers from going out on strike:

> What the hell'll they do for you? Pull you out and run away when trouble starts. Give those birds a chance and they'll have your sisters and wives in the whore houses, like they done in Russia. They'll tear Christ off his bleeding cross. They'll wreck your homes and throw your babies in the river. You think that's bunk? Read the papers.[8]

In keeping with agit-prop conventions, Fatt, who also appears in flashback scenes as the industrialist Fayette and the Broadway producer Grady, is a two-dimensional caricature, but in the vignettes, Odets steps beyond the narrow confines of agit-prop and creates relatively complex characters whose experiences highlight the fundamental contradictions of consumer capitalism and whose relationships and lives are the testing ground for the economic system in which they live.

As each strike committee member rises in turn, we see a recurring theme – they are fighting an uphill battle to gain a foothold in their world, to achieve the promise held out to them by the American Dream. In the first scene, Joe and Edna have just had their furniture repossessed, they barely have enough to make ends meet, their kids are physically suffering and their marriage is falling apart. What makes this even more bitter for Edna is the contrast between her expectations that hard work would lead to the material rewards of full participation in society, and the difficulty of their situation: 'Everything was gonna be so ducky! A cottage by the waterfall, roses in Picardy. You're a four-star bust!'[9] Part of Edna's bitterness comes from her knowledge that plenty exists, even in the middle of the Depression; their banishment from the Edenic promise of democracy is made more poignant by the abundance that surrounds them:

> Sure, I see it in the papers, how good orange juice is for kids. But damnit our kids get colds one on top of the other. They look like little ghosts. Betty never saw a grapefruit. I took her to the store last week and she pointed to a stack of grapefruits. 'What's that!' she said. My God, Joe, this world is supposed to be for all of us![10]

For Odets, consumer capitalism, while far from ideal, offers its participants real rewards in addition to social prestige: health, better food and clothing, and security. Even more importantly, it co-opts the imagery of utopia as its own, so that even by the time the play was written, it had become difficult to imagine a system outside of consumer culture; Edna measures her success by material goods. Thus, Edna and Joe's inability to purchase the shoes and food they need does not indict the need but rather calls into question a system which does not allow it to be fulfilled. Their inability to live fully, furthermore, is characterized in both physical and emotional terms: Edna suffers sleepless nights and wrinkles, the children are plagued by colds and in danger of developing rickets, and Joe is hungry and tired and beaten down by the daily grind of existence.

The juxtaposition of wealth and scarcity – which was being played out on a national scale as people suffered hunger and eviction on a level never before seen in the United States, even after production capacity had greatly increased during the 1920s – is echoed in other scenes in *Waiting for Lefty*, where the desires expressed by the characters are already conditioned by the marketplace in which they participate. Sid and Florrie dream of getting married, an impossibility given the financial situation of their families. But Florrie's dogged assertion to her brother that she deserves pleasure recognizes that there are human needs, socially determined, that go beyond mere physical survival and connect standard of living with consumerist pleasures: 'I gotta right to have something out of life. I don't smoke, I don't drink. So if Sid wants to take me to a dance, I'll go.'[11] Sid's long speech condemning the 'money man' who cheats the promise by dealing him nothing more than 'a pair of tens' is juxtaposed with his playful banter with Florrie about the 'fifty or sixty dozen' roses he would bring her if they were in the movies. There is no place to which Sid and Florrie can escape, and their dream of a place to sit together is rendered as unreachable as a desire for a fancy gown or dozens of roses.

Perhaps most damningly, Odets uses the play to condemn those who neglect the human costs of a system in favour of profit. The 'money man' uses Sid's brother as cannon fodder to further his own economic ends; the charity ward of the hospital is closed because it costs too much; the industrialist Fayette glibly remarks on the importance of creating more consumers even as he makes poison gas, dismissing the death of Miller's brother in the First World War:

> **Fayette** The world is an armed camp today. One match sets the whole world blazing in forty-eight hours. Uncle Sam won't be caught napping!
> **Miller** They say 12 million men were killed in that last one and 20 million more wounded or missing.
> **Fayette** That's not our worry. If big business went sentimental over human life there wouldn't be big business of any sort![12]

As Agate Keller, who wears his glass eye as a proud reminder of his roots in the working class, remarks in the final speech of the play, the value of such an exploitative system must be measured not just in the rewards it offers – which are real and desirable – but in the costs it exacts from those trying to achieve those rewards:

> This is your life and mine! It's skull and bones every incha the road! Christ, we're dyin' by inches! For what? For the debutant-ees to have their sweet comin' out parties in the Ritz! Poppa's got a daughter she's gotta get her picture in the papers. Christ, they make 'em with our blood. Joe said it. It's slow death or fight. It's war![13]

After Lefty Costello, the absent member of the strike committee, is found murdered, Keller exhorts the audience to action:

> HELLO AMERICA! HELLO. WE'RE STORMBIRDS OF THE WORKING-CLASS. WORKERS OF THE WORLD ... OUR

BONES AND BLOOD! And when we die they'll know what we did to make a new world. Christ, cut us up into little pieces. We'll die for what is right! Put fruit trees where our ashes are![14]

Keller's speech conflates images of Christian martyrdom with socialist sacrifice by the working class. Perhaps most importantly, the play makes it clear that the system is corrupt and must be torn down – though what is erected in its place is less clear. Keller's paradisiacal vision of fruit trees echoes the language of consumer abundance that Edna uses earlier in the play and suggests that, at the very least, the images of natural abundance and the marketplace are inextricably mixed.

Clurman characterized the play as the 'birth cry of the thirties', which is somewhat inaccurate. The themes that Odets addresses in *Waiting for Lefty* – the economic basis of war, the failed promises of consumer capitalism, the dangers of unchecked corporate greed – had been mainstays of leftist drama for years. But Clurman and others recognized in Odets's play a new voice, one that more effectively than any other playwright of the period was able to crystallize the complexity of what Sid calls 'the 1935 blues' and put it onstage. Brooks Atkinson of the *New York Times* called it 'one of the most dynamic dramas of the year in any department of our theatre' and noted that 'People who want to understand the times through which they are living can scarcely afford to ignore it.'[15] The play's appearance marked the cry of an important new voice in American drama.

Awake and Sing!

Economics comes down like a ton of coal on the head.
Jacob, *Awake and Sing!*

The one-act *Waiting for Lefty* was Odets's first play to reach the stage, but his first full-length play, *Awake and Sing!*, was written first. In fact, *Awake and Sing!* was already in rehearsals when *Waiting for Lefty* debuted; it opened just a few weeks later. The origins of *Awake and Sing!* reach back to Odets's childhood and time spent with his Uncle Israel and Aunt Esther. In 1932, while

Odets was labouring to find a home as an actor in the Group and living with several other actors in a small brownstone, he began a Jewish family drama, which he titled 'I Got the Blues' in early drafts. Drawing on his experience with his family and those he had known growing up, he constructed the play to have six or seven parts of relatively equal size, a structure based on his experience of Group ensemble training and, to a lesser extent, the influence of Chekhov, whom Odets admired. Odets worked on and off on the script over the course of two years, desperately trying to interest Clurman and Strasberg in the play. Clurman liked it but thought it needed work on both the first and third acts; Strasberg thought that the ethnicity of the characters limited it too much to make it effective. The Group actors, however, were more enthusiastic, and a summer reading of the play showed that it was perfectly suited to their style. Still, Clurman and Strasberg demurred, and despairing of his own theatre ever producing the play, Odets optioned it to another producer.

Finally in December 1934, the Group directors agreed to do the play as much from a lack of other viable scripts as a sense that Odets's play would succeed. Set in a lower middle-class household on Longwood Avenue in the Bronx – one of the streets in which Odets lived as a child – the play chronicles the extended Berger family as the comfort of their world is challenged by the ongoing deprivations of the Great Depression. As Odets characterizes the play in his prefatory note, 'All of the characters in *Awake and Sing!* share a fundamental activity: a struggle for life amid petty conditions.'[16] Act One begins with the family in relative comfort, though cracks are already beginning to show in the façade. Ralph, the son, complains that he can't get ahead in the world or buy even simple consumer pleasures like black and white shoes; he characterizes his life as 'every other day to sit around with the blues and mud in your mouth'.[17] His dream of marrying his poor girlfriend, Blanche, is met with fierce opposition from Bessie, his eminently pragmatic mother, who rules the family through a combination of guilt and iron will. Bessie's socialist father, Jacob, coaches Ralph throughout the play to break free of the strictures that are placed on him; ironically, though, Jacob by his own admission is never to do more than talk:

> Look on me and learn what to do, boychick. Here sits an old man polishing tools. You think maybe I'll use them again! Look

on this failure and see for seventy years he talked, with good ideas but only in his head ... you should act. Not like me. A man who had golden opportunities but drank instead a glass tea.[18]

Myron, Bessie's husband, is a virtual nonentity in his own home, wandering aimlessly from room to room and spouting empty platitudes about Teddy Roosevelt and the rewards that come from merit and hard work. The central plotline of the play centres on Hennie, Ralph's sister, who reveals in the first act that she is pregnant and abandoned by the baby's father. In response, Bessie conspires to trick Sam Feinschreiber, a newly-arrived immigrant, into marrying Hennie, while Myron and Jacob weakly protest.

In Act Two, a year has passed. Hennie and Sam are unhappily married and the Bergers have been forced to take in a lodger to defray costs: Moe Axelrod, a cynical war veteran who works in various rackets, but who is in love with Hennie and who has a soft spot for Jacob and Ralph. Ralph is finally rejected by his girlfriend's family, and when he asks Myron and Bessie for permission to bring her home to live with them, Myron inadvertently blurts out the truth about Hennie and Sam's marriage. Stung by the hypocrisy of his whole family, Ralph lashes out at them, including his grandfather, and in a climactic fit of pique, Bessie smashes Jacob's records, which serve as his refuge and comfort during the play. Shortly after, Jacob leaves to take the dog out and news comes back that he has fallen off the roof and died. Act Three is set on the day that the insurance adjuster is coming to pay on Jacob's life insurance policy. Jacob has left the money to Ralph, a down payment on the life Jacob always imagined but never was able to achieve. Bessie wants Ralph to use the money for the family, but Moe tricks her by pretending to have a suicide note from Jacob, jeopardizing the insurance claim. At the end of the play, Ralph rejects the money, vowing instead to work so that 'life won't be printed on dollar bills',[19] while Hennie and Moe escape to the South, leaving the baby behind in the hopes of finding a new paradise for themselves.

Like *Waiting for Lefty*, *Awake and Sing!* wrestles with the effects of the Depression on an ordinary family. Both plays are calls to action, but *Awake and Sing!*, which takes its title from Isaiah 26.19, is firmly realistic in style and structure, borrowing plot devices – secret insurance money, marital infidelity, fake suicide notes – from the tradition of the well-made play. Both plays also end optimistically; indeed, this optimistic ending was a source of contention for many critics who saw in Hennie and Moe's abandonment of the baby not liberation, but rather self-indulgent abdication of responsibility. They also saw Ralph's assertions as nothing more than vague idealism unconnected to anything in his character. Odets was aware of these criticisms of the optimistic endings to his plays – the same charges were levelled later at *Paradise Lost* and *Rocket to the Moon* – but he maintained that in the case of Hennie and Moe, 'Young people can go through an experience and have their eyes opened, and determine from it to live in a different way.'[20] Tying their fates to Moe's idealistic vision of a new paradise, their escape rejects the known to seek a utopian vision somehow existing outside the marketplace. He tells Hennie, 'Paradise, you're on a big boat headed south. No more pins and needles in your heart, no snake juice squirted in your arm. The whole world's green grass, and when you cry it's because you're happy.'[21] The scepticism of the critics measures the desire to escape against the likelihood of doing so, and so we are left to hope, pushing the achievement into a future that lies outside the scope of the play.

The fundamental struggle in *Awake and Sing!* is a struggle for respect, but Odets connects respectability to material goods, and ultimately to participation in the marketplace. For Bessie, the ability to offer food is both a symbol of middle-class respectability and a means of control. She decides that Sam can be invited to dinner but Blanche cannot, and thus she codifies through the most basic form of consumption, eating, who is allowed to be part of the family. Actual food and references to food almost overwhelm the play, so much that the Group's property man, Moe Jacobs, remarked to a reporter that 'for him the play was "one long meal"'.[22] Other characters measure respectability both through food and through other consumer goods. Moe's derision of the Bergers' house cuts directly against Bessie's measure of self-worth: 'No oranges, huh? – what a dump.'[23] Ralph longs for a pair of black and white shoes, and Jacob takes refuge in his records. For each character, the symbolic value of those objects is far greater than their material value. For Jacob, his recordings, particularly Caruso's recording of 'O Paradiso', are a refuge, the physical manifestation of his socialist ideals. Though he has not achieved his ideals, he is able to maintain them by shifting their ideological weight to the imaginary world created by the music: 'Caruso stands on the ship and looks on a Utopia. You hear? "Oh, paradise! Oh Paradise on earth!"'[24] When Bessie smashes the records at the end of Act Two, then, she destroys the last vestige of his idealism. Jacob has nowhere to turn and nothing to live for, and so he passes his legacy on to Ralph. Ultimately, *Awake and Sing!* is Ralph's play; his response to Bessie's cynical remark at the end of the play is Odets's assertion that Jacob's utopian vision is not completely lost:

> **Ralph** We don't want life printed on dollar bills, Mom!
> **Bessie** So go out and change the world if you don't like it.
> **Ralph** I will. And why? 'Cause life's different in my head. Gimme the earth in two hands. I'm strong.[25]

The struggle for life amid petty conditions has become, once again, a hope for a new life. As *Waiting for Lefty* does, *Awake and Sing!* juxtaposes the deprivation that the family faces with the prospect of abundance promised by the world around them – the bolts of fabric that Ralph feels he will drown in at the warehouse, the new car that Morty drives – and couches the vision of change in the utopian language that is a hallmark of all of Odets's plays.

Paradise Lost

> This is about the richest city in the world. A person starves to death in it every other day.
>
> Pike, *Paradise Lost*

Odets's next full-length play, *Paradise Lost*, makes even more explicit the Edenic metaphor; in this case, however, the idea of paradise is used allegorically to examine the disillusionment and dissolution of the American middle class. The Gordon family is in many ways similar to the Bergers, but Odets shifts away from making them overtly Jewish, and they are, at least at the beginning of the play, less constrained by economic difficulties. Odets attempted to make the play more broadly appealing by making the family more generically American. *Paradise Lost*, which always remained Odets's favourite play, also shows the influence of Chekhov, not only in its creation of several roles of equal size, but in its depiction of a feckless group of intelligent, sensitive people incapable of adjusting to changing conditions.

The central movement of the play is indicated in the title; it is a gradual stripping away of the family's material possessions, but also of its illusions about itself and about the nature of the consumer marketplace and the democracy in which they participate. Odets suffuses his realistic family drama with allegory, and the sometimes heavy-handed symbolism irritated some early reviewers of the play. Certainly critics on the political left, who had helped to champion Odets's earlier work, were befuddled by the aimlessness of the dialogue and the lack of a clear leftist solution to the problems the play presents. In the play, Leo Gordon, who owns a small manufacturing plant, faces bankruptcy when he discovers that his partner, Sam Katz, has been embezzling money to pay for treatments for Katz's impotence. Leo briefly considers, and then rejects, a plan to commit arson for the insurance money and watches as the business slowly sinks under the weight of its debts. Clara Gordon, like Bessie Berger, is a tough, pragmatic matriarch who controls the household and maintains a sense of family pride, but her fight against the disease and decay afflicting the family is doomed to failure. The family loses everything, including their two sons – one is dead by the end of the play and the other is dying – and is evicted from their home in Act Three. The cycle of destruction is complete, and we are left with the unflinching verdict of Paul, a homeless man, who tells the Gordons, 'You had a sorta little paradise here. Now you lost the paradise. That should teach you something. But no! You ain't awake yet ... You have been took like a bulldog takes a pussy cat! Finished!'[26] Their demise is as much the result of their ineffectual response to the changes around them as it is the economic pressures they face.

Paul's assessment of the Gordons is not wrong: except for Clara, they are hapless and ineffectual when they should be vigorous; they talk when they should fight. For example, the fiancé of the Gordons' daughter, Pearl, is forced to leave town to find a job, and she withdraws from life completely, retreating in self-pity to her room to play her piano. Their older son, Ben, is an Olympic gold medallist, now retired because of a heart condition. A victim of his own cult of personality, he expects a 'big berth in Wall Street',[27] but is incapable of holding down a job; even Clara admits that he's never worked a day in his life. Eventually, Ben is reduced to selling

Mickey Mouse wind-up toys on the street and is supplanted in his marital bed by his friend Kewpie. Kewpie, a man of action, is driven by a conflict between a sense of inferiority and a deep love for Ben; as the Gordons become weaker, he grows more violent, disgusted by their passivity: 'You gimme worms, the whole bunch ... I don't stop to say it ain't my cake. I cut a piece without asking.'[28] In many ways, Ben, who is killed during a failed robbery attempt at the end of the play, can be seen as an early version of Biff Loman in Arthur Miller's *Death of a Salesman*, an idol of physical prowess, frozen in time (much like the statue of Ben that dominates the Gordons' living room), incapable of moving beyond early success.

Despite the futility of their response to the changes taking place around them, the Gordons somehow remain sympathetic, as Clurman recognized:

> The play ... represented the search for reality. The little people of the small middle-class world were fumbling about in an environment they didn't control or understand, their hearts full of fond dreams, their eyes beclouded with illusions inherited from the past, while their hands groped in a void that was full of terror. When facts finally confronted them with unmistakable concreteness, they were the facts of bankruptcy and destitution, a house empty of all its foolish and kindly furniture, forever shaken and damaged in its ancient comfort.[29]

What brings the Gordons to ruin, Clurman hints, is their idealism, but it is also what keeps them from being simply a source of ridicule or an object lesson. Leo Gordon is vague and romantic, out of place in the kind of world in which people like Kewpie succeed. But Leo's idealism nevertheless remains a redeeming trait. He responds positively to his factory workers who request better working conditions, telling his partner, 'I would not want my life built up on the misery of these people.'[30] And at the end of the play, in response to Paul, Leo closes with a vision:

> No! There is more to life than this! Everything he said is true, but there is more. That was the past, but there is a future ... Oh, yes, I tell you the whole world is for men to possess. Heartbreak and terror are not the heritage of mankind! The world is beautiful. No fruit tree wears a lock and key.[31]

As with the end of *Awake and Sing!*, Leo's closing speech shifts the horror of their loss towards hope for the future.

The unmistakably utopian vision that Leo espouses was difficult for some critics to countenance, especially coming from the meek and passive Leo. And to a certain extent, their criticism is valid, but the unlocked fruit tree as a symbol of easy abundance is a direct answer to the images of corruption and decay presented by Kewpie's rapacious consumption. At one point, for example, Kewpie tells Ben, 'I'm in you like a tape worm!'[32] Conversely, the character of Pike, the Gordons' furnace man, operates as a clear-eyed realist in a world of romantics like Leo. He compiles statistics about poverty and unemployment and spends his time sketching dead people. He responds bitterly both to a jingoistic radio commentator who urges her listeners to prepare for another war and to the glib politician Foley, who suggests that people's weariness stems from an unbalanced diet: 'This is about the richest city in the world. A person starves to death in it every other day. Not enough alkaline. That's what it means! Hunger and degradation – eighty-twenty.'[33] Pike once again juxtaposes the idealism of a free market with the horrors of those excluded from it. At the last, however, Odets uses *Paradise Lost* to look at American life from several different angles, tempering Leo's romantic dream with Pike's cynical clarity, suggesting that any vision of a utopia in 1930s America demands significant, even brutal, sacrifice from those who wish to participate.

Golden Boy

Do you think I like this feeling of no possessions?
Joe Bonaparte, *Golden Boy*

After *Paradise Lost* failed at the box office, Odets accepted an offer to write screenplays in Hollywood for a time. Given the rapid expansion of the sound film industry and the concomitant need for writers who could script convincing dialogue, virtually every American playwright and fiction writer of note was presented with similar opportunities. For Odets, the decision was complicated. He hoped the money would help support *Paradise Lost* until it found an audience, but he also wanted to get away from the pressure of New York and the Group for a time. On the other hand, as a playwright who had written so much about the dangers of selling out to moneyed interests and who had exalted the cause of the common man, he knew that even a temporary move to California would be seen as hypocrisy. At the same time, Odets was genuinely interested in the potential of film to reach a mass audience. In 1937, he wrote an article in the *New York Times* calling film the 'folk theatre' of America, and arguing that film's ability to speak to and for the common man should be hailed as a model for the theatre, rather than dismissed out of hand. He continued to move between New York and Los Angeles for the next twenty years in search of that kind of mass audience.

Odets's first play after *Paradise Lost* was a union play called *The Silent Partner*, a large-scale drama focusing on a labour dispute. But when Clurman saw a draft, he knew that it would not be commercially successful and would be expensive for the Group to produce. He asked Odets to rewrite the play, but gave no assurance that the Group would produce it. Odets, frustrated, scrapped the play, and instead turned his attention to *Golden Boy*, the idea for which he had gotten while attending a prizefight in California. *Golden Boy* would turn out to be one of the most commercially and critically successful plays ever produced by the Group. It is the story of Joe Bonaparte, a young, bookish second-generation Italian immigrant. Joe is both a talented violinist and a talented boxer. Torn between the violin that feeds his soul and the boxing ring that gives him material comfort, Joe gradually drifts further and further away from his family and his music. Eventually, after killing another fighter in the ring, Joe himself ends up dying in a car accident (possibly a suicide) as he tries to escape what he has become.

Clurman, who directed the play on Broadway, saw it as an example of the 'great fight' that faced everyone in the 1930s: to maintain a sense of self in the face of the increasing impersonality of American society. In staging *Golden Boy*, then, he repeated the motif of the fight, physically staging many of the scenes to mirror the movements of boxers squaring off in the ring. The structure of the play supports Clurman's interpretation; it contains a number of relatively short scenes, but even more importantly, it consciously pits the two halves of Joe's nature against each other, reinforcing the idea that the biggest fight in the play doesn't happen in the ring but in Joe's psyche. From the beginning of the play, Joe is divided. In the early scenes, he speaks of his frustration both with his lack of opportunities and with his status as an outsider: 'People have hurt my feelings for years. I never forget. You can't get even with people by playing the fiddle. If music shot bullets I'd like it better – artists and people like that are freaks today. The world moves fast and they sit around like forgotten dopes.'[34] Joe sees boxing not only as a way to get ahead financially, but also as a way to match the speed of the world he lives in, to mark his place in society. Just as his boxing style is predicated on speed more than power, he longs for a car like the one driven by film star Gary Cooper: 'those cars are poison in my blood. When you sit in a car and speed you're looking down at the world. Speed, speed, everything is speed – nobody gets me!'[35] The image of the car as poison foreshadows Joe's eventual death by automobile, but he sees in speed both a means of fitting into society and a means of escape. Ironically, just as the burgeoning advertising industry of the 1930s promised, purchasing the mass-produced consumer item is a way to be recognized, to avoid being a 'forgotten dope', but it is also an expression of Joe's personality, a marker of his individuality within that social order. The car both makes him one of the crowd and sets him apart.

Nowhere else in his plays does Odets so clearly present the battle lines of modern culture: commerce against art; the individual against the communal; the machine against the organic. It is no accident that Joe's father, kindly and supportive even when he doesn't understand Joe's decision, makes his modest living as a fruit seller. Here, Odets returns to the comforting image of the natural world as a source of nurture and sustenance, directly in contrast to the way Joe imagines himself as a machine in the ring. When he is rejected by his girlfriend Lorna, his transformation to a soulless commodity is complete, all human connection lost: 'Now I'm alone ... I'll show them all – nobody stands in my way ... When a bullet sings through the air it has no past – only a future – like me! Nobody, nothing, stands in my way!'[36] Lorna's love, which promises redemption and real human connection, comes too late for Joe; he has travelled too far, too fast, and only in death can his father 'bring-a him home ... where he belong'.[37]

Rocket to the Moon and *Night Music*

> It's getting late to play at life; I want to live it ... none of you can give me what I'm looking for, a whole full world, with all the trimmings!
>
> Cleo Singer, *Rocket to the Moon*

Odets's next two plays, *Rocket to the Moon* and *Night Music*, were his last plays produced by the Group. *Rocket to the Moon* opened in early 1938 to mixed reviews. Set over the course of a hot New York summer, the play focuses on Ben Stark, a middle-aged dentist trapped in a difficult marriage and a stalled career. Ben's wife, Belle, relies on his steady income and his solid companionship, but when he proposes moving to a new, bigger practice, Belle refuses. She doesn't want to be beholden to her estranged father, Mr Prince, who has offered to finance the move. Thwarted in his career ambitions, Ben contemplates an affair with his receptionist, Cleo Singer, a young, naive and hopelessly romantic girl who aspires to be a dancer. For Ben, Cleo represents everything that has gone missing from his life: hope, excitement and freedom; she is, potentially, his rocket to the moon. His pursuit of Cleo is at first encouraged by his father-in-law, Mr Prince – he challenges Ben, to get 'out of the coffin by Labor Day'.[38] As the play progresses, however, Prince begins to see in Cleo both a companion for his older years and also a girl he can mould and shape: 'My girl, I studied you like a scientist. I understand your needs ... A man to help you learn and grow. A man of maturity and experience in everything – love, what to eat, where, what to wear and where to buy it – money to buy it – an eye turned out to the world.'[39]

At the end of the play, Cleo is left with the choice of being Ben's mistress or Prince's ornament; she chooses neither. Rather, she insists on pursuing her own sense of identity, an identity that, in typically Odets fashion, is directly connected to images of abundance and community: 'It's getting late to play at life; I want to live it ... none of you can give me what I'm looking for, a whole full world, with all the trimmings!'[40] Her decision to reject both men in favour of self-determination is a decision to break free of the commodification that they demand of her. Her youth and vitality – she is the only vital character in the play – are connected specifically in the play with the natural world. The men in the play repeatedly objectify her in images of consumption, vainly attempting to subdue and control the natural energy she possesses. For example, Prince tells her, 'You're a girl like candy, a honeydew melon – a delicious girl', and comments to Ben that she has 'womanhood fermenting through her veins'.[41] But Cleo ultimately resists her own commodification – 'No man can take a bite out of me, like an apple and throw it away.'[42] *Rocket to the Moon* is less directly concerned with economic pressures than Odets's earlier plays, but the issue of commodification and the place of the idealistic individual in modern society remain central concerns.

In *Night Music*, Odets's final play of the 1930s, he once again returns to a rootless, second-generation immigrant, Steve Takis, looking for love, opportunity and connection in a world haunted by the looming spectre of another world war. *Night Music*, which is structured episodically in twelve scenes, borrows from the Hollywood romantic comedy; Steve and Fay Tucker, an actress, meet when the trained monkeys he is watching for a film company escape and steal her necklace. He loses his job, and the two of them try to figure out where they fit into a changing world. Guided by a variety of oddball characters including a wise, benevolent detective assigned to help find the monkeys, they travel through New York, even ending up at the World's Fair; they are, of course, happily united at the end of the play. The play is also Steve's journey from bitterness and deprivation to hope, though any hope is tempered by the knowledge that the United States is soon to be drawn into another war. At the beginning of the play, Steve reveals he has been on the outside his whole life, never at home, never given an opportunity to fully realize himself, and his bitterness almost consumes him. Rosenberger, however, serves as a counterpoint to Steve's anger, telling him at one point:

> There are two ways to look, Mr. Takis – to the past or the future. We know a famous case in history where a woman kept looking back and turned to a salt rock. If you keep looking back on a mean narrow past, the same thing can happen to you. You are feeling mad. Why shouldn't you feel mad? In your whole life you never had a pretzel ... But your anger must bear children or it's hopeless.[43]

Rosenberger's metaphorical call to arms is much less militant than those in earlier Odets plays, perhaps because the real threat of armed conflict had turned the focus away from strictly economic issues. But the tone of *Night Music* is closer to *Paradise Lost* and *Awake and Sing!* in its support for those trapped in a consumer culture which they can neither escape nor make fully their own.

Instead of fulfilment, Steve and the 'millions' of others he says he represents are given the *image* of fulfilment. The World's Fair is a self-conscious commodity, presenting a utopian vision of the future but at a cost that many cannot afford – as Steve points out: 'They call this place the world of the future ... The world of tomorrow, don't they? It don't feel any different from than the present an' past, I couldn't get in here without the buck ... I don't respect that world of the future. Here's the Fair – it don't guarantee me meals.'[44] Not only does Steve recognize the irony inherent in that commercialized vision of utopia, the irony is doubled when the Fair is juxtaposed with the threatened destruction of another world war. In one of the most poignant moments in the play, Roy Brown, a homeless man who in an earlier scene had confessed his desire to see the Fair, meets Fay and Steve inside. Roy ruefully tells them that now he's in, he can't find his way out, and when Steve invites him to join them for some ice cream, Roy tells them, 'that don't mix with mustard'.[45] Given Roy's plan to join the army, the reference to mustard gas further underscores the ambivalence that Steve – and Odets – feels about the Fair and all it represents. There is a shadow hanging over the play. Still, when Rosenberger praises the beauty of the Fair, Steve agrees, and the play moves, like *Awake and Sing!*, *Paradise Lost* and *Rocket to the Moon*, towards an ending that is seemingly more hopeful than the events that precede it. As sharp as Odets was in his criticism of American culture and politics of the 1930s, he always returned to its utopian roots, and in doing so captured both the despair and promise of the decade.

6

Lillian Hellman: *The Children's Hour* (1934), *Days to Come* (1936), *The Little Foxes* (1939)

Anne Fletcher

> God forgives those who invent what they need.
> Ben Hubbard, *The Little Foxes*[1]

Born Lillian Florence Hellman in 1905, in New Orleans, the playwright's early years were split between that city, with its concomitant Southern grit and charm, where her family lived in a boarding house operated by her father's sisters – women who greatly influenced the girl – and New York City, where her mother Julia Newhouse Hellman's family resided. The Newhouses were wealthier than the Hellmans, but they held less interest for precocious young Lillian. Hellman's Jewish heritage derived from both sides of her family, yet was drawn upon in her life and for her writing only when it proved efficacious in the moment. A self-described lacklustre student, Hellman attended New York University (much before its heyday; the facilities comprised little more than one floor of a building in Greenwich Village).[2] She never graduated from college, leaving out of boredom, she alleges, after only two years.

Hellman recounted a story that, by luck, at a party, she was discovered by an editor who offered her a job as a manuscript reader with the publishing firm of Boni and Liveright. From the age of nineteen or twenty to twenty-nine in 1934, when her first hit, *The Children's Hour*, premiered, she worked first in New York at the publishing company, taking a brief hiatus from the workforce when she married Arthur Kober, an aspiring young writer (her only husband and lifelong friend), before moving to Hollywood for employment as a reader at MGM Studio for $50 a week.[3] *The Children's Hour* catapulted Hellman to the equivalent of stardom for a playwright. Until her death in 1984, Lillian Hellman accomplished the somewhat auspicious task, especially as a woman, of earning her living as a writer – of plays and screenplays, and later as a memoirist.

Hellman composed eight plays,[4] two of which won the New York Drama Critics' Circle Award: *The Children's Hour* (the award was created, it is said, because the play lost the Pulitzer Prize to Zöe Akin's *The Old Maid*) and *Watch on the Rhine*. She completed four stage adaptations, including one of Jean Anouilh's *The Lark* (1955), and worked on numerous screenplays, including *Dark Angel* (1935), *Dead End* (1937), *The North Star* (1944) and *The Chase* (1966). Hellman's one truly collaborative venture – collaborative in the sense of a process that necessitated the rapid-fire adjustments and rewrites required for the Broadway opening of a musical – was with Leonard Bernstein's *Candide* in 1956. The playwright herself admits that collaboration 'was truly not my nature'.[5] Like another grand dame of American theatre and film, Katharine Hepburn (who it is rumoured declined membership in the Group Theatre in the 1930s), Lillian Hellman, with the exception of accepting criticism from long-time lover and mentor Dashiell Hammett, insisted on working alone. While other playwrights aligned themselves with cooperative ventures in the spirit of the time, like the Group Theatre, the Theatre Union or even the more conservative Theatre Guild, Hellman always wrote solo and always for Broadway.

Early in her career Lillian Hellman emerged as equally infamous for her alleged plagiarism, 'red' politics and prevarication as she was famous for her writing. For all her days, Hellman elided the truth, inventing and reinventing herself, blaming inconsistencies and inaccuracies in her accounts on her poor memory. Of four memoirs (five including a compilation in a single volume, *Three*, published in 1980): *An Unfinished Woman* (1969), *Pentimento* (1973), *Scoundrel Time* (1976) and *Maybe: A Story* (1980), the first two were initially received as factually correct or at least 'true' as far as memory can be accurate. *Scoundrel Time* met with some 'push back' from people who were present during the HUAC days, and *Maybe* is generally considered Hellman's apology, in the original sense of the word, or equivocation in which she defends her view of truth. They all came under fire from multiple angles when allegations surfaced that Julia, the title character in the pivotal story in *Pentimento*, was based on a woman named Muriel Gardiner, who wrote to Hellman pointing out the similarities between her story and Hellman's creation.[6] And then, in a 1979 appearance on *The Dick Cavett Show*, author Mary McCarthy uttered a now famous proclamation about Hellman's veracity: 'Every word she [Lillian Hellman] writes is a lie, including "and" and "the".'[7] With little chance of winning and a *pro bono* attorney in hand, Hellman launched a libel suit against McCarthy. The court case remained unresolved when the playwright died five years later, in 1984, in ignominy.

Lillian Hellman's life was filled with dichotomies. She took on the role of truth-teller and moralist, a word she repeatedly used in describing herself and her writing, yet, to all intents and purposes, she lied, or at least coloured the truth. Dashiell Hammett's daughter, among others, believed that Hellman's rapid shifts in time and place when she regaled her audience with a good story – as demonstrated in the narrative forms of both *Pentimento* and *Maybe* – constituted a strategy for deflecting questions, avoiding or outright altering facts and embellishing her role in the docu-fiction she composed. Curiously, Hellman's anti-Semitic remarks belied the playwright's Jewish heritage, while on occasions she laid claim to her Jewishness with a vengeance. Her view toward women was bifurcated as well: although the creator of strong-willed female characters – 'juicy' roles – strangely, she eschewed feminism.

Hellman appears an unlikely candidate to represent American dramatic literature of the 1930s, generally exemplified by dramas of 'attack' or theatre as a 'weapon'.[8] Across the decade, a critical debate ensued over art versus politics, manifesting in articles and production reviews in the leftist (often communist) and mainstream press alike, a rehash of the age-old argument over the nature and purpose of the theatre, but with higher political (and often personal) stakes. Although less affected by this controversy than more politically engaged playwrights, Hellman is implicated in the deliberations, as what we would call today a social dramatist – one commenting on what critic Timothy J. Wiles dubs the 'inertia and complacency indulged by the neurotic rich'.[9]

In fact, the decade that begins with the stock market crash, is dominated by the Great Depression and culminates with impending war boasts a wide variety of drama in form, style and subject matter. Wide-ranging works of the period from an array of perspectives – agit-prop to drawing room – reached a variety of audiences, from union hall to Broadway. Nevertheless, one has to delve deeply into a Hellman script, apart from *Days to Come* (her only 'strike play'), to find material traces of the 1930s. On the surface at least, it appears that Hellman missed the Great Depression altogether, that the 1930s were, for her, somebody else's 'fervent years'.[10] Certainly, with the sudden success of *The Children's Hour* (1934) and her subsequent $2,500 a week salary at Samuel Goldwyn Productions,[11] she spent most of the 1930s as a very wealthy young woman. *The Little Foxes* (1939) contributed to Hellman's wealth before the outset of the Second World War, as did the 1943 film adaptation starring Bette Davis. Blacklisting, however, would lower her income considerably.[12]

Her political engagement – anti-fascist in nature; moral, humanistic, not overtly influenced by economics or politics, partisan or other – came late in the 1930s. Like many of the literati of her day, Lillian Hellman appears to have been politically confused – a practising humanist, a believer in social justice, a civil rights activist, she failed to fully comprehend the subtleties and complexities of ideologies of the time and ignored the bald cruelty of a changing Russia under Stalin.[13] For a time she was a communist. Nevertheless, *The Children's Hour*, *The Little Foxes*, and even *Days to Come* to a lesser degree, almost completely disregard the financial despondency that followed the Crash and reflect no particular political point of view.

Hellman's social consciousness, if not her palpable politics, like that of many in the 1930s, follows the build-up to and the denouement of the Popular Front. During her brief time in the Communist Party, which she later claimed as being from 1938 to 1940,[14] the playwright worked for or lent her name to many leftist social causes, her cause célèbre always the Spanish Civil War. Her investment in *The Spanish Earth* – a documentary film about the

Republican Loyalist side in the dispute, with a narration penned by Ernest Hemingway – her travel to Spain and her writing about it are illustrative of her involvement.[15] However, Hellman sustained her support of Russia as a Spanish Loyalist ally despite Stalin's annihilation of his own people, fuelling the long-standing and negative notion of her as stalwart Stalinist. Regardless of the playwright's political affiliation, the characters in her plays of 1930s are alternatively unaware of economics and politics or unaffected by them.

Typically, in retrospect, Hellman ascribes romance (and morality) to the decade and, by implication, as was her habit, she situates herself in the midst of the action, at times as its heroine. Hellman biographer Alice Kessler-Harris refers to Hellman's practice of placing herself at the centre as 'self-dramatizing'.[16] The playwright reminisced in a 1965 interview for *The Paris Review*, the implication, of course, being that the playwright stood by her beliefs:

> There were always X number of clowns, X number of simple-minded fools, X number of fashionables who just went along with what was being said and done, but there were also remarkable people, people of belief, people willing to live by their beliefs.[17]

Lillian Hellman would take umbrage at the thought that she might be included in a volume like this because of her gender, and, surely, that has been the rationale behind her representation elsewhere in the past. The playwright's alleged proto-feminism, when brought to her attention decades later, vexed her greatly. Hellman would want to be represented for her work itself, not as simply a woman playwright. From the outset of her career, she combated critics and reviewers who assessed her work with even a nod to her gender: 'I am a *playwright*. You wouldn't refer to Eugene O'Neill as one of America's foremost *male* playwrights.'[18] To justify her inclusion in this chapter, then, requires that we examine not only the subject matter, thematic concerns and structure of Hellman's plays, but that we reflect upon her tone and style as indicative of the 1930s – perhaps, even as bound by the time. Dramaturgical similarities exist between her Depression and Second World War plays, extending to Hellman's very last piece, *Toys in the Attic* (1960) – similarities that point to the playwright as, perhaps, stuck in a particular era. After *Toys in the Attic* met with a mediocre response, the playwright abandoned writing for the stage and, after a period of retreat and reassessment (and critical neglect), she refashioned herself as an award-winning memoirist.[19]

Although we readily recall the poverty and political turmoil of Depression-era America, it would be as inequitable to exclude the period's dramas depicting 'haves' and speak only of the 'have nots' as it would be to omit great movie musicals, like *42nd Street* or *Top Hat*, in a discussion of the films of the decade. Lillian Hellman's plays of the era are populated by wealthy characters who employ servants; she sets several of her plays in the South, and the servants are often black. The playwright proclaimed her intention to have been 'to write about nice, well-born people ... with good intentions', additionally stating, 'I've never been interested in political messages ...'.[20]

Always contradictory and ever an enigma, Hellman may well have skilfully separated her personal views on politics from her profession; the plays themselves indicate that this is the case. Her sparing use of topical allusions may be a factor in the survival of her work across the decades. On the one hand, the scarcity of specific references may give the scripts a longer shelf life, leaving the texts open for [re]production. On the other hand, in the context of the 1930s, this non-specificity left the playwright open to the same kind of criticism from the radical left that plagued John Howard Lawson, a fellow organizer of the Screen Writers Guild. Leftist critics deemed Lawson's Marxist ideology too tame, and mainstream critics the opposite, finding them 'red'. Ironically, criticism aimed at Hellman's lack of social conscience in her plays of the decade came from Lawson's pen.

It was Hellman's politics, though – as indeterminate or illusive as they may have been – that marred her career, for, when the House Un-American Activities Committee loomed large, she was blacklisted and lost potentially lucrative screenwriting work. Across, the 1940s, then, Hellman relied mostly on her playwriting for income – no real hardship, however – as she had by now amassed quite a good deal of money. The playwright's actions, like those of many fellow travellers in the 1930s, had an impact on her in the 1950s and across the Cold War years. No doubt, as she worked on her revival of *The Children's Hour* in 1952, while not to the extent of Arthur Miller with *The Crucible* and certainly not that of Bertolt Brecht, Hellman compared the dramatic action of the play to her HUAC experience. Certainly it manifested in her adaptation of Jean Anouilh's *The Lark* and in her work on the libretto for *Candide*.[21]

The Children's Hour

> Look: everybody lies all the time. Sometimes they have to, sometimes they don't.
>
> Joe Cardin, *The Children's Hour*, 52

Acclaim came early to the young playwright: her first play, *The Children's Hour*, opened on 20 November 1934 and ran for 691 performances. Its lesbianism subject matter, although the word is never uttered in the text, created a stir, and while Mayor LaGuardia made no move to block the New York production, the play was banned in Boston and Chicago. It was not easy to get the production off the ground as, due to the play's controversial topic, the producers faced difficulty in casting. The show therefore opened with a cast of relative 'unknowns'.

The playwright contributed her own screenplay for *These Three*, the 1936 film version of the story, directed by William Wyler. In this version, to avoid censorship, all hints at lesbianism were expunged, and the plot focused on a heterosexual love triangle. Hellman remounted a slightly altered incarnation of the play on Broadway in 1952,[22] directing it herself. A notable film version in 1961 starred Audrey Hepburn and Shirley MacLaine.

Based on a true story that appeared in a book entitled *Bad Companions* by William Roughead, 'Closed Doors, or the Great Drumsheugh Case', *The Children's Hour* dramatizes the irreversible effects of a lie, the penultimate damage a rumour can cause. Ironically, the play takes its title from Henry Wadsworth Longfellow's poem of the same name that rather sweetly evokes the time between afternoon and evening. The plot centres on two schoolmistresses, Karen Wright and Martha Dobie, and the accusation of lesbianism levelled at them by a troublesome student named Mary Tilford. Supporting characters include Dr Joseph Cardin, Karen's fiancé; Lily Mortar, a has-been actress, aunt to Martha; and Amelia Tilford, the child's grandmother. The cast is rounded out by an assortment of little girls; Agatha, Mrs Tilford's maid; and a grocery boy.

The girl, Mary – bully of the boarding school – blackmails another student, Rosalie, into corroborating her story of suspicious sounds emanating from one of the teacher's rooms that point to a lesbian alliance between the two women. When the grandmother broadcasts this innuendo to the parents of the other students, the boarding school is evacuated before the teachers have even been informed why. The young women lose their libel suit against Mrs Tilford and retreat to their boarding school home, ostracized by everyone in the small New England community besides a creepy grocery boy who makes daily deliveries. Joe admits he doubts Karen, and their engagement is broken; Martha, driven to an emotional brink, confesses that she loves Karen 'that way' and then walks offstage to kill herself. In the play's final scene, Mrs Tilford recants, apologizing to Karen.

The Children's Hour is seminal in a discussion of the playwright, in its own right as a groundbreaking stage depiction of a taboo subject and as riveting drama, and in Hellman's *oeuvre*, because the play set the stage so to speak for all her works to come. Hellman critic/biographer Katherine Lederer asserts that the play has been accorded 'undue weight' and that all of the playwright's subsequent work 'has been forced to fit the image created by *The Children's Hour*'.[23] Indeed, Hellman's later plays suffer from some of the same defects and exhibit some of the same strengths as her first.

Hellman's talent lay in her storytelling and the pace at which she propelled the play's action. Like a meticulous mystery writer in her timing of 'reveals', Hellman skilfully puts forth and alternately withholds information. One of the play's enduring characteristics is her adroit deployment of interrupted action, leaving the audience/reader musing about what might have been – if only Rosalie had stood up to Mary; if only Karen or Martha had answered the telephone when Mrs Tilford called. While by today's standards (or audience attention span) some scenes drag and might warrant cutting in production, the plot unfolds apace, culminating in the final Act Two scene at Mrs Tilford's home, with all the principals onstage as Mary is questioned. The play climaxes, and the curtain falls with Rosalie's lines, 'Yes. Yes. I did see it. I told Mary. What Mary said was right. I said it, I said it – .'[24]

As Lederer notes, 'the "knee-jerk" critical stereotypes ever after associated with her [Hellman's] work emerged in critical reception of *The Children's Hour*'.[25] The most glaring of these critical stereotypes – and an accurate observation of Hellman's writing – regards the playwright's deployment of 'Melodrama' and elements of the 'Well-Made Play'.

Maybe too well-made

Hellman's works, particularly those of the 1930s, are almost always referred to by critics as Well-Made Plays and as Melodramas. Often Henrik Ibsen, considered by many the 'father' of modern drama, is cited as an influence on her writing. Some comment on Hellman's fondness for Anton Chekhov (she edited his letters in 1955), which at face value seems contradictory to her appropriation of Ibsen-like structure in her works. Her use of multiple protagonists and her thematic concern with by-gone days nod to Chekhov as progenitor. A few, with regard to novelesque aspects of her writing, note a Jamesian quality in her plays. In particular, Thomas P. Adler recognizes Hellman's drawing-room settings, like James's, 'as sites where old-world values meet new, where niavete [sic] and innocence are challenged by experience and corruption, and where ... self-determination is pursued through moral (or immoral) choices'.[26]

The moniker 'Well-Made Play' (*pièce bien faite*) is glaringly (mis)used as a pejorative in contemporary critical parlance, when, in fact, elements of the Well-Made Play, carefully deployed, create tension and suspense and accelerate the running time of a script that might otherwise languish in production. Consider August Wilson's climactic scene at the end of Act One in *The Piano Lesson* when Maretha screams, having seen Sutter's ghost, a moment that leaves audience/reader eager to learn what is to come – a strong curtain.

Critics repeatedly conflate the Well-Made Play with Melodrama, viewed as an equally negative genre today. Historically, Melodrama flourished even before the Well-Made Plays of Eugène Scribe and Victorien Sardou. Playwrights like Henrik Ibsen, most notably, infused the Well-Made Play with social conscience, retaining specific structural elements like the *clou* (the small object upon which the play's action hinges)[27] and, at the same time, maintained the 'teeter-totter' technique or 'punch and counter punch' of Melodrama, which amounts to alternate scorings of points for the 'good guy' versus the 'bad', and the strong curtain. Perhaps it is Ibsen to whom we owe the confusion between the Well-Made Play and Melodrama. Both genre classifications are used by critics, disparagingly, about Lillian Hellman's corpus of plays.

The Well-Made Play, of course, follows a linear structure, with causal action that progresses in chronological order. As with any play structured according to Gustav Freytag's pyramid or triangle, it follows the typical order of Exposition, Rising Action, Conflicts, Complications, Mini-Climaxes/Crisis, Climax, Falling Action and Denouement. Additionally, the overall action of the Well-Made Play is replicated in the structure of each act. In a Well-Made Play, the major climax is in the middle – for a three-act play it falls at the end of the second act; for a five-act play, at the end of Act Three. The plot is based on a secret known to the audience and withheld from some characters, revealed to them in a climactic scene. The play closes with a *scène à faire* or obligatory scene that characteristically hinges on the disclosure of secrets – the scene necessary to provide resolution.

Mrs Tilford's visit to Karen, in which the elderly woman explains that she knows Mary has lied about Karen and Martha's alleged homosexuality, apologizes and offers restitution, constitutes the *scène à faire* in *The Children's Hour*, and the efficacy of that scene has been debated by critics, beginning with Brooks Atkinson's evaluation of the play's premiere:

> In the last ten or fifteen minutes of the final act she [Hellman] tries desperately to discover a mettlesome conclusion ... Please, Miss Hellman, conclude the play before the pistol shot and before the long arm of coincidence starts wabbling in its socket.[28]

Hellman responded in her introduction to the published version of the play:

> The play probably should have ended with Martha's suicide: the last scene is tense and over-burdened. I knew this at the time, but I could not help myself. I am a moral writer, often too moral a writer, and I cannot avoid, it seems, that last summing-up.[29]

The playwright reconsidered the ending prior to her 1952 revival and, once again, she could not bring herself to change it.

At the conclusion of *The Little Foxes*, Alexandra expresses her notion that she would rather 'be fighting ... some place where people don't just stand around and watch'.[30] As with Nora's door slamming in Ibsen's *A Doll House*, she leaves us wondering what will become of Alexandra after the curtain falls. When later asked whether the kind of plays she wrote, namely the Well-Made Play, would survive, Hellman commented that 'survival won't have anything to do with well made or not well made, or words like "melodrama." I don't like labels and isms. They are for people who raise or lower skirts because that's the thing you do for this year.'[31] Vestiges of the Well-Made Play (and of Melodrama), of course, manifest in half-hour television shows, films and even in some successful plays of the twenty-first century. Whether the amalgamation of characteristics of these forms as they appear in Hellman's work continues to enthral contemporary audiences is questionable.

In its construction, complete with the bracelet stolen by Rosalie as its *clou*, *The Children's Hour* is almost the perfect Well-Made Play – almost. A Well-Made Play in the manner of Ibsen, which Lederer and others claim *The Children's Hour* to be, requires detailed plot preparation.[32] On at least one count, in this regard, Lillian Hellman utterly fails to offer adequate exposition, and that has to do with the gun: it receives no mention and makes its one and only appearance as an offstage sound effect when Martha shoots herself.

Each published version of the text reveals multiple minor inconsistencies, particularly in the final scene of the third act. Hellman handles preparation for the *scène à faire* a little differently in each, but in neither does she completely succeed. In the 1934 edition, Agatha, the maid, enters before Mrs Tilford (Agatha is omitted from this scene in the 1981 acting edition), telling Karen that she (Agatha) has been 'phoning and phoning' 'all the time'.[33] In the other two versions used for reference here, it is Mrs Tilford who telephoned. Regardless, the mention of offstage telephone calls is undoubtedly included to emphasize Mrs Tilford's urgent desire to reach the young women, but, in all versions of the play, it seems self-conscious, carelessly inserted, especially since an onstage telephone figured so prominently earlier in the play's action. In the acting edition, the grocery boy states that there is a car outside that has been there every time he has come up the road, and Mrs Mortar identifies Mrs Tilford as the person in the car. Upon her entrance, Mrs Tilford explains, 'I've been outside all day ... I've been to the door ... I've been phoning you ... I've been waiting for you to come out.'[34] In this version, she claims to have been telephoning, apparently at the same time that she has been sitting outside, as both the grocery boy and Mrs Mortar informed the audience/reader of the car. Earlier in the play, the children leave for class while the boarding school's only apparent instructors – Karen, Martha and Mrs Mortar – remain onstage. These instances may appear inconsequential, but they are indicative of imperfections in the crafting of this Well-Made Play.

Other blemishes in the play are more illustrative of stage conventions of the time(s) rather than of inconsistencies in playwriting. *The Children's Hour* was written at a time of literal 'strong curtains' whereby the house curtain was rung in to indicate passage of time, or to allow for complete scene changes, and productions typically included two intermissions, making for a rather long theatre-going experience. Act One of *The Children's Hour* occurs at the boarding school; Act Two takes place in Mrs Tilford's living room; and in Act Three, the action returns to the Wright–Dobie school. A trickier shift in time, although not in space, transpires between Act Two, Scene One and Scene Two: Mary has exited, Mrs Tilford has placed her telephone calls to the other parents and guardians, and Mary is then immediately discovered onstage, lounging. Ringing in the curtain between these two scenes, as was customary in the past, breaks the action and draws today's audience out of the play. Additionally, in *The Children's Hour*, and later in *Watch on the Rhine*,[35] Hellman leaves the stage empty, a felony on the contemporary stage. The playwright's stage directions make this unpeopled stage deliberate in the latter piece, but in *The Children's Hour*, occurring when it does, directly after the gun shot and before Mrs Mortar or Karen's entrance, the moment is puzzling.

Despite its premiere at the height of the Depression, *The Children's Hour* bears little evidence of the period. The teachers are working women, and characters comment on how they have scrimped and saved in getting the school on its feet, but they now have ample money to send Mrs Mortar off to London. Joe comments on his medical school loans as being the reason for his protracted engagement to Karen. One of the little girls, wrangled out of her money by Mary, confesses that she has very little. Apart from these brief allusions to finance, the play depicts the upper crust existence and values of Mrs Tilford, the small New England town's dowager, and the power of her word. She employs the aforementioned maid and a chauffeur who remains offstage. Hellman's description of Mrs

Tilford's home reflects 'old money'. John Howard Lawson criticizes the playwright for her 'inability to dramatize the social roots of the action', and finds this lack of a 'solid social framework' the reason for the play's 'abstract and undynamic'[36] nature.

The Children's Hour remains relevant in terms of its messages about suspicion, mendacity, innuendo, gossip and intolerance. However, Hellman's handling of lesbianism remains even more problematic today. Characters' repeated use of the word *unnatural* in reference to Karen and Martha, use of the term *wrong*, Martha's expression of guilt and her use of the phrase *feeling dirty*[37] in her confession scene, and Karen's use of the word *sin*[38] leave the playwright's attitude toward same-sex relationships ambiguous at best.

In her 1996 essay 'The Lesbian Rule: Lillian Hellman and the Measures of Realism' in *Modern Drama*, Anne Fleche presents a case for Hellman's rhetoric of absence, avoidance, negation and silence in the play, but her expert analysis, employing contemporary critical lenses, in view of Hellman's attitude toward feminism, would likely have met with the playwright's disapproval. Nevertheless, criticism like Fleche's, Sally Shedd's discussion of visibility and the marked in 'There is No Keyhole on My Door', Tanfer Tunc's examination of Mary in light of childhood anxiety, and Mary Titus's 'Murdering the Lesbian …' are invaluable in approaching contemporary mountings of the play.

Days to Come

All the things we know were there to know a long time ago.
Andrew Rodman, *Days to Come*[39]

Days to Come, Lillian Hellman's second play, was an unmitigated 'flop'. Her only attempt at labour drama ran for only seven performances. The playwright admitted defeat and, perhaps uncharacteristically, assumed some responsibility for the production's failure: '*Days to Come* was botched. The whole production was botched, including my botching …'.[40]

Its plot concerns a brush manufacturer, Andrew Rodman, who naively places trust in union busters and scabs because his workers' strike, his poor business acumen and his desire to support his wife in the style to which she is accustomed have coalesced, presently pointing toward financial ruin. Deception and self-delusion characterize the Rodman family: Julie Rodman, Andrew's wife, is having an affair with his best friend; Rodman's 'sensitive' sister keeps the affair secret until the play's end; and Hannah, the family maid, has had the 'goods' on these people for decades. Leo Whalen, a pragmatic union organizer, arrives in the Ohio factory town and Julie fantasizes about how he might 'show her the way'.[41] Despite Whalen's admonition that the workers not succumb to taunts from the scabs, a fight ensues in which Firth's (Rodman's top man in shop) daughter is killed. In her 1978 study of Hellman, Doris V. Falk offers an even more unflattering plot summary of the play than is presented here, culminating with the statement that 'All these characters, good and bad, are ineffectual; and their efforts, along with the plot, just peter out.'[42]

John Howard Lawson's March 1937 *New Theatre and Film* article compares *Days to Come* with *The Children's Hour* in terms of both structure and subject matter. He finds the two 'almost identical' in structure.[43] *The Children's Hour* follows two separate lines of action: one concerns the Karen–Martha–Joe relationship, the other Mary's scheming.[44] The two strains meet in the climactic scene at the end of Act Two, but, in Lawson's words, 'The third act fizzles out in futile despair.'[45] Lawson identifies the dual pattern in *Days to Come* as comprised of the story of Julie Rodman versus that of the strike breakers. Again, he finds that they converge at a single point, but the play's action is 'broken sharply by the planting of the body of the murdered gangster', thus (as in *The Children's Hour*), leading to a 'desultory and retrospective' final act.[46]

The script bears the potential for exhibiting class against class warfare and faith in the future that characterized Marxist dramas of the decade, but it falls short of succeeding for a number of reasons, most importantly because the playwright was overly ambitious in terms of both plot and theme. As Hellman put it, 'I wanted to say too much.'[47] She continued:

> I knew a woman like Cora and I hated her, and *that* hate had to get into the play; I knew a woman like Julie, I pitied her, and *that* pity had to go into the play; I had been raised with the Ellicotts

of the world, and what I felt about them had to go into the play, too; I knew Leo Whalen ...[48]

As a result of this overreaching, Hellman fails to flesh out either the story of the Rodmans and their delusions or the workers' tale. In *American Drama 1900–1940*, Christopher Bigsby places Andrew Rodman's 'moral imagination' at the centre of the play, explicating how the character's fundamental misunderstanding of the machinations of socio-economics and his belief that he could continue to 'play the game of wealth', bestowing benevolence upon his workers, blinded him. Bigsby aptly asserts that the major problem with *Days to Come* stems from the idea that 'this moral tale'[49] is buried within the confines of the strike play form. All of the strike action transpires offstage, outside the purview of the play's staged action, and apart from Firth, no workers are directly introduced. A thin subplot concerning the maid, Hannah, smuggling food for them from the Rodmans' kitchen indicates class unity, but in her depiction of the effects of the Depression or class struggle, Hellman never rises to the height of Clifford Odets's combination of poetry and agit-prop, or even to the level of social realism exhibited by lesser-known Theatre Union playwrights. *Days to Come*, her strike play, maintains no martyr and omits the hope for a better day that is the hallmark of Marxist writing of the era. The play limps to its conclusion, with Cora, the fragile and selfish sister, dining on a robust breakfast as truths about the other characters are revealed in rapid-fire succession. Andrew Rodman resigns himself to both his wife and friend's philandering and the potential for future worker unrest.

The playwright never settles on a coherent form or message, only hinting at social justice and missing the mark in her depiction of family feuds, frailties and delusions in the manner Tennessee Williams or Arthur Miller would offer in the next decade. Although Hellman claimed that *Days to Come* was centred on the family, with the strike and social conflicts purely as background,[50] she muddied the family drama with the social issues. Consequently, her one attempt to infuse a play with some, albeit not much, topicality failed as decidedly with the mainstream audience as with those on the left. In 'Lillian Hellman's Political Theater: The Thirties and Beyond', Timothy J. Wiles attempts to build a case for the playwright as Marxist, but, just as we see with Hellman's creation of female characters and feminism, her use of material and economic conditions is not enough to establish Marxism as the ideological framework for her plays.

Strangely, John Howard Lawson, who spent the early to middle part of the decade facing critical abuse from both left and right, gives Hellman somewhat of a 'pass' regarding her inchoate form, finding the play an improvement on *The Children's Hour* and identifying the flaws in *Days to Come* as occurring 'due to the intensity of the author's growth' as a socially conscious playwright.[51] Yet in essence he found her to be 'beyond her present ability to organize and unify her material',[52] concluding that, 'One cannot interpret a living social process without a living social philosophy.'[53] Hellman would never return to the drama of the working class. Her specialty would remain creating commentaries on the lives of the rich and often bored, and always with realism as her dramatic form of choice.

The Little Foxes

> Take us the foxes, the little foxes, that spoil the vines; for our vines have tender grapes.
> Song of Solomon 2.15, used as the epigram to
> *The Little Foxes*

> There are people who eat the earth and eat all the people on it like in the Bible with the locusts. Then there are people who stand around and watch them eat it. Sometimes I think it ain't right to stand and watch them do it.
> Addie, *The Little Foxes*[54]

Lillian Hellman is lauded for her knack of dealing with evil forces incarnate in her characters. While the playwright was somewhat surprised at the almost universal reaction to Mary Tilford in *The Children's Hour* as innately evil, as what would become known later as a 'bad seed' type, she purposefully presented the Hubbards (Regina, Ben and Oscar) in *The Little Foxes* (1939) as cunning, malicious and self-serving. No sibling bond curbs their respective conniving, as each attempts to out-scheme the other, all in the name of money.

The play is set at the turn of the twentieth century, as the Industrial Revolution takes hold in the deep, agricultural South. While critics agree that the play addresses the changing South, sometimes the nature of that focus is misconstrued as referring to the broken and conquered post-Civil War plantation aristocracy. In the play, we learn that Birdie Hubbard (née Bagtry) grew up amidst plantation wealth and longingly looks back to that genteel existence. Conversely, the Hubbards, around whom the action revolves, grew up in another social stratum, hardly 'Old South' – one from which, despite their airs, they will never escape. As evidenced in Hellman's 1946 prequel, *Another Part of the Forest*, their father acquired his money in a most distasteful way, swindling Confederates, acting as turncoat and running with the Ku Klux Klan, barely escaping tar and feathers. The Hubbard boys, particularly Ben, in *The Little Foxes* have likewise increased their fortune riding on the backs of others, and through Oscar's marriage to Birdie. They point to the future, as Ben proclaims, 'The century's turning, the world is open. Open for people like you and me ... There are hundreds of Hubbards ... and they will own the country someday.'[55] In some respects, then, in theme (as requiem to the past and harbinger of the future) while not in structure, the play is somewhat Chekhovian. Although many articulate the message of *The Little Foxes* as anti-capitalistic, and Hellman's intention to critique the socio-economic transition underway, her depiction of the family's servants undermines that critique, incriminating both the playwright and her characters as part of the history of slavery.

The Hubbard siblings desire a piece of the manufacturing action, and the brothers have arranged a deal with a Chicago businessman. As Ben espouses, they intend to 'bring the machine to the cotton and not the cotton to the machine'.[56] Regina, their sister, has a long-standing resentment toward her brothers because, as the female child, she failed to inherit her fair share of the family fortune. This plot point becomes crucial to the play's denouement in which she seeks revenge.

While *The Little Foxes* follows an intriguing traditional well-made[57] linear progression – complications arising and building to one crisis after another as information unfolds – it is the movement of the characters 'like chessman',[58] as they attempt to outmanipulate and double-cross one another, that is most interesting to follow. Hellman has carefully crafted a triangular arrangement in which two siblings 'gang up' on the third, except when all are threatened and unite against an outsider.

Hellman's characters are precisely drawn, especially that of Regina, a role that has remained a star turn since the play premiered with Tallulah Bankhead. Lederer attributes Hellman's creation of fleshed out characters, clearly differentiated one from another, to the playwright's developed deployment of rhythm and individual idiom (*The Children's Hour*, for example, is less successful in creation of character – some of the play's set speeches could be uttered by almost any character in the play), praising the dialogue in Hellman's later plays: 'At its best, Hellman's dialogue is poetry of the theatre, a quality not often appreciated in her work.'[59] At times the playwright's prose does soar, but by contemporary standards (as one might say of even Tennessee Williams), her syntax can be cumbersome, challenging actors in terms of line delivery.

The cast includes, in addition to the Hubbard siblings, Horace Giddens, Regina's bank-owner husband who, at curtain rise, is in a Baltimore hospital being treated for heart disease; Alexandra ('Zan'), their daughter; Birdie, Oscar's sensitive, alcoholic wife, who is very close to Zan; Leo, Oscar and Birdie's crass and callous – in fact, cruel – son, a natural deceiver; Mr Marshall, the northern businessman with whom the brothers are cutting their deal; and two wise long-time servants, Addie, who has always cared for Zan, and Cal, the house man who serves as both butler and messenger. Another third servant is alluded to but remains offstage.

Ben and Oscar have secured their share of the funds necessary to join Marshall in business; Regina's share will assure that the family maintains 51 per cent of the company. All of them have written to Horace (Regina's only source for the money), and he has failed to respond. The siblings taunt each other and jostle for control of the conversation and of the family wealth. Regina proclaims that perhaps her husband is holding out for a bigger share. Then she and Ben agree that perhaps money should be taken from Oscar's share to 'pay off' Horace. Oscar is appeased when he persuades Regina to consider marrying off her daughter to Leo, his son, her cousin. Alexandra is sent to Baltimore to fetch Horace. Meanwhile – just in case Horace refuses to contribute to the investment – at Leo's suggestion, the brothers plot to steal an $88,000 Union Pacific bond from Horace's safe deposit box. When Horace, a dying man, returns, he discovers the theft and rather than holding it over the brothers' heads as his wife prefers, he concocts a plan whereby he will say nothing and simply leave the bond to Regina in his will, thus aborting his wife's eager scheme to gain control of the Hubbard fortune. However, Horace does not live to execute his plan, as when he grasps for his medicine bottle, it falls, and Regina deliberately stands by as he suffers a fatal heart attack.

Stylistically and in tone, once again, Hellman's execution fails to match her stated intentions. In the case of *The Little Foxes*, perhaps her most autobiographical play,[60] she says, 'I had meant to half-mock my own youthful high-class innocence in Alexandra ... I had meant people to smile at, and to sympathize with, the sad, weak Birdie, certainly I had not meant them to cry.'[61] Again, the playwright emerged dismayed by audience reactions, for example to Birdie, who reads and plays as a precursor to the Blanche Dubois type perfected later by Tennessee Williams. As for the other characters, Hellman wished for audience members to identify with them to a certain extent, although not fully. Audiences almost unilaterally judged the Hubbards as evil.

Hellman also hoped to infuse the play with both irony and humour. Irony is apparent early in the play when Ben describes the Hubbards and Giddens as 'close knit', and Mr Marshall responds, 'That is very pleasant. Keeping your family together to share each other's lives',[62] but is not until later that the reader/audience learns there is no love lost among members of this family, who are merely putting on a show for their guest. As for comedy, Hellman believed it would surface in the dialogue where characters interpret for each other, and in some of the overlapping passages that drive Ben to exclaim, 'Four conversations are three too many.'[63] As with the irony, although the playwright saw the characters in *The Little Foxes* as 'funny in their role-playing ... funny but dangerous',[64] the comedy falls flat. The play is generally categorized as melodrama.

All of this said, *The Little Foxes* is meritorious for a number of reasons, and it continues in production every year at regional theatres across the country.[65] Once again, as with *The Children's Hour*, Hellman skilfully spins her tale, leading the reader/audience in one direction, then offering surprising twists and turns. Particularly complex is the action following Horace's discovery of the theft, when he cleverly sends the servant Cal to the bank with instructions to find the bank manager and convey the message that his safe deposit box arrived safely (a fact the manager already knows as he delivered it himself). In this way, much as Hamlet observes Claudius at the play-within-a-play – only in this case through offstage revelation narrated by a messenger – Horace learns of Leo's telling reactions. Timing is crucial to the play's final scenes as Regina must have stage time alone with Horace to assure he suffers his fatal attack. Consequently, Addie must be working in another room, Cal and Alexandra be elsewhere, and the brothers must arrive after Horace has been helped upstairs. The action drives to its conclusion where Regina ultimately takes revenge and wins out over her brothers, an action she determined to accomplish many years previously, as we learn from *Another Part of the Forest*. Shortly after this, Alexandra confronts her mother, and, with the play's final line we are left pondering Regina's future – surely not the debut on the Chicago social register that she imagined for herself.

Set as it is at the turn of the century, *The Little Foxes* has little to say about 1939 America. The play articulates an almost always apropos anti-capitalist message, but in no way does it depict the Depression or foreshadow the Second World War. It constitutes, nevertheless, in construction and in character development, one of Lillian Hellman's finest dramas. The play also, as expressed by Addie's line in the above epigram, fully establishes a frequent Hellman concern in both life and art: passivity.

In championing anti-fascism, and in taking a stand before HUAC, Hellman took personal identifiable action. She resented those who stood by idly and, on more than one occasion, espoused moral rectitude to be a focal point in her plays. In *The Children's Hour*, Lily Mortar's refusal to return as witness on the teachers' behalf constitutes both passivity and physical absence. John Howard Lawson identifies Leo Whalen in *Days to Come* as playing 'no dynamic role' because he urges the workers not to strike and the critic deduces that 'Whalen is *more passive* ... than any of the other characters.'[66] *Days to Come* is peopled with passive personalities, self-deluded individuals who allow life to happen to them: Andrew in his belief that he can find harmony with the workers; Ellicott in his continued affair with Julie, a relationship that is going nowhere; and Julie as she aimlessly meanders from man to man looking for fulfilment, but bearing no responsibility to that end.

The plays today

May I drive tonight, Uncle Ben, please? ... Leo always –
Alexandra Giddens, *The Little Foxes*[67]

Early in *The Little Foxes*, when she and her cousin set off to escort Mr Marshall to the train, Zan wants to drive the horses, an act of which she is deprived.[68] Upon her return she confides to Birdie that, once again, Leo beat the horses.[69] The situation of Alexandra, Leo and the horses can be taken as a metaphor for thematic concerns across Lillian Hellman's corpus of plays and might even reflect some of the playwright's desires and fears about life itself – notions of gender roles, silencing and marginalization.

Critics seldom if ever address Hellman's anomalous depiction of female characters, but the playwright herself comments extensively on her attitudes towards women and second-wave feminism in interviews and memoirs. From *The Children's Hour* across her career, Hellman continued to draw female characters, ranging across a spectrum from delicate or docile to domineering and downright dastardly, more often than not falling on one extreme or the other.

The playwright's overall characterization of women, 'women's work' and the female domain is equally troublesome, and dichotomous as well. In the opening scene of *The Children's Hour*, for example, Mrs Mortar encourages the young women to develop 'tricks'[70] and, in the acting edition, speaks of what 'man' desires of 'woman'.[71] Hellman, of course, may have intended, in this play, to contrast the negative example of Mrs Mortar with the behaviour of the girls' teachers. Julie Rodman in *Days to Come* appears as a vestigial 'true woman', subject to the 'cult of domesticity' – a woman who has no sense of self and seeks identity or self-actualization through others. Christopher Bigsby pinpoints Andrew Rodman's self-centred sister, Cora, as a 'reprise' of Mrs Mortar from *The Children's Hour* and as a potential precursor to Regina in *The Little Foxes*.[72] In the same play, more fragile than Cora in *Days to Come* and, unlike Cora, not at all narcissistic, the delicate Birdie Hubbard spends most of her hours under the effects of alcohol, reminiscing. Her drinking fails to obscure the sad truths of her existence, and she expresses her hope that Alexandra, with whom she is often compared and whom she loves, not follow her path. Hellman was surprised by audience reception of Zan: many viewed her position at the play's conclusion as powerful, but that was not the playwright's plan. In fact, Hellman concludes not one of her original plays with a female character in a totally triumphant position.[73] The playwright troubles female success, even when a character is identifiably the play's protagonist, like Regina. Hellman undermines the women's happiness and sometimes subverts expectations at the last second, as with Alexandra in *The Little Foxes* asking Regina, 'Are you afraid, Mama?'[74]

For detractors of realism – those who find its form and structure imitative of canonical male playwrights – Lillian Hellman's works seem retrograde. But, as Judith Barlow points out in her chapter 'Feminism, Realism, and Lillian Hellman', in *The Little Foxes*, the playwright interrogates male supremacy. Although from the outset of the play until she is widowed Regina has no control over personal wealth, she actively participates in financial planning – and plotting. Barlow comments on Hellman's insertion of economic discussions (inherently male at the time) into the domestic sphere (the home), subverting normative views of the female domain. The play's prequel, produced seven years later, operates similarly. In *Another Part of the Forest*, set in 1880, Lavinia Hubbard, emotionally disturbed wife of the Hubbard patriarch, Marcus, and mother to Ben, Regina and Oscar, functions as catalyst for Marcus's demise and the revelation of his sordid past to the children. The playwright paints a portrait of a stereotypically fragile Southern woman while, at the same time, skilfully allowing that allegedly weak character to assume a pivotal place in the play's plot.

Interestingly, and related to domesticity, throughout her *oeuvre* Hellman includes gendered imagery. For example, in *The Little Foxes*, Regina uses a confection to express her surprise, and perhaps even pride, at Alexandra's mettle: 'Well, you have spirit after all. I used to think you were all sugar water.'[75] In *Watch on the Rhine*, Fanny, the family matriarch, when facing what will be 'a hard day',[76] determines that she and her son have been 'shaken out of the magnolias' and concludes, 'I'm not put together with flour paste',[77] an allusion to both cooking and holding power.

Thomas Adler describes Hellman's feminism as 'narrow' and her notion of power for women as 'purely economic' and achieved solely through 'economic independence',[78] a weak display of liberal feminism. In her words, often repeated by the playwright (Hellman's habit was to cite herself), 'I don't think it's of any great moment who carries out the garbage. I think it is important that people can be economically equal.'[79] Hellman was fearful of economic dependence and, although she spent the bulk of her lifetime financially secure, she behaved alternately as spendthrift and miser, idiosyncratically splitting financial hairs and placing undue constraints on her material possessions and artistic properties.

Speech acts, secrets and silence figure prominently in Lillian Hellman's plays. An internet search for images using '*The Children's Hour* + production' yields myriad advertisements and production photographs depicting Mary's whispered lie to her grandmother. Again, suspicions raised against Karen and Martha in the play are never spoken aloud. Also, Mary employs silence regarding Rosalie's theft of the bracelet as a tool to ensure that Rosalie speaks on her behalf. As noted above, *Days to Come* is replete with secrets, whose far-reaching consequences culminate in Andrew's title line 'for all the days to come'.[80] In *The Little Foxes*, speaking versus silence can be viewed, at least in part, from a class conscious perspective, as well as a racial one. Oscar (nouveaux riche at best) silences Birdie (old money) with a slap. Yet the black servants, Addie and Cal, are allowed to speak truth to power, especially in their more intimate conversations with Horace and Alexandra.

Alexandra describes speech(es) as crucial to her discovery of truths concerning her family: 'Addie *said* there were people who ate the earth ... and just now Uncle Ben *said* the same thing ... he *said* the same thing. Well, *tell* him for me, Mama ... *Tell* him'[81] (emphasis mine). Alexandra lauds her power of potentially speaking the truth over Regina ('What was Papa doing on the staircase?').[82] Throughout the play, the Hubbards threaten to expose each other's wrongdoings through the act of speaking. It is significant that it is the servant Cal's message that could expose Leo, his father and his uncle's craftiness, and that the quotation about 'eating the earth' and passivity is assigned to Addie, the other black servant.

Growing up in the South, in the teens and twenties, Lillian Hellman's attitudes toward people of colour were, of course, much different from the majority of those held today. Like many of her generation, Hellman was tended to by a black nurse, Sophronia, to whom she remained devoted. Nevertheless, Hellman's depiction of people of colour in her plays, right through to *Toys in the Attic* (produced in 1960), places them exclusively in subservient roles. *Toys*, however, includes two interracial relationships, one offstage and largely in the past, the other onstage and in the present, in full view, between a wealthy Southern woman and her manservant. Significantly, neither of these relationships ends happily, and the last line of the play, in fact, is uttered by Henry, servant to his long-time employer and love, Albertine. That line is simply, 'Good-bye.'[83]

In many respects, Lillian Hellman's plays of the 1930s were thematically prescient at the time, yet their durability in production is questionable in part because of the playwright's treatment of gender and race. Surprisingly, feminist critic Jill Dolan found the 2011 production of *The Children's Hour*, starring Kiera Knightley and Elisabeth Moss, engaging, 'compelling' in fact.[84] University productions have cast the play 'colour blind' and capitalized on the issue of bullying inherent in the script.[85] A 2017 Broadway revival of *The Little Foxes* is in its initial planning stages.[86]

Regardless, the feisty personality of Lillian Hellman will endure through her memoirs, and her plays will live on as historical antecedents for the work of other playwrights, male and female, for days to come.

Afterword

Anne Fletcher

The robust legacy of American theatre of the 1930s comes as no surprise since the forms, styles, genres and subject matter that comprise the decade's drama, discussed in Chapter 2, are disparate. In part because of this variety, the impact of 1930s theatre is far reaching: some elements (re)emerge almost immediately, while others manifest later, especially in the socially turbulent and theatrically innovative decade of the 1960s, and beyond.

As Chrystyna Dail argues in her new book, *Stage for Action: U.S. Social Activist Theatre in the 1940s*, the traditional theatre history narrative that radical theatre died with the 1930s warrants questioning. While producing agencies such as the Theatre Collective, Theatre Union, Federal Theatre Project and Group Theatre disbanded at the decade's close, social and political theatre persisted across the 1940s and on to the present. Collectivity marked the work of the Open Theatre in the 1960s, and continued with companies like the Omaha Magic Theatre (founded by former Open Theatre actress Jo Ann Schmidman and playwright Megan Terry). Today, ensemble, collective approaches and political awareness play integral roles in the ongoing work of companies like the Bread and Puppet Theater, Double Edge Theatre, the SITI Company, Teatro Campesino, the Wooster Group and more.

Individual playwrights addressed earlier in this book remained active to varying degrees and, of course, as the subsequent volumes of this series illustrate, many more joined their ranks, some of whom, like Arthur Miller – hailed by many as the United States' pre-eminent dramatist – paid homage to their predecessors from the 1930s. Dail and, earlier, Brenda Murphy, in *Congressional*

Theatre (1999), both explore Arthur Miller's 1946 *You're Next*, for example, as dramaturgically reminiscent of Clifford Odets's *Waiting for Lefty*. Odets and other Theatre Union and Group Theater playwrights placed emphasis on the struggles of the everyday man (and woman) during the Depression, allowing space for Miller to follow them with not only his seminal play *Death of a Salesman*, but with his important essay 'Tragedy and the Common Man'. It may not be hyperbolic to view Odets's humanist, realist, social drama as the instigator for the pervading dramatic substance and form for much of the remainder of the twentieth century. Of course earlier American dramatists imbued their plays with social concerns, but they often returned to melodrama and the Well-Made Play for dramatic form. Odets's concern with changing form not only manifests in his dramatic writings, but is one of the most frequently discussed topics in his 1940 journal. In his retrospective *Timebends: A Life*, Arthur Miller not only comments on Odets but compares himself to others of his predecessors, and he contemplates dramatic form in his memoir as well. American social drama, following on the heels of Miller, is, of course, alive and well in US theatre of the later twentieth century and into the twenty-first.

Thornton Wilder's (see the 1940s volume of this series) depiction of time and his ontological leanings serve as tribute to his close friendship with and admiration for Gertrude Stein. He attests to her influence in his non-dramatic writings as well. In her use of language, Stein also foreshadowed the non-linear, often polyvocal, circumlocutious dialogue that would characterize future women's playwriting in particular: Ntozake Shange's choreopoems, the language of Suzan-Lori Parks as well as her contrast between absence and presence, and Adrienne Kennedy's (often surreal) landscapes, to name a few.

While it would remain for Megan Terry to somewhat uncomfortably wear the mantle of 'mother' of American feminist drama, and for other women playwrights to take up the gauntlet after her, surely Lillian Hellman helped pave the way for them, as illustrated by the tribute paid to her by playwrights Marsha Norman, Julia Jordan and Theresa Rebeck, in the spring of 2010, with their creation of the Lilly Awards, to honour the work of women in the American theatre.

While appropriate representatives of the decade's drama, Gertrude Stein, Langston Hughes, Clifford Odets and Lillian Hellman may be viewed, at the same time, as 'outliers', rebels of sorts, and individuals who, in one way or another, paid a price for expressing their beliefs through their actions or in their writing. At various points in their lives, each suffered political persecution, and each faced artistic challenges. In the 1950s, three of the playwrights examined here (Hughes, Odets and Hellman) and many, many others faced formal interrogations before the House Un-American Committee (HUAC). Stein's controversy arose after her death in retrospective speculation on her activities during the Second World War, when she translated the speeches of Marshal Philippe Pétain.

American-born Gertrude Stein (1874–1946), because she lived abroad throughout her writing career (apart from one trip to the US, that being by and large a publicity tour), might be considered as something of an anomaly amidst the other playwrights and plays selected for discussion regarding American drama of the 1930s. Nonetheless, even if (and perhaps *because*) she 'staged' her Americanism in later life, she warrants emphasis in this volume on *American* playwrights. As Leslie Atkins Durham reminds us in her 2005 book on Stein, *Staging Gertrude Stein: Absence, Culture, and the Landscape of American Alternative Theatre*, the playwright viewed her work as 'quintessentially American'.[1] Durham's study contextualizes seminal productions and critical reception of Stein's work across the second half of the twentieth century, pointing into the twenty-first. She analyses how the cultural moment of each production she discusses affected the director's particular vision, concept and execution, and how the American social landscape of the time is reflected in each.

As a result of her living abroad from 1903 until her death from stomach cancer on 27 July 1946 (she is buried in France), Stein did not experience the Great Depression first-hand, although her much heralded celebrity tour of the US transpired in 1934–5, in the midst of the economic crisis (Karen Lieck traces Stein's fame in her 2009 book, *Gertrude Stein and the Making of an American Celebrity*). Stein spent the Second World War, as Laura Schultz explains in her chapter on the playwright, almost imprisoned in her own home, bereft of information from a US perspective regarding the current international situation. Despite the urging of friends States-side, Stein and same-sex partner Alice B. Toklas remained in France, a dangerous choice, and their survival there remains somewhat shrouded in political intrigue – some might say it has precipitated a 'witch hunt'[2] on a smaller, more individual scale, perhaps akin to that experienced by the other playwrights covered here in their encounters with HUAC, only from a different political perspective. Biographies and critical studies of Stein present conflicting views of the author's socio-political leanings. All told, she emerges as progressive in some ways, yet, on the other hand, not without personal prejudices.

Similarly, Stein's work initially met with both critical praise and derision, but, regardless, as F. W. Dupee notes in his General Introduction to *The Selected Writings of Gertrude Stein*, her famous syntax, 'Steinese' as he calls it, 'her little sentences' were 'originally quoted in scorn' but, over time, came 'to be repeated from something like affection; and thus the very theory that underlay her technique of reiteration was proved; what people loved they repeated, and what people repeated they loved'.[3]

Stein's theatrical vindication would come several decades later, with a resurgence of interest in her work, especially in *Doctor Faustus Lights the Lights*, as a result of the blossoming of a new avant-garde in the American theatre and the rise of the field of Performance Studies and, later, dramatic theory relating to Postmodernism and post-dramatic theatre.[4] During her lifetime, Stein was prolific as poet, fiction writer, playwright and librettist. Beginning with *Three Lives* in 1909, her literary output outlived her, continuing for some eight decades, with several of her last works published posthumously by her literary executor and long-time friend Carl Van Vechten, noted music and dance critic, mostly remembered in theatrical circles for his celebrity photography (and inspiration for one of Gertrude Stein's 'portraits' discussed in the chapter on Stein). Gertrude Stein, as noted later in this Afterword, remains an iconic persona on the American cultural landscape, and her work is staged with somewhat surprising frequency.

Langston Hughes's career commenced during the Harlem Renaissance of the 1920s, with which he is most frequently associated, but his playwriting blossomed in the 1930s, as did his political activism. Hughes, like Odets and Hellman, was called to testify before the House Committee on Un-American Activities in 1953. Like Odets, Hughes objected to party demands regarding his writing – the sort to which playwright John Howard Lawson often acquiesced – before he turned his attention almost exclusively to the Communist Party (CP-USA). Hughes stated, 'I did not believe political directives could be successfully applied to creative writing.'[5] No doubt the experience of testifying affected the activist and former communist sympathizer, as Hughes excluded his more radical, even socialist verse from his *Selected Poems* in 1959 and moved toward more lyrical writing later in his career.[6]

Cast in the role of 'Other' as a black man of mixed racial descent, Hughes may also have attempted to avoid further marginalization by choosing to live as a closeted homosexual. Hughes scholars remain divided as to the poet/playwright/activist's sexual orientation. Regardless, Langston Hughes's influence lives on in the generations of black poets, playwrights and activists who follow him, and, of course, his poem 'A Dream Deferred' is immortalized as inspiration for the title of Lorraine Hansberry's *A Raisin in the Sun*, reprinted in the introductory pages of most editions of the play.

Clifford Odets, while prolific in the 1930s, after bursting onto the Broadway scene with *Awake and Sing!* (in 1935, the same season as Hughes's *Mulatto*) and the legendary premiere of *Waiting for Lefty*, remained tortured by his subsequent move to Hollywood, his failed marriages, his HUAC testimony and his inability to recapture the heady success and artistic achievements of his early writing. Like his friend director Elia Kazan, following his 1952 testimony, Odets was shunned by many in the Hollywood community. The playwright never recovered from the Cold War questioning. He is said to have even had created a bound copy of his testimony.[7] Odets never again attained the critical praise at which he rejoiced during the 1930s. Several accounts of his final days, sadly, describe the dying playwright raising his fist, as Agate did at the end of *Lefty*, and exclaiming, 'Clifford Odets, you have so much still to do!'[8]

While very different in their choice of subject matter (with Lillian Hellman's focus on, often Southern, upper- to middle-class characters, and Odets's overt, even Marxist, concentration on the visible effects of socio-political circumstances on lower- to middle-class urban dwellers), both Hellman and Odets addressed economics in their works. And, both cast their plays in a realistic style. Perhaps more importantly, although they were not friends, the two experienced similar career trajectories and some personal parallels. Hellman's first Broadway play, *The Children's Hour* (1934), premiered at the same time that Odets was penning *Awake and Sing!* Critics have compared both playwrights to Anton Chekhov: Odets for his use of language and tendency to introduce his audience to given circumstances in progress, with little exposition

(Odets, a classical music aficionado, viewed his plays like musical compositions); Hellman in her later plays, especially *The Autumn Garden* and *Toys in the Attic*, for her evocation of mood. Unlike Odets, Lillian Hellman was blacklisted during the McCarthy era, and, as a result, deprived of lucrative screenwriting opportunities across the late 1940s into the early 1950s. Despite carefully crafting her 1952 HUAC hearing response for the benefit of the press, throughout her days she remained subject to political scrutiny, due to her early alliance with Communist Party members and affiliates, and because of her outspoken nature. Hellman's playwriting career – quite successful in the 1940s – took a markedly downward turn long before she abandoned the medium altogether and emerged as memoirist. Of the playwrights examined in this volume, Hellman lived the furthest into the twentieth century, dying at her home on Martha's Vineyard, Massachusetts, on 30 June 1984.

Due, in part, to anniversaries of the playwrights' births (Hellman, 1905; Odets, 1906) and of the original productions of their seminal plays (*The Children's Hour*, 1934; *Waiting for Lefty* and *Awake and Sing!*, 1935), and likely because of their socio-political currency, interest in producing their works accelerated in the 1990s and 2000s. For Odets, this renewed fascination in his work meant Broadway revivals of *Awake and Sing!* (2006), *The Country Girl* (2008), *Golden Boy* (2012) and *The Big Knife* (2013). Chicago productions include not only *Lefty* and *Awake and Sing!*, but also the less often produced *Rocket to the Moon*, *Clash by Night* and *Paradise Lost*.

Hellman's *The Little Foxes* continues as her most widely produced play and has graced the New York stage in revival, as star vehicle, three times: in 1967, starring Anne Bancroft; 1981, featuring Elizabeth Taylor; 1997, with Stockard Channing – and a projected production in 2017, with Laura Linney and Cynthia Nixon as suggested alternates in the role of Regina. Washington DC's Arena Stage has announced a Lillian Hellman Festival for its 2016–17 season. A 2011 London production of *The Children's Hour* (as mentioned in the chapter on Hellman) featured Kiera Knightley and Elisabeth Moss.

As fashion historians have long reminded us, a decade's zeitgeist often subsequently re-emerges with alterations some years later, and, as we can see with the playwrights included in this book, such has been the case with American drama of the 1930s.

Gertrude Stein – 'What is the answer?'[9]

As she was born decades before the other three playwrights addressed in this volume and remained largely unrecognized for the first half of her writing career, the number of works Gertrude Stein published between the 1930s and her death in 1946 might appear, at first glance, surprisingly small. Of course, the Second World War intervened and influenced Stein's writing. She completed four Second World War pieces: *Paris France* (1940), her memoir that blends childhood memory and commentary on what it means to be 'French', which was, ironically, published on the day France fell to Germany; *In Savoy; or, Yes Is For a Very Young Man: A Play of the Resistance in France*; *Wars I Have Seen* (1945), which Stein dubbed her 'war autobiography';[10] and *Brewsie and Willie* (1946), based on her post-war encounters in France with American GIs.

Stein completed *Ida A Novel* in 1939 (published 1940), her unique construction of a female character's identity; *Three Sisters Who Are Not Sisters* in 1943, a children's murder-mystery melodrama that plays with identity construction as well; and her masterful libretto *The Mother of Us All* in 1946. She did not live to see production of this last piece, her opera in honour of quintessential suffragette Susan B. Anthony, with music by Virgil Thomson.

Subsequently, Stein influenced composers, playwrights, production companies and even children's theatre (*Three Sisters Who Are Not Sisters* appears, with a cogent commentary, in noted children's theatre expert Lowell Swortzell's *Around the World in 21 Plays: Theatre for Young Audiences*, 2000). Her own writings have been reprinted numerous times, her libretti adapted and performed to new music, and a few works have been performed by dance companies.[11]

Composer Virgil Thomson, as explained in the chapter on Stein, was a crucial player in the inaugural staging of *Four Saints in Three Acts* in 1934. The premiere featured an African-American cast, which Leslie Atkins Durham contends referenced codes of primitivism at the time, so reception of it was understandably changed when Thomson remounted the production in 1952, an entirely different era with regard to race in the US.[12] In 1950, the Living Theatre (Judith Malina and Julian Beck) selected *Doctor Faustus Lights the Lights* as their first public performance. Another piece of note was created by Al Carmines (director, *Doctor Faustus Lights the Lights*, 1979), *In Circles*, which premiered in 1967 at the Judson Poet's Theatre. Portions of it were subsequently performed in the mid-1990s at the Algonquin Hotel in New York City[13] and it was revived for a limited run in its entirety in 1997.[14] Carmines explains his relationship with Stein's work in the 'Documents' chapter. Director Lawrence Kornfeld, former Managing Director of the Living Theatre and founder of the Judson Poet's, directed eleven different Stein productions, with eight more repeat productions.[15] Durham claims of these last two productions (Living Theatre and Judson Poet's) that, while in large measure they captured Stein's 'abstraction and openness', 'the concerns of Cold War culture crept in'.[16] In 1970, film director Perry Miller Adato created *Gertrude Stein: When This You See, Remember Me*, still lauded as one of the first biography documentaries constructed entirely of still photography and narration.[17]

In 1995, Frank Galati adapted Stein's *Each One As She May*, which he staged in 1997. The Santa Fe Opera mounted *The Mother of Us All* in 1976, and it was produced at the Glimmerglass Opera Festival in 1998. The first coincided with the United States bicentennial celebration and, as a result, its focus did not target the piece's latent messages regarding homosexuality or even women's rights, which was more overtly displayed in the Glimmerglass production on the 150th anniversary of the Seneca Falls Women's Conference. Subsequently, the latter moved to the New York City Opera.[18] In fact, the 1990s saw a rebirth of interest in Gertrude Stein, represented by Robert Wilson's 1992 production of *Doctor Faustus Lights the Lights* (discussed at some length by Laura Schultz in the Stein chapter), no surprise because of Wilson and Stein's shared interest in time and landscape. The year 1999 saw both the Wooster Group's *House/Lights* that drew on Stein's *Faustus* and Anne Bogart's *Gertrude and Alice*. Durham takes the abstract and imagistic vision and concept of German composer/director Heiner Goebbels in his 2003 piece, *Hashirigaki*, adapted from Stein's *Making of Americans*, as her case study for returning Stein to the global stage of the twenty-first century. A 2015 production of Stein's 1921 40-minute play 'Reread Another A Play to Be Played Indoors or Out I Wish to Be a School', by Target Margin, received an extraordinarily positive review from Ben Brantley in the *New York Times*.[19] (The company did not fare so well in critic Christopher

Isherwood's review of their 2009 staging of Stein's 'A Family of Perhaps Three'.[20]) Of the current theatre practitioners influenced by Gertrude Stein, Richard Foreman foregrounds his indebtedness to the playwright (see the 'Documents' chapter),[21] which is discussed by Marvin Carlson in his chapter 'After Stein: Traveling the American Theatrical "Langscape"'. In fact, a great deal of attention is paid to Stein's pervasive influence in the volume in which this chapter appears, Elinor Fuchs and Uda Chaudhuri's *Land/Scape/Theatre* (2002), which also includes a chapter by Jane Palatini Bowers (whose 1991 piece is referenced in the Stein chapter). Stein was the subject of a symposium at New York University in 2001, and the 2002 *Theater* article based on the symposium proceedings, 'A Play That Must Be Performed' (excerpted in the 'Documents' chapter), features frank comments by Maria Irene Fornes and Mac Wellman, both of whom once considered Stein 'cute'.

Well over 100 books have been published on Gertrude Stein. She has been immortalized on stage and screen numerous times, and her place as an American cultural icon is undeniable. From gracing the cover of *Time* magazine on 11 September 1933 onward to the present, Stein is ubiquitous. Her phrase 'There is no there there'[22] is uttered by individuals who do not even know its source! With every production of the popular musical *Mame*, an audience somewhere hears the actress performing the role of Vera sing, 'I'll always be Alice Toklas, if you'll be Gertrude Stein' ('Bosom Buddies', *Mame*). Stein's name appears in 'La Vie Boheme' from *Rent* as well.

Not only did Gertrude Stein's plays and prose meet with many stage adaptations in the later part of the twentieth century, but she (and Alice B. Toklas) continues to grace the stage as characters as well. Stein serves as a featured character, played by actress Kathy Bates, in Woody Allen's film *Midnight in Paris* (2011). Solo pieces that incorporate a Stein character or her works abound, from *Gertrude Stein, Gertrude Stein, Gertrude Stein* (1980, starring Pat Carroll who won both the Drama Desk Award for her live performance as Stein and a Grammy in the spoken word category for her recording of the piece) to less familiar pieces like Jade Eseban Estrada's one-hander musical *ICONS: The Lesbian and Gay History of the World, Vol. 1* and Brazilian actor/director Luiz Päetow's *Plays*. The Frank Galati and Stephen Flaherty chamber musical, *Loving Repeating* (Chicago, 2003/2011), takes one of Stein's 1934 Chicago lectures as its inspiration. *Chicago Tribune* critic Chris Jones included mention of a piece at Jacob's Pillow in which dancers performed to a recitation of Stein's poem 'If I Told Him: A Completed Portrait of Picasso' in his 22 July 2015 review of a production of *Loving Repeating*. Gertrude Stein is even a featured character in a graphic novel, Nick Bertozzi's *The Salon* (St Martin's Press, 2007). The title of Ricky Ian Gordon and Royce Vavrek's original opera, *27*, derives from the Paris address of Stein's salon, 27 rue de Fleurus. The piece premiered at Opera of St Louis in 2014. Another original opera on Stein and Toklas opened at Pittsburgh Opera in February 2016.[23] Productions of Stein's work and about Stein occur at such a rapid pace that it is impossible to track them.

The examples above fail to take into account Stein's enormous impact – like that of the abstract artists she admired, whose work she collected and who served as beacons for her pioneering work in imagistic theatre – on the worlds of fiction, poetry and creative writing. Nor does it give more than a nod to the ways in which Gertrude Stein is championed by the LBGTQ community and in women's rights circles.

Stein moved fluidly across genres, remarkably. As Richard Howard stated in reviewing her complete works in 1998,

> It is evident ... that she transformed and often renewed every genre she ventured upon. Her theater – which sallied forth as opera, as antiphon, as ballet, as film and ultimately, even classically, as a dialogue of persons – became, whenever it reached the stage, something else: circus, singing games, a cross between voodoo and bullfighting.[24]

On her death bed, Stein asked, 'What is the answer?' Approaching death as she had life, Gertrude Stein questioned everything around her: the very viewing of the landscape before her, traditional syntax, dramatic form, life itself. Persistent questioning, then, for Gertrude Stein, might be viewed, paradoxically (and characteristically), as her unique way of *answering*. Her persona, theatrical forms and styles manifest in performance of the twenty-first century; her questions spiral across the decades, and continue to push boundaries as her query continues to reverberate, 'What is the answer?'

Langston Hughes – 'I, too, am America'[25]

While Gertrude Stein often took as her subject the quotidian, the everyday people and places she encountered with seldom a reference to politics or economics, Langston Hughes joins the other playwrights in this volume in his earnest defence of liberty and freedom, in his case primarily African-American, and his emphasis on the economic peril in which the average American of the 1930s and beyond has lived.

Of the playwrights discussed here, apart from Odets's successful combination of realist form and agit-prop in *Waiting for Lefty*, it is Hughes who presages later protest drama with *Scottsboro* and *Don't You Want to be Free* (1938), which also introduced expressionism and the Russian staging techniques Hughes studied on his trip abroad to black theatre.[26] As Adrienne Macki mentions in the Hughes chapter, Scottsboro's focus on black youths and their unfair treatment by an apparently 'rigged' judicial system reverberates in the United States today, with recent and contested racial encounters with police in Fergusson, Missouri; Baltimore, Maryland; and other US cities. The Black Lives Matter movement has precipitated numerous professional theatrical productions and shows on college campuses that utilize Hughes's polyvocality, poetry and techniques like placards and slides similar to those used in the workers' theatre movement of the 1930s. Indeed, Langston Hughes is the only one of the playwrights on which we focus who himself participated in the workers' theatre movement, and his force is evident in the twenty-first century.

Although Hughes died in 1967 at the age of only sixty-five, his writing career, across multiple genres, constituted a full three-quarters or more of the years he lived, and he published steadily, something almost every year. Perceived gaps in the poet/playwright's literary productivity occur when he was most actively engaged in guest teaching positions, which he only occasionally accepted, or, more frequently, when he was editing *Common Ground* or writing regularly for the *Chicago Defender*. Hughes contributed to and served on the editorial board of *Common Ground*, a literary magazine with focus on ethnicity, from 1942 to 1949. His column in the *Defender* appeared for twenty consecutive years (c. 1941–61). It was for the *Defender* that Hughes first crafted stories featuring the character Jesse B. Semple (often spelled 'Simple'); these stories presented the prototypical Harlem common man and his perceptions of current events. They were subsequently published in collections.

During the late 1950s and 1960s, Hughes was sometimes at odds with more militant factions of the Black Power movement, but his objections were related to the participants' tactics of anger rather than emanating from a disagreement with their demonstrations of black pride. His internal conflict (externally he supported young black artists) is representative of the split regarding the mission of black theatre initiated in the long-standing philosophical argument between Alain Locke and W. E. B. Du Bois earlier in the century – the two sides representing 'folk' versus 'protest' art, or termed later, more boldly perhaps, 'integrationist' versus 'separatist', that characterized twentieth-century black drama and later erupted in an extended debate between critic Robert Brustein and playwright August Wilson. Despite Hughes's misgivings about some contemporary black theatre and poetry, he served as a valuable mentor for young black writers; he discovered Alice Walker, for example.[27]

The Off-Broadway production of *Black Nativity* (1961) can be viewed as an extension of Hughes's early notion of community-based theatre because, with its flexible cast number, chorus, dancers and drummers, mute roles (Mary, Joseph) and narrator, it welcomes incorporation of local choruses, dance groups and neighbourhood associations, offering opportunity to cast guest artists or community leaders in featured roles. The piece intertwines gospel spirituals Hughes selected (and some composed for the production) with retelling of the traditional 'Christmas Story'. *Black Nativity*, with its chorus of upwards to 150 participants, is still produced annually in Boston and other US cities. A cast album, *Black Nativity – In Concert: A Gospel Celebration*, popular during the Christmas season, was released and, in 2004, a documentary on the original production was created. The performance piece was refashioned as a film in 2013, starring Angela Bassett, Jennifer Hudson and Forest Whitaker, that incorporates a family story centred on a black youth raised by a single mother who visits his relatives in New York City where one of them, a reverend played by Forest Whittaker, is staging an annual Christmas pageant. Hughes's *Black*

Nativity anticipated Off-Broadway productions like Al Carmines's *In Circles* and Lee Breuer's 1983 *Gospel at Colonus*.

Until only recently, the connection between the poetry of Langston Hughes and the speeches of Dr Martin Luther King, Jr was only alluded to and not fully explored. W. Jason Miller's 2015 book, *Origins of the Dream: Hughes's Poetry and King's Rhetoric*, introduces archival support that makes this vital connection explicit. Miller is clear that he does not question the originality of King's ideas, nor does he intend to privilege Hughes as their originator. Rather, he suggests that their interrelationship constitutes 'the twentieth century's most visible integration of poetry and politics'.[28] Moreover, Miller's identification of specific instances in which the relationship between the two men's bodies of work exhibit reciprocity is useful for the purpose of commenting on Langston Hughes's legacy. That is to say, not only did Hughes influence King but vice versa. According to Miller, eight of Hughes's poems, most expressly 'Dream of Freedom' because of its evocation of dreaming, respond to King's rhetoric.[29] This intertextuality demonstrates the socio-political power of the arts at its most potent.

Hughes's extensive *oeuvre* includes not only poetry and plays, but operas, journalistic writing (essays, commentaries, critiques), children's books and autobiographies (*The Big Sea* and *I Wonder as I Wander*). Like Gertrude Stein, and perhaps because, like her, he left a large body of poetry ripe for adaptation, Hughes's posthumous shelf life (and performance life) continues into the twenty-first century. His *Ask Your Mama: 12 Moods for Jazz* (1960), first performed in 2009 at Carnegie Hall, serves as the centrepiece of the Langston Hughes Project.[30]

Clifford Odets – 'The last sixteen wasted years'[31]

By 1950, Clifford Odets had fallen victim to the 'consumer capitalism' he depicted in his early work, as explicated by Chris Herr in his chapter on the playwright. Sixty years later, in 2010, the playwright's son, Walt Odets (named after American poet Walt Whitman), explained how his father felt pressured to complete *The*

Country Girl (1950) as a commodity, as a play of appeal to a wider audience, in order to make money.[32] By then divorced from second wife, actress Bette Grayson, Walt's mother, Odets was supporting his two children, and Nora, his daughter, was developmentally delayed. Grayson died four years later, leaving Walt and Nora in the playwright's sole custody as Nora's medical bills mounted.

The private struggle of Clifford Odets, as single parent, with one disabled child and another in need of proper attention and an education, faced with the choice of earning $100,000 a week in Hollywood as a 'ghost writer' or making a mere $4,000 for a play in New York,[33] is overshadowed by images of the playwright as 'sell out', even 'stool pigeon', and as having never attained his full potential as a playwright. Odets's *New York Times* obituary, on 16 August 1963, perpetuated these depictions, begun in much earlier articles and reviews, like Frank Nugent's 'Odets, Where is Thy Sting?',[34] claiming, 'His failure to outgrow the adjective "promising" was a constant source of chagrin for the writer.'[35] Just nine weeks after the playwright's death, as Elia Kazan assembled his Lincoln Center Repertory cast of Arthur Miller's *After the Fall*, he defended his friend's reputation, affirming, 'Cliff wasn't "shot." ... The mind and talent were alive in the man.'[36] Two years later, in a piece for the *New York Times*, Odets biographer Margaret Brenman-Gibson excoriated the press for their representations of the playwright in the majority of obituaries that appeared, targeting *Time* magazine's coverage in particular, stating that the publication 'took the cake for its smart-aleck illiteracy'.[37] She noted protests by the likes of Irwin Shaw, John Houseman, Jerome Robbins, Gore Vidal and more, as well as making mention of some private apologies. Nevertheless, the public damage was done.

Like so many other writers and performers, Clifford Odets left New York for Hollywood – for the first time in 1936 – but he remained loyal to his artistic progenitor, the Group Theatre, continuing to write for them and sending financial contributions until the company disbanded in 1941. The playwright spent the remainder of his life ('the sixteen wasted years' to which he alluded on his deathbed) struggling between desire for commercial and financial success and artistic freedom and integrity: 'The monk and the winking courtier were perpetually at war inside him.'[38] As early as 1940, in diary entries that were published almost a half-century later, Odets already acknowledged that his meteoric rise – four plays on Broadway in one year, a brand new Cadillac, his face on the cover of *Time* magazine – foretold a fall. He sought in his life the classical balance that all tragic heroes fail to achieve. In his 1940 journal, Odets related the explanation of the 'creative personality' he gave to playwright Bill Kozlenko on a long car ride:

> the artist has in him many elements. Some, if they were isolated, would be bad, some good. But all of these must be held in a firm **balance** ... If he carries this load carefully – in **balance** – its power for good work and use is enormous ... Abuse – out of **balance** – is suicide and a bitter grave ... the artist, if he makes a proper amalgam, is beyond good and evil, for everything in him is for creation and life ... Inner contradictions are not solved by throwing out half of the personality, but by keeping both sides tearing and pulling ... until an *amalgam on a high level of life and experience is achieved*.[39] (emphasis mine)

The author wrote frequently of his never-ending internal battle, expressed as a war between 'heart and appetite' in the 2006 *New Yorker* article, 'Stage Left: The Struggles of Clifford Odets'.[40] For the playwright that 'amalgam' was never reached, the balance and moderation required to avert tragedy never attained. Elia Kazan's 1963 statement, 'The tragedy of our times is the tragedy of Clifford Odets', may well serve as this playwright's epitaph.

Issued in 1939, *Six Plays by Clifford Odets* failed to prove a harbinger of playwriting success to come. After so many productions in rapid-fire succession across the 1930s, Odets's last play for The Group Theatre, *Night Music* (1940, 20 performances),[41] and *Clash by Night* (1941–2, 49 performances, produced by Billy Rose, directed by Lee Strasberg), his last on Broadway until 1949, despite a favourable review of the first act,[42] were failures.

Odets was occupied with screen work across the 1940s; some of his most notable projects included his directorial debut with *None but the Lonely Heart* (1944) and the screenplay for *Humouresque* (1946), starring Joan Crawford and John Garfield. There were others for which he did not receive screen credit, and, in keeping with the Hollywood 'system', under contract, Odets contributed numerous rewrites of the work of others, including an early version of the perennial Christmas favourite *It's a Wonderful Life* (released in 1946). Clifford Odets was 'facile', as his son explains, able to work quickly and efficiently in the role of script doctor: 'In four or five days he could rewrite the whole thing – get rid of the line an actress objected to and reconstruct the relevant things around it. And then they'd pay him $100,000 for a week of work.'[43] At decade's close, Odets returned to the Broadway stage with *The Big Knife* (1949), his condemnation of the Hollywood scene, which, like his last two plays, met with a mixed review from Atkinson in the *New York Times*. As with *Clash by Night* eight years earlier, the critic praised Odets's characters and the playwright's ability to craft individual scenes, but this time he went so far as to take Odets to task for moving to Hollywood to earn a living and apparently 'wanting to have his cake and eat it too'.[44] *Clash by Night* was adapted for screen, large (1952) and small (1957), and the film version of *The Big Knife* was released in 1955.

Unlike Lillian Hellman, and like his friend Kazan, who, despite his artistic achievements and fame, remained ostracized by many until his death at the age of 94, Odets escaped blacklisting in the film industry because technically he 'named names' in his 1952 appearance before HUAC. Odets chose not to invoke his Fifth Amendment right at the hearings, insisting he had nothing to hide, so, following Kazan's lead, he identified individuals he believed had participated in communist activities. The playwright pinpointed only people who had been previously named, including Kazan as they agreed to 'name' each other. Despite his defiant demeanour at the hearings during his long testimony, Odets's cooperation as a 'friendly witness' caused irreparable damage to many of his relationships and to his career. According to his son, Odets awakened one day not long after his appearance before the committee to discover fine pieces of art he had loaned to friends piled outside his door, an overt snub by his former friends.[45] Unlike another 'moralist' playwright, Lillian Hellman (see below), Odets spoke his true conscience, but his political naivety[46] allowed him to become 'used' by the committee, unlike Hellman for whom the reverse can be said to be true. Nevertheless, Odets's testimony enabled him to remain gainfully employed as a screenwriter. He did not live to achieve the public vindication he sought, which may have been derived years later with the release of the committee's transcripts in which his bold statements were recorded.

Clifford Odets's last Broadway play, *The Flowering Peach* – better known in its next incarnation as the 1970 musical *Two by Two*, with music by the inimitable Richard Rodgers, and starring Odets's friend Danny Kaye – premiered in 1954, nine years before the playwright's death from colon cancer on 14 August 1963. Odets directed the play himself.

Critics in 1954 saw the play as a comedy, recasting the family of Noah as a modern-day middle-class Jewish family. Only Brooks Atkinson glimpsed the seriousness underneath the comic veneer, commenting on Noah's 'totalitarianism' and Odets's 'message of hope for the sullen world of today'.[47] The seemingly innocuous biblically inspired tale of infighting among Noah's family warrants more critical attention than it has received. Indeed, *The Flowering Peach* is a historiographer's dream, a fine example of how time and distance allow the theatre historian an opportunity to re-evaluate forgotten plays, unearthing sometimes exquisite and enlightening cultural artefacts. Viewed through the lens of Cold War containment theory,[48] Noah's ark may be paralleled with the 1950s American phenomenon the 'bomb shelter', and the contentiousness, selfishness and even hoarding of family members aboard as indicative of the paranoia of the period. Might Clifford Odets, as with *Night Music*, which looked back on the 1930s and forward to the Second World War, have straddled an era with this play? Might Noah's dove of peace become, then, emblematic of a day when the wall would fall and of a world (as yet to come) devoid of nuclear arms?[49] If so, then, while Clifford Odets never basked in theatrical fame again, he may have ultimately outwitted his audience and critics with this Cold War-era parable.

Following commercial failure of *The Flowering Peach*, which was surprisingly the Pulitzer Prize judges' initial selection, overruled by the Pulitzer committee, Odets returned to Hollywood where he continued to work from 1955 to 1963, according to his son, moving from one furnished rental home to another, always thinking he would soon move the family back to New York City to resume his playwriting career.[50] During this period, *Sweet Smell of Success* (1957), starring Burt Lancaster, whose character was loosely based on Walter Winchell, was released, a film that has gained in stature over time (recast as a musical in 2002 by Marvin Hamlisch, Craig Carnelia and John Guare). Instead, the playwright turned to the up-and-coming medium of television, which at times he lamented as the 'come down' his detractors suggested it to be and, at others, he defended as having the great potential it has, in some aspects, attained. At the time of his death, Odets was employed by NBC as scriptwriter and script supervisor for *The Richard Boone Show*, which ran rather dismally opposite rival station CBS's wildly popular *Petticoat Junction*.

Clifford Odets's body of dramatic work is not only socio-political and at the same time autobiographical; it chronicles the dilemmas faced by Americans across some quarter of a century. The Depression-era plays most vividly capture the American experience discussed in Chapter 1, but his later works illustrate the nuanced struggles faced by many as they grappled to maintain personal integrity in the midst of commodification and bigger and bigger business, and as they faced the ever present fear of nuclear warfare that pervaded the 1950s and beyond.

Lillian Hellman – 'No secrets about her feelings'[51]

Historian Alice Kessler-Harris opens *A Difficult Woman: The Challenging Life and Times of Lillian Hellman* (2012) with an iconic photograph of the playwright late in life – characteristically smoking, clad only (it appears) in a fur coat, staring boldly and directly into the camera. The subject's reputation precedes her; her name need not appear in the advertisement, part of the famous 'What becomes a legend most?' series. Kessler-Harris then poses questions regarding the author's celebrity, pondering why Hellman's accomplishments have been overshadowed by her legendary temper and predilection for reshaping the truth. Kessler-Harris employs the craft of the New Historian as she carefully unpacks the playwright's public (and private) persona(s), in her own words, 'by thinking through her relationship to the twentieth century'.[52] In so doing, the biographer reminds her readers of changes, contrasts and contradictions across the 1900s, oppositions, even dichotomies that parallel those in Hellman herself.

Despite periodic revivals of Hellman's plays, her writing, including her memoirs, which were bestsellers in the 1970s, is often dwarfed by her enormous personality. Hellman seems most remembered for the controversy surrounding the veracity of her words that emanated from Mary McCarthy's comment on *The Dick Cavett Show*, referenced in the Hellman chapter of this volume, her litigious nature and her abiding anger. Even William Styron's graveside eulogy of the playwright mentions Hellman's propensity for feuds. By no means should her behaviour diminish Hellman's worth as a writer, but her conduct has called into question her credibility as a memoirist, her chosen profession later in life.

Hellman closed out the decade of the 1930s with production of *The Little Foxes* (1939), dealt with in the Hellman chapter, and she ended her association with actress Tallulah Bankhead, who scored a hit performing the leading role, the now legendary scheming Regina. Their ongoing quarrel – one that appears at least in part to have constituted a competition between two very public and strong-minded women, each craving the spotlight – ended in a political dispute turned 'cat fight' à la that depicted in Clare Booth Luce's *The Women*. Bankhead and the cast had accepted an offer to perform in a benefit for Finnish Relief after Russia invaded Finland and were dismayed when Hellman refused to grant permission for it. Legend has it – recorded by critic Joseph Wood Krutch – that Hellman struck Bankhead with her handbag![53] Perhaps merely one of many apocryphal anecdotes about Hellman, nonetheless, the incident reflects the playwright's reputation on two levels, pointing to her personality and her political views. (Her alleged pro-Stalinist leanings, exhibited by unflattering comments she made concerning Finland and Russia at the time of the incident, haunted her across her lifetime.)

The first three-quarters of the decade of the 1940s were productive and rewarding years for the playwright. Her war play, *Watch on the Rhine*, received the 1941 New York Drama Critics' Award (Dashiell Hammett wrote the screenplay for the movie version, released in 1944); Hellman's screenplays for *The Little Foxes* and *The North Star* garnered Oscar nominations in 1944; and *The Searching Wind*, starring Montgomery Clift and Sylvia Sidney, was produced on Broadway in 1944 (with a more than respectable 318 performances), with the film version two years later starring Robert Young. *Another Part of the Forest*, the prequel to *The Little Foxes*, opened in 1946. In this piece, Hellman turns to another era, casting the action of the play in Reconstruction

Alabama, allowing her to trace the roots of the Hubbards' family fortune to patriarch Marcus Hubbard's dishonest business deals and inappropriate behaviour during the Civil War. In it we see how heredity and environment moulded the characters of Regina and her brothers and the ways in which their duplicity and greed derived from their early life in a dysfunctional family, one in which their mother's mental capacity was challenged by her husband as she remained locked in a loveless marriage. We also meet a young Birdie and witness how she is eventually coerced into the marriage that will affect her sanity in *The Little Foxes*. *Another Part of the Forest* is not, however, a historical drama, as its setting serves merely as a backdrop to, rather than as an integral part of, the play's action. Neither is the play a parable placed in the past to illuminate present-day conditions.

Hellman was inducted as a member of the National Institute of Arts and Letters in 1947, the season in which *Another Part of the Forest* was produced, and 1947 also marked the HUAC appearances of the 'Hollywood Ten' and the film industry's response. Hellman refused to sign a contract with Columbia Pictures that contained a 'loyalty' clause,[54] and her blacklisting followed. The playwright did speak out, in an editorial she submitted to the Screen Writers' Guild magazine, which she titled, 'The Judas Goats'.[55] By her own account, Hellman's loss of income lasted some eight years, and her blacklisting eventually cost her the beloved farm she shared with Dashiell Hammett.[56]

After adapting and directing *Monserrat* (1949), the playwright entered the 1950s with completion of her favourite play, *The Autumn Garden*, and its Broadway production in 1951. With *The Autumn Garden*, Hellman veered from her usual path of melodrama and the Well-Made Play structure into more of a composite structure, akin to Chekhov, whose work she had come to admire. With its seasonal metaphor, autumn being the time of perhaps an Indian summer followed by decay, the play, an ensemble piece, tells the story of disappointments, lost loves and the wasted lives of its characters.

The year 1952 constituted a watershed for the playwright, with Hellman's appearance before the House Un-American Activities Committee. Library of Congress historian and Cold War expert John Earl Haynes summarizes and analyses the playwright's testimony in his article 'Lillian Hellman and the Hollywood Inquisition:

The Triumph of Spin-Control over Candour', explaining how she succeeded in testifying that she was not a communist while also refusing to discuss what she knew of communist activities or identifying those communists she knew.⁵⁷ He continues:

> Her testimony was also done with such adroitness that her refusal to answer Committee questions escaped a contempt citation while also avoiding the stigma of being identified as a 'fifth-amendment Communist', i.e. one who refused to answer questions about Communism by claiming the fifth-amendment right against self-incrimination, a claim regarded by the public as indicating that the claimant had something incriminating to hide.⁵⁸

In this piece, written long after the fact in 1998, Haynes reveals a draft of Hellman's statement to the press (included in the 'Documents' chapter), submitted by her to her attorney, Joseph Rauh, in which she admits to having been a member of the Communist Party from 1938 to 1940. According to Hellman, she was a 'casual member' who 'drifted away' from the party. She claims her 'maverick spirit' was compatible with neither the extreme political left nor the extreme conservative right. In both the draft and her final letter to Committee Chair John Wood, Hellman discusses the complexities of testifying before HUAC, and the incomprehensibility of the intricacies for the 'layman'.⁵⁹ While they may have struggled with parsing the particulars of the processes, participants from the film industry were no doubt aware of the professional stakes involved in their appearances before HUAC. Lillian Hellman simply 'played her cards right' and, while she endured blacklisting and a life swathed in suspicion, unlike Odets (or Kazan) she was deemed neither 'friendly' nor uncooperative. On a personal level, her sometime consort John Melby suffered the collateral damage of Hellman's involvement. He was dismissed from his position at the State Department.⁶⁰

Coincidentally, *L'Alouette* or *The Lark*, Jean Anouilh's play about the French martyr Joan of Arc, with its ambiguous ending in which Joan is granted at least temporary reprieve, appeared in the same year that Lillian Hellman testified, and Hellman provided Broadway with its English adaptation in 1955, one in which she 'developed Anouilh's play as an analogy for her own well-known refusal to 'cut [her] conscience to fit this year's fashions' when asked to name names before HUAC.[61] Leonard Bernstein composed incidental music for the production, and he and Hellman collaborated again on *Candide* in 1957. Hellman recalled the creating and mounting of *Candide* as unpleasant, confessing that she found collaboration stressful. As librettist for the comic opera, she again emphasized HUAC, this time, as explained by Brenda Murphy in *Congressional Theatre*, even more blatantly, in fact, burlesquing committee proceedings.[62]

For her next project, *Toys in the Attic* (1960), and for her last Broadway play, in 1963, *My Mother, My Father, and Me*, adapted from Bert Belchman's novel *How Much?*, the playwright returned to working solo.

With *Toys in the Attic*, Hellman continued to employ the Chekhovian tactics with which she experimented in *The Autumn Garden*. It includes poetic and touching speeches unlike those in some of her earlier plays. In fact, the New Orleans Bernier sisters have been compared to the characters in Chekhov's *The Three Sisters*.[63] *My Mother, My Father, and Me* (1963) constituted an ignominious conclusion to Hellman's playwriting career, running for a total of only seventeen performances.

Lillian Hellman's plays, mined by feminist critics in recent years, and in the case of *The Children's Hour* examined from a gay and lesbian perspective, offer fodder for new and exciting exploration from a variety of critical lenses. A review of the playwright's work reveals how (probably unintentionally) Hellman sprinkled her plays with characters, for example, that exhibit deviance or abnormal behaviours, certainly conduct that challenges society's conventions, well beyond the pathological little Mary or the perceived sexual orientation of Martha. These characters and situations, ripe for further exploration, range from Cora in *Days to Come*, to the alcoholic personality of Birdie, the 'unwomanly behavior' of Regina and Alexandra's constructed gender (she wanted to drive the horses) in *The Little Foxes*, to the 'abnormal' attachment of sister to brother and the interracial class-crossing relationship of a matriarch to her employee in *Toys in the Attic*.

Hellman briefly returned to screenwriting, for example with *The Chase*, starring Marlon Brando, in 1965, but her interest in stage and film had dwindled. Other forms of writing occupied her attention: the editing of a collection of Hammett's stories (1966), and before that, an edition of Chekhov's letters (1955), followed by a whole new career as a memoirist with *An Unfinished Woman: A Memoir* (1969), *Pentimento: A Book of Portraits* (1973), *Scoundrel Time* (1976), *Maybe: A Story* (categorized as fiction) and *Three* (both in 1980). At the time of her death in 1984, long a gourmet aficionado, the playwright was collaborating with long-time friend and sometime lover Peter Feibleman on *Eating Together: Recipes and Recollections*.

Lillian Hellman was the recipient of many, many honours and awards across her lifetime, including the National Book Award for *An Unfinished Woman* (1969), the Edward MacDowell Medal for her contribution to literature (1976) and the Paul Robeson Award from Actors' Equity (also 1976). Hellman herself serves as a character in several plays, among them *Lillian*, the one-woman show performed by Zoe Caldwell in 1986; Peter Feibleman's 1993 *Cakewalk*, starring Elaine Stritch; and Nora Ephron's *Imaginary Friends* (2002), based on the personal and legal battle between Hellman and Mary McCarthy.

At least ten biographies – some critical, some strictly biographical and some sensational – have been written about Lillian Hellman. Kessler-Harris's subtitle, 'A Difficult Woman', and Dorothy Gallagher's 'An Imperious Life' convey, to some extent at least, popular opinion of the playwright. 'Tell-alls' exist, some written by Hellman's alleged allies. No matter the manner in which she (or others who wrote about her) may have 'misremembered' or characterized events of her life, as Hellman biographer William Wright concludes, this playwright's colourful life and her *oeuvre* certainly 'justify' her 'outsized legend'.[64]

Documents

Excerpts from the Gertrude Stein Symposium at New York University (2001)

Bevya Rosten, Anne-Marie Levine, Catharine Stimpson, Richard Howard, Wendy Steiner, Maria Irene Fornes, Mac Wellman, Al Carmines, Richard Foreman, Charles Bernstein, Jane Bowers

Theater 12 (2) (Summer 2002): 2–25 (Duke University Press).

This selection is chosen for many reasons alluded to across this text, one being that so much of Gertrude Stein's writing is readily available in print. The piece included here, then, is not in Stein's words, but rather in those of her successors. It is taken from a twenty-first-century gathering of Stein scholars and theatre practitioners, some noted in the Stein chapter or in the Afterword. Bevya Rosten convened the symposium and accompanying performance. Below are comments from playwrights Maria Irene Fornes and Mac Wellman, and directors Al Carmines and Richard Foreman. The day's panels were titled 'Stein's Landscape: Politics, Love, and Art', 'Stein's Influence on Contemporary Performance Practices' and 'Stein's Legacy in Language'.

From Panel 2: 'Stein's Influence on Contemporary Performance Practices', pages 17–18

MARIA IRENE FORNES: I never liked Stein. I couldn't understand why people were so in love with her writing. I thought that it was too cute, too charming, too playful. I don't mean that I hated her, but I didn't find that very special attraction that other people felt for her. When the Acting Company asked me if I would do an adaptation for the stage of *The Autobiography of Alice B. Toklas*, I said yes because I wanted to find out what there was about Gertrude Stein that I didn't see, and what other people saw. So many people have such high respect for Gertrude Stein that I wanted to see how I had failed. She had managed to hypnotize people, and maybe she would hypnotize me, too.

ROSTEN: You said at one point that Stein's repetition really irritated you, and then, after you began to work on the adaptation, you discovered that it was tremendously profound.

FORNES: I wouldn't say that it was profound, but I do believe that she was not being precious, she was not being cute. I felt that the repetitions were part of her experience of things. They were sincere.

MAC WELLMAN: I think I have a similarly complex relationship to Stein. When I first read her, I simply didn't get it. The tautologies really irritated me. I thought it was cute. I couldn't read it. It actually wasn't until I came to New York City and began to see shows by this genius [*gestures to Al Carmines*] ... that the whole thing just completely opened up for me. So I really do think of her as a profound theatrical force ...

AL CARMINES: ... I was a fervent disciple of Tillich ... When I came to Judson, I had planned only to stay for a couple of years and go back and study with Tillich and get my doctorate. But, when I got to Judson, I discovered Gertrude Stein. She was not only fascinating to me, not only clear to me, but a great threat to my Tillichianism ... And the only way I could respond to that threat was by composing ... When I first read her works I was so threatened by this this-worldly person, this un-Tillian woman, this totally complex human being without any visible god, that I was frightened ... I was so frightened that she might be right, that maybe this world was enough.

From Panel 3: 'Stein's Legacy in Language', pages 20–2

RICHARD FOREMAN: I am one of those many workers in the fields of language and art today when we are indeed making the *materiality*, making the *continual present* of art and literature and theater erupt in our work. Gertrude Stein was mother, Brecht was my father, and just at a certain point I felt the pouring forth of obvious great genius, I was smothered by the mother's milk of language pouring out of Stein.

... I'm very worried about the future. I'm very worried about the computerization of all of us, and of us the computerization of our language ... The continual present of everything being available in this web of information that we have – Stein, to me, is a kind of precursor of that in a strange way.

... Stein was also introducing ... a kind of dailiness. We are forgetting how mundane, how daily, language writing is ... Stein is saying, 'No, to escape the present, wait. Focus on these tiny, meaningless things that seem to come from nowhere from the unconscious.'

... I hate, in Stein productions, a kind of cuteness in relation to her language, delivering it as if these were witty things that are being said. To me, it is a suffocated person, as all artists are, trying to find a way to assert an alternative reality.

Langston Hughes, 'The Negro Artist and the Racial Mountain' (1926)

The Nation, 23 June 1926, 692–4.

Although this, Langston Hughes's 'manifesto', has been widely reprinted, it is crucial in placing the playwright in context. It predates and presages his work as both an artist and a civil rights advocate in the 1930s and beyond.

One of the most promising of the young Negro poets said to me once, 'I want to be a poet – not a Negro poet,' meaning, I believe, 'I want to write like a white poet'; meaning subconsciously, 'I would like to be a white poet'; meaning behind that, 'I would like to be white.' And I was sorry the young man said that, for no great poet has ever been afraid of being himself. And I doubted then that, with his desire to run away spiritually from his race, this boy would ever be a great poet. But this is the mountain standing in the way of any true Negro art in America – this urge within the race toward whiteness, the desire to pour racial individuality into the mold of American standardization, and to be as little Negro and as much American as possible.

But let us look at the immediate background of this young poet. His family is of what I suppose one would call the Negro middle class: people who are by no means rich yet never uncomfortable nor hungry – smug, contented, respectable folk, members of the Baptist church. The father goes to work every morning. He is a chief steward at a large white club. The mother sometimes does fancy sewing or supervises parties for the rich families of the town. The children go to a mixed school. In the home they read white papers and magazines. And the mother often says 'Don't be like niggers' when the children are bad. A frequent phrase from the father is, 'Look how well a white man does things.' And so the word white comes to be unconsciously a symbol of all virtues. It holds for the children beauty, morality, and money. The whisper of 'I want to be white' runs silently through their minds. This young poet's home is, I believe, a fairly typical home of the colored middle class. One sees immediately how difficult it would be for an artist born in such a home to interest himself in interpreting the beauty of his own people. He is never taught to see that beauty. He is taught rather not to see it, or if he does, to be ashamed of it when it is not according to Caucasian patterns.

For racial culture the home of a self-styled 'high-class' Negro has nothing better to offer. Instead there will perhaps be more aping of things white than in a less cultured or less wealthy home. The father is perhaps a doctor, lawyer, landowner, or politician. The mother may be a social worker, or a teacher, or she may do nothing and have a maid. Father is often dark but he has usually married the lightest woman he could find. The family attend a fashionable church where few really colored faces are to be found. And they themselves draw a color line. In the North they go to white theaters and white movies. And in the South they have at least two cars and [a] house 'like white folks.' Nordic manners, Nordic faces, Nordic hair, Nordic art (if any), and an Episcopal heaven. A very high mountain indeed for the would-be racial artist to climb in order to discover himself and his people.

But then there are the low-down folks, the so-called common element, and they are the majority – may the Lord be praised! The people who have their hip of gin on Saturday nights and are not too important to themselves or the community, or too well fed, or too learned to watch the lazy world go round. They live on Seventh Street in Washington or State Street in Chicago and they do not particularly care whether they are like white folks or anybody else. Their joy runs, bang! into ecstasy. Their religion soars to a shout. Work maybe a little today, rest a little tomorrow. Play awhile. Sing awhile. O, let's dance! These common people are not afraid of spirituals, as for a long time their more intellectual brethren were, and jazz is their child. They furnish a wealth of colorful, distinctive material for any artist because they still hold their own individuality in the face of American standardizations. And perhaps these common people will give to the world its truly great Negro artist, the one who is not afraid to be himself. Whereas the better-class Negro would tell the artist what to do, the people at least let him alone when he does appear. And they are not ashamed of him – if they know he exists at all. And they accept what beauty is their own without question.

Certainly there is, for the American Negro artist who can escape the restrictions the more advanced among his own group would put upon him, a great field of unused material ready for his art. Without going outside his race, and even among the better classes with their 'white' culture and conscious American manners, but still Negro enough to be different, there is sufficient matter to furnish a black artist with a lifetime of creative work. And when he chooses to touch on the relations between Negroes and whites in this country, with their innumerable overtones and undertones surely, and especially for literature and the drama, there is an inexhaustible supply of themes at hand. To these the Negro artist can give his racial individuality, his heritage of rhythm and warmth, and his incongruous humor that so often, as in the Blues, becomes ironic laughter mixed with tears. But let us look again at the mountain.

A prominent Negro clubwoman in Philadelphia paid eleven dollars to hear Raquel Meller sing Andalusian popular songs. But she told me a few weeks before she would not think of going to hear 'that woman,' Clara Smith, a great black artist, sing Negro folksongs. And many an upper-class Negro church, even now, would not dream of employing a spiritual in its services. The drab melodies in white folks' hymnbooks are much to be preferred. 'We want to worship the Lord correctly and quietly. We don't believe in 'shouting.' Let's be dull like the Nordics,' they say, in effect.

The road for the serious black artist, then, who would produce a racial art is most certainly rocky and the mountain is high. Until recently he received almost no encouragement for his work from either white or colored people. The fine novels of Chesnutt go out of print with neither race noticing their passing. The quaint charm and humor of Dunbar's dialect verse brought to him, in his day, largely the same kind of encouragement one would give a sideshow freak (A colored man writing poetry! How odd!) or a clown (How amusing!).

The present vogue in things Negro, although it may do as much harm as good for the budding artist, has at least done this: it has brought him forcibly to the attention of his own people among whom for so long, unless the other race had noticed him beforehand, he was a prophet with little honor.

The Negro artist works against an undertow of sharp criticism and misunderstanding from his own group and unintentional bribes from the whites. 'Oh, be respectable, write about nice people, show how good we are,' say the Negroes. 'Be stereotyped, don't go too far, don't shatter our illusions about you, don't amuse us too seriously. We will pay you,' say the whites. Both would have told Jean Toomer not to write *Cane*. The colored people did not praise it. The white people did not buy it. Most of the colored people who did read *Cane* hate it. They are afraid of it. Although the critics gave it good reviews the public remained indifferent. Yet (excepting the work of Du Bois) *Cane* contains the finest prose written by a Negro in America. And like the singing of Robeson, it is truly racial.

But in spite of the Nordicized Negro intelligentsia and the desires of some white editors we have an honest American Negro literature already with us. Now I await the rise of the Negro theater. Our folk music, having achieved world-wide fame, offers itself to the genius of the great individual American composer who is to come. And within the next decade I expect to see the work of a growing school of colored artists who paint and model the beauty of dark faces and create with new technique the expressions of their own soul-world. And the Negro dancers who will dance like flame and the singers who will continue to carry our songs to all who listen – they will be with us in even greater numbers tomorrow.

Most of my own poems are racial in theme and treatment, derived from the life I know. In many of them I try to grasp and hold some of the meanings and rhythms of jazz. I am as sincere as I know how to be in these poems and yet after every reading I answer questions like these from my own people: Do you think Negroes should always write about Negroes? I wish you wouldn't read some of your poems to white folks. How do you find anything interesting in a place like a cabaret? Why do you write about black people? You aren't black. What makes you do so many jazz poems?

But jazz to me is one of the inherent expressions of Negro life in America; the eternal tom-tom beating in the Negro soul – the tom-tom of revolt against weariness in a white world, a world of subway trains, and work, work, work; the tom-tom of joy and laughter, and pain swallowed in a smile. Yet the Philadelphia clubwoman is ashamed to say that her race created it and she does not like me to write about it. The old subconscious 'white is best' runs through her mind. Years of study under white teachers, a lifetime of white books, pictures, and papers, and white manners, morals, and Puritan standards made her dislike the spirituals. And now she turns up her nose at jazz and all its manifestations – likewise almost everything else distinctly racial. She doesn't care for the Winold Reiss' portraits of Negroes because they are 'too Negro.' She does not want a true picture of herself from anybody. She wants the artist to flatter her, to make the white world believe that all Negroes are as smug and as near white in soul as she wants to be. But, to my mind, it is the duty of the younger Negro artist, if he accepts any duties at all from outsiders, to change through the force of his art that old whispering 'I want to be white,' hidden in the aspirations of his people, to 'Why should I want to be white? I am a Negro – and beautiful'?

So I am ashamed for the black poet who says, 'I want to be a poet, not a Negro poet,' as though his own racial world were not as interesting as any other world. I am ashamed, too, for the colored artist who runs from the painting of Negro faces to the painting of sunsets after the manner of the academicians because he fears the strange unwhiteness of his own features. An artist must be free to choose what he does, certainly, but he must also never be afraid to do what he must choose.

Let the blare of Negro jazz bands and the bellowing voice of Bessie Smith singing the Blues penetrate the closed ears of the colored near intellectuals until they listen and perhaps understand. Let Paul Robeson singing 'Water Boy,' and Rudolph Fisher writing about the streets of Harlem, and Jean Toomer holding the heart of Georgia in his hands, and Aaron Douglas's drawing strange black fantasies cause the smug Negro middle class to turn from their white, respectable, ordinary books and papers to catch a glimmer of their own beauty. We younger Negro artists who create now intend to express our individual dark-skinned selves without fear or shame. If white people are pleased we are glad. If they are not, it doesn't matter. We know we are beautiful. And ugly too. The tom-tom cries and the tom-tom laughs. If colored people are pleased we are glad. If they are not, their displeasure doesn't matter either. We build our temples for tomorrow, strong as we know how, and we stand on top of the mountain, free within ourselves.

'Langston Hughes Proposes an Oath to End All Oaths for Americans' (1951)

The Chicago Defender, 10 March 1951, 6.

This selection, one of Hughes's hundreds of pieces for the Chicago Defender, *was written two decades after the 1930s, but before Hughes's testimony before HUAC. It anticipates the civil rights battle across the United States, and it stands as a reminder in the troubled times of the 2010s.*

Since this is the Year of Oaths – Loyalty Oaths, Anti-Communist Oaths, Behave-Yourself Oaths – as an American Negro citizen, I hereby propose a series of oaths I would I [sic] love to see my fellow Americans take – providing one could guarantee them working:

I solemnly swear that I will no longer hold in my heart contempt of [sic] hatred for any human being on account of race, color, creed, poverty or previous condition of servitude. I will treat everybody with courtesy and decency, rich or poor, black or white, Jew or Gentile, Catholic or Protestant, foreign-born or 201% American, whether of Mayflower, refugee, or slave ship origin.

I also swear and affirm that I will no longer Jim crow anybody or patronize any hotel, restaurant, railroad, or steamship line that practices the segregation of my fellow human beings.

I will not attend motion picture or dramatic theatres where fellow citizens of color have to sit in the gallery. I will not teach in nor send my children to schools where Negro, Mexican-American, or Indian children may not study, or where my colored fellow-citizens, if qualified, may not teach.

I further swear that I will have no part of churches that draw the color line, because it seems to me wrong to talk religion and not practice it, to believe in Christ and not try to act like Christ, to pray and not mean my prayers. I will open my arms to all mankind and welcome all who might wish to enter my churches in fellowship and reverence.

I do solemnly swear that I will never use insulting epithets toward my fellow-citizens of other racial or religious groups. I will not interfere in the ways of worship of those whose creed may not be my own, but I will let all men worship according to their lights and find heaven in their own way. And I will try to prepare myself for a heaven in which there is no color line, and try to make a better world before I leave this earthly home.

I swear and affirm that I will not refuse to work side by side with other Americans if I am a worker. If I am an employer, I will employ in my shop, plant, factory, foundry, or whatever establishment I own or manage any man or woman capable of doing the work required without regard to the color of the face or the religious creed of the worker. I will institute immediately an individual Fair Employment Practice Act of my own, and see that it [is] carried out.

I further swear I will never tell mammy jokes, or any other type of offensive joke that may hurt or humiliate any fellow citizen. I will not laugh at stereotypes on the stage or in the movies. My embarrassed silence will indicate to producers on Broadway or in Hollywood how shameful it is to ridicule unkindly any people in our commonwealth.

I will not buy for my children books to [sic] which other children are caricatured in an unkind racial fashion or pictured as funny little varmints because of their color or religious background.

On the positive side I swear I will support motion pictures, plays, and books which seek to portray minority groups as human beings with no more sins or faults than all human beings have – which are many. I will buy the products of those firms that employ in their plants and factories all peoples without discrimination. I will give aid and comfort to all groups trying to make a better, more decent America. I will take no part in Ku Klux Klans, pseudo-100% American groups seeking to make an exclusively white Protestant Gentile society along Hitler lines excluding millions of other Americans from their plans for prosperity. I will actively oppose such organizations.

I swear that henceforth when I pledge allegiance to the flag, I will really mean what I say 'with liberty and justice for all.' A-L-L – ALL – EVERYBODY in these United States of America. I swear to make America mean all that its Constitution indicates – for ALL. So help me God.

Excerpts from Clifford Odets's HUAC testimony (1952)

'Communist Infiltration of the Hollywood Motion Picture Industry – Part 8', Hearings Before the Committee on Un-American Activities, House of Representatives, Eighty-Second Congress, Second Session, 20, 21, 22 May 1953.

The following is excerpted from Clifford Odets's second day of testimony before HUAC on 20 May 1952. Odets had already admitted his membership in the Communist Party at his earlier appearance before the committee. The focus of this portion of his questioning is on Waiting for Lefty, *and the excerpt illustrates the manner in which witnesses were repeatedly asked about events that transpired almost twenty years before. Later on in his testimony, Odets was asked repeatedly about productions of* Lefty *at which he was not present, copyright regarding use of his play by alleged communist organizations, and his participation in charitable*

Popular Front (Odets uses the phrase 'broad front') events. The section reproduced here is useful for understanding the decade of the 1930s in how it illustrates the interrelationship of theatre practitioners, communist, leftist and liberal. Odets exhibits the common knowledge of the era regarding Marxist criticism as well. In his subsequent session, in his defence, Odets stated that while he knew cabbies, he 'made up' the play, drawing on vernacular he had heard rather than on a specific strike.

[Mr. TAVENNER.] You have stated today in your testimony that the criticisms that your productions received from the Communist press were instrumental in your taking the stand, and finally determining that you would break with the Communist Party ... You spoke of the severity of the criticisms. The criticisms that you referred to were criticisms of a technical character regarding your plays, were they not, as distinguished from the criticism of your ability and your skill in portraying the characters?

Mr. ODETS. Well, I would like to ask this, if I may: I would like to read you a few of them, and put a few of them in the record by reading them, and then let you make your own judgment ... I think they are generally all around very bad notices.

Mr. TAVENNER. You say generally bad. Was there a period of time in which the Communist press seemed to change its attitude regarding your plays?

Mr. ODETS. Well, I can only say that from the very first play, from Waiting for Lefty, on until my plays of a year ago, the criticisms were sometimes good and sometimes bad, shockingly bad.

Mr. TAVENNER. What was the purpose of the criticism, do you know?

Mr. ODETS. The purpose, I would think, would be to say 'This man has gone off the track and while he has talent and we mourn his loss,' so to speak, 'we wish we could get him back.'

Mr. TAVENNER. Did it also take on the character of a challenge to you to produce more plays depicting the strike episode as in your play 'Waiting for Lefty'?

Mr. ODETS. That was in the beginning ... It was suggested that I produce or write another strike play.

Mr. TAVENNER. Did that go beyond the cell of the Communist Party of which you were a member?

Mr. ODETS. I should think that I might meet people in the theater and they would say 'When are you going to write another play like Waiting for Left[y]? We need more strike plays ...' However, in the reviews ...

Mr. TAVENNER. Let us come to that in a few minutes ... Did you have the feeling ... that the type of criticism received through the Communist press constituted on the part of the Communist Party to direct you in your course of writing ...

Mr. ODETS. I would say that some of the criticisms were open to that interpretation ...

Mr. TAVENNER. During the period of your membership in the Communist Party did you meet and associate with functionaries of the Communist Party who were interested particularly in the cultural activities of the party, other than members of your OWN cell?

[*Under questioning, Odets mentions meeting V. J. Jerome, one of the founders of the CP-USA, Nathaniel Buchwald, co-founder of the Artef workers theatre group and for the* Daily Worker, *Joe North from the* New Masses, *and Tavenner asks him about Michael Blankfort, director, playwright, critic and the screenwriter who later 'fronted' blacklisted Albert Maltz in the film* The Broken Arrow.]

Mr. TAVENNER. Well, he [Blankfort] placed you highly, too, didn't he?

Mr. ODETS. Well, when he had to he did. But when he could get away from it he didn't. As I said before, there was not always unanimity of opinion, so that a play of mine might be reviewed very badly and then someone else on the left would say 'Just a minute, this play is much better than you put in New Masses, so you must let me write a second article.'

Mr. TAVENNER. Can you assign any reason for that change of attitude?

Mr. ODETS. No, sir ... they wanted to keep me there. They would have liked to have had me write what they might call, with quotes around the word, 'progressive plays.' ...

Mr. TAVENNER. And they attempted to direct you in that course of writing ... did you follow the suggestion which you received by way of criticism through the Communist press, and other ways?

Mr. ODETS. I am afraid I never did ... I didn't believe it. I didn't respect any person or any party or any group of people who would say to a young creative-writer 'Go outside your experience and write outside your experience a play.' I knew as fumbling as my beginnings were, and they certainly were, that I could only write out of my own experience, out of my own incentive.

Mr. TAVENNER. If I understand you correctly, you rebelled against that type of Communist Party discipline.

Mr. ODETS. I did ...

Mr. TAVENNER. Now let us return at this point to the criticisms of your plays because it is rather difficult to follow those criticisms. At times the reviewers praised your works very highly. At other times they criticized usually in matters of form, according to my study of them ...

Mr. ODETS. ... may I go ahead?

[*Given permission to do so, Odets quotes negative portions of a review by Nathaniel Buchwald.*]

Mr. TAVENNER. ... now the same reviewer, in the issue of January 12, 1935, which is some time earlier than the one you referred to, had this to say:

> Propelled by his burning revolutionary fervor, and by essentially clear-guiding idea, this young playwright swept the audience off its feet by the sheer power and sincerity of dramatic utterance,

which was amplified and given vibrant resonance by the magnificent performance of the Group Theater players.

[*This line of questioning continued for some time, during which Tavenner presented left-wing dramatic criticism that was favorable to Odets's work, and the playwright, in his defence, presented that which was negative.*]

[Mr. TAVENNER, cont.] In the issue of January 5, 1935, the same reviewer, that is Nathaniel Buchwald, does criticize certain technical matters which he set forth, but he also says this. He concedes that Odets will learn and that he is splendidly equipped for a young revolutionary dramatist, and that the play is,

> A high watermark of revolutionary drama and probably the most effective agit-prop play written in this country thus far ...

... what is meant by agit-prop play, when he says it is a most effective agit-prop play?

Mr. ODETS. Agit-prop is short for the phrase agitational propaganda.

Mr. TAVENNER. Though he criticized certain technical aspects of your plays, would you not say that at that time, in January of 1935, that the Communist Part was very enthusiastic about Waiting for Lefty?

Mr. ODETS. Yes, I remember telling you distinctly in our last meeting that they were delighted with the play ... very clear to make the point that they thought it was a wonderful play.

Mr. TAVENNER. I find the New Masses review in its issue of January 29, 1935 Mr. Burnshaw had this to say:

> On January 5, when the curtain ran down on the first performance of Clifford Odets' Waiting for Lefty the audience cheered, whistled, and screamed with applause ... he states that 'Some persons referred to the play as a disjointed, structurally arbitrary piece of playwriting' ... that is about what John Howard Lawson had said about it, is that correct?

Mr. ODETS. You have very good notes there ... I remember Jack Lawson. I don't remember what he said.

Mr. TAVENNER. It says:

> Yet a second seeing by the New Masses reviewer provides sufficient perspective – For discerning in the juxtaposition of scenes a clear logic ...

So there was a commendation by the New Masses. Now, John Howard Lawson, according to our study, was concerned in his criticism with the technique, as he referred to it, but he does not question your talent about which he says it is of 'outstanding significance, his skill, his vitality, and honesty rarely found in the current theatre.' ... And he predicts for you a great future. Well, that certainly is not a severe criticism of your work from the standpoint of the Communist Party.

Mr. ODETS. Well, may I say a few words ... They may have interest. A Marxist believes that if you would straighten out your ideology in terms of Marxist orientation ... you will no longer have structural flaws ... I happen to know from reading a book or two that John Howard Lawson very thoroughly believes that. I do not. I have respect in many areas for Jack Lawson as, for instance, a once very, very talented playwright, but the part I am discussing is, I think arrant nonsense.

Mr. TAVENNER. So your position is that these various items of criticism and praise were designed to pressure you as a member of the party into writing more in line with the party dictates and the party policy, is that what I am to understand?

Mr. ODETS. Yes, I would say that they would want me to write more from their world point of view.

Draft of Lillian Hellman's letter to HUAC, written in the form of a public statement, to be issued in the event Hellman refused to testify (1952)

John Earl Haynes, 'Hellman and the Hollywood Inquisition: The Triumph of Spin-Control Over Candor', *Film History* 10 (1998): 408–14.

Lillian Hellman's final letter to Committee Chair John Wood is widely available, but the document below is not. In his book, Lillian Hellman: Her Life and Legend *(2008), Carl Rollyson discusses his discovery of the letter in the Joseph Rauh papers at the Library of Congress (237). Some phrases, in particular the paragraphs about the playwright's traditional American upbringing, appear in all three versions in the Rauh collection. The letter(s) illustrates Hellman's rhetorical strategies, apparent in every autobiographical piece she crafted. In terms of content, without 'naming names' in the letter reprinted here, Hellman gives her opinion of those who did 'name names' in their testimonies (among them, in the context of this volume, Clifford Odets).*

This morning I refused to answer questions put to me by the House Un-American Activities Committee. I wanted to answer the questions because I have nothing to hide and nothing to be ashamed of. But a few weeks ago I learned from the Committee's counsel that if I answered questions about myself I would also be forced to answer questions about other people, and that if I refused to do that I would be cited for contempt. That was difficult for a layman to understand. But there is one thing I do understand: I am not willing now or in the future to serve as an informer and thus to save myself at the expense of people who committed no wrong except that they once held unpopular political opinions. I do not believe any government anywhere on earth has a right to ask a citizen to hand over his conscience, and I will not make myself today's cheap favourite by doing so.

My own story is simple. I joined the Communist Party in 1938 and left it sometime in 1940. I was a most casual member. I attended very few meetings and saw and heard nothing more than people sitting around a room talking of current events or discussing the books they had read. I drifted away from the Communist Party because I seemed in the wrong place. My own maverick nature was no more suitable to the political left than it had been to the conservative background from which I came. No pressure were [sic] ever brought on me or my work, and no suggestion was ever made that I return to the Party.

Since that time I have, entirely on my own judgment, joined many organizations. I heard much that I disagreed with, and I disagreed very loudly, but I have never heard anything sub[v]ersive, or disloyal or unpatriotic. I do not like subversion in any form and I would have considered it my duty to have reported it to the proper authorities.

My own work is the proof that I have always gone in an independent direction. I wrote 'Watch on the Rhine' at the height of the Nazi–Soviet pact. As a matter of fact, my work has most often been attacked by the Left press, but I felt that they had as much right to their opinions as did any other group, and that I, in turn, had a right to ignore their opinions.

I went to Russia in the autumn of 1944 as a guest of the Soviet Cultural groups. I was frightened of the dangerous fourteen-day flight across Siberia, but I took the trip because members of our government thought that any friendly contact was desirable. I travelled a great deal in Russia and I was the only foreigner every [sic] permitted to go [to] the Russian front and live with the army. I immediately made it clear to the Russians that I must feel free to speak about the trip with my own government. I did exactly that, and I was told that my travels had been most valuable to our country. I saw horrible destruction in Russia, and incredible suffering. I came to the conclusions that the Russians could not want another war, and that we would all have to find a way to peace. There were no secrets about my feelings. I spoke about them and I wrote them down. I still believe my trip was of some small value, and I quote from a speech printed in the Russian press: 'We are accustomed to foreigners who hate us and to foreigners who love us too much. But Miss Hellman is our first visitor who deeply loves her own country and does not hate us.'

Because I believe in peace I have joined many organizations. Certainly there were Communists in these organizations. I decided long ago that people who were going my way could perfectly well come along. I am not a child and I cannot be led astray, nor did anybody every [sic] try to do so. My last organizational activity was the Progressive Party. I resigned from the Progressive Party because I came to the conclusion, finally, that I am not a political person and that I have no place in any political group. I do not ever again wish to have any political connections, but I have no guilt about those in my past, bitterness, and no blame for anybody.

For me it was all a long time ago. But I was raised in an old-fashioned American tradition and that meant the right to think, to speak and to write with full freedom, and to allow others to do the same. And there were certain other homely things that were taught to me: to try to tell the truth, to be loyal to my friends and to my country, not to destroy my neighbor, and so on. In general, I accepted the Christian ideals of honor. It is not my fault if today many of those ideals are being twisted to suit the convenience of men who do not truly love their country, and who hold it in disrespect.

There is nothing good in not [sic?] betraying innocent people. It simply cannot be done. And those who have done it, and those who have urged them to do it, owe their God and their country a lifetime of prayers.

Workers' theatre: Excerpts from Mordecai Gorelik,'Theatre is a Weapon' (1934)

Theatre Arts Monthly 18 (June 1934): 421–33.

Designer, theatre historian and educator Mordecai Gorelik began his Broadway career with a 1925 production by John Howard Lawson for the Theatre Guild. He also worked at the Neighborhood Playhouse and with the famed Provincetown Players. He designed most of Lawson's plays, and most of those produced by the Group Theatre. He taught at the Theatre Collective and designed for the

Theatre Union. He was hired by the Federal Theatre Project as well. His was the designer for the premiere of Arthur Miller's All My Sons. *He authored the seminal theatre history text* New Theatres for Old *(1940) and wrote widely for both workers' periodicals and journals of the stage. This article is selected for several reasons: 1) as a theatre historian, he chronicles the history of the workers' theatre movement even as he lived it; 2) he mentions several of the plays, playwrights and companies referenced in this book; 3) he was acquainted with all of the people and companies about whom he writes; 4) he offers a 'leftist' perspective but he was never a communist, considering himself to be a 'bleeding heart liberal'; and 5) he considered himself a worker and fought for fair pay for actors, designers and technicians. He serves as a representative for other participants in the amateur and professional companies that addressed working- and middle-class issues of the 1930s.*

The theatre, in the course of its long history, has many times changed its forms, because society has changed its forms. Today one must be blind to deny that society is once more undergoing tremendous changes. These changes bear hardest upon the working class, making it a sensitive barometer of social and political storm. Into what new conception are we moving? The militant workers – whom Karl Marx called the advance guard of the proletariat – have their answer: *Theatre is a weapon!*

What is the meaning of this sentence, which appears sometimes on the banners formally hung across the prosceniums of the American workers' theatres? What, indeed, are the workers' theatres? Until lately Broadway has not even known of their existence.

To understand the workers' theatres of this country, one must first take into account their opinion of the economic crisis and the relation of this crisis to the commercial theatre. The bankruptcies, strikes and revolts that convulse most of the world are proof to them that capitalism has entered its last phase. 'In the Soviet Union,' they declare, 'this exploitative system has been overthrown, and the workers are building a socialist state. Elsewhere fascist dictatorships attempt to prolong the life of capitalism by means of terror.'

The art of the theatre of any period springs from the social and economic institutions of its audience. Accordingly, the revolutionary observers maintain that the world theatre cannot be unaffected by such a cataclysm, nor is the American theatre an exception. They estimate that the American commercial theatre, in its most prosperous times, never played to even twenty per cent of the population of this country, and that at present it does not play to even ten per cent. If so, it is this small, comparatively well-circumstanced audience which determines the themes and ideals of Broadway plays ...

In the matter of plays, the crisis has been responsible for two divergent trends in Broadway playwriting ... There is a movement away from realism to a nostalgic idealization of the past, in the form of romantic costume drama. On the other hand political questions in one form or another are beginning to take place alongside of problems of the individual psyche; the commercial theatre is involved to some extent in the general problems of the day, and casts about for a message to its audience. Thus Elmer Rice, in *We, the People* has suggested a return to Jeffersonian democracy as the way out of the national dilemma, while Eugene O'Neill seems to reach back still further to the implicit faith of the Catholic Church.

Economically the Broadway theatre is dominated by realty concerns, each production is a desperate gamble with an 82 per cent prospect of failure, labor troubles are on the increase, and more than three-fourths of all stage employees are out of work. Faced with this dilemma, the commercial theatre managers propose to establish a 'national theatre', a highly centralized institution, partly subsidized by public funds, which will endeavor to retain what is left of the commercial theatre audience, eliminating wasteful competition, limiting the number of employees, and cutting overhead expenses to the bone. Such a program, of course, closely parallels that of other industrial owners.

It is precisely in this matter of a national program that the objectives of the workers' theatres become clear. For to the workers' theatres and community playhouses alike, there is a difference between a national theatre and a national theatre monopoly.

The workers' theatres ask: 'Has the term "national theatre" any meaning when it leaves out of reckoning a national audience, when it ignores in its plays all the great national conflicts? What does such a "national theatre" mean to the broad American population, the farmers and the industrial workers who cannot afford to buy

even second-balcony seats, and whose chief concern is not with inward musings but with the bitter struggle for bread?'...
Commercial managers as a rule do not give much time to the study of their second- balcony audiences ... it might be a revelation [for them] to learn ... the reactions of a class-conscious worker who is able to see a typical Broadway play. 'Who is this hero in a dress suit?' asks the worker, 'and why is he always hanging around rooms and bedrooms? Who are the clowns in overalls, the soubrettes in maids' aprons? Are they supposed to be self-respecting workers? Still more puzzling, all the characters in the play never stop thinking, yet they do not seem to think about anything more concrete than romantic love. It is quite clear that this theatre and its audience have had no experience with breadlines, evictions, strikes or lynchings. It is clear, in fact, that this theatre is the theatre of my employers, that it represents their point of view, is concerned with their problems, and proposes their own idea of a solution.'

[...] the comment of culturally developed revolutionary workers is ten times more incisive. For them the theatre is no abstract art but a weapon of persuasion, to be used in the worldwide struggle between the owners of industry and the working population. 'Theatre is a weapon,' say the worker-actors, 'but it is a weapon for both sides.' The capitalists, although they insist the theatre is pure art, use it more and more to mislead and stupefy the population. When O'Neill and Barry point to the moral that implicit faith is the solution to our ills, they enable our rulers to continue their war preparations and wage-cuts with no embarrassing questions asked. No doubt these playwrights have the best of intentions; the fact remains that they add their efforts to the sum total of propaganda which either justifies the aims of the capitalist oppressors or shields them from investigation ...

[...] change ... has come over the radical theatres since the days of the Provincetown Players and the New Playwrights Theatre. It is significant that while both the Provincetown and the New Playwrights grew out of rebellious middle-class groups sympathetic to labor, the new theatres stem from workers' organizations. The cultural leadership of the working class has definitely passed out of the hands of sympathetic intellectuals into those of the revolutionary workers themselves, to whom it is a truism that the class war exists in the cultural field ...

The first evidence of this change was hardly more than the emergence of the slogan, 'Theatre is a weapon!' But this was a slogan with the power to unite isolated groups, and to invest them with a new determination. Dramatic units which had hitherto limited themselves to occasional entertainments for the trade unions or relief agencies ... took on permanence and an identity of their own. Two New York units were especially engaged in the pioneer work of this period – the Workers Laboratory Theatre, one of the cultural sections of the Workers International relief; and the Prolet-Bühne, a German-speaking troupe; they jointly issued a mimeographed monthly bulletin entitled Workers Theatre, and supplied the initiative for the first national conference of workers' theatres, April 1932.

Today the League of Workers Theatres (L.O.W.T.), established at that conference, has contact with four hundred groups in this country and Canada ... dramatic troupes have originated in varied revolutionary bodies – trade unions, social and athletic clubs, farm leagues, student organizations, culture clubs, foreign-language societies.

Almost penniless, rehearsing and playing evenings after a hard day's work or search for work, the worker-players continue to add to their number, put on productions and gather devoted audiences while the commercial theatre, with comparatively every material resource, settles into a decline. On their stages the voice of the worker speaks so his own class can hear ... Workers and farmers facing eviction, strikers on the picket lines, negroes threatened by lynch gangs, have not the time to wait until the commercial theatre, by a vision of abstract beauty, shall teach the world to become a beautiful place to live in. All that in good time, after the classless society has been established ...

Professional theatre managers who know the difficulties encountered in producing plays even when there is plenty of money available, would throw up their hands at the situation in the workers' theatres ...

The undertaking of a full-length play presents obstacles that are all but insurmountable. Scenery, costumes, lighting and scene-shifting are reduced to the absolute minimum ... The amount of money raised is never adequate, and the theatres are usually in debt for sums which would appear trifling to Broadway ... How the worker-actors long for some of that 'Moscow gold,' so diligently rumored to be the source of all radical propaganda!

Without exception the workers' form of organization is the co-operative, the general policy as to plays and funds being vested in the membership itself. This type of organization is a guarantee against dictatorship and opportunism ...

One might think ... that there would be no time for the subtleties of technique or craftsmanship. On the contrary, there is increasing emphasis on this aspect of the theatre. A play without artistry is a bad weapon, propaganda which is not convincing is sometimes damaging ...

Three years ago, at the time of the initial reaction against the ideals of the upper-class theatre, the usual form of the workers' theatres was that of the so-called agit-prop (theatre of agitation and propaganda). These were portable productions whose actors brought their settings and costumes to union meetings, strike headquarters, street corners, parks, or workers' social affairs. Their repertory, one-act pieces for the most part, consisted almost entirely of political satires in which the capitalist in a silk hat was the invariable villain and the worker in overalls the shining hero ...

[Here, in a lengthy paragraph, Gorelik, using his quotation-mark questioning style established earlier, addresses the workers' theatres acknowledgement of the crudity of their craft and their desire to learn stage techniques. He continues:]

The start has already been made. Last year witnessed the first production – a revival of Claire and Paul Sifton's *1931* – by the Theatre Collective, of New York, a semi-professional group organized to do full-length plays ... A new dramatic group, the Theatre Collective of Chicago, has just begun work. This season ... the New York Artef, one of the oldest stationary theatres in the country, gave the premiere of Paul Peters and Charles R. Walker's *The Third Parade* ...

It is worth remembering that these producing units are organized on the basis of permanent companies, and that unlike practically all the casts of commercial plays, which disband when the plays are over, they continue to build their repertory and their ensemble playing, and create studios for additional training ...

The developing artistry of the workers' theatres has not been less noticeable in the portable units ... the Workers Laboratory Theatre performed Newsboy in a technique which they called 'theatre-montage', a form probably new to the American stage ...

One reason for such a rapid advance has been the friendly contact set up between the people of the workers' theatre and those of the commercial and community theatre ... A growing section of the former commercial-theatre audience is no longer able to afford tickets to Broadway presentations and has, in fact, lost interest in the Broadway theatre, which in its themes largely ignores the ruin that has overtaken sections of the middle class. This audience is turning to the workers' stage, where an immediate, electrifying bond seems to exist between play and audience ...

Hundreds of young people wanting stage training now get their start in the workers' troupes, and many alert professional theatre people have found in the rising theatre a new source of interest. The workers in turn eagerly welcome the opportunity to have the playwrights, actors and technicians of the professional stage as their instructors in the arts and crafts of the theatre ...

That the contact is having a profound effect can be inferred from at least two instances – the case of the Theatre Union, which drew an unprecedented workers' audience to its anti-war play, *Peace on Earth* ... and the Theatre Guild's *They Shall Not Die*, written by John Wexley ...

What is the ultimate aim of the workers' theatres? To accept the challenge of the worst period of trial in human history. They wish to help build a drama which will reevaluate the standards of the past, seek out the truth despite all obstacles, and hearten the mass of people to the momentous task of founding a new society free of exploitation.

They wish to aid in the building of an audience greater than any ever envisaged before, a theatre of the whole people instead of a theatre of the fortunate few ... If the theatre is to expand instead of contract, if it is to include the interests of the whole working population, if it is to provide employment for all professional stage people, a really national theatre will have to be one which plays to the whole population.

Finally, but perhaps most immediately important, the workers' theatres wish, through enlightenment, to solidify the resistance of workers and middle class against the threat of fascism.

Theatre is a weapon for the liberation of humanity. No honest culture can be destroyed that lives in the minds and the hearts of millions of people ... In the case of the American theatre the process of widening and deepening has already begun ...

NOTES

1 Introduction to the 1930s

1. William H. Leuchtenberg, *Franklin D. Roosevelt and the New Deal* (New York: Harper Perennial, 2009), 23.
2. Symbolically, premier novelist of the 1920s, F. Scott Fitzgerald's *The Great Gatsby* went out of print in 1939, and the author died in 1940. (Peter Conn, *The American 1930s: A Literary History*. (Cambridge: Cambridge University Press, 2009), 29.
3. William H. and Nancy K. Young, *The 1930s* (Westport, CT: Greenwood Press, 2002), 7.
4. Ibid., 6
5. Conn, *The American 1930s*, 2.
6. Ibid., 2.
7. Young and Young, *The 1930s*, 7.
8. In the 25th anniversary edition of his book *The Great Depression: America, 1929–1941* (2009), historian Robert S. McElvaine offers an extensive comparison between conditions building to the 1929 Crash and its aftermath and the socio-economic state before, during and immediately after the banking failure under the George W. Bush administration. In his study, McElvaine takes to task another work on the Depression, *The Forgotten Man* by Amity Shlaes, in which the author uses the past (1930s) to reflect upon the present, vilifying FDR's approach to the Depression and defending George Bush's behaviour in 2008.
9. Conn, *The American 1930s*, 3.
10. Ibid., 30.
11. David E. Kyvig, *Daily Life in the United States, 1920–1940* (Chicago: Ivan R. Dee, 2004), 138–9.
12. Ibid., 209.

13. Ibid., 224.
14. Conn, *The American 1930s*, 6.
15. Young and Young, *The 1930s*, 6.
16. Ibid., 83.
17. Ibid., 99.
18. Ibid., 111.
19. Ibid., 102–4.
20. Ibid., 105.
21. Ibid., 102.
22. Ibid., 48.
23. Ibid., 77.
24. http://affordableaccoutrements.blogspot.com/2009/09/1930s-dinner-party.html (accessed 17 March 2016).
25. http://www.pbs.org/opb/historydetectives/feature/1930s-high-society/ (accessed 17 March 2016).
26. Young and Young, *The 1930s*, 24.
27. Ibid.
28. Marc McCutcheon, *The Writer's Guide to Everyday Life from Prohibition through World War II* (Cincinnati: Writer's Digest Books, 1995), 66–7.
29. Randy McBee, *Dance Hall Days: Intimacy and Leisure among Working-Class Immigrants in the United States* (New York: New York University Press, 2000), 171.
30. Young and Young, *The 1930s*, 19.
31. http://www.history.com/topics/civilian-conservation-corps (accessed 17 March 2016).
32. http://www.encyclopedia.com/topic/National_Youth_Administration.aspx (accessed 17 March 2016).
33. http://www.retrowaste.com/1930s/sports-in-the-1930s/ (accessed 17 March 2016).
34. http://www.ehow.com/info_8736180_sports-1930s-america.html (accessed 17 March 2016).
35. http://www.ushmm.org/wlc/en/article.php?ModuleId=10005680 (accessed 17 March 2016).
36. *The American Experience: The 1930s*, Public Broadcasting System.
37. Young and Young, *The 1930s*, 128.

38   Ibid., 126.
39   Ibid., 132.
40   Ibid., 121.
41   'The 1930s: Science and Technology: Overview', in Judith S. Baughman et al. (eds), *American Decades, Vol. 4, 1930–1939* (Detroit: Gale, 2001).
42   http://www.history.com/this-day-in-history/worlds-first-parking-meter-installed (accessed 17 March 2016).
43   http://xroads.virginia.edu/~1930s2/Time/timefr.html (accessed 17 March 2016).
44   http://www.healthcentral.com/dailydose/2013/2/18/alka_seltzer_born_feb_21_1931/ (accessed 17 March 2016).
45   http://inventors.about.com/od/timelines/a/twentieth_4.htm (accessed 17 March 2016).
46   http://www.digipro.co.uk/print-news/history-of-the-photocopier-machine/ (accessed 17 March 2016).
47   http://www.ncbi.nlm.nih.gov/pmc/articles/PMC1293286/pdf/jrsocmed00123-0045.pdf (accessed 17 March 2016).
48   http://www.scielo.br/scielo.php?pid=S0102-67202013000400001&script=sci_arttext&tlng=en (accessed 17 March 2016).
49   https://profiles.nlm.nih.gov/ps/retrieve/Narrative/LW/p-nid/138/p-docs/true (accessed 17 March 2016).
50   http://www.rsc.org/chemistryworld/2015/03/sodium-thiopental-mk-ultra-truth-serum-lethal-injection-podcast (accessed 17 March 2016).
51   http://www.defibhub.co.uk/pages/defibrillation-a-history-of-discovery (accessed 17 March 2016).
52   Bruce Lambert, 'John H. Lawrence, 87: Led in Radiation Research', *New York Times*, 9 September 1991, http://www.nytimes.com/1991/09/09/us/john-h-lawrence-87-led-in-radiation-research.html (accessed 17 March 2016).
53   http://xroads.virginia.edu/~ma02/30s/1932/1932.html (accessed 17 March 2016). David Eldridge, *American Culture in the 1930s* (Edinburgh: Edinburgh University Press, 2008), 126.
54   http://www.chemheritage.org/discover/online-resources/chemistry-in-history/themes/public-and-environmental-health/food-chemistry-and-nutrition/emerson.aspx (accessed 17 March 2016).

55 http://www.tuskegee.edu/about_us/centers_of_excellence/bioethics_center/about_the_usphs_syphilis_study.aspx (accessed 17 March 2016).
56 http://www2.lbl.gov/Science-Articles/Archive/early-years.html (accessed 17 March 2016).
57 https://www.sciencenews.org/article/90th-anniversary-issue-1930s (accessed 17 March 2016).
58 https://www.cap.ca/pic/archives/56.5(2000)/volkoff-sept00.html (accessed 17 March 2016).
59 https://physics.aps.org/story/v13/st23 (accessed 17 March 2016).
60 'The 1930s: Science and Technology'.
61 http://www.cmog.org/article/birth-new-industry-fiberglass (accessed 17 March 2016).
62 http://pubs.acs.org/doi/abs/10.1021/cen-v088n015.p046 (accessed 17 March 2016).
63 http://www.chemheritage.org/discover/online-resources/chemistry-in-history/themes/petrochemistry-and-synthetic-polymers/synthetic-polymers/plunkett.aspx (accessed 17 March 2016).
64 See Eldridge, *American Culture in the 1930s*, 5.
65 Ibid., 126.
66 Ibid., 157.
67 Ibid., 173.
68 Conn, *The American 1930s*, 54–6.
69 Ibid., 38.
70 Ibid., 92.
71 Eldridge, *American Culture in the 1930s*, 54–5.
72 Ibid., 32.
73 Conn, *The American 1930s*, 31.
74 Susan Meisenhelder, 'Conflict and Resistance in Zora Neale Hurston's Mules and Men', *Journal of American Folklore* 109 (433) (Summer 1996): 267–88.
75 Eldridge, *American Culture in the 1930s*, 33–4.
76 https://www.poets.org/poetsorg/book/us-1-featuring-book-dead (accessed 17 March 2016).
77 Young and Young, *The 1930s*, 258.
78 Conn, *The American 1930s*, 70–1
79 Ibid., 39

80 The Mexican influence felt elsewhere in the arts was manifested in Aaron Copeland's suite *El Salon in Mexico* (1936).
81 Eldridge, *American Culture in the 1930s*, 61.
82 Ibid., 84.
83 Young and Young, *The 1930s*, 59.
84 https://bfi.org/about-fuller/biography (accessed 17 March 2016).
85 Eldridge, *American Culture in the 1930s*, 127; Young and Young, *The 1930s*, 76.
86 Young and Young, *The 1930s*, 178.
87 Ibid., 176.
88 D. Kyvig, *Daily Life in the United States, 1920–1940* (Chicago: Ivan R. Dee, 2004), 205.
89 http://www.musicalamerica.com/mablogs/?p=8053; http://marthagraham.org/about-us/our-history/ (accessed 17 March 2016).
90 Young and Young, *The 1930s*, 160.
91 Ibid., 162
92 http://www.pulpmags.org/history_page.html (accessed 17 March 2016); advertisement and table of contents http://www.amazon.com/Classic-Era-American-Pulp-Magazines/dp/1556523890/ref=sr_1_9?ie=UTF8&qid=1448471442&sr=8-9&keywords=pulp+magazines (accessed 17 March 2016).
93 Mervyn Rothstein, 'Isaac Asimov, Whose Thoughts and Books Traveled the Universe, Is Dead at 72', *New York Times*, 7 April 1992, https://www.nytimes.com/books/97/03/23/lifetimes/asi-v-obit.html (accessed 17 March 2016).
94 Young and Young, *The 1930s*, 153.
95 Ibid., 268–9, 274.
96 Kyvig, *Daily Life in the United States*, 71.
97 Ibid., 88.
98 Young and Young, *The 1930s*, 207.
99 Eldridge, *American Culture in the 1930s*, 95.
100 Young and Young, *The 1930s*, 214.
101 Conn, *The American 1930s*, 193.
102 Kvyig, *Daily Life in the United States*, 100.
103 See Cheryl Black and Anne Fletcher, 'Moving the World Toward Brotherhood: Representations of Cultural "Otherness" in the Theatre Union's Black Pit (1935)', in Cheryl Black and Jonathan

Shandell (eds), *Experiments in Democracy: Interracial and Cross-Cultural Exchange in the American Theatre, 1912–1945* (Carbondale, IL: Southern Illinois University Press, 2016), 84–104.
104   Eldridge, *American Culture in the 1930s*, 79–80.
105   Young and Young, *The 1930s*, 249.
106   Kyvig, *Daily Life in the United States*, 99.
107   M. McCutcheon, *The Writer's Guide to Everyday Life from Prohibition through World War II* (Cincinnati: Writer's Digest Books, 1995), 65; Young and Young, *The 1930s*, 186.
108   Eldridge, *American Culture in the 1930s*, 104.

2 American theatre in the 1930s

1   Lyrics from 'Wall Street' in the 1966 spoof on 1930s movie musicals, *Dames at Sea*.
2   The New Playwrights Theatre operated for only three years and produced *The Moon is a Gong* by John Dos Passos; *Loud Speaker* by John Howard Lawson; Em Jo Basshe's *Earth*; Basshe's *The Centuries*; Lawson's *The International*; Michael Gold's *Fiesta*; *The Belt* by Paul Sifton; Gold's *Hoboken Blues*; Upton Sinclair's *Singing Jailbirds*; and Dos Passos's *Airways, Inc.*
3   O'Neill's expressionistic pieces, *The Hairy Ape* and *The Emperor Jones*, were produced at the Provincetown. Other of his experimental pieces, like *The Great God Brown* and *Marco Millions*, premiered on Broadway. Elmer Rice's *The Subway* and *The Adding Machine* as well as Sophie Treadwell's *Machinal* are classic examples of American expressionism.
4   This approach to the decade was tentatively taken in 'Reading Across the 1930s', in David Krasner (ed.), *A Companion to Twentieth-Century American Drama* (Malden, MA; Blackwell Publishing Ltd., 2005), but it is greatly expanded and reconsidered here.
5   Anne Fletcher, 'Reading Across the 1930s', 106.
6   Sam Smiley, *The Drama of Attack: Didactic Plays of the Depression* (Columbia, MO: University of Missouri Press, 1972).
7   Susan Duffy, *Labor on Stage: Dramatic Interpretations of the Steel and Textile Industries in the 1930s* (Westwood, CT: Greenwood Press, 1996).
8   Christopher Herr, 'American Political Drama, 1910–45', in Jeffrey

H. Richards and Heather Nathans (eds), *The Oxford Handbook of American Drama* (Oxford: Oxford University Press, 2014).
9 Smiley, *The Drama of Attack*, 63.
10 Herr, 'American Political Drama, 1910–45', 281.
11 Ibid., 280.
12 C. W. E. Bigby, *A Critical Introduction to Twentieth Century American Drama: 1900–1940* (New York: Cambridge University Press, 1982), 143.
13 Characteristics of agit-prop include mass recitation; mobile staging; cartoon-like, exaggerated characters; direct address. Pieces were generally short. They might be staged on a street corner or in a union hall, and performances were by amateurs, generally labourers.
14 See Colette A. Hyman, *Staging Strikes: Workers' Theatre and the American Labor Movement* (Philadelphia: Temple University Press, 1997).
15 The Theatre Collective produced *Marion Models* by Jack and Olga Shapiro; Philip Barber's *The Klein-Ohrbach Strike*; Walter Anderson's *Hunger Strike*; Jack Shapiro's *For People Who Think*; Clifford Odets's *Till the Day I Die*; Albert Maltz's *Private Hicks*; an adaptation of Lope de Vega's *The Pastrycook*; Philip Stevenson's *You Can't Change Human Nature*; and a militant revival of Claire and Paul Sifton's *1931–*, originally produced by the Group Theatre. There may have been other plays and productions.
16 Daniel Opler, 'Monkey Business in Union Square: A Cultural Analysis of the Klein-Ohrbach Strikes of 1934–5', *Journal of Social History* 36 (1) (2002): 149.
17 See specific reviews cited in Anne Fletcher, *Rediscovering Mordecai Gorelik: Scene Design and the American Theatre* (Carbondale: Southern Illinois University Press, 2009), 107.
18 *The Young Go First* programme.
19 Fletcher, 'Reading Across the 1930s', 99–100.
20 *Theatre Arts Monthly* 18 (1934): 420–33.
21 Ilka Saal, *New Deal Theater: The Vernacular Tradition in American Political Theater* (New York: Palgrave MacMillan, 2007), 90.
22 Both Peters and John Howard Lawson, like many other advocates for freeing the black youth, were white. See Adrienne Macki's chapter on Langston Hughes for detail on the black poet/playwright activist's participation.

23 Paul Peters and George Sklar, *Stevedore* (New York: Covici-Fried Publishers, 1934), 122.
24 The terms 'villains' and 'good guys' are not intended to belittle the characters or the play; these words are used here as recognizable attributes of the form of melodrama.
25 For an in-depth analysis of the play, see Anne Fletcher and Cheryl Black, 'Staging a Tripartite Oppression: Race, Class, and Gender in the Theatre Union's *Stevedore* (1934)', *New England Theatre Journal* 22 (2011): 23–51; and Anne Fletcher, 'Fighting One "ISM" with Another – The Communist Party Fights Racism in the South: Scottsboro Dramatizations and *Stevedore*', *Theatre Symposium* 11 (Southeastern Theatre Conference and University of Alabama Press, 2003), 50–62.
26 On the first trip he was harassed by the White Legion Knights and run out of town; on the second he was arrested and charged with criminal libel. Jonathan L. Chambers, *Messiah of the New Technique: John Howard Lawson, Communism, and American Theatre, 1923–1937* (Carbondale: Southern Illinois University Press, 2006), 177. John Howard Lawson, *Marching Song* (New York: Dramatists Play Service, 1937), 83.
27 Ibid., 158.
28 'The Living Newspaper', http://xroads.virginia.edu/~ma04/mccain/play/intro.htm (accessed 10 January 2016).
29 Broadway's Dreamers: The Legacy of The Group Theatre About the Group Theatre, 29 December 1997, http://www.pbs.org/wnet/americanmasters/group-theatre-about-the-group-theatre/622/ (accessed 7 January 2016).
30 See Wendy Smith, *Real Life Drama: The Group Theatre and America, 1931–1940* (New York: Grove Press, 1994) and Helen Krich Chinoy, *The Group Theatre: Passion, Politics, and Performance in the Depression Era*, ed. Don B. Wilmeth and Milly S. Barranger (New York: Palgrave Macmillan, 2013).
31 Chambers, *Messiah of the New Technique*, 4.
32 Ibid., 137.
33 John Howard Lawson, 'Communism in Relation to *Success Story*', August 1932, Lawson Papers, Morris Library Special Collections Research Center, Southern Illinois University, Carbondale.
34 Chambers, *Messiah of the New Technique*, 140, and *The Daily Worker,* 3 October 1932, 1, as cited in Chambers, *Messiah of the New Technique*, 140.

35 John Howard Lawson, Autobiography, Lawson papers, as cited in Chambers, *Messiah of the New Technique*, 166.
36 Chinoy, *The Group Theatre*, 14.
37 Jordan Y. Miller and Winifred L. Frazer, *American Drama between the Wars* (Boston: Twayne Publishers, 1991), 142.
38 Scott R. Irelan, 'Plays, Production, and Politics: The Lincoln Legend of Dramatic Literature and Performance as Staged During FDR's Second Presidential Term by the Federal Theatre Project and the Playwrights' Producing Company', PhD diss., Southern Illinois University, Carbondale, IL, 2006, 254.
39 John F. Wharton, *Life Among the Playwrights* (New York: Quadrangle, 1974), 37.
40 Brenda Murphy, 'Plays and Playwrights: 1915–1945', in Don B. Wilmeth and Christopher Bigsby (eds), *The Cambridge History of American Theatre, Volume II* (New York: Cambridge University Press, 1999), 332.
41 Miller and Frazer, *American Drama between the Wars*, 130.
42 Fonzie D. Geary II, 'A Plague on Both Your Houses: Mr. Anderson Goes to Washington', *New England Theatre Journal* 22 (2011): 1–22.
43 Fonzie D. Geary II, 'Social Critiques in Three Prose Plays by Maxwell Anderson: *Saturday's Children*, *Both Your Houses*, and *The Star-Wagon*', PhD diss., University of Missouri, Columbia, MO, 2011, 97.
44 Ibid., 117.
45 S. N. Behrman, *No Time for Comedy* (New York: Samuel French, Inc., 1938), 122.
46 Kenneth T. Reed, *S. N. Behrman* (Boston: G. K. Hall & Co., 1975), 47.
47 S. N. Behrman, *Brief Moment* (New York: Farrar & Rinehart, 1931), 8.
48 Ibid., 212.
49 S. N. Behrman, *Biography*, in *4 Plays by S. N. Behrman* (New York: Random House, reprint 1952), 180.
50 S. N. Behrman, *End of Summer*, in *4 Plays by S. N. Behrman* (New York: Random House, reprint 1952), 294.
51 Ibid., 322.
52 Ibid., 342.
53 Ibid., 326.

54 Charles Kaplan, 'S. N. Behrman: the Quandary of the Comic Spirit', *College English* 11 (6) (March 1950): 317–23.
55 Charles Isherwood, 'No, Mr. Kaufman, Satire Lives On, If It's Yours', *New York Times*, 24 September 2009.
56 Ibid.
57 Ibid.
58 See Jeffrey D. Mason, *Wisecracks: The Farces of George S. Kaufman* (Ann Arbor, MI: UMI Research Press, 1988).
59 'Stage Door', http://georgeskaufman.com/play-catalogue/15-play-catalogue/library-of-america-collection/65-stage-door.html (accessed 9 January 2016).
60 Ibid.
61 Fletcher, 'Reading Across the 1930s', 110.
62 George S. Kaufman and Moss Hart, *You Can't Take it With You*, in *Three Plays by Kaufman and Hart* (New York: Grove Press, 1980), 121.
63 Ibid., 200.
64 Ibid., 130.
65 Ibid., 166.
66 Ibid., 201.
67 Miller and Frazer, *American Drama between the Wars*, 217.
68 George S. Kaufman and Moss Hart, *The Man Who Came to Dinner*, in *Three Plays by Kaufman and Hart*(New York: Grove Press, 1980), 257; Lewis was the long-term president of the United Mine Workers and an advocate for the creation of the Congress of Industrial Organizations (CIO).
69 Kaufman and Hart, *The Man Who Came to Dinner*, 254.
70 Miller and Frazer, *American Drama between the Wars*, 221.
71 Brooks Atkinson, 'Henry Hull in "Tobacco Road" Based on the Novel by Erskine Caldwell', *New York Times*, 5 December 1933, 31.
72 Kenneth Jones, 'Tobacco Road, Rarely Staged Hit of Yesteryear, Gets Fresh Paving by NC's Triad Stage', *Playbill*, 14 June 2007, http://www.playbill.com/news/article/tobacco-road-rarely-staged-hit-of-yesteryear-gets-fresh-paving-by-ncs-triad-141518 (accessed 10 January 2016).
73 Mark Fearnow, *The American Stage and the Great Depression: A Cultural History of the Grotesque* (Cambridge: Cambridge University Press, 1997), 110.

74 Leah D. Franks, 'Shocks Dissipated in "Tobacco Road"', *New York Times*, 13 October 1985, LI27.
75 William Saroyan, *My Heart's in the Highlands* (New York; Harcourt, Brace and Company, 1939), 9.
76 Ibid., 9.
77 John Anderson quoted in Saroyan, *My Heart's in the Highlands*, 111.
78 Ibid., 115.
79 The author was present and participated in such a reaction to the play, when, en masse, the audience rose to their feet and a young stranger grabbed her hand. She also had the pleasure of speaking briefly with Edward Albee at the First International Thornton Wilder Society Conference, in Ewing, NJ, October 2008. His response to her comment, 'I cried at the end of "The Goat"', was 'I hope you laughed too', his quick-witted acknowledgement of the play's hybridity.
80 Fletcher, 'Reading Across the 1930s', 124.
81 Anne Fletcher, 'Precious Time: An Alternative Reading of Thornton Wilder's *Our Town* and William Saroyan's *The Time of Your Life*', *Theatre Symposium* 14 (2006): 51.

3 Gertrude Stein

1 Steven Watson, *Prepare for Saints: Gertrude Stein, Virgil Thomson, and the Mainstreaming of American Modernism* (New York: Random House, 1998), 4.
2 Quoted in Hans-Thies Lehmann, *Postdramatic Theatre* (London and New York: Routledge, 2006), 50.
3 Gertrude Stein, *Everybody's Autobiography* (Cambridge, MA: Exact Change, [1937] 1993), 72.
4 Ibid., 72–3.
5 Gertrude Stein, 'Portraits and Repetition', in Gertrude Stein, *Writings 1932–1946*, ed. Catharine R. Stimpson and Harriet Chessman (New York: Library of America, 1998), 290–1.
6 Ibid., 289.
7 Gertrude Stein, *The Making of Americans* (Normal, IL: Dalkey Archive Press, [1925] 1999), 184.
8 Stein, 'Portraits and Repetition', 293.

9   Gertrude Stein, *Orta Or One Dancing*, in Gertrude Stein, *A Stein Reader*, ed. Ulla E. Dydo (Evanston, IL: Northwestern University Press, 1993), 121.
10 The portrait of the word *play* is simply called *Play*. It appeared first in Gertrude Stein, *Portraits and Prayers* (New York: Random House, 1934), where it is dated '1909'. Ulla Dydo, however, dates it '1911(?)' in the list of contents of *A Stein Reader*, v.
11 It was British linguist J. L. Austin who first discovered the performative aspect of language: that utterances like 'I promise', or 'I do' at a marriage ceremony, are actually producing something that did not exist prior to the utterance of the words: the promise, the marriage. Austin's research has been crucial to the work of philosophers Jacques Derrida and Judith Butler in their exploration of how identity categories like race, sex and gender, among others, are socially constructed rather than biologically given.
12 Gertrude Stein, *Tender Buttons*, in Gertrude Stein, *Writings 1903–1932*, ed. Catharine R. Stimpson and Harriet Chessman (New York: Library of America, 1998), 320.
13 Gertrude Stein, *The Autobiography of Alice B. Toklas*, in *Writings 1903–1932*, 794; and Gertrude Stein, 'Plays', in *Writings 1932–1946*, 260.
14 Ulla Dydo in *A Stein Reader*, 268.
15 Ibid.
16 Gertrude Stein, *What Happened. A Five Act Play*, in *A Stein Reader*, 269.
17 Stein, 'Plays', 261.
18 Ibid.
19 Ulla Dydo in *A Stein Reader*, 273.
20 In fact, Van Vechten had already visited her the week before: cf. *The Autobiography of Alice B. Toklas*, 797; and Edward Burns, *The Letters of Gertrude Stein and Carl Van Vechten 1935–1946* (New York: Columbia University Press, 1986), 847–53.
21 Stein, *The Autobiography of Alice B. Toklas*, 829.
22 Jane Palatini Bowers, *'They Watch Me as They Watch This': Gertrude Stein's Metadrama* (Philadelphia: University of Pennsylvania Press, 1991), 8–24; and Cyrena N. Pondrom, 'An Introduction to the Achievement of Gertrude Stein', in Gertrude Stein, *Geography and Plays* (Madison: University of Wisconsin Press, [1922] 1993), li–lii.

23 Gertrude Stein, *Ladies' Voices*, in *A Stein Reader*, 306–7.
24 Stein, 'Plays', 267.
25 Ulla Dydo, *Gertrude Stein: The Language That Rises 1923–34* (Evanston, IL: Northwestern University Press, 2003), 44–6.
26 Robert Wilson in 1996 staged a marvellous production of *Saints and Singing* at the Hebbel Theater in Berlin with music by Hans Peter Kuhn. With the subtitle *an operetta*, Kuhn and Wilson strike precisely the light note of Stein's play, where saints are like Hollywood starlets, as Ulla Dydo writes in her introduction to the play in *A Stein Reader*. In Stein's text, words move around like beads in a kaleidoscope, creating momentary patterns of beauty and meaning just in order to continuously dissolve and reassemble into new patterns of sound and vision. Wilson and Kuhn create a similar effect when they make each scene dissolve into surprising new scenes of completely different tone, colour and meaning. The whole piece is kept together by a musical refrain and choreographic pattern that is repeated throughout the performance, albeit performed from different angles: from behind with the performers turning their back on the audience, sideways or even from below with the performers hopping like frogs and croaking in the green light.
27 Stein, 'Plays', 269.
28 Dydo, *The Language That Rises*, 440.
29 *An Historic Drama in Memory of Winnie Eliot*; *Will He Come Back Better: Second Historic Drama*; *In the Country: Third Historic Drama*. All written in 1930 and printed in Gertrude Stein, *Last Operas and Plays* (Baltimore and London: Johns Hopkins University Press, [1949] 1995).
30 Bowers, *'They Watch Me as They Watch This'*, 70.
31 Gertrude Stein, *Identity A Poem*, in *A Stein Reader*, 588.
32 Stein also experimented with children's books in the 1930s and 1940s: *The World Is Round* (1938), *To Do: A Book of Alphabets and Birthdays* (1940), as well as three children's plays written during the war: *In A Garden: A Tragedy in One Act*; *Three Sisters Who Are Not Sisters: A Melodrama*; and *Look and Long: A Play in Three Acts* – all three written in 1943 and published in *The Gertrude Stein First Reader and Three Plays* (Dublin: Maurice Fridberg, 1946).
33 Stated in an interview the author conducted with Goebbels in 2011 on *Songs of Wars I Have Seen*. Published in Danish: 'Sange om krigen – Om Komponisten Heiner Goebbels', in *peripeti.dk*, http://www.peripeti.dk/2011/05/28/1189/ (accessed 17 March 2016).

34 See reproductions of Indiana's costume designs in Wanda M. Corn and Tirza True Latimer, *Seeing Gertrude Stein: Five Stories* (Berkeley: University of California Press, 2011), the catalogue to the 2010–11 exhibitions at the Contemporary Jewish Museum in San Francisco and the National Portrait Gallery, Smithsonian Institution, Washington, DC.
35 Dydo in *A Stein Reader*, 268.
36 Gertrude Stein, *Four Saints in Three Acts*, in Gertrude Stein, *Last Operas and Plays* (Baltimore and London: Johns Hopkins University Press, [1949] 1995), 444. In fact, Hitchcock and Fussel count as many as sixty-five different names of saints mentioned in Stein's text. See Hitchcock and Fussel in Virgil Thomson and Gertrude Stein, *Four Saints in Three Acts*, ed. H. Wiley Hitchcock and Charles Fussel, *Music of the United States of America*, Vol. 18 (Middleton, WI: A-R Editions, Inc. for the American Musicological Society, 2008), xx.
37 Stein, *Four Saints*, 458.
38 Ibid., 447.
39 Ibid., 449.
40 Ibid., 463.
41 Ibid., 455.
42 Ibid., 460.
43 Bowers, 'They Watch Me as They Watch This', 52.
44 Richard Bridgman claims that 'almost two-thirds of the text is composed of authorial statement and commentary'. Richard Bridgman, *Gertrude Stein in Pieces* (New York: Oxford University Press, 1970), 187.
45 The prologue is itself a device added by Thomson.
46 Stein, *Four Saints*, 444–5.
47 Ibid., 450.
48 Ibid., 447.
49 Ibid., 450.
50 Ibid., 472.
51 Ibid., 473.
52 Dydo, *The Language That Rises*, 185–6.
53 Stein, *Four Saints*, 440.
54 Ibid.
55 Ibid., 441.

56 Ibid.
57 Ibid., 442.
58 Bowers, 'They Watch Me as They Watch This', 50.
59 Ibid. 56.
60 Stein, *Everybody's Autobiography*, 199.
61 Andrzej Wirth, 'Gertrude Stein and her Critique of Dramatic Reason', in Sarah Posman and Laura Luise Schultz (eds), *Gertrude Stein in Europe: Reconfigurations Across Media, Disciplines, and Traditions* (London and New York: Bloomsbury, 2015), 202; Stein, *Four Saints*, 444.
62 The four lectures on *Narration* were published in 1935 by the University of Chicago Press.
63 Later Wilder would be very inspired by James Joyce, *Finnegan's Wake*, e.g. in *The Skin of Our Teeth*, 1942.
64 Lehmann, *Postdramatic Theatre*; Andrzej Wirth, 'Stein and Witkiewicz: Critique of Dramatic Reason', in Timothy Wiles (ed.), *Poland Between the Wars: 1918–1939: A Collection of Papers and Discussions from the Conference 'Poland between the Wars: 1918–1939' held in Bloomington, Indiana February 21–23, 1985* (Bloomington: Indiana University Polish Studies Center, 1989).
65 Dydo in *A Stein Reader*, 595.
66 Gertrude Stein, *Doctor Faustus Lights the Lights*, in *A Stein Reader*, 597.
67 Ibid., 610.
68 Ibid., 614.
69 Ibid., 615.
70 Ibid.
71 Ibid., 624.
72 Ibid.
73 See George Cotkin, *Feast of Excess: A Cultural History of the New Sensibility* (Oxford and New York: Oxford University Press, 2016), 20.
74 Andrzej Wirth, 'Die Auflösung der dramatischen Figur oder: "I am I because my little dog knows me"', in Andrzej Wirth and Thomas Irmer (eds), *Flucht nach Vorn* (Leipzig: Spector Books, 2013), 210.
75 Sarah Bay-Cheng, *Mama Dada: Gertrude Stein's Avant-Garde Theater* (New York and London: Routledge, 2004), 65.
76 Wirth, 'Auflösung der dramatischen Figur', 212. Original German

text: 'Es war der wohl radikalste Schritt, durch die Auflösung der Figur das Drama abstrakt zu machen ...'.
77 Wirth, 'Gertrude Stein and her Critique of Dramatic Reason', 209.
78 It is the same deconstruction of the logic of drama that Hans-Thies Lehmann traces in his book *Postdramatic Theatre*.
79 Gertrude Stein, *Listen To Me*, in Stein, *Last Operas and* Plays, 387.
80 Ibid., 388.
81 Ibid., 388–9.
82 Ibid., 403.
83 Ibid., 404.
84 Bowers, 'They Watch Me as They Watch This', 91.
85 Wirth, 'Gertrude Stein and her Critique of Dramatic Reason', 208.
86 Stein, *Listen To Me*, 388.
87 Ibid., 390.
88 Ibid.
89 Ibid.
90 Stein, *Everybody's Autobiography*, 250; and Bowers, 'They Watch Me as They Watch This', 95.
91 Bowers, 'They Watch Me as They Watch This', 96.
92 Gertrude Stein, *The World is Round* (London: B.T. Batsford Ltd, 1939).

4 Langston Hughes

1 Kevin Gaines, *Uplifting the Race: Black Leadership, Politics, and Culture in the Twentieth Century* (Chapel Hill: University of North Carolina Press, 1996), 3.
2 'Signifying' is a term, derived from Henry Louis Gates's seminal book *The Signifying Monkey: A Theory of African-American Literary Criticism* (1988), used in literary criticism in reference to rhetorical strategies employed by African-American writers in their deployment of irony and indirection to express ideas and opinions.
3 Jeffrey Stewart, 'New Negro as Citizen', in *The Cambridge Companion to The Harlem Renaissance*, ed. George Hutchinson (Cambridge: Cambridge University Press, 2007), 15.
4 Arnold Rampersad, *The Life of Langston Hughes, Vol. 1,*

1902–1941: I, Too, Sing America (New York: Oxford University Press, 1986), 7, 12.
5   Susan Duffy, *The Political Plays of Langston Hughes* (Carbondale: Southern Illinois University Press, 2000), 2.
6   Joseph McLaren, *Langston Hughes: Folk Dramatist in the Protest Tradition, 1921–1943* (Westport, CT: Greenwood Press, 1997), 33.
7   Eric J. Sundquist, 'Who Was Langston Hughes?', *Commentary* 102 (6) (December 1996): 57.
8   William A. Sundstrom, 'Last Hired, First Fired? Unemployment and Urban Black Workers during the Great Depression', *Journal of Economic History* 52 (2) (June 1992): 420.
9   Arnold Rampersad et al. (eds), *Selected Letters of Langston Hughes* (New York: Knopf, 2015), 125.
10 Langston Hughes, *Scottsboro, Limited*, in *The Political Plays of Langston Hughes*, ed. Susan Duffy (Carbondale: Southern Illinois University Press, 2000), 47.
11 Katy Ryan, 'Prison, Time, Kairos in Langston Hughes's Scottsboro, Limited', *Modern Drama* 58 (2) (Summer 2015): 173.
12 Michelle Alexander, *The New Jim Crow: Mass Incarceration in the Age of Colorblindness* (New York: New York Press, 2012), 2.
13 Andrew Hemingway, *Artists on the Left: American Artists and the Communist Movement 1926–1956* (New Haven, CT: Yale University Press, 2002).
14 Langston Hughes, *I Wonder as I Wonder* (New York: Hill and Wang, 1993), 199.
15 Ibid., 199–200.
16 Louise Thompson, Interview, 19 February 1988, Tape 15, Louise Thompson Project. Emory University Rare Books and Archives.
17 Rampersad, *The Life of Langston Hughes*, 356; Thompson, Interview.
18 Anne Donlon, '*Don't You Want to be Free?*': Questions of Emancipation in 1930s African American Theatre, Presentation at the American Literature Association Conference, American Literature Association, Boston, MA, May 2013.
19 Rampersad et al., *Selected Letters*, 200–1.
20 For discussion of three seminal community-based theatres in Harlem, see Adrienne Macki Braconi, *Harlem's Theaters, A Staging Ground for Community, Class, and Contradiction, 1923–1939* (Evanston, IL: Northwestern University Press, 2015).

21 Louise Thompson Project, Tape 16.
22 Ibid.
23 'Herndon Lauds "Suitcase" Play', *New York Amsterdam News*, 7 May 1938, 16. Hughes wrote a play, *Angelo Herndon Jones* (1936), responding to Herndon's legal case, the travesty of justice in the South and interracial organizing. Susan Duffy argues that the piece represents 'a turning point in the development of Hughes's work, his last attempt to write a serious didactic play with traditional dramatic structure' (138).
24 Peggy Howard, '"Sing Out the News" to Open Saturday: Critic Sees Play as a Sure Hit When it Reaches Broadway', *Chicago Defender*, 1 October 1938, 19.
25 Langston Hughes to Carl Van Vechten as quoted in Emily Bernard (ed.), *Remember Me to Harlem: The Letters of Langston Hughes and Carl Van Vechten, 1925–1962* (New York: Alfred A. Knopf, 2001), 68.
26 Hughes, *I Wonder as I Wonder*, 311–12, as cited in Rampersad, *The Life of Langston Hughes*, 440.
27 Set in West Africa, Gordon's *White Cargo* was a hit on Broadway and in London in the 1920s and later adapted to a film with Hedy Lamarr in the role of the racially-mixed seductress, Tondeleyo. For production photos and background on its British premiere, see Leon Gordon, 'WHITE CARGO', *Play Pictorial* 45 (270): 47–62. For discussion of the play's treatment of African primitivism, see Stephanie Newell, *Literary Culture in Colonial Ghana: 'How to Play the Game of Life'* (Manchester: Manchester University Press, 2002), 119–34. On the play's representation of the white colonizer, see Daniel Stephen, *The Empire of Progress: West Africans, Indians, and Britons at the British Empire Exhibition, 1924–25* (New York: Palgrave Macmillan, 2013), 117–19.
28 Michele Birnbaum, *Race, Work, and Desire in American Literature, 1860–1930* (New York: Cambridge University Press, 2003), 135–6.
29 Harry J. Elam, Jr and Michele Elam, 'Blood Debt: Reparations in Langston Hughes's Mulatto', *Theatre Journal* 61 (1) (March 2009): 87.
30 Ibid.
31 Brooks Atkinson, 'Race Problems in the South the Theme of "Mulatto" a "New Drama" by Langston Hughes', *New York Times*, 25 October 1935, 25.
32 Ibid.

33 See 'Philadelphia Clamps Down on "Mulatto"', *New York Amsterdam News*, 18 November 1939, 2; 'Mulatto is Storm Center', *New York Amsterdam News*, 9 December 1939, 1.
34 'Mercedes Gilbert Tops – "Mulatto" New Experience in Boston', *New York Amsterdam News*, 30 March 1940, 16.
35 'Mercedes Gilbert Tops', 16; 'The Stage: Copley Theatre, "Mulatto"', *Daily Boston Globe*, 25 March 1940, 9.
36 Charles Collins, '"Mulatto" a Dismal Tragedy of Woes of Racial Problem', *Chicago Daily Tribune*, 28 December 1936, 15.
37 Birnbaum, *Race, Work, and Desire*, 140.
38 Nelson B. Bell, '"Mulatto" Tells Tragic Story of Half-Caste: Acted by Mixed Cast Play Interests Large Houses at the Belasco', *Washington Post*, 22 February 1937, 11.
39 M. Oakley Christoph, '"Mulatto" Shows Capitol Players at their Peak Form', *Hartford Courant*, 15 July 1938, 4.
40 Hughes initially offered the script to the Gilpin Players in 1930, shortly after he completed writing it at the Hedgerow Theatre. They were 'unwilling to accept it' at first, perhaps because it was too controversial, writes Karamu Theatre scholar Reuben Silver (243).
41 For further information regarding the 1967 revival, see Dan Sullivan, '"Mulatto" Staged at Theater Club: Langston Hughes Hit of '35 Revived for "Members"', *New York Times*, 16 November 1967, 61.
42 Webster Smalley (ed.), *Five Plays by Langston Hughes* (Bloomington: Indiana University Press, 1963), xi.
43 Elam and Elam, 'Blood Debt', 88.
44 McLaren, *Langston Hughes*, 61.
45 Elam and Elam, 'Blood Debt', 87.
46 Langston Hughes, *Mulatto*, in *Five Plays by Langston Hughes*, ed. Webster Smalley (Bloomington: Indiana University Press, 1963), 10.
47 Ibid., 18.
48 Ibid., 23.
49 Ibid.
50 Ibid., 24.
51 Shea Coulson, 'Funnier Than Unhappiness: Adorno and the Art of Laughter', *New German Critique* 34 (1) (Winter 2007): 142.
52 This idea regarding avenging the rape of black women forms one of the central conflicts in Willis Richardson's *Compromise* (1925).

Likewise, this play's investment in Cora's struggle between her loyalty to Colonel Tom and to her children also amends what Koritha Mitchell describes as the 'silence about rape' to suggest how black women attempted to protect their families from further violence. *Living with Lynching: African American Lynching Plays, Performance, and Citizenship, 1890–1930* (Urbana: University of Illinois Press, 2011), 152. For discussion of *Compromise*'s representation of miscegenation, protection of black womanhood and lynching, see Macki Braconi, *Harlem's Theaters*, 36–41.

53 Previous lynching dramas such as Angelina Weld Grimké's *Rachel* and George Douglas Johnson's *Safe* illustrate how mothers condone (their own or their children's) death to escape lynching. On mothers in lynching dramas, see Mitchell, *Living with Lynching*, Ch. 5; Koritha Mitchell, 'Sisters in Motherhood(?): The Politics of Race and Gender in Lynching Drama', in *Gender and Lynching: The Politics of Memory*, ed. Evelyn Simien (New York: Palgrave Macmillan, 2011), 37–60.

54 James M. Cone, *The Cross and the Lynching Tree* (Maryknoll, NY: Orbis Books, 2011), 11–12.

55 Hughes, *Mulatto*, 34.

56 Bernard, *Remember Me to Harlem*, 78.

57 Hurston and Hughes were neighbours in Westfield, NJ, and colleagues supported by Charlotte Osgood Mason, who was referred to as 'Godmother'.

58 Bernard, *Remember Me to Harlem*, 73.

59 Ibid., 75.

60 Ibid., 76.

61 McLaren, *Langston Hughes*, 20.

62 For a more detailed discussion of the failed collaboration between Hurston and Hughes, see Henry Louis Gates, Jr, 'A Tragedy of Negro Life', in Langston Hughes and Zora Neale Hurston, *Mule Bone: A Comedy of Negro Life*, ed. George Houston Bass and Henry Louise Gates, Jr (New York: Harper Perennial, 2008), 5–23.

63 John Lowe, 'Hurston, Toomer, and the Dream of a Negro Theatre', in Deborah G. Plant (ed.), *'The Inside Light': New Critical Essays on Zora Neale Hurston* (Santa Barbara, CA: Praeger, 2010), 79–92, 83.

64 Ibid., 83.

65 Henry Louis Gates, Jr, 'Why the "Mule Bone" Debate Goes On', *New York Times*, 10 February 1991, H5, 8.

66 Lynda M. Hill, 'Staging Hurston's Life and Work', in Lynda Hart and Peggy Phelan (eds), *Acting Out: Feminist Performances* (Ann Arbor: University of Michigan Press, 1993), 295–314, 303.
67 John Beaufort, '"Mule Bone" Debuts after 60 Years Rescued Three Years Ago, the Play Delights '90s Audiences', 26 February 1991, *Christian Science Monitor*, search.proquest.com.proxy.lib.siu.edu/docview/291177605?accountid=13864 (accessed 3 July 2016).
68 Frank Rich, 'A Difficult Birth for "Mule Bone"', *New York Times*, 15 February 1991, C1.
69 Ibid., C24.
70 Hurston to Hughes, quoted in Henry Louis Gates, Jr, 'Why the "Mule Bone' Debate Goes On', *New York Times*, 10 February 1991, H5, 8.
71 Henry Louis Gates, Jr (2008), 'A Tragedy of Negro Life', in Langston Hughes and Zora Neale Hurston, *Mule Bone: A Comedy of Negro Life*, ed. George Houston Bass and Henry Louise Gates, Jr (New York: Harper Perennial, 2008), 20.
72 Ibid.
73 Zora Neale Hurston and Langston Hughes, *Mule Bone: A Comedy of Negro Life* (New York: Harper Perennial, 2008), 60–1.
74 Ibid., 67.
75 Carme Manuel, 'Mule Bone: Langston Hughes and Zora Neale Hurston's Dream Deferred of an American-American Theatre of the Black Word', *African American Review* 35 (1) (Spring 2001): 84.
76 Hurston and Hughes, *Mule Bone*, 116.
77 Ibid., 122.
78 Ibid., 112.
79 Ibid.
80 Jennifer Stapleton, 'Zora Neale Hurston's Construction of Authenticity Through Ethnographic Innovation', *Western Journal of Black Studies* 30 (1) (Spring 2006): 66.
81 Ibid., 66.
82 Gates, 'A Tragedy of Negro Life', 20.
83 Hughes, *Mule Bone*, 147
84 Ibid., 146.
85 Ibid., 147.
86 Ibid.

87 Ibid., 150.
88 Ibid.
89 Ibid., 151.
90 Manuel, 'Mule Bone', 84.
91 Gates, 'A Tragedy of Negro Life', 22.
92 Ibid.
93 Rampersad et al., *Selected Letters*, 189.
94 Van Vechten as quoted in Bernard, *Remember Me to Harlem*, 135.
95 Leslie Sanders, 'Little Ham's Self Invention: Teaching Langston Hughes', in Maryemma Graham, Sharon Pineault-Burke and Marianna White Davis (eds), *Teaching African American Literature: Theory and Practice* (New York: Routledge, 1998), 66.
96 McLaren, *Langston Hughes*, 84.
97 Sanders, 'Little Ham's Self Invention', 66.
98 Sharyn Emery, 'The ~~Philadelphia~~ Harlem Story: Langston Hughes's Screwy Play *Little Ham*', *Modern Drama* 66 (3) (Fall 2012): 374.
99 Sanders, 'Little Ham's Self Invention', 68.
100 Ibid.
101 Hughes as quoted in Bernard, *Remember Me to Harlem*, 136.
102 *Cleveland Plain Dealer*'s McDermott as quoted in McLaren, *Langston Hughes*, 85.
103 Ibid., 88.
104 *Variety*'s Glenn Pullen as quoted in McLaren, *Langston Hughes*, 88.
105 Arthur Spaeth of the *Cleveland News* as quoted in Bernard, *Remember Me to Harlem*, 137.
106 'Cleveland Gets Poet's Comedy: Efforts of Gilpin Players with Picture of Harlem Life Win Audience', *New York Amsterdam News*, 28 March 1936, 8.
107 Review quoted in Reuben Silver, 'A History of the Karamu Theatre of Karamu House, 1915–1960', diss., Ohio State University, 1961, 234. *Stevedore* was cast across race and produced by the Theatre Union.
108 McLaren, *Langston Hughes*, 89. For example, writing about the May 1936 revival, the *Cleveland Call and Post* stated that the playwright 'leaves all serious purpose behind', creating a play 'with no social purpose', quoted in Silver, 'A History of the Karamu Theatre of Karamu House, 1915–1960', 232.

109 Hughes as quoted in Rampersad, *The Life of Langston Hughes*, 326.
110 Shane White, Stephen Garton, Stephen Robertson and Graham White, *Playing the Numbers: Gambling in Harlem Between the Wars* (Cambridge, MA: Harvard University Press, 2010), 21.
111 Review quoted in Silver, 'A History of the Karamu Theatre of Karamu House, 1915–1960', 232.
112 Coulson, 'Funnier Than Unhappiness', 142
113 McLaren, *Langston Hughes*, 107.
114 Sundquist, 'Who Was Langston Hughes?', 58.
115 Ibid.
116 Duffy, *The Political Plays of Langston Hughes*, 4.

5 Clifford Odets

1 Alfred Kazin, *Starting Out in the Thirties* (Boston: Little, Brown and Company, 1962), 80–1.
2 Clifford Odets, *The Time Is Ripe: The 1940 Journal of Clifford Odets* (New York: Grove Press, 1988), 334.
3 John Gassner 'The American Galaxy', *Masters of the Drama* (New York: Random House, 1940), 689.
4 Thomas Gale Moore, *The Economics of the American Theatre* (Durham, NC: Duke University Press, 1968), 14, 147.
5 Margaret Brenman-Gibson, *Clifford Odets, American Playwright: The Years From 1906–1940* (New York: Atheneum, 1981), 496.
6 Ibid., 515.
7 Harold Clurman, *The Fervent Years: The Story of the Group Theatre and the Thirties* (New York: Hill and Wang, 1945), 138–9.
8 Clifford Odets, *Six Plays* (New York: Methuen, [1939] 1982), 6.
9 Ibid., 9.
10 Ibid., 10.
11 Ibid., 17.
12 Ibid., 15.
13 Ibid., 30.
14 Ibid., 31.

15 Brooks Atkinson, 'Waiting for Lefty', *New York Times*, 27 March 1935, 24.
16 Odets, *Six Plays*, 37.
17 Ibid., 42.
18 Ibid., 77–8.
19 Ibid., 97.
20 Michael J. Mendelsohn, 'Odets at Center Stage', *Theatre Arts* (May 1962): 16–19, 74–6, 28–30, 78–80.
21 Odets, *Six Plays*, 99.
22 Wendy Smith, *Real Life Drama: The Group Theatre and America, 1931–1940* (New York: Grove Press, 1990), 279–80.
23 Odets, *Six Plays*, 49.
24 Ibid., 51.
25 Ibid., 95.
26 Odets, *Six Plays*, 229.
27 Ibid., 171.
28 Ibid., 223.
29 Clurman, *The Fervent Years*, 166.
30 Odets, *Six Plays*, 187.
31 Ibid., 229–30.
32 Ibid., 204.
33 Ibid., 168.
34 Ibid., 264.
35 Ibid., 266.
36 Ibid., 299.
37 Ibid., 321.
38 Ibid., 350.
39 Ibid., 414.
40 Ibid., 416–17.
41 Ibid., 369–70.
42 Ibid., 411.
43 Clifford Odets, *Night Music* (New York: Random House, 1940), 189.
44 Ibid., 161.
45 Ibid.

6 Lillian Hellman

1. Lillian Hellman, *The Little Foxes* in *Six Plays by Lillian Hellman* (New York: Vintage Books, 1979), 162. Quotations from *The Children's Hour*, *Days to Come* and *The Little Foxes*, unless otherwise noted, are drawn from *Six Plays by Lillian Hellman* (New York: Vintage Books, 1934, reprint 1979).
2. Alice Kessler-Harris, *A Difficult Woman: The Challenging Life and Times of Lillian Hellman* (New York: Bloomsbury Press, 2012), 31.
3. William Wright, *Lillian Hellman: The Image, the Woman* (New York: Simon and Schuster, 1986), 103.
4. *The Children's Hour* (1934), *Days to Come* (1936), *The Little Foxes* (1939), *Watch on the Rhine* (1941), *The Searching Wind* (1944), *Another Part of the Forest* (1946), *The Autumn Garden* (1951), *Toys in the Attic* (1960).
5. Jerome Weidman, 'Lillian Hellman Reflects on the Changing Theater', *Dramatists Guild Quarterly* 7 (Winter 1970): 22.
6. Kessler-Harris, *A Difficult Woman*, 335.
7. Transcript from Dick Cavett interview as quoted in Kessler-Harris, *A Difficult Woman*, 323.The transcript is housed in the Mary McCarthy Collection, Vassar College.
8. See Sam Smiley, *The Drama of Attack* (Columbia: University of Missouri Press, 1972) and Mordecai Gorelik, 'Theatre is a Weapon', *Theatre Arts Monthly* 18 (1934): 420–33.
9. Mark W. Estrin, *Critical Essays on Lillian Hellman* (Boston: G. K. Hall & Co., 1989), 94.
10. See Harold Clurman, *The Fervent Years: The Group Theatre and the Thirties* (Cambridge, MA: Da Capo Press, 1983).
11. Wright, *Lillian Hellman*, 103.
12. J. Bryer, *Conversations with Lillian Hellman* (Jackson: University Press of Mississippi, 1986), 257.
13. Hellman biographer Alice Kessler-Harris offers an alternative contextualization of Hellman's anti-fascism, determining it 'misguided to imagine that she [Hellman] espoused antifascism to obscure her sympathy for communism ... Rather, in the context of the moment, these commitments converged ... In 1936 and 1937, the heyday of the Popular Front and the moment when the New Deal seemed to be veering leftward, Hellman found in a broadly

defined socialism the value system she found dear' (Kessler-Harris, *A Difficult Woman*, 121).

14 Kessler-Harris, *A Difficult Woman*, 378.
15 Ibid., 116–21.
16 Ibid., 307.
17 Anne Hollander and John Marquand, 'Lillian Hellman: The Art of Theatre No. 1', *The Paris Review* 33 (Winter–Spring 1965): 8. Available online: http://www.theparisreview.org/interviews/4463/the-art-of-theater-no-1-lillian-hellman (accessed 10 June 2015).
18 Wright, *Lillian Hellman*, 98.
19 Hellman was awarded the National Book Award in 1969 for *An Unfinished Woman* and received a nomination in 1974 for *Pentimento: A Book of Portraits*.
20 Hollander and Marquand, 'Lillian Hellman: The Art of Theatre No. 1', 12.
21 Brenda Murphy (ed.), *The Cambridge Companion to American Women Playwrights* (New York: Cambridge University Press, 2006), 170–2.
22 The most noticeable change in the text is the exchange of the Shakespeare reading in the first scene – from the *Merchant of Venice* in the first edition to *Antony and Cleopatra* in the latter. Additionally, Agatha, the maid, has less stage time and involvement in the plot in the 1952 version. There are other alterations of minor details, such as the addition of references to a strapless dress in the acting edition.
23 Hellman, *The Children's Hour*, in *Six Plays by Lillian Hellman*, 18.
24 Hellman, *The Children's Hour*, 57.
25 Katherine Lederer, *Lillian Hellman* (Boston: Twayne Publishers, 1979), 22.
26 Thomas P. Adler, 'Lillian Hellman: Feminism, Formalism, and Politics', in Brenda Murphy (ed.), *The Cambridge Companion to American Women Playwrights* (New York: Cambridge University Press, 2006), 122.
27 The *clou* was the staple of pieces of the Boulevard theatres of Paris and of earlier nineteenth-century Well-Made Plays such as the glass of water in Sardou's *A Glass of Water* or the letter in Scribe's *A Scrap of Paper*.
28 Brooks Atkinson, '"The Children's Hour," Being a Tragedy of Life in a Boarding School', *New York Times*, 21 November 1934, 23.

29 Lillian Hellman, *Four Plays by Lillian Hellman* (New York: Random House, 1934), x.
30 Hellman, *The Little Foxes*, 225.
31 Hollander and Marquand, 'Lillian Hellman: The Art of Theatre No. 1', 5.
32 Hellman, *The Children's Hour*, 31.
33 Hellman, *The Children's Hour*, in *Six Plays by Lillian Hellman*, 74. Perhaps the maid's telephoning was originally an indication of the power and status of the wealthy Mrs Tilford that Hellman felt could be eliminated in later versions of the play.
34 Lillian Hellman, *The Children's Hour* (New York: Dramatists Play Service, 1981), 69.
35 In *Watch on the Rhine*, the stage is left empty early in the play, in the middle of Act One, presumably to highlight the entrance of Sara and her family (Hellman, *Watch on the Rhine*, 241).
36 John Howard Lawson, 'A Comparative Study of "The Children's Hour" and "Days to Come"', *New Theatre and Film* (March 1937): 15.
37 Hellman, *The Children's Hour*, in *Four Plays*, 79.
38 Ibid., 78.
39 Hellman, *Days to Come*, in *Six Plays by Lillian Hellman*, 145.
40 Holland and Marquand, 'Lillian Hellman: The Art of Theatre No. 1', 5.
41 Hellman, *Days to Come*, 119.
42 Doris V. Falk, *Lillian Hellman* (New York: Frederick Unger Publishing Co., 1978), 48.
43 Lawson, 'A Comparative Study', 15.
44 After a rehearsal for a recent Southern Illinois University production of *The Children's Hour*, J. Thomas Kidd – a director quite familiar with the play – exclaimed, 'I kept wanting the little girls to come back!', indicative of the two-plot structure.
45 Lawson, 'A Comparative Study', 15.
46 Ibid.
47 Hellman, *Four Plays*, xi.
48 Ibid.
49 C. W. E. Bigsby, *A Critical Introduction to Twentieth Century American Drama: 1900–1940* (New York: Cambridge University Press, 1982), 279.

50 Lederer, *Lillian Hellman*, 34.
51 Lawson, 'A Comparative Study', 15.
52 Ibid.
53 Ibid., 61.
54 Hellman, *The Little Foxes*, 205.
55 Ibid., 222–3.
56 Ibid., 159.
57 *The Little Foxes*'s climax occurs late, not at the end of the second act, but rather, near the play's close when Regina withholds his medicine and Horace dies.
58 Falk, *Lillian Hellman*, 51.
59 Lederer, *Lillian Hellman*, 28.
60 Hellman stated on many occasions that the Hubbards are loosely based on her mother's family.
61 Lillian Hellman, *Pentimento* (Boston: Little, Brown and Company, 1973), 180.
62 Hellman, *Six Plays*, 155.
63 Hellman, *The Little Foxes*, 165.
64 Lederer, *Lillian Hellman*, 46.
65 The play is more problematic regarding selection for production at colleges and universities because of its use of the 'n' word.
66 Lawson, 'A Comparative Study', 16.
67 Hellman, *The Little Foxes*, 159–60.
68 Ibid., 159.
69 Ibid., 173.
70 Lillian Hellman, *The Children's Hour* (New York: Dramatists Play Service, Inc., 1981), 6.
71 Ibid., 11.
72 Bigsby, *A Critical Introduction to Twentieth Century American Drama*, 278.
73 Karen in *The Children's Hour* has lost both her friend and her fiancé, and Mrs Tilford is left to care for Mary; Julie is left adrift at the conclusion of *Days to Come*. *Watch on the Rhine* could be argued as an exception because Sara and her mother remain strong in the face of adversity, but Sara's husband rejoins the anti-fascists in Germany and likely will not return alive. In *The Searching Wind*, Emily's son has recognized her and her husband for the

vacuous individuals they are; Regina has lost out to brother Ben once again in *Another Part of the Forest*; *The Autumn Garden*'s Constance continues in self-delusion: 'Nevermind. Most of us lie to ourselves ...' (494), and at the conclusion of *Toys in the Attic* the old maid sisters return to life basically as before, young Lily faces an eventual rejection and Albertine's long-time lover says good-bye.

74 Hellman, *The Little Foxes*, 225.
75 Ibid., 225.
76 Hellman, *Watch on the Rhine*, 301.
77 Ibid.
78 Adler, 'Lillian Hellman', 119.
79 Bryer, *Conversations with Lillian Hellman*, 205.
80 Hellman, *Days to Come*, 146.
81 Hellman, *The Little Foxes*, 225.
82 Ibid., 221.
83 Lillian Hellman, *Toys in the Attic* (New York: Random House, 1959), 116.
84 Jill Dolan, 'The Children's Hour, Comedy Theatre, London, March 12, 2011', *The Feminist Spectator*, http://feministspectator.princeton.edu/2011/03/17/the-childrens-hour/ (accessed 31 May 2016).
85 Southern Illinois University Carbondale production, April 2015; Texas Tech University production, 2014.
86 https://www.ibdb.com/Production/View/508257 (accessed 26 June 2016).

Afterword

1 Leslie Atkins Durham, *Staging Gertrude Stein: Absence, Culture, and the Landscape of American Alternative Theatre* (New York: Palgrave Macmillan, 2005), 1.

2 Renate Stendhal, 'Why the Witch-Hunt Against Gertrude Stein?', *Tikkun*, 4 June 2012, http://www.tikkun.org/nextgen/why-the-witch-hunt-against-gertrude-stein (accessed 26 June 2016). See also accompanying Editor's Note. In her chapter for this volume, Laura Schultz contextualizes the experience of Stein as a US citizen in France during the war. Historian Barbara Will addresses links between the avant-garde and fascist thought in 'The Strange Politics

of Gertrude Stein', *Humanities* 33 (2) (March/April 2012), and her more recent full-length study *Unlikely Collaboration: Gertrude Stein, Bernard Faÿ, and the Vichy Dilemma* (New York: Columbia University Press, 2011).
3. F. W. Dupee, 'General Introduction', in Carl Van Vechten (ed.), *The Selected Writings of Gertrude Stein* (New York: Vintage Books, 1962), ix.
4. See Hans-Thies Lehmann: *Postdramatic Theatre* (London and New York: Routledge, 2006*)*.
5. Langston Hughes, *The Collected Works of Langston Hughes, Volume 14: Autbiography: I Wonder as I Wander* (Columbia: University of Missouri Press, 2002), 140.
6. Laurie Leach, *Langston Hughes: A Biography* (Santa Barbara, CA: Greenwood, 2004), 118–19.
7. Odets's former student Leslie Wiener as quoted in Victor S. Navasky, *Naming Names* (New York: Penguin Books, 1991), 376.
8. Elia Kazan as quoted in 'The Fight Back: The Battles of Clifford Odets and Thurgood Marshall', *The New Yorker*, 12 May 2008, http://www.newyorker.com/magazine/2008/05/12/the-fight-back (accessed 16 June 2016); Margaret Brenman-Gibson, 'How Clifford Odets Spent His Last, Desperate Days', *New York Times*, 18 October 1981, D1.
9. Reported to have been Gertrude Stein's last words to partner Alice B. Toklas.
10. Edward M. Burns, Ulla E. Dydo and William Rice (eds), *The Letters of Gertrude Stein and Thornton Wilder* (New Haven, CT: Yale University Press, 1996), 417.
11. Lowell Swortzell, *Around the World in 21 Plays: Theatre for Young Audiences Applause* (Milwaukee, WI: Hal Leonard Publishing Corporation, 2000), 131.
12. Durham, *Staging Gertrude Stein*, 6
13. Actress/Singer Susan Patrick Benson, interview with the author, 23 June 2016.
14. 'Al Carmines' Gertrude Stein Musical Revived Feb. 15', *Playbill*, 11 February 1997, http://www.playbill.com/article/al-carmines-gertrude-stein-musical-revived-feb-15-com-69537 (accessed 26 June 2016).
15. 'Gertrude Stein: Online Dramaturgy', http://www.tenderbuttons.com/gsonline/theater/lkdramanotes.html (accessed 26 June 2016).

16 Durham, *Staging Gertrude Stein*, 6.
17 Perry Miller Adato Collection, 'Chapter 3 – Gertrude Stein: When This You See Remember Me' (1970), https://www.youtube.com/watch?v=wMn5bxk7d4U (accessed 1 July 2016). Miller Adato was also a founder of Stage for Action, socio-political theatre of the 1940s.
18 Durham, *Staging Gertrude Stein*, 6.
19 Ben Brantley, 'Review: Revisiting Gertrude Stein's Writings in Rereading Another', *New York Times*, 23 September 2015, http://www.nytimes.com/2015/09/29/theater/review-revisiting-gertrude-steins-writings-in-reread-another.html?_r=1 (accessed 26 June 2016).
20 Christopher Isherwood, 'The There That's There: Mapping a Modernist's Way With Words', *New York Times*, 2 June 2009.
21 Marvin Carlson, 'After Stein', in Elinor Fuchs and Uda Chaudhuri, *Land/Scape/Theatre* (Ann Arbor: University of Michigan Press, 2002), 147.
22 Gertrude Stein, *Everybody's Autobiography* (New York: Random House, 1937), 289.
23 Mark Kanny, 'Review: Pittsburgh Opera about Gertrude Stein a Winner', TRIBLIV, 21 February 2016, http://triblive.com/aande/moreaande/9979368-74/opera-stein-act (accessed 29 June 2016).
24 Richard Howard, 'There Is a Lot of Here Here', *New York Times*, 3 May 1998, https://www.nytimes.com/books/98/05/03/reviews/980503.03howardt.html (accessed 26 June 2016).
25 Adapted from Hughes's poem 'I, Too, Sing America'. The phrase 'I, too, am America' serves as the title for several anthologies of African-American poetry as well as the title of the Coretta Scott King Award winner for illustration, a children's collection of Hughes's poetry.
26 Samuel Hay, *African American Theatre: An Historical and Critical Analysis* (Cambridge: Cambridge University Press, 1994), 24.
27 Alice Walker: The Official Website, http://alicewalkersgarden.com/books/ (accessed 26 June 2016).
28 W. Jason Miller, *Origins of the Dream: Hughes's Poetry and King's Rhetoric* (Gainesville: University Press of Florida, 2015), 2.
29 Ibid., 4, Figure 1.
30 'Ask Your Mama: 12 Moods for Jazz', http://www.ronmccurdy.com/about_hudges_project.htm (accessed 26 June 2016).

31 Clifford Odets as quoted in Brenman Gibson, 'How Clifford Odets Spent His Last, Desperate Days', *New York Times*, 18 October 1981, D1.
32 'Interview: Walt Odets', *Jewish Chronicle Online*, 12 November 2010, http://www.thejc.com/lifestyle/lifestyle-features/41116/interview-walt-odets (accessed 15 June 2016).
33 'Stage Left: The struggles of Clifford Odets', *The New Yorker*, 17 April, 2006, http://www.newyorker.com/magazine/2006/04/17/stage-left (accessed 29 June 2016).
34 Frank S. Nugent, 'Odets, Where is Thy Sting?', *New York Times*, 6 September 1936, X3.
35 'Clifford Odets, Playwright Dies', *New York Times*, 16 August 1963, 27.
36 'Stage Left'.
37 Brenman-Gibson, 'Odets: Failure or Not?', *New York Times*, 13 June 1965, X1.
38 'Stage Left'.
39 Clifford Odets, *The Time is Ripe: The 1940 Journal of Clifford Odets* (New York: Grove Press, 1988), 98.
40 'Stage Left'.
41 *Night Music* was revived in 1951, ANTA Playhouse.
42 Brooks Atkinson, 'Drama About League of Nations and Woodrow Wilson Opens', *New York Times*, 29 December, 1941, 20.
43 'Struggling with Integrity: An Interview with Walt Odets by Jon Robin Baitz', http://johnshaplin.blogspot.com/2010/03/struggling-with-integrity-interview.html (accessed 16 June 2016).
44 Brooks Atkinson, 'The Big Knife: If Hollywood Has Not Helped Odets It Has Apparently Done Him No Harm', *New York Times*, 6 March 1949, X1.
45 'Struggling with Integrity', http://johnshaplin.blogspot.com/2010/03/struggling-with-integrity-interview.html (accessed 29 June 2016).
46 Ibid.
47 Brooks Atkinson, 'Theatre: Family Life in Noah's Ark: "The Flowering Peach" Opens at Belasco', *New York Times*, 29 December 1954, 19.
48 Bruce McConachie, *American Theater in the Culture of the Cold War: Producing and Contesting Containment, 1947–1962* (Iowa City: University of Iowa Press, 2003).

49 For a variant of this interpretation, and how this work compares to Odets's plays of the 1930s, see Christopher J. Herr, *Clifford Odets and American Political Theatre* (Westport, CT: Praeger, 2003), 140–1.
50 'Struggling with Integrity'.
51 Lillian Hellman, Draft of Statement to be issued to the press following her testimony, sent to her attorney, Joseph Rauh, as quoted in John Earl Haynes, 'Hellman and the Hollywood Inquisition: The Triumph of Spin-Control Over Candour', *Film History* 10 (1998): 412.
52 Alice Kessler-Harris, *A Difficult Woman: The Challenging Life and Times of Lillian Hellman* (London: Bloomsbury Press, 2013), 3.
53 Joseph Wood Krutch as quoted in D. Martinson, *Lillian: A Life with Foxes and Scoundrels* (Berkeley, CA: Counterpoint Press, 2005), 148.
54 Loyalty clauses or 'oaths' required their signers to swear they were not and never had been members of the Communist Party and that they would not associate with radicals or 'subversives'.
55 Lillian Hellman, 'The Judas Goats', as quoted by William Wright in *Lillian Hellman: The Image, the Woman* (New York: Simon & Schuster, 2000), 212.
56 Hellman as quoted in Dan Rather, 'A Portrait of Lillian Hellman', in Jackson Bryer (ed.), *Conversations with Lillian Hellman* (Jackson: University Press of Mississippi, 1986), 211.
57 Haynes, 'Hellman and the Hollywood Inquisition', 409.
58 Ibid.
59 Hellman as quoted in Haynes, 'Hellman and the Hollywood Inquisition', 412.
60 See Robert P. Newman, *The Cold War Romance of Lillian Hellman and John Melby* (Chapel Hill: University of North Carolina Press, 2011), 261.
61 Brenda Murphy, *Congressional Theatre: Dramatizing McCarthyism on Stage, Film, and Television* (Cambridge: Cambridge University Press, 1999), 170.
62 Ibid., 172.
63 See, Júnia De Castro Magalhães Alves, 'Miss Hellman's Mood Plays: *The Autumn Garden* and *Toys in the Attic*', December 1984, https://www.researchgate.net/publication/287930114_Miss_Hellman's_mood_plays_The_Autumn_Garden_and_Toys_in_

the_Attic (accessed 16 June 2016). Hellman herself made this comparison when she edited Chekhov's letters.

64 William Wright, 'Why Lillian Hellman Remains Fascinating', *New York Times*, 3 November 1996, http://www.nytimes.com/1996/11/03/theater/why-lillian-hellman-remains-fascinating.html?pagewanted=all (accessed 26 June 2016).

BIBLIOGRAPHY

1. Introduction to the 1930s

American Experience: 1930s. Public Broadcasting System, DVD.
Baughman, J., ed. *American Decades, Vol. 4: 1930–1939*. Student Resources in Context. Detroit: Gale, 2001.
Black, C. and Jonathan Shandell, eds. *Experiments in Democracy: Interracial and Cross-Cultural Exchange in the American Theatre, 1912–1945*. Carbondale, IL: South Illinois University Press, 2016.
Conn, P. *The American 1930s: A Literary History*. Cambridge: Cambridge University Press, 2009.
Eldridge, D. *American Culture in the 1930s*. Edinburgh: Edinburgh University Press, 2008.
Kyvig, D. *Daily Life in the United States, 1920–1940*. Chicago: Ivan R. Dee, 2004.
Leuchtenberg, W. *Franklin D. Roosevelt and the New Deal*. New York: Harper Perennial, 2009.
McBee, R. *Dance Hall Days: Intimacy and Leisure among Working-Class Immigrants in the United States*. New York: New York University Press, 2000.
McCutcheon, M. *The Writer's Guide to Everyday Life from Prohibition through World War II*. Cincinnati: Writer's Digest Books, 1995.
McElvaine, R. *The Great Depression: America, 1929–1941*. New York: Three Rivers Press, 2009.
Meisenhelder, Susan. 'Conflict and Resistance in Zora Neale Hurston's Mules and Men', *Journal of American Folklore* 109 (433) (Summer 1996): 267–88.
Young, W. H. and Nancy K. Young. *The 1930s*. Westport, CT: Greenwood Press, 2002.

2. American Theatre in the 1930s

Plays

Anderson, M. *Both Your Houses.* New York: Samuel French, 1933.
Anderson, M. *Elizabeth the Queen,* in *Four Verse Plays by Maxwell Anderson.* New York: Harcourt, 1959.
Anderson, M. *Mary of Scotland,* in *Four Verse Plays by Maxwell Anderson.* New York: Harcourt, 1959.
Anderson, M. *Winterset,* in *Four Verse Plays by Maxwell Anderson.* New York: Harcourt, 1959.
Behrman, S. N. *Brief Moment.* New York: Farrar & Rinehart, 1931.
Behrman, S. N. *No Time for Comedy.* New York: Samuel French, Inc., 1938.
Behrman, S. N. *Biography,* in *4 Plays by S. N. Behrman.* New York: Random House, 1952.
Behrman, S. N. *End of Summer,* in *4 Plays by S. N. Behrman.* New York: Random House, 1952.
Bein, A. *Let Freedom Ring.* New York: Samuel French, 1936.
Kaufman, G. and Moss Hart. *The Man Who Came to Dinner,* in *Three Plays by Kaufman and Hart.* New York: Grove Press, 1980.
Kaufman, G. and Moss Hart. *You Can't Take it With You,* in *Three Plays by Kaufman and Hart.* New York: Grove Press, 1980.
Kirkland, J. *Tobacco Road.* New York: Viking Press, 1934.
Lawson, J. H. *Marching Song.* New York: Dramatists Play Service, 1937.
Lawson, J. H. *Success Story,* in *The 'Lost' Group Theatre Plays,* Vol. 1. New York: ReGroup Theatre Company, 1932/2011.
Maltz, A. *Black Pit.* New York: G.P. Putnam's Sons, 1935.
Peters, P. and George Sklar. *Stevedore.* New York: Covici-Fried Publishers, 1934.
Saroyan, W. *My Heart's in the Highlands.* New York: Harcourt, Brace and Company, 1939.
Saroyan, W. *The Time of Your Life.* New York: Samuel French, 1941.
Sherwood, R. *Reunion in Vienna.* New York: Dramatists Play Service, Inc., 1931.
Sherwood, R. *Idiot's Delight.* New York: Dramatists Play Service, Inc., 1936.
Sherwood, R. *The Petrified Forest.* New York: Scribners, 1936.
Sherwood, R. *Abe Lincoln in Illinois.* New York: Dramatists Play Service, Inc., 1939.
Sklar, G. and Albert Maltz. *Peace on Earth.* New York: Samuel French, 1934.

Recommended books and articles

Atkinson, Brooks. 'Henry Hull in "Tobacco Road" Based on the Novel by Erskine Caldwell'. *New York Times*, 5 December 1933, 31.

Bigby, C. W. E. *A Critical Introduction to Twentieth Century American Drama: 1900–1940*. New York: Cambridge University Press, 1982.

Broadway's Dreamers: The Legacy of the Group Theatre About the Group Theatre, 29 December 1997. Available online: http://www.pbs.org/wnet/americanmasters/group-theatre-about-the-group-theatre/622/ (accessed 7 January 2016).

Chambers, J. *Messiah of the New Technique: John Howard Lawson, Communism, and American Theatre, 1923–1937*. Carbondale: Southern Illinois University Press, 2006.

Chinoy, H. *The Group Theatre: Passion, Politics, and Performance in the Depression Era*, ed. Don B. Wilmeth and Milly S. Barranger. New York: Palgrave Macmillan, 2013.

Duffy, S. *Labor on Stage: Dramatic Interpretations of the Steel and Textile Industries in the 1930s*. Westwood, CT: Greenwood Press, 1996.

Fearnow, M. *The American Stage and the Great Depression: A Cultural History of the Grotesque*. Cambridge: Cambridge University Press, 1997.

Fletcher, A. 'Fighting One "ISM" with Another – The Communist Party Fights Racism in the South: Scottsboro Dramatizations and *Stevedore*'. *Theatre Symposium* 11 (2003): 50–62.

Fletcher, A. 'Reading Across the 1930s', in David Krasner (ed.), *A Companion to Twentieth Century American Drama*, 106–26. Malden, MA: Blackwell, 2005.

Fletcher, A. 'Precious Time: An Alternative Reading of Thornton Wilder's *Our Town* and William Saroyan's *The Time of Your Life*'. *Theatre Symposium* 14 (2006): 51.

Fletcher, A. *Rediscovering Mordecai Gorelik: Scene Design and the American Theatre*. Carbondale: Southern Illinois University Press, 2009.

Fletcher, A. and Cheryl Black. 'Staging a Tripartite Oppression: Race, Class, and Gender in the Theatre Union's *Stevedore* (1934)'. *New England Theatre Journal* 22 (2011): 23–51.

Franks, Leah D. 'Shocks Dissipated in "Tobacco Road"', *New York Times*, 13 October 1985, L127.

Geary, F. 'A Plague on Both Your Houses: Mr. Anderson Goes to Washington'. *New England Theatre Journal* 22 (2011): 1–22.

Geary, F. 'Social Critiques in Three Prose Plays by Maxwell Anderson:

Saturday's Children, Both Your Houses, and *The Star-Wagon*'. PhD diss., University of Missouri, Columbia, 2011.

Herr, C. 'American Political Drama, 1910–45', in Jeffrey H. Richards and Heather Nathans (eds), *The Oxford Handbook of American Drama*. Oxford: Oxford University Press, 2014: 280–94.

Hyman, C. *Staging Strikes: Workers' Theatre and the American Labor Movement*. Philadelphia: Temple University Press, 1997.

Irelan, S. 'Plays, Production, and Politics: The Lincoln Legend of Dramatic Literature and Performance as Staged During FDR's Second Presidential Term by the Federal Theatre Project and the Playwrights' Producing Company'. PhD diss., Southern Illinois University, 2006.

Isherwood, Charles. 'No, Mr. Kaufman, Satire Lives on, If It's Yours', *New York Times*, 24 September 2009.

Jones, Kenneth. 'Tobacco Road, Rarely Staged Hit of Yesteryear, Gets Fresh Paving by NC's Triad Stage', *Playbill*, 14 June 2007. Available online: http://www.playbill.com/news/article/tobacco-road-rarely-staged-hit-of- yesteryear-gets-fresh-paving-by-ncs-triad-141518 (accessed 10 January 2016).

Kaplan, Charles. 'S. N. Behrman: The Quandary of the Comic Spirit'. *College English* 11 (6) (1950): 317–23.

Levine, I. *Left Wing Dramatic Theory in the American Theatre*. Ann Arbor, MI: UMI Research Press, 1985.

'The Living Newspaper'. Available online: http://xroads.virginia.edu/~ma04/mccain/play/intro.htm (accessed 10 January 2016).

Mason, J. *Wisecracks: The Farces of George S. Kaufman*. Ann Arbor, MI: UMI Research Press, 1988.

Miller, J and Winifred L. Frazer. *American Drama between the Wars*. Boston, MA: Twayne Publishers, 1991.

Murphy, Brenda. 'Plays and Playwrights: 1915–1945', in Don B. Wilmeth and Christopher Bigsby (eds), *The Cambridge History of American Theatre*, Volume II, 332. New York: Cambridge University Press, 1999.

Opler, Daniel. 'Monkey Business in Union Square: A Cultural Analysis of the Klein-Ohrbach Strikes of 1934–5'. *Journal of Social History* 36 (1) (2002): 149.

Reed, K. *S. N. Behrman*. Boston, MA: G. K. Hall & Co., 1975.

Saal, I. *New Deal Theater: The Vernacular Tradition in American Political Theater*. New York: Palgrave MacMillan, 2007.

Smiley, S. *The Drama of Attack: Didactic Plays of the Depression*. Columbia: University of Missouri Press, 1972.

Smith, W. *Real Life Drama: The Group Theatre and America, 1931–1940*. New York: Grove Press, 1994.

Wharton, J. *Life Among the Playwrights*. New York: Quadrangle, 1974.

3. Gertrude Stein

Plays and other writing

Stein, G. *Geography and Plays*. Madison: The University of Wisconsin Press, 1922/1993.
Stein, G. *The Making of Americans*. Normal, IL: Dalkey Archive Press, 1925/1999.
Stein, G. *Portraits and Prayers*. New York: Random House, 1934.
Stein, G. *Narration: Four Lectures*. Chicago: University of Chicago Press, 1935.
Stein, G. *Everybody's Autobiography*. Cambridge, MA: Exact Change, 1937/1993.
Stein, G. *The World is Round*. London: B.T. Batsford Ltd, 1939.
Stein, G. *The Gertrude Stein First Reader and Three Plays*. Dublin: Maurice Fridberg, 1946.
Stein, G. *Last Operas and Plays*. Baltimore and London: Johns Hopkins University Press, 1949/1995.
Stein, G. *Writings 1932–1946*, ed. C. Stimpson and Harriet Chessman. New York: Library of America, 1998.
Wiley Hitchcock, H. and Charles Fussel, eds. *Four Saints in Three Acts*. Music of the United States of America, Volume 18, xx. Middleton, WI: A-R Editions, Inc. Published for the American Musicological Society, 2008.

Recommended books and articles

Bay-Cheng, S. *Mama Dada: Gertrude Stein's Avant-Garde Theater*. New York and London: Routledge, 2004.
Bowers, J. *They Watch Me as They Watch This: Gertrude Stein's Metadrama*. Philadelphia: University of Pennsylvania Press, 1991.
Bridgman, R. *Gertrude Stein in Pieces*. New York: Oxford, 1970.
Burns, E. *The Letters of Gertrude Stein and Carl Van Vechten 1935–1946*. New York: Columbia University Press, 1986.
Corn, W. and Tirza True Latimer. *Seeing Gertrude Stein. Five Stories*. Catalogue to the 2010–11 exhibitions at the Contemporary Jewish Museum in San Francisco and the National Portrait Gallery, Smithsonian Institution, Washington DC. Oakland: University of California Press, 2010–11.
Cotkin, G. *Feast of Excess: A Cultural History of the New Sensibility*. Oxford and New York: Oxford University Press, 2016.

Dydo, U. *A Stein Reader*. Evanston, IL: Northwestern University Press, 1993.
Dydo, U. *Gertrude Stein: The Language That Rises 1923–34*. Evanston, IL: Northwestern University Press, 2008.
Lehmann, H. *Postdramatic Theatre*. London and New York: Routledge, 2006.
Posman, S. and Laura Luise Schultz, eds. *Gertrude Stein in Europe: Reconfigurations Across Media, Disciplines, and Traditions*. London and New York: Bloomsbury, 2015.
Watson, Steven. *Prepare for Saints: Gertrude Stein, Virgil Thomson, and the Mainstreaming of American Modernism*. New York: Random House, 1998.
Wirth, A. 'Stein and Witkiewicz: Critique of Dramatic Reason', in Timothy Wiles (ed.), *Poland Between the Wars: 1918–1939. A Collection of Papers and Discussions from the Conference 'Poland between the Wars: 1918–1939' held in Bloomington, Indiana, February 21–23, 1985*, 280–96. Bloomington: Indiana University Polish Studies Center, 1989.
Wirth, A. 'Die Auflösung der dramatischen Figur oder: "I am I because my little dog knows me"', in A. Wirth and Thomas Irmer, *Flucht nach Vorn*, 210. Leipzig: Spector Books, 2013.

4. Langston Hughes

Plays and other writing

Hughes, Langston. *Little Ham*, in *Five Plays by Langston Hughes*, ed. Webster Smalley, 43–112. Bloomington: Indiana University Press, 1963.
Hughes, Langston. *Mulatto* in *Five Plays by Langston Hughes*, ed. Webster Smalley, 1–36. Bloomington: Indiana University Press, 1963.
Hughes, Langston. *I Wonder as I Wonder*. New York: Hill and Wang, 1993.
Hughes, Langston. *Scottsboro, Limited*, in *The Political Plays of Langston Hughes*, ed. Susan Duffy, 37–49. Carbondale: Southern Illinois University Press, 2000.
Hurston, Z. and Langston Hughes. *Mule Bone: A Comedy of Negro Life*. New York: Harper Perennial, 2008.

Recommended books and articles

Alexander, M. *The New Jim Crow: Mass Incarceration in the Age of Colorblindness*. New York: New York Press, 2012.

Atkinson, Brooks. 'Race Problems in the South the Theme of "Mulatto," a "New Drama" by Langston Hughes', *New York Times*, 25 October 1935, 25.

Beaufort, John. '"Mule Bone" Debuts After 60 Years Rescued Three Years Ago, the Play Delights '90s Audiences', *Christian Science Monitor*, 26 February 1991, http://search.proquest.com.proxy.lib.siu.edu/docview/291177605?accountid=13864 (accessed 17 March 2016).

Bell, Nelson B. '"Mulatto" Tells Tragic Story of Half-Caste: Acted by Mixed Cast, Play Interests Large House at the Belasco', *Washington Post*, 22 February 1937, 11.

Bernard, E., ed. *Remember Me to Harlem: The Letters of Langston Hughes and Carl Van Vechten, 1925–1962*. New York: Alfred A. Knopf, 2001.

Birnbaum, M. *Race, Work, and Desire in American Literature, 1860–1930*. New York: Cambridge University Press, 2003.

Christoph, M. Oakley. '"Mulatto" Shows Capitol Players At Their Peak Form', *Hartford Courant*, 15 July 1938, 4.

'Cleveland Gets Poet's Comedy: Efforts of Gilpin Players with Picture of Harlem Life Win Audience', *New York Amsterdam News*, 28 March 1936, 8.

Collins, Charles. '"Mulatto" a Dismal Tragedy of Woes of Racial Problem', *Chicago Daily Tribune*, 28 December 1936, 15.

Cone, J. *The Cross and the Lynching Tree*. Maryknoll, NY: Orbis Books, 2011.

Coulson, Shea. 'Funnier Than Unhappiness: Adorno and the Art of Laughter'. *New German Critique* 34 (1) (Winter 2007): 141–63.

Donlon, Anne. '*Don't You Want to be Free?*: Questions of Emancipation in 1930s African American Theatre'. Presentation at the American Literature Association Conference, American Literature Association, Boston, MA, May 2013.

Duffy, S. *The Political Plays of Langston Hughes*. Carbondale: Southern Illinois University Press, 2000.

Elam, Harry J., Jr and Michele Elam. 'Blood Debt: Reparations in Langston Hughes's Mulatto'. *Theatre Journal* 61 (1) (March 2009): 85–103.

Emery, Sharyn. 'The ~~Philadelphia~~ Harlem Story: Langston Hughes's Screwy Play *Little Ham*'. *Modern Drama* 66 (3) (Fall 2012): 373–85.

Gaines, K. *Uplifting the Race: Black Leadership, Politics, and Culture in the Twentieth Century*. Chapel Hill: University of North Carolina Press, 1996.

Gates, Henry Louis, Jr. 'Why the "Mule Bone" Debate Goes On', *New York Times*, 10 February 1991, H5, 8.

Gates, Henry Louis, Jr. 'A Tragedy of Negro Life', in Langston Hughes and Zora Neale Hurston, *Mule Bone: A Comedy of Negro Life*, ed. George Houston Bass and Henry Louise Gates, Jr, 5–23. New York: Harper Perennial, 2008.

Hemenway, Robert E. 'From *Zora Neale Hurston: A Literary Biography*', in Langston Hughes and Zora Neale Hurston, *Mule Bone: A Comedy of Negro Life*, ed. George Houston Bass and Henry Louise Gates, Jr, 161–89. New York: Harper Perennial, 2008.

Hemingway, A. *Artists on the Left: American Artists and the Communist Movement 1926–1956*. New Haven, CT: Yale University Press, 2002.

'Herndon Lauds "Suitcase" Play', *New York Amsterdam News*, 7 May 1938, 16.

Hill, Lynda M. 'Staging Hurston's Life and Work', in Lynda Hart and Peggy Phelan (eds), *Acting Out: Feminist Performances*, 295–314. Ann Arbor: University of Michigan Press, 1993.

Howard, Peggy. 'Sing Out the News to Open Saturday: Critic Sees Play As A Sure Hit When It Reaches Broadway', *Chicago Defender*, 1 October 1938, 19.

Klein, Alvin. 'Musical Depicts Harlem of 1930s', *New York Times*, 30 August 1987, WC16.

Klein, Alvin. '"Ham" Survives a Move', *New York Times*, 20 October 2002, NJ10.

Leach, L. *Langston Hughes: A Biography*. Westport, CT: Greenwood Press, 2004.

Lowe, John. 'Hurston, Toomer, and the Dream of a Negro Theatre', in Deborah G. Plant (ed.), *'The Inside Light': New Critical Essays on Zora Neale Hurston*, 79–92. Santa Barbara: Praeger, 2010.

Manuel, Carme. 'Mule Bone: Langston Hughes and Zora Neale Hurston's Dream Deferred of an American-American Theatre of the Black Word'. *African American Review* 35 (1) (Spring 2001): 77–92.

McLaren, J. *Langston Hughes: Folk Dramatist in the Protest Tradition, 1921–1943*. Westport, CT: Greenwood Press, 1997.

'Mercedes Gilbert Tops – "Mulatto" New Experience in Boston', *New York Amsterdam News*, 30 March 1940, 16.

Mitchell, K. *Living with Lynching: African American Lynching Plays, Performance, and Citizenship, 1890–1930*. Urbana: University of Illinois Press, 2011.

Mitchell, K. 'Sisters in Motherhood(?): The Politics of Race and Gender in Lynching Drama', in Evelyn Simien (ed.), *Gender and Lynching: The Politics of Memory*, 37–60. New York: Palgrave Macmillan, 2011.

Rampersad, A. *The Life of Langston Hughes. Vol. 1, 1902–1941: I, Too, Sing America*. New York: Oxford University Press, 1986.

Rampersad, A. *Selected Letters of Langston Hughes*. New York: Knopf, 2015.

Rich, Frank. 'A Difficult Birth for "Mule Bone"', *New York Times*, 15 February 1991, C1, C24.

Ryan, Katy. 'Prison, Time, Kairos in Langston Hughes's Scottsboro, Limited'. *Modern Drama* 58 (2) (Summer 2015): 171–93.

Sanders, Leslie. '"Interesting Ways of Staging Plays": Hughes and Russian Theatre'. *Langston Hughes Review* 15 (1) (Spring 1997): 4–12.

Sanders, Leslie. 'Little Ham's Self Invention: Teaching Langston Hughes', in Maryemma Graham, Sharon Pineault-Burke and Marianna White Davis (eds), *Teaching African American Literature: Theory and Practice*, 65–74. New York: Routledge, 1998.

Silver, Reuben. 'A History of the Karamu Theatre of Karamu House, 1915–1960'. Diss., Ohio State University, 1961.

Smalley, W., ed. *Five Plays by Langston Hughes*. Bloomington: Indiana University Press, 1963.

'The Stage: Copley Theatre, "Mulatto"', *Daily Boston Globe*, 25 March 1940, 9.

Stapleton, J. 'Zora Neale Hurston's Construction of Authenticity Through Ethnographic Innovation'. *Western Journal of Black Studies* 30 (1) (Spring 2006): 62–8.

Stewart, Jeffrey. 'New Negro as Citizen', in George Hutchinson (ed.), *The Cambridge Companion to the Harlem Renaissance*, 13–27. Cambridge: Cambridge University Press, 2007.

Sullivan, Dan. '"Mulatto" Staged at Theater Club: Langston Hughes Hit of '35 Revived for "Members"', *New York Times*, 16 November 1967, 61.

Sundquist, Eric J. 'Who Was Langston Hughes?', *Commentary* 102 (6) (December 1996): 55–9.

Sundstrom, William A. 'Last Hired, First Fired? Unemployment and Urban Black Workers during the Great Depression'. *Journal of Economic History* 52 (2) (June 1992): 415–29.

Van Vechten, C. 'Carlos to Langston Hughes, 4 January 1936', in Emily Bernard (ed.), *Remember Me to Harlem: The Letters of Langston Hughes and Carl Van Vechten, 1925–1962*. New York: Alfred A. Knopf, 2001.

Weber, Bruce. 'Crime and Comeuppance with a Sassy, Jazzy Heart:

Langston Hughes's Little Ham', *New York Times*, 24 December 2001, E5.
White, S., Stephen Garton, Stephen Robertson and Graham White. *Playing the Numbers: Gambling in Harlem Between the Wars.* Cambridge, MA: Harvard University Press, 2010.

5. Clifford Odets

Plays and other writing

Odets, C. *Six Plays.* New York: Methuen, 1939/82.
Odets, C. *Night Music.* New York: Random House, 1940.
Odets, C. *The Time Is Ripe: The 1940 Journal of Clifford Odets.* New York: Grove Press, 1988.

Recommended books and articles

Brenman-Gibson, M. *Clifford Odets, American Playwright: The Years From 1906–1940.* New York: Atheneum, 1981.
Cantor, H. *Clifford Odets: Playwright-Poet.* Metuchen, NJ: Scarecrow, 1978.
Chinoy, H. *The Group Theatre: Passion, Politics and Performance in the Depression Era.* London: Palgrave Macmillan, 2013.
Clurman, H. *The Fervent Years: The Story of the Group Theatre and the Thirties.* New York: Hill and Wang, 1945.
Frick, John W. '"Odets, Where is Thy Sting?" Reassessing the "playwright of the proletariat"', in William W. Demastes (ed.), *Realism and the American Dramatic Tradition*, 123–38. Tuscaloosa: University of Alabama Press, 1996.
Gassner, J. *Masters of the Drama.* New York: Random House, 1940.
Herr, C. *Clifford Odets and American Political Theatre.* Westport, CT: Praeger, 2003.
Kazin, A. *Starting Out in the Thirties.* Boston: Little, Brown, 1962.
Mendelsohn, Michael J. 'Odets at Center Stage'. *Theatre Arts* (May 1963): 16–19, 74–6, 28–30, 78–80.
Miller, G. *Clifford Odets.* New York: Continuum, 1989.
Moore, T. *The Economics of the American Theatre.* Durham, NC: Duke University Press, 1968.
Murphy, Brenda. 'Plays and Playwrights, 1915–1945', in Don B. Wilmeth and Christopher Bigsby (eds), *The Cambridge History of*

American Theatre, Volume II: 1870–1945, 289–342. Cambridge: Cambridge University Press, 1989.
Novick, J. *Beyond the Golden Door: Jewish American Drama and Jewish American Experience.* New York: Palgrave Macmillan, 2008.
Smith, W. *Real Life Drama: The Group Theatre and America, 1931–1940.* New York: Grove Press, 1990.
Weales, G. *Odets, The Playwright.* London: Methuen, 1985.

6. Lillian Hellman

Plays and other writing

Hellman, L. *Four Plays by Lillian Hellman.* New York: Random House, 1934.
Hellman, L. *The Searching Wind.* New York: Viking Press, 1944.
Hellman, L. *Toys in the Attic.* New York: Random House, 1959.
Hellman, L. *An Unfinished Woman.* Boston: Little, Brown and Company, 1969.
Hellman, L. *Pentimento.* Little, Brown and Company, 1973.
Hellman, L. *Scoundrel Time.* Boston: Little, Brown and Company, 1976.
Hellman, L. *Six Plays by Lillian Hellman.* New York: Vintage Books, 1979.
Hellman, L. *Maybe.* Boston: Little, Brown and Company, 1980.
Hellman, L. *The Children's Hour.* New York: Dramatist Play Service, 1981.

Recommended books and articles

Adler, Thomas. 'Lillian Hellman: Feminism, Formalism, and Politics', in Brenda Murphy (ed.), *The Cambridge Companion to American Women Playwrights*, 118–33. New York: Cambridge University Press, 1999.
Atkinson, Brooks. '"The Children's Hour", Being a Tragedy of Life in a Boarding School', *New York Times*, 21 November 1934, 23.
Barlow, Judith. 'Into the Foxhole: Feminism, Realism, and Lillian Hellman', in William W. Demastes (ed.), *Realism and the American Dramatic Tradition*, 156–71. Tuscaloosa: University of Alabama Press, 1996.
Bigsby, C. W. E. *A Critical Introduction to Twentieth Century American*

Drama: American Drama 1900–1940. New York: Cambridge University Press, 1982.

Broe, Mary Lynn. '"Bohemia Bumps into Calvin": The Deception of Passivity in Lillian Hellman's Drama', in Mark W. Estrin (ed.), *Critical Essays on Lillian Hellman*, 78–89. Boston: G. K. Hall & Co., 1989.

Bryer, J., ed. *Conversations with Lillian Hellman*. Jackson: University Press of Mississippi, 1986.

Dolan, Jill. 'The Children's Hour, Comedy Theatre, London, March 12, 2011', http://feministspectator.princeton.edu/author/jill/ (accessed 17 March 2016).

Estrin, M. *Critical Essays on Lillian Hellman*. Boston: G. K. Hall & Co., 1989.

Falk, D. *Lillian Hellman*. New York: Frederick Unger Publishing Co., 1978.

Fleche, Anne. 'The Lesbian Rule: Lillian Hellman and the Measures of Realism'. *Modern Drama* 39 (1) (1996): 16–30.

Hollander, Anne and John Marquand. 'Lillian Hellman: The Art of Theatre No. 1'. *Paris Review* 33 (Winter–Spring 1965): 1–19, http://www.theparisreview.org/interviews/4463/the-art-of-theater-no-1-lillian-hellman (accessed 10 June 2015).

Kessler-Harris, A. *A Difficult Woman: The Challenging Life and Times of Lillian Hellman*. New York: Bloomsbury Press, 2012.

Lawson, John Howard. 'A Comparative Study of "The Children's Hour" and "Days to Come"'. *New Theatre and Film* (March 1937): 15–16, 60–1.

Lederer, K. *Lillian Hellman*. Boston: Twayne Publishers, 1979.

Murphy, B. *Congressional Theatre: Dramatizing McCarthyism on Stage, Film, and Television*. New York: Cambridge University Press, 2003.

Weidman, Jerome. 'Lillian Hellman Reflects on the Changing Theater'. *Dramatists Guild Quarterly* 7 (Winter 1970): 22.

Wiles, Timothy J. 'Lillian Hellman's American Political Theater: The Thirties and Beyond', in Mark W. Estrin (ed.), *Critical Essays on Lillian Hellman*, 90–112. Boston: G. K. Hall & Co., 1989.

Wright, W. *Lillian Hellman: The Image, the Woman*. New York: Simon and Schuster, 1986.

Afterword

Adato, P. 'Chapter 3 – Gertrude Stein: When This You See Remember Me', Perry Miller Adato Collection, https://www.youtube.com/watch?v=wMn5bxk7d4U (accessed 1 July 2016).

'Al Carmines' Gertrude Stein Musical Revived Feb. 15', *Playbill*, 11 February 1997.

Alves, Júnia De Castro Magalhães. 'Miss Hellman's Mood Plays: *The Autumn Garden* and *Toys in the Attic*', December 1984, https://www.researchgate.net/publication/287930114_Miss_Hellman's_mood_plays_The_Autumn_Garden_and_Toys_in_the_Attic (accessed 1 July 2016).

Atkinson, Brooks. 'Drama About League of Nations and Woodrow Wilson Opens', *New York Times*, 29 December 1941, 20.

Atkinson, Brooks. 'The Big Knife: If Hollywood Has Not Helped Odets It Has Apparently Done Him No Harm', *New York Times*, 6 March 1949, X1.

Atkinson, Brooks. 'Theatre: Family Life in Noah's Ark: "The Flowering Peach" Opens at Belasco', *New York Times*, 29 December 1954, 19.

Brantley, Ben. 'Review: Revisiting Gertrude Stein's Writings in Rereading Another', *New York Times*, 23 September 2015, http://www.nytimes.com/2015/09/29/theater/review-revisiting-gertrude-steins-writings-in-reread-another.html?_r=1 (accessed 26 June 2016).

Brenman-Gibson, Margaret. 'Odets: Failure or Not?', *New York Times*, 13 June 1965, X1.

Brenman-Gibson, Margaret. 'How Clifford Odets Spent His Last, Desperate Days', *New York Times*, 18 October 1981, D1.

Burns, E., Ulla E. Dydo and William Rice, eds. *The Letters of Gertrude Stein and Thornton Wilder*. New Haven, CT: Yale University Press, 1996.

Durham, L. *Staging Gertrude Stein: Absence, Culture, and the Landscape of American Alternative Theatre*. New York: Palgrave Macmillan, 2005.

'The Fight Back: The Battles of Clifford Odets and Thurgood Marshall', *New Yorker*, 12 May 2008, http://www.newyorker.com/magazine/2008/05/12/the-fight-back (accessed 15 June 2016).

Fuchs, E. and Uda Chaudhuri, eds. *Land/Scape/Theatre*. Ann Arbor: University of Michigan Press, 2002.

Hay, S. *African American Theatre: An Historical and Critical Analysis*. Cambridge: Cambridge University Press, 1994.

Haynes, John Earl. 'Hellman and the Hollywood Inquisition: The Triumph of Spin-Control Over Candour'. *Film History* 10 (1998): 408–14.

Howard, Richard. 'There Is a Lot of Here Here', *New York Times*, 3 May 1998.

'Interview: Walt Odets', *Jewish Chronicle Online*, 12 November 2010, http://www.thejc.com/lifestyle/lifestyle-features/41116/interview-walt-odets (accessed 15 June 2016).

Isherwood, Christopher. 'The There That's There: Mapping a Modernist's Way With Words', *New York Times*, 2 June 2009.

Kanny, Mark. 'Review: Pittsburgh Opera about Gertrude Stein a Winner', TRIBLIV, 21 February 2016, http://triblive.com/aande/moreaande/9979368-74/opera-stein-act (accessed 29 June 2016).

Martinson, D. *Lillian: A Life with Foxes and Scoundrels*. Berkeley, CA: Counterpoint Press, 2005.

McConachie, B. *American Theater in the Culture of the Cold War: Producing and Contesting Containment 1947–1962*. Iowa City: University of Iowa Press, 2003.

Miller, J. *Origins of the Dream: Hughes's Poetry and King's Rhetoric*. Gainesville: University Press of Florida, 2015.

Murphy, B. *Congressional Theatre: Dramatizing McCarthyism on Stage, Film, and Television*. Cambridge: Cambridge University Press, 1999.

Navasky, V. *Naming Names*. New York, Penguin Books, 1991.

Newman, R. *The Cold War Romance of Lillian Hellman and John Melby*. Chapel Hill: University of North Carolina Press, 2011.

Nugent, Frank S. 'Odets, Where is Thy Sting?', *New York Times*, 6 September 1936, X3.

'Stage Left: The Struggles of Clifford Odets', *New Yorker*, 17 April 2006.

Stendhal, Renate. 'Why the Witch-Hunt Against Gertrude Stein?', *Tikkun*, 4 June 2012, http://www.tikkun.org/nextgen/why-the-witch-hunt-against-gertrude-stein (accessed 26 June 2016).

'Struggling with Integrity: An Interview with Walt Odets by Jon Robin Baitz', http://johnshaplin.blogspot.com/2010/03/struggling-with-integrity-interview.html (accessed 16 June 2016).

Swortzell, L. *Around the World in 21 Plays: Theatre for Young Audiences*. New York: Applause, 2000.

Van Vechten, C., ed. *The Selected Writings of Gertrude Stein*. New York: Vintage Books, 1962.

Wright, William. 'Why Lillian Hellman Remains Fascinating', *New York Times*, 3 November 1996.

INDEX

1930s
  architecture and design 21–2
  arts and culture 14–15
  dance 23–4
  domestic life 6–8
  education 8–10
  film 26–8
  labour and the working class 13–14
  life in the 1–4
  literature 16–19
  media 24–5
  music 15, 22–3
  painting 20–1
  photography 15, 21
  poetry 19–20
  radio 25–6
  science and technology 11–13
  sports and recreation 10–11
  theatre see theatre
1931– (Sifton, Paul/Sifton, Claire) 48, 49, 241
20-Minute Meals (cookbook) 7
27 (opera) (Gordon, Ricky Ian/Vavrek, Royce) 204

Abe Lincoln in Illinois (Sherwood, Robert E.) 31, 54, 56–7
acting 54
actor, unity with character 114–15
Adams, Ansel 21
Adams, James Truslow: *Epic of America, The* 16
Adato, Perry Miller: *Gertrude Stein: When This You See, Remember Me* 202
Adler, Luther 50
Adler, Stella 50, 52, 150
Adler, Thomas P. 179, 192–3
Adler Planetarium 13
'Advertisement for the Waldorf Astoria' (Hughes, Langston) 19
advertising 7, 25–6
AFL (American Federation of Labor) 14
AFL-CIO 14
African-Americans *see* race/racism
'After Stein: Traveling the Amercan Langscape' (Carlson, Marvin) 203
After the Fall (Miller, Arthur) 208
Agee, James/Evans, Wallace: *Let Us Now Praise Famous Men* 16, 21
agit-prop 36, 38–9, 232
agriculture 46
Akins, Zoë: *Old Maid, The* 32, 172
Albee, Edward: *Goat, or Who is Sylvia, The* 78
alienation 115

Alison's House (Glaspell, Susan) 31
All My Sons (Miller, Arthur) 237
All Quiet on the Western Front (film) 27
All This and Heaven Too (Field, Rachel) 18
Allen, Fred 26
Allen, Frederick Lewis: *Only Yesterday: An Informal Study of the 1920s* 16
Allen, Gracie 26
Allen, Harbor 40 see also Peters, Paul
Allen, Woody: *Midnight in Paris* 203
American 1930s: A Literary History, The (Conn, Peter) 3
American Drama 1900–1940 (Bigsby, Christopher) 185
American Dream 16, 17, 147, 154
American Guide Series 16
American Humor: A Study of the National Character (Rourke, Constance) 16
American Jitters (Wilson, Edmund) 17
American Landscape (Rice, Elmer) 35, 55
American Madness (film) 27
American myth 78–9
American novel, the 18 see also literature
'American Political Drama, 1910–45' (Herr, Christopher) 33
American theatre see theatre
American Tragedy, An (Dreiser, Theodore) 48
American Tragedy (Evergood, Philip) 21

Amos 'n' Andy (radio show) 2, 26
Anderson, Carl David 13
Anderson, John 78
Anderson, Maxwell 34, 58–61
  Anne of a Thousand Days 59
  Bad Seed, The 59
  Both Your Houses 59–60
  Elizabeth the Queen 58
  Gods of the Lightning 58
  High Tor 58–9
  Key Largo 55, 59
  Lost in the Stars 59
  Mary of Scotland 58
  Night Over Taos 48
  Valley Forge 58
  What Price Glory 58
  Winterset 58
Anderson, Maxwell/Weill, Kurt: *Knickerbocker Holiday* 54–5
Anderson, Sherwood: *Puzzled America* 17
Animal Kingdom, The (Barry, Philip) 74
Anne of a Thousand Days (Anderson, Maxwell) 59
Another Part of the Forest (Hellman, Lillian) 187, 190, 192, 213–14
Anouilh, Jean: *Lark, The* 172, 215–16
Anthony, Susan B. 99
architecture and design 21–2
Ardrey, Robert 55
  Casey Jones 48, 53, 54
  Thunder Rock 48, 53–4
'Are You Makin' Any Money?' (Hupfield, Herman) 23
Arena Stage 200
Around the World in 21 Plays: Theatre for Young Audiences (Swortzell, Lowell) 201

INDEX

art 20–1, 85
Artaud, Antonin 93
arts and culture 14–15
Asimov, Isaac 24
Ask Your Mama: 12 Moods for Jazz (Hughes, Langston) 207
Astaire, Fred 23
astronomy 13
Atkinson, Brooks 129, 157, 210, 211
atom smasher 13
Autobiography of Alice B. Toklas, The (Stein, Gertrude) 81–2, 90, 95, 220
Autumn Garden, The (Hellman, Lillian) 200, 214
aviation films 28
Avignon Festival 112
Awake and Sing! (Odets, Clifford) 32, 48, 146, 147, 157–61, 199, 200

Bacharach, Ernest 21
Back Street (Hurst, Fannie) 17–18
Bad Companions (Roughead, William) 177
Bad Seed, The (Anderson, Maxwell) 59
Balanchine, George 23
ballroom dance 24
Bancroft, Anne 200
Bankhead, Tallulah 188, 213
banking crisis (2008) 2
Banks, Richard 112
Barlow, Judith: 'Feminism, Realism, and Lillian Hellman' 192
Barrier, The (Hughes, Langston/ Meyerowitz, Jan) 130
Barry, Philip 74–5
Animal Kingdom, The 74

Bright Star 74
Here Come the Clowns 74
Hotel Universe 74
Joyous Season, The 74
Philadelphia Story, The 74–5
Spring Dance 74
Tomorrow and Tomorrow 74
baseball 10
basketball 10
Bass, George Houston 135
Bassett, Angela 206
Bates, Kathy 203
Bausch, Pina 117
Bay-Cheng, Sarah 114
Beck, Julian 118
Behrman, S. N. 34, 61–7
Biography 63–4, 65, 67
Brief Moment 63, 67
End of Summer 65–7
No Time for Comedy 55, 61–2, 64, 67
race 35
Rain from Heaven 64–5, 67
Bein, Albert: *Let Freedom Ring* 41, 42, 43
Bel Geddes, Norman
Futurama 4
Horizon 22
Bell, Nelson B. 130
Benedict, Ruth: *Patterns of Culture* 3
Benét, Stephen Vincent 19
Benny, Jack 26
Benton, Thomas Hart 20
Social History of Indiana, A 20
Berchet, Gérard 13
Berkeley, Busby 27
Berlin, Irving: 'Cheek to Cheek' 23
Berners, Lord 108
Bernstein, Leonard
Candide 172, 216

Lark, The 216
Bertozzi, Nick: *Salon, The* 204
Big Bear Super Market 6
Big Knife, The (Odets, Clifford) 200, 210
Big Night, The (Powell, Dawn) 48
Big Sea, The (Hughes, Langston) 207
Bigsby, Christopher 191
  American Drama 1900–1940 185
  Biography (Behrman, S. N.) 63–4, 65, 67
Birds Eye 7
Birnbaum, Michele 128, 129–30
Bisquick 7
Bitter Stream (Wolfson, Victor) 41
black Americans *see* race/racism
Black Fury (film) 27, 43
black holes 13
Black Lives Matter movement 205
Black Mask (pulp magazine) 24
Black Nativity (Hughes, Langston) 206
Black Nativity – In Concert: A Gospel Celebration 206
Black Power movement 206
Black Pit (Maltz, Albert) 41, 42–3
Black Reconstruction (Du Bois, W. E. B.) 3
Black Thunder (Bontemps, Arna) 3
Blankfort, Michael 42, 230
Blitzstein, Mark: *Cradle Will Rock, The* 21
Blockade (film) 27
'Blue Moon' (Rodgers, Richard/Hart, Lorenz) 23
Bodas de Sangre (*Blood Wedding*) (Lorca, Frederico Garcia) 142

Bogart, Anne: *Gertrude and Alice* 202
'Bone of Contention, The' (Hurston, Zora Neale) 134
Bontemps, Arna
  Black Thunder 3
  God Sends Sunday 142
Bontemps, Arna/Cullen, Countee: *St. Louis Woman* 142
'Book of the Dead, The' (Rukeyser, Muriel) 20
Both Your Houses (Anderson, Maxwell) 59–60
Bottom Dogs, The (Dahlberg, Edward) 17
Bourke-White, Margaret 21, 24, 74
  You Have Seen Their Faces 21
Bowers, Jane Palatini 104–5, 116, 118, 203
  'They Watch Me as They Watch This': Gertrude Stein's Metadrama 94
boxing 11
Brando, Marlon 216
Brantley, Ben 202
Bread and Puppet Theater 195
Brecht, Bertolt 115
  Mother, The 41
Breen, Joseph 28
Brennan-Gibson, Margaret 208
Breuer, Lee: *Gospel at Colonus* 207
Brewsie and Willie (Stein, Gertrude) 97, 201
Brides (magazine) 8
Bridgeman, Richard 256 n.44
Brief Moment (Behrman, S. N.) 63, 67
Bright Eyes (film) 27
Bright Star (Barry, Philip) 74
Broadway 151
Broken Arrow, The (film) 230

Brooks, Cleanth/Warren, Robert Penn: *Understanding Poetry* 19
'Brother, Can You Spare a Dime?' (Gormy, Jay/Harburg, Yip) 23
Browder, Earl 3
Brown, John Mason 78
Brustein, Robert 206
Buchwald, Nathaniel 230, 231–2
Buck, Pearl S.
 Good Earth, The 18
 House Divided, A 18
 Sons 18
Bull, Clarence Sinclair 21
Burck, Jacob: *Lord Provides, The* 21
Burns, Edward/Dydo, Ulla: *Letters of Gertrude Stein and Thornton Wilder, The* 97, 107
Burns, George 26
Burnshaw, Stanley 232–3
business 47

Cage, John 118–19
 Living Room Music 118–19
 Three Songs 118
Cakewalk (Feibleman, Peter) 217
Caldwell, Erskine: *Tobacco Road* 17, 75
Caldwell, Zoe 217
Can You Hear Their Voices? A Play of Our Time (Flanagan, Hallie/Clifford, Margaret) 36
'Can You Make Out Their Voices' (Chambers, Whittaker) 36
cancer 12
Candide (Hellman Lillian/Bernstein, Leonard) 172, 216
candy 7

Cane (Toomer, Jean) 224
Cantor, Eddie 26
capitalism 155
Capra, Frank 27
Carlson, Marvin: 'After Stein: Traveling the Amercan Langscape' 203
Carmichael, Hoagy 23
Carmines, Al 112, 118, 202, 219, 220
 In Circles 207
Carnegie, Dale: *How to Win Friends and Influence People* 3
Carnelia, Craig 211
Carnovsky, Morris 37, 150
Carothers, Wallace 13
Carr, John Dickson 18
Carroll, Pat 203
Case of Clyde Griffiths, The (Goldschmidt, Lena/Piscator, Erwin) 48, 53
Casey Jones (Ardrey, Robert) 48, 53, 54
Cattaneo, Ann 135
CCC *see* Civilian Conservation Corps
cellar clubs 9
censorship 28, 177
 Ethiopia (Rice, Elmer) 35, 46
Chambers, Jonathan: *Messiah of the New Technique: John Howard Lawson, Communism, and American Theatre 1923–1937* 49–50
Chambers, Whittaker: 'Can You Make Out Their Voices' 36
Channing, Stockard 200
character, unity with actor 114–15
Chase, The (Hellman, Lillian) 216
Chaudhuri, Uda/Fuchs, Elinor: *Land/Scape/Theatre* 203

'Cheek to Cheek' (Berlin, Irving) 23
Chekhov, Anton 179, 199–200
  Three Sisters, The 216
Chesnutt, Charles W. 224
Chicago Defender (newspaper) 205
Chicago World's Fair 3–4
Child, Nellise: *Weep for the Virgins* 48, 53
Children's Hour, The (Hellman, Lillian) 32, 176–8, 181–3, 190, 199, 200
  character 186, 188
  feminism 191, 194
  homosexuality 36, 177, 183, 216
  scène à faire 180
  speech acts 193
  structure 184
  success of 172, 174
Children's Hour, The (Longfellow, Henry Wadsworth) 177
chips 7
'Chronicle' (Graham, Martha) 23
Chrysler Building, New York City 22
cinemas 28
CIO *see* Congress of Industrial Organizations
Civilian Conservation Corps (CCC) 5, 9, 38
Clash by Night (Odets, Clifford) 200, 209, 210
class 1, 36
Clift, Montgomery 213
Clifford, Margaret Ellen/Flanagan, Hallie: *Can You Hear Their Voices? A Play of Our Time* 36
'Closed Doors, or the Great Drumsheugh Case' (Roughead, William) 177

clothing 6
clubs 9
Clurman, Harold 38, 47, 51, 77, 157
  Awake and Sing! 158
  Golden Boy 165
  Group Theatre 149, 152, 153
Cocoanuts (film) 27
Collins, Charles 129
comedy 61–7
  Barry, Philip 74–5
  Hellman, Lillian 189
  Kaufman, George S. 67–74
  Kirkland, Jack 75–7
comic books 25
comic strips 24–5
Common Ground (magazine) 205
communism 3, 51 *see also* House Un-American Activities Committee
  Group Theatre 39
  Hellman, Lillian 174–5, 215
  Hughes, Langston 125
Communist Party USA (CP-USA) 39
Cone, James H. 132
Congress of Industrial Organizations (CIO) 14
Congressional Theatre (Murphy, Brenda) 195, 216
Conn, Peter: *American 1930s: A Literary History, The* 3
Connelly, Marc: *Green Pastures* 31
Conroy, Jack: *Disinherited, The* 17
Contrast, The (Tyler, Royall) 59
convenience foods 7
Coughlin, Charles E. 26
Counting Her Dresses. A Play (Stein, Gertrude) 91
Country Girl, The (Odets, Clifford) 200, 207–8

Cowley, Malcolm: *Exile's Return* 16
Cowley, Malcolm/Hughes, Langston/Wilson, Edmund: *Culture in Crisis* 3
CP-USA *see* Communist Party USA
Cradle Will Rock, The (Blitzstein, Mark) 21, 47
Cradle Will Rock, The (Robbins, Tim) 21
Cradle Will Rock, The (Welles, Orson) 47
Crane, Hart 19
Crawford, Cheryl 37, 47, 149
Crawford, Joan 21, 209
Crocker, Betty 7
Crohn's syndrome 12
Crucible, The (Miller, Arthur) 176
Cullen, Countee/Bontemps, Arna : *St. Louis Woman* 142
Culture in Crisis (manifesto) (Wilson, Edmund/Cowley, Malcolm/Hughes, Langston) 3
Culture of Cities, The (Mumford, Lewis) 12
cummings, e. e. 19
Cushing's syndrome 12
cyclotron 13

Dahlberg, Edward
  Bottom Dogs, The 17
  dance 23–4
Dail, Chrystyna 195
  Stage for Action: U.S. Social Activist Theatre in the 1940s 195
Daily Worker (newspaper) 39
dance 23–4
dance marathons 11
Daughters of the Revolution (Woods, Grant) 20

Davidman, Joy 20
Days to Come (Hellman, Lillian) 174, 183–6, 190, 191, 193, 216
Dead End (film) 27
Death of a Salesman (Miller, Arthur) 163, 196
Death of Character, The (Fuchs, Elinor) 114
Deeter, Jasper 128
defibrillation 12
Depression *see* Great Depression, the
diet 6–7, 8
Difficult Woman: The Challenging Life and Times of Lillian Hellman, A (Kessler–Harris, Alice) 212, 217
DiMaggio, Joe 10
Dinner at Eight (Ferber, Edna/ Kaufman, George S. 68, 69–70
Dinner at Eight (film) 70
Disinherited, The (Conroy, Jack) 17
Doctor Faustus Lights the Lights (Stein, Gertrude) 96, 108–14, 114
  productions 112–14, 201–2
documentary films 27
Dolan, Jill 194
Doll's House, A (Ibsen, Henrik) 180
domestic life 6–8
Donlon, Anne 126
Don't You Want to be Free (Hughes, Langston) 123, 126–7, 128, 205
Dorgman, Zelda 41
Dos Passos, John 16, 17, 29
Double Edge Theatre 195
Douglas, Aaron 226

Dracula and Frankenstein (film) 27
'Dream Deferred, A' (Hughes, Langston) 199
'Dream of Freedom' (Hughes, Langston) 207
Dreiblatt, Martha 41
Dresier, Theodore
  American Tragedy, An 48
  Tragic America 17
Dreyfuss, Henry 22
Du Bois, W. E. B. 18, 123, 206
  Black Reconstruction 3
Duck Soup (film) 27
Duffy, Susan 32–3
  Political Plays of Langston Hughes, The 123
Dunbar, Paul Laurence 224
Dupree, F. W.: *Selected Writings of Gertrude Stein, The* 198
Durham, Leslie Atkins 201, 202
  Staging Gertrude Stein: Absence, Culture, and the Landscape of American Alternative Theatre 197
Dust Be My Destiny (film) 27
Dust Bowl Ballads 23
Dydo, Ulla 89
  Stein Reader, A 109
Dydo, Ulla/Burns, Edward: *Letters of Gertrude Stein and Thornton Wilder, The* 97, 107

Each One As She May (Stein, Gertrude) 202
Eating Together: Recipes and Recollections (Hellman, Lillian/Feibleman, Peter) 217
economy *see* Great Depression, the

Edmonds, George D.: *Guns Along the Mohawk* 17
education 8–10
'Eight Who Lie in the Death House' (Peters, Paul [Harbor Allen]) 42
Elam, Harry, Jr 130–1
Elam, Michele 130–1
Eldridge, David 15
Elizabeth the Queen (Anderson, Maxwell) 58
Ellington, Duke: 'It Don't Mean a Thing (If It Ain't Got That Swing)' 22
Elliot, T. S. 19
Em-Fuehrer Jones (Hughes, Langston) 142
Emerson, Gladys Anderson 12
Emery, Sharyn 140
Empire State Building, New York City 22
End of Summer (Behrman, S. N.) 65–7
Ephron, Nora: *Imaginary Friends* 217
Epic of America, The (Adams, James Truslow) 16
Estrada, Jade Eseban: *ICONS: The Lesbian and Gay History of the World, Vol 1* 203
Ethiopia (Rice, Elmer) 35, 46
Evans, Herbert M. 12
Evans, Wallace/Agee, James: *Let Us Now Praise Famous Men* 16, 21
Evergood, Philip: *American Tragedy* 21
Everybody's Autobiography (Stein, Gertrude) 95, 118
Exile's Return (Cowley, Malcolm) 16
expositions 3–4

fabric 6
Fair Labor Standards Act 14
fairs 3–4
Falk, Doris V. 184
family life 4
'Family of Three Perhaps' (Stein, Gertrude) 203
farce 68
Farmer, Virginia 37
Faulkner, William 18
Faÿ, Bernard 96–7
Fearing, Kenneth 20
Fearnow, Mark 76
Federal Art Project 15, 21
Federal Music Project 15
Federal Theatre Companies 15
Federal Theatre Project (FTP) 45–7, 195
Federal Writers Project 15
Feibleman, Peter: *Cakewalk* 217
Feibleman, Peter/Hellman, Lillian: *Eating Together: Recipes and Recollections* 217
feminism 175, 191–3, 196 *see also* gender
'Feminism, Realism, and Lillian Hellman' (Barlow, Judith) 192
Ferber, Edna/Kaufman, George S.
  Dinner at Eight 68, 69–70
  Stage Door 68, 70
Fibber Magee and Molly (radio show) 26
fibreglass 13
Field, Rachel: *All This and Heaven Too* 18
Fields, Dorothy 23
Fiesta Ware 8
film 26–8, 69, 164–5, 172
Film and Photo League (FPL) 27
Fisher, Rudolph 226
Fitzgerald, F. Scott 243 n.2

Flaherty, Stephen/Galati, Frank: *Loving Repeating* 203–4
Flanagan, Hallie 45, 47
Flanagan, Hallie/Clifford, Margaret Ellen: *Can You Hear Their Voices? A Play of Our Time* 36
Fleche, Anne: 'Lesbian Rule: Lillian Hellman and the Measures of Realism, The' 183
Fleeing from a Dust Storm (Rothstein, Arthur) 21
Flowering Peach, The (Odets, Clifford) 211
fluxus movement 119
food 6–7, 8
football 10
Foreman, Richard 112, 118, 203, 219, 221
Forgotten Man, The (Shlaes, Amity) 243 n.8
Fornes, Maria Irene 203, 219–20
Fortune magazine 16, 24
Foster, William Z. 3
Four Saints in Three Acts (Stein, Gertrude) 99–106, 107, 113, 201
  history 94–5
  landscape play 92, 93
  success 82–3
FPL *see* Film and Photo League
Franklin D. Roosevelt and the New Deal (Leuchtenberg, William H.) 1
Franks, Leah D. 76–7
Free Volksbühne: *Doctor Faustus Lights the Lights* 112
Front Page, The (film) 27
Front Porch (Hughes, Langston) 142
Frost, Robert 19

FTP *see* Federal Theatre Project
Fuchs, Elinor: *Death of Character, The* 114
Fuchs, Elinor/Chaudhuri, Uda: *Land/Scape/Theatre* 203
Fugitive from a Chain Gang (film) 27
Fuller, Buckminster 22
Futurama (exhibit) (Bel Geddes, Norman) 4

Galati, Frank 202
Galati, Frank/Flaherty, Stephen: *Loving Repeating* 203–4
Gallagher, Dorothy: 'Imperious Life, An' 217
gambling 11
games 11
gangster films 26
Garbo, Greta 21
Gardiner, Muriel 173
Gardner, Erle Stanley 18
Garfield, Julie (John) 38, 150, 209
Garland, Judy 27
Gassner, John 148
Gates, Henry Louis, Jr 135, 136, 138
Geary, Fonzie D., II
 'Plague on Both Your Houses: Mr. Anderson Goes to Washington, A' 60
 'Social Critiques in Three Prose Plays by Maxwell Anderson: *Saturday's Children, Both Your Houses,* and *The Star-Wagon*' 59
Gehrig, Lou 10
gender 36, 175
genre 76, 77
Gentle People, The (Shaw, Irwin) 48, 54

Gentlewoman (Lawson, John Howard) 48, 50, 51–2
Geographical History of America, Or, The Relation of Human Nature to the Human Mind (Stein, Gertrude) 95
Geography and Plays (Stein, Gertrude) 92, 93
George White's Scandals of 1931 23
Gerber foods 7
Germany 10
Gershwin, George/Gershwin, Ira
 Of Thee I Sing 60
 Strike Up the Band 68
Gershwin, Ira/Gershwin, George
 Of Thee I Sing 60
 Strike Up the Band 68
Gertrude and Alice (Bogart, Anne) 202
Gertrude Stein and the Making of an American Celebrity (Lieck, Karen) 197
Gertrude Stein, Gertrude Stein, Gertrude Stein (Martin, Marty) 203
Gertrude Stein Symposium 219–21
Gertrude Stein: When This You See, Remember Me (Adato, Perry Miller) 202
Gibbons, Cedric 22
Glaspell, Susan 30
 Alison's House 31
Glimmerglass Opera Festival 202
Goat, or Who is Sylvia, The (Albee, Edward) 78
God Sends Sunday (Bontemps, Arna) 142
Gods of the Lightning Anderson, Maxwell 58
Goebbels, Heiner
 Hashirigaki 98, 202

Wars I have Seen 97
Gold, Mike 40
  Jews Without Money 17
Gold Piece, The (Hughes, Langston) 123
Golden Boy (Odets, Clifford) 48, 147, 164–6, 200
Golden Eagle Guy (Levy, Melvin) 48, 53
Goldschmidt, Lena/Piscator, Erwin: *Case of Clyde Griffiths, The* 48, 53
Gomez, Manuel 40
Gone With the Wind (film) 55
Gone with the Wind (Mitchell, Margaret) 17
Good Earth, The (Buck, Pearl S.) 18
'Good Morning Revolution' (Hughes, Langston) 125
Goodman, Benny 26
Gordon, Leon: *White Cargo: A Play of the Primitive* 128
Gordon, Ricky Ian/Vavrek, Royce: *27 (opera)* 204
Gorelik, Mordecai 37, 52, 236–7
  1931– 49, 241
  Casey Jones 54
  Gentle People, The 54
  Men in White 53
  Success Story 50
  'Theatre is a Weapon' 39–40, 236–42
  Thunder Rock 54
Gorky, Arshile 21
Gormy, Jay/Harburg, Yip: 'Brother, Can You Spare a Dime?' 23
Gospel at Colonus (Breuer, Lee) 207
government subsidies 45
Graham, Martha 23
  'Chronicle' 23

'Platform for the American Dance, A' 23
Gramont, Elisabeth de 97
Granich, Irwin *see* Gold, Mike
Grapes of Wrath, The (Steinbeck, John) 2, 17
Grayson, Bette 208
Great Depression, the 1–2, 4–6, 14
  film 27
  Gorelik, Mordecai 237–9
  Stock Market Crash 1–2, 4, 29
Great Depression: America, 1929–1941, The (McElvaine, Robert S.) 243 n.8
Green, Paul
  House of Connelly, The 48, 150
  Johnny Johnson 48, 53
Green Pastures (Connelly, Marc) 31
Griffith Observatory 13
Gropper, William: *Miners* 21
Grotowski, Jerzy 117
Group Theatre 34, 37, 38, 47–54, 149–50, 195
  Awake and Sing! 158
  Clurman, Harold 149, 152, 153
  communism 39
  Crawford, Cheryl 149
  financial position 151–2
  Lawson, John Howard 48–52
  My Heart's in the Highlands 76
  Odets, Clifford 48, 149–53, 208
  Strasberg, Lee 149, 150
Guare, John 211
Guns Along the Mohawk (Edmonds, George D.) 17
Gussow, Mel 76

Guthrie, Woodie: 'So Long, It's
  Been Good to Know Ya' 23

Hamlisch, Marvin 211
Hammett, Dashiell 172, 213, 214
  Maltese Falcon, The 18, 24
  Thin Man, The 18
Handke, Peter 117
Hansberry, Lorraine: *Raisin in the
  Sun, A* 129, 199
Harburg, Yip/Gormy, Jay:
  'Brother, Can You Spare a
  Dime?' 23
Harlem (Thurman, Wallace/Rapp,
  William Jordan) 140
Harlem Renaissance 18
Harlem Suitcase Theatre (HST)
  126–7, 142
Hart, Lorenz. Rodgers, Richard
  'Blue Moon' 23
  I'd Rather Be Right 60–1
Hart, Moss 38
Hart, Moss/Kaufman, George S.
  I'd Rather Be Right 60–1
  *Man Who Came to Dinner,
  The* 32, 68, 72–4
  Once in a Lifetime 68, 69
  You Can't Take it With You
  32, 35, 68, 71–2
Hashirigaki (Goebbels, Heiner)
  98, 202
Havoc, June 11
Hawk's Nest Tunnel disaster 20
Hayden Planetarium 13
Hayes, Alfred 20
Haynes, John Earl: 'Lillian
  Hellman and the
  Hollywood Inquisition: The
  Triumph of Spin-Control
  over Candour' 214–15
Hebbel Theater: *Doctor Faustus
  Lights the Lights* 112
Helburn, Theresa 133

Hellman, Julia Newhouse 171
Hellman, Lillian 27, 31, 171–6,
  196, 199–200, 212–17
  Another Part of the Forest
  187, 190, 192, 213–14
  anti-Semitism 173
  Autumn Garden, The 200,
  214
  Bankhead, Tallulah 213
  biographies 217
  Candide 172, 176
  Chase, The 216
  Days to Come 174, 183–6,
  190, 191, 193, 216
  deviant characters 216
  *Eating Together: Recipes
  and Recollections* 217
  Feibleman, Peter 217
  feminism 175, 191–3
  honours and awards 217
  House Un-American Activities
  Committee 176, 197, 200,
  214–16, 234–6
  influences 179
  'Judas Goats, The' 214
  Lark, The 172, 176, 215–16
  legacy 217
  Little Foxes, The 174, 186–94,
  200, 213, 216
  Maybe: A Story 172–3, 217
  Melodramas 178–9, 181
  Monserrat 214
  *My Mother, My Father, and
  Me* 216
  North Star 213
  passivity 190
  Pentimento 172–3, 217
  plagiarism 172–3, 213, 217
  politics 173–6, 184–5, 196–7,
  199–200, 215, 235–6
  race 35, 193–4
  reputation 212–13
  Scoundrel Time 172–3, 217

Searching Wind, The 213
Spanish Earth, The 174–5
speech acts, secrets and silence 193
Three 172, 217
Toys in the Attic 175, 194, 216
Unfinished Woman, An 172, 217
Watch on the Rhine 172, 182, 192, 213, 235
Well-Made Plays 178–83
Hellman Lillian/Bernstein, Leonard: *Candide* 172, 176
Hellman, Lillian/Feibleman, Peter: *Eating Together: Recipes and Recollections* 217
Hemingway, Ernest 27, 93, 175
Hepburn, Audrey 177
Hepburn, Katharine 172
Here Come the Clowns (Barry, Philip) 74
Herndon, Angelo 127
Heroes for Sale (film) 27
Herr, Christopher 32, 33
'American Political Drama, 1910–45' 33
Hickok, Lorena 16–17
High Tor (Anderson, Maxwell) 58–9
Hill, Lynda M. 135
Hindenburg disaster 25
His Girl Friday (film) 27
Hitler, Adolf 3, 10
Holliday, Billie: 'Strange Fruit' 23
Hollywood Production Code 28
Hollywood Ten 16
homosexuality 36, 177–8, 183, 199
Hoover, Herbert 4
Hopkins, Harry 45
Hopper, Edward 20

Horizon (Bel Geddes, Norman) 22
horse racing 10–11
Hotel Universe (Barry, Philip) 74
House Divided, A (Buck, Pearl S.) 18
House in the Country, A (Levy, Melvin) 53
House/Lights (Wooster Group) 112–14, 202
House of Connelly, The (Green, Paul) 48, 150
House Un–American Activities Committee (HUAC) 197
Hellman, Lillian 176, 197, 200, 214–16, 234–6
Hughes, Langston 125, 197, 198
Odets, Clifford 197, 199, 210, 228–33
Houseman, John 47, 208
housing 47
How to Win Friends and Influence People (Carnegie, Dale) 3
Howard, Richard 204
Howard, Sidney 34, 55
Gone With the Wind 55
Madam, Will You Walk 55
Silver Cord, The 55
They Knew What They Wanted 55
Howard Johnson's 7
HST *see* Harlem Suitcase Theatre
HUAC *see* House Un-American Activities Committee
Hudson, Jennifer 206
Hughes, Langston 16, 19, 31, 121–7, 198–9, 205–7
'Advertisement for the Waldorf Astoria' 19
Ask Your Mama: 12 Moods for Jazz 207

Barrier, The 130
Big Sea, The 207
Black Nativity 206–7
Bodas de Sangre (*Blood Wedding*) 142
Chicago Defender (newspaper) 205
Common Ground (magazine) 205
communism 125, 198–9
Deeter, Jasper 128
Don't You Want to be Free 123, 126–7, 128, 205
'Dream Deferred, A' 199
'Dream of Freedom' 207
Em-Fuehrer Jones 142
Front Porch 142
Gold Piece, The 123
'Good Morning Revolution' 125
Harlem Suitcase Theatre 126–7, 142
homosexuality 199
House Un–American Activities Committee 125, 197, 198
Hurston, Zora Neal 133–5
I Wonder as I Wander 207
Jones, Martin 127–8
King, Martin Luther, Jr 207
Langston Hughes Project 207
'Langston Hughes Proposes an Oath to End All Oaths for Americans' 226–8
Limitations of Life 142
Little Eva's End or Colonel Tom's Cabin 142
Little Ham 122, 139–42
McClendon, Rose 128
Mulatto 122, 123, 127–33, 199
Mule Bone: A Comedy of Negro Life, The 122, 133–40

'My America' 143
'Negro Artist and the Racial Mountain, The' 123, 221–6
New Negro Theatre 126
New Song, A 126
'One More "S" in the U.S.A' 125
Organizer, De 142
Peterson, Dorothy
politics 125, 196–9
race 19–20, 122–3, 199, 205–6, 221–8
St Louis Woman 142
Scarlet Sister Barry 142
Scottsboro Limited: Four Poems and a Play in Verse 19–20, 124–5, 205
Selected Poems 199
Simple Stakes a Claim 143
Skyloft Players 126
Soviet Union 125–6
Spain 126
Thompson, Louise 126, 127
translations 142
'Waiting on Roosevelt' 20
'What the Negro Wants' 143
Hughes, Langston/Cowley Malcolm/Wilson, Edmund: *Culture in Crisis* 3
Hughes, Langston/Muse, Clarence: *Way Down South* 142–3
Hugo, Victor 148
Miserables, Les 148
Humouresque (Odets, Clifford) 209
Hupfield, Herman: 'Are You Makin' Any Money?' 23
Hurrell, George 21
Hurst, Fannie: *Back Street* 17–18
Hurston, Zora Neal 18
'Bone of Contention, The' 134

Mule Bone: A Comedy of Negro Life, The 133–5
Mules and Men 18
Their Eyes Were Watching God 18–19
Hutton, Barbara 8
hybridity 76, 77

I Wonder as I Wander (Hughes, Langston) 207
Ibsen, Henrik 179
 Doll's House, A 180
Iceman Cometh, The (O'Neill, Eugene) 78
ICONS: The Lesbian and Gay History of the World, Vol 1 (Estrada, Jade Eseban) 203
I'd Rather Be Right (Hart, Lorenz/Rodgers, Richard) 60–1
I'd Rather Be Right (Hart, Moss/Kaufman, George S.) 60–1
Ida A Novel (Stein, Gertrude) 96, 108, 111, 201
Identity A Poem (Stein, Gertrude) 95–6
Idiot's Delight (Sherwood, Robert E.) 34, 55, 56
'If I Told Him: A Completed Picture of Picasso' (Stein, Gertrude) 204
Imaginary Friends (Ephron, Nora) 217
immigration 3, 146–8
'Imperious Life, An' (Gallagher, Dorothy) 217
In Circles (Stein, Gertrude) 202
 Carmines, Al 207
In Dubious Battle (Steinbeck, John) 17
In Savoy: or, Yes Is For a Very Young Man (Stein, Gertrude) 98, 201

Injunction Granted (Living Newspaper play) 46, 47
inventions 12
Irelan, Scott R. 57
irony 189
Isherwood, Charles: 'No, Mr Kaufman, Satire lives on, if it's Yours' 68
Isherwood, Christopher 203
'It Don't Mean a Thing (If It Ain't Got That Swing)' (Ellington, Duke) 22
It's a Wonderful Life (film) 209–10

James, Henry 179
James, William 85
Jefferson Memorial 22
Jerome, V. J. 230
Jews Without Money (Gold, Mike) 17
John Reed Clubs 3
Johnny Johnson (Green, Paul) 48, 53
Johnson, James Weldon 18
Johnson, Lyndon 60
Jones, Chris 204
Jones, James Earl 126
Jones, Martin 127–8
Jones, Robert Earl 126
Jordan, Jim 26
Jordan, Julia 196
Jordan, Marion 26
Joyous Season, The (Barry, Philip) 74
'Judas Goats, The' (Hellman, Lillian) 214
Judson Poets' Theatre 118
 Doctor Faustus Lights the Lights 112
jukeboxes 23
junk food 7
Just Around the Corner (film) 27

Kaplan, Charles: 'S. N. Behrman: The Quandary of the Comic Spirit' 67
Kaufman, George S. 67–8
  Merrily We Roll Along 68, 70
  Stage Door 68
Kaufman, George S./Ferber, Edna
  Dinner at Eight 68, 69–70
  Stage Door 68, 70
Kaufman, George S./Hart, Moss
  I'd Rather Be Right 60–1
  Man Who Came to Dinner, The 32, 68, 72–4
  Once in a Lifetime 68, 69
  You Can't Take it With You 32, 35, 68, 71–2
Kaye, Danny 211
Kazan, Elia 38, 53, 54, 208, 210
Kennedy, Adrienne 196
Kessler-Harris, Alice 175
  Difficult Woman: The Challenging Life and Times of Lillian Hellman, A 212, 217
Key Largo (Anderson, Maxwell) 55, 59
King, C. C. 12
King, Martin Luther, Jr 207
King Kong (film) 27
King Kullen Market 6
Kingsley, Sidney: *Men in White* 48, 52–3, 150, 151
Kirkland, Jack: *Tobacco Road* 75–7
Kitchen, S. F. 12
Knickerbocker Holiday (Weill, Kurt/Anderson, Maxwell) 54–5
Knightly, Keira 194, 200
Kober, Arthur 172
Kooning, William de 21
Kornfield, Lawrence 112, 118, 202
Krasnya Presnya 125–6
Kroger 7
Krutch, Joseph Wood 213
Kuhn, Hans Peter

labour drama 37–49, 237–42
labour movement 13–14 *see also* working class
Ladies' Voices (Stein, Gertrude) 91–2
Lancaster, Burt 211
landscape plays 83
Land/Scape/Theatre (Fuchs, Elinor/Chaufhuri, Uda) 203
Lane, Preston 76
Lange, Dorothea
  Migrant Mother 21
  White Angel Breadline, The 21
Langston Hughes Project 207
'Langston Hughes Proposes an Oath to End All Oaths for Americans' 226–8
language
  performative aspects of 88
  Stein, Gertrude 88, 89
Laning, Edward: *Unlawful Assembly, Union Square* 21
Lark, The (Anouilh, Jean) 172, 215–16
Larkin, Margaret 41, 43
Lawrence, Ernest 13
Lawrence, John H. 12
Lawson, John Howard 16, 27, 29, 35, 198, 233
  criticism of 176
  Gentlewoman 48, 50, 51–2
  Group Theatre 48–52
  Hellman, Lillian 183, 184, 186, 190
  Marching Song 41, 44–5
  Processional 52
  Pure in Heart, The 50
  Success Story 48, 50–1

Theory and Technique of Playwriting 50
League of Workers Theatres 240
LeCompte, Elizabeth 114
Lederer, Katherine 178, 188
Left Wing Dramatic Theory (Levine, Ira A.) 37
Lehmann, Hans-Thies 107
'Lesbian Rule: Lillian Hellman and the Measures of Realism, The' (Fleche, Anne) 183
Let Freedom Ring (Bein, Albert) 41, 42, 43
Let Us Now Praise Famous Men (Agee, James/Evans, Wallace) 16, 21
Letters of Gertrude Stein and Thornton Wilder, The (Burns, Edward/Dydo, Ulla) 97, 107
Leuchtenberg, William H.: *Franklin D. Roosevelt and the New Deal* 1
Levine, Ira A.: *Left Wing Dramatic Theory* 38
Levy, Melvin
  Golden Eagle Guy 48, 53
  House in the Country, A 53
Lieck, Karen: *Gertrude Stein and the Making of an American Celebrity* 197
Life (magazine) 24
Life Among the Playwrights (Wharton, John) 55, 67–8
life expectancy 2
'Life is Just a Bowl of Cherries' (Henderson, Ray/Brown, Lew) 23
Lillian (Luce, William) 217
'Lillian Hellman and the Hollywood Inquisition: The Triumph of Spin-Control over Candour' (Haynes, John Earl) 214–15
Lillian Hellman: Her Life and Legend (Rollyson, Carl) 234
'Lillian Hellman's Political Theater: The Thirties and Beyond' (Wiles, Timothy J.) 185
Lilly Awards 196
Limitations of Life (Hughes, Langston) 142
Lindbergh, Charles 24
Linney, Laura 200
Listen To Me (Stein, Gertrude) 96, 114–18
literature 16–19
Little Eva's End or Colonel Tom's Cabin (Hughes, Langston) 142
Little Foxes, The (Hellman, Lillian) 174, 186–94, 200, 213, 216
Little Ham (Hughes, Langston) 122, 139–42
Little House on the Prairie, The (Wilder, Laura Ingalls) 18
liver therapy 12
Living Newspapers 46
  Injunction Granted 46, 47
  One-Third of a Nation 46, 47
  Power 46, 47
  Triple-A Plowed Under 46–7
Living Room Music (Cage, John) 118–19
Living Theatre 118, 201
  Doctor Faustus Lights the Lights 112, 201–2
Lloyd, Wray 12
Locke, Alain 206
Loewy, Raymond 22
Long, Huey 2
Long Christmas Dinner, The (Wilder, Thornton) 107–8

Longfellow, Henry Wadsworth: *Children's Hour, The* 177
Lorca, Frederico Garcia: *Bodas de Sangre (Blood Wedding)* 142
Lord Provides, The (Burck, Jacob) 21
Lost in the Stars (Anderson, Maxwell) 59
Loving Repeating (Galati, Frank/Flaherty, Stephen) 203–4
Luce, Clare Booth: *Women, The* 213
Lumpkin, Grace 43
To Make My Bread 17, 41, 43
lynching dramas 132

Macbeth (Welles, Orson) 47
McCarthy, Mary 173, 213, 217
McClendon, Rose 128, 129
McDermott, William 141
McElvaine, Robert S.: *Great Depression: America, 1929–1941, The* 243 n.8
Macki, Adrienne 205
MacLaine, Shirley 177
McLaren, Joseph 123, 140
MacLeish, Archibald 19
Madam, Will You Walk (Howard, Sidney) 55
magazines 24, 39
Making of Americans, The (Stein, Gertrude) 82, 86–7, 93, 98, 202
Malina, Judith 118
Maltese Falcon, The (Hammett, Dashiell) 18, 24
Maltz, Albert 40, 41, 230
Black Pit 41, 42–3
Maltz, Albert/Sklar, George
Merry-Go-Round 41
Peace on Earth 40, 41–2, 242

Mame (musical) 203
Man Who Came to Dinner, The (Kaufman, George S./Hart, Moss) 32, 68, 72–4
Manuel, Carme 137, 139
Marching Song (Lawson, John Howard) 41, 44–5
Marx Brothers 27
Marxism 19, 34, 39, 42, 43
Mary of Scotland (Anderson, Maxwell) 58
Mawra, Joseph
Maybe: A Story (Hellman, Lillian) 172–3, 217
media 24–5, 39
medicine 12
Meisner, Sanford 37
Melby, John 215
Meller, Raquel 224
Melodramas 178–9, 181
Men in White (Kingsley, Sidney) 48, 52–3, 150, 151
Mercer, Johnny 23
Merrily We Roll Along (Kaufman, George S.) 68, 70
Merry-Go-Round (Sklar, George/Maltz, Albert) 41
Messiah of the New Technique: John Howard Lawson, Communism, and American Theatre 1923–1937 (Chambers, Jonathan) 49–50
Mexico (Stein, Gertrude) 91
Meyerhold, Vsevolod 125–6
Meyerowitz, Jan/Hughes, Langston: *Barrier, The* 130
Mickey Mouse 11
Midnight in Paris (Allen, Woody) 203
Mielzener, Jo 57
Migrant Mother (Lange, Dorothea) 21

Miller, Arthur 185, 195
  After the Fall 208
  All My Sons 237
  Crucible, The 176
  Death of a Salesman 163, 196
  Timebends: A Life 196
  'Tragedy and the Common
    Man' 196
  You're Next 195
Miller, Glenn 26
Miller, W. Jason: *Origins of the
  Dream: Hughes's Poetry
  and King's Rhetoric* 207
Miners (Gropper, William) 21
Minot, George R. 12
Miserables, Les (Hugo, Victor)
  148
Mr. Smith Goes to Washington
  (film) 27, 60
Mitchell, Margaret: *Gone with
  the Wind* 17
Modernism 15
'Monkey Business in Union
  Square: A Cultural Analysis
  of the Klein-Ohrbach
  Strikes of 1934–5' (Opler,
  Daniel) 38
Monserrat (Hellman, Lillian) 214
Moore, Marianne 19
Morrison, Herb 25
Mosher, Gregory 135
Moss, Elisabeth 194, 200
Mother, The (Brecht, Bertolt) 41
Mother of Us All, The (Stein,
  Gertrude) 98–9, 201, 202
Moving Day (film) 27
Mulatto (Hughes, Langston) 122,
  123, 127–33, 199
*Mule Bone: A Comedy of
  Negro Life, The* (Hughes,
  Langston) 122, 133–40
Mules and Men (Hurston, Zora
  Neal) 18

Müller, Heiner 83
Mumford, Lewis: *Culture of
  Cities, The* 12
mural art 20–1
Murphy, Brenda: *Congressional
  Theatre* 195, 216
Murphy, William P. 12
Muse, Clarence/Hughes,
  Langston: *Way Down South*
  142–3
music 11, 15, 22–3
'My America' (Hughes, Langston)
  143
My Heart's in the Highlands
  (Saroyan, William) 48, 77–8
My Mother, My Father, and Me
  (Hellman, Lillian) 216

Nancy Drew detective series 18
National Association of
  Manufacturers 14
National Endowment for the Arts
  15
National Labor Relations Act 14
national theatre 238–9
National Youth Administration
  (NYA) 9
Native Son (Wright, Richard) 19
'Negro Artist and the Racial
  Mountain, The' (Hughes,
  Langston) 123, 221–6
Neighborhood Players 30
neutron stars 13
New Criticism 19
New Deal 4–6
  arts and culture 15
  Civilian Conservation Corps
    (CCC) 5, 9
  National Youth Administration
    (NYA) 9
  Works Progress Administration
    (WPA) 5, 9
New Masses (magazine) 39

New Negro Renaissance 122
New Negro Theatre 126
New Playwrights Theatre 29–30
New Song, A (Hughes, Langston) 126
New Theatre (magazine) 39
New York World's Fair 4
Newsweek (magazine) 24
'Night and Day' (Porter, Cole) 23
Night Music (Odets, Clifford) 48, 147, 148, 168–9, 209, 211
Night Over Taos (Anderson, Maxwell) 48
Nixon, Cynthia 200
'No, Mr Kaufman, Satire lives on, if it's Yours' (Isherwood, Charles) 68
No Time for Comedy (Behrman, S. N.) 55, 61–2, 64, 67
Nolan, Lloyd 52
None but the Lonely Heart (Odets, Clifford) 209
Norman, Marsha 196
North, Joe 230
North Star (Hellman, Lillian) 213
Northwest Passage (Roberts, Kenneth) 17
Nugent, Frank: 'Odets, Where is Thy Sting?' 208
NYA *see* National Youth Administration
nylon 13

Oak, Liston 40
Obama, Barack 60
Odets, Clifford 27, 31, 145–53, 196, 199–200, 207–12
  Awake and Sing! 32, 48, 146, 147, 157–61, 199, 200
  Big Knife, The 200, 210
  Clash by Night 200, 209, 210
  Consumer capitalism 155, 207–8
  Country Girl, The 200, 207–8
  death 211
  family 146, 207–8
  Flowering Peach, The 211
  Golden Boy 48, 147, 164–6, 200
  Group Theatre 48, 149–53, 208
  Hollywood 164–5, 208, 209–10, 211
  House Un-American Activities Committee 197, 199, 210, 228–33
  Hugo, Victor 148
  Humouresque 209
  immigrant experience 146–8
  It's a Wonderful Life 209–10
  Jewish influence 146–7
  modern culture 166
  Night Music 48, 147, 148, 168–9, 209, 211
  None but the Lonely Heart 209
  obituaries 208
  Paradise Lost 48, 160, 161–4, 200
  politics 148–9, 155, 196–7, 199, 228–33
  Pulitzer Prize 211
  Richard Boone Show, The 212
  Rocket to the Moon 48, 147, 148, 160, 167–8, 200
  Silent Partner, The 165
  Six Plays by Clifford Odets 209
  Sweet Smell of Success 211
  television 211–12
  Theatre Collective 37
  Theatre of Action 38
  Till the Day I Die 48
  Waiting for Lefty see Waiting for Lefty
Odets, Lou 146
Odets, Nora 208

Odets, Pearl Geisinger 146
Odets, Walt 207–8
'Odets, Where is Thy Sting?'
  (Nugent, Frank) 208
Of Thee I Sing (Gershwin,
  George/Gershwin, Ira) 60
Okhlopkov, Nikolai 125–6
Old Maid, The (Akins, Zoë) 32,
  172
Olga's House of Shame (Mawra,
  Joseph) 113
Olympics, the 10
Omaha Magic Theatre 195
Once in a Lifetime (Hart,
  Moss/Kaufman, George S.)
  68, 69
One Carl Van Vechten (Stein,
  Gertrude) 90
'One More "S" in the U.S.A'
  (Hughes, Langston) 125
One Per Cent 4, 8
One-Third of a Nation (Living
  Newspaper play) 46, 47
O'Neill, Eugene 30, 238
  Iceman Cometh, The 78
O'Neill, Tip 60
*Only Yesterday: An Informal
  Study of the 1920s* (Allen,
  Frederick Lewis) 16
Open Theatre 195
Operas and Plays (Stein,
  Gertrude) 94
Opler, Daniel: 'Monkey Business
  in Union Square: A Cultural
  Analysis of the Klein–
  Ohrbach Strikes of 1934–5'
  38
Oppenheimer, J. Robert 13
Organizer, De (Hughes, Langston)
  142
*Origins of the Dream: Hughes's
  Poetry and King's Rhetoric*
  (Miller, W. Jason) 207

Orozco, Jose 20
Orta Or One Dancing (Stein,
  Gertrude) 87
Our Daily Bread (film) 27
Our Town (Wilder, Thornton)
  107
Owens, Jessie 10

Päetow, Luiz: *Plays* 203
painting 20–2
Palin, Sarah 60
Paradise Lost (Odets, Clifford)
  48, 160, 161–4, 200
Paris France (Stein, Gertrude) 95,
  201
Parks, Suzan-Lori 196
patriotism 3
Patterns of Culture (Benedict,
  Ruth) 3
Patterson, Louise *see* Thompson,
  Louise
Peace on Earth (Sklar, George/
  Maltz, Albert) 40, 41–2,
  242
Pentimento (Hellman, Lillian)
  172–3, 217
Pétain, Marshal Philippe 97
Peters, Paul/Walker, Charles
  Rumford: *Third Parade,
  The* 241
Peters, Paul (Harbor Allen) 42
  'Eight Who Lie in the Death
  House' 42
Peters, Paul (Harbor Allen)/Sklar,
  George: *Stevedore* 35–6,
  41, 42
Petrified Forest, The (Sherwood,
  Robert) 56
Petticoat Junction (TV show) 212
Philadelphia Story, The (Barry,
  Philip) 74–5
photography 15, 21
physics 13

Piano Lesson, The (Wilson, August) 179
Picasso, Pablo 85
  Demoiselles d'Avignon, Les 85
Piscator, Erwin/Goldschmidt, Lena: *Case of Clyde Griffiths, The* 48, 53
'Plague on Both Your Houses: Mr. Anderson Goes to Washington, A' (Geary, Fonzie D., II) 60
Plain Edition 94
plastic 13
'Platform for the American Dance, A' (Graham, Martha) 23
Play (Stein, Gertrude) 87
Play, A (Stein, Gertrude) 91
play structure 180
'Play That Must Be Performed, A' (*Theater* article) 203
'Plays' (Stein, Gertrude) 90, 101
Plays (Päetow, Luiz) 203
playwrights 34–5
Playwrights Producing Company Inc. 34, 54–8, 62
Pluto (planet) 13
poetry 19–20
political drama 33, 36, 39, 59–61 *see also* labour drama
Political Plays of Langston Hughes, The (Duffy, Susan) 123
politics 3, 5–6 *see also* communism
  agit-prop 36, 38–9, 232
  Anderson, Maxwell 59–60
  capitalism 155
  Communist Party USA 39
  film 27
  Gorelik, Mordecai 238
  Group Theatre 39, 149–50
  Hellman, Lillian 173–6, 184–5, 196–7, 199–200, 215, 235–6
  Hughes, Langston 125, 196–9
  Marxism 19, 34, 39, 42, 43
  Odets, Clifford 148–9, 155, 196–7, 199, 228–33
  playwrights 34–5, 51
  political drama 33, 36, 39, 59–61 *see also* labour drama
  Stein, Gertrude 97, 196–8
  Waiting for Lefty 153–7
Pollack, Jackson 21
Pollard, Red 11
Porter, Cole 23
  'Night and Day' 23
positrons 13
Post, Marion 21
Postmodernism 15
Powell, Dawn: *Big Night, The* 48
Power (Living Newspaper play) 46, 47
Prepare for Saints – Gertrude Stein, Virgil Thomson and the Mainstreaming of American Modernism (Watson, Steven) 82
Processional (Lawson, John Howard) 52
Prolet-Bühne 37, 38, 240
proletarian realism 17
Provincetown Players 30
Public Enemy, The (film) 26
Pulitzer Prize 32, 211
Pullen, Arthur 141
pulp magazines 24
Pure in Heart, The (Lawson, John Howard) 50
Puzzled America (Anderson, Sherwood) 17

Queen, Ellory 18

race/racism 2, 18–19, 35
  bias 124
  Black Lives Matter movement 205
  Black Power movement 206
  culture 122
  Four Saints in Three Acts 201
  Hellman, Lillian 193–4
  Hughes, Langston 19–20, 122–3, 205–6, 221–8
  literature 18–19
  Little Ham 122, 139–42
  lynching 132
  Mulatto 122, 123, 127–33
  Mule Bone: A Comedy of Negro Life, The 122, 133–9
  music 23
  New Negro Renaissance 122
  radio 26
  rape 132
  Scottsboro Boys case 3, 42, 124
  theatre 35, 206
radio 10, 11, 25–6
radio astronomy 13
Rain from Heaven (Behrman, S. N.) 64–5, 67
Raisin in the Sun, A (Hansberry, Lorraine) 129, 199
Rampersad, Arnold 135
rape 261 n.52
Rapp, William Jordan/Thurman, Wallace: *Harlem* 140
Rauh, Joseph 215
Ray, Nicholas 38
Reagan, Sylvia 41
Rebeck, Theresa 196
Regionalism 20
'Regular Regularly In Narrative' (Stein, Gertrude) 103
Reiss, Winold 225

Rent (musical) 203
'Reread Another A Play to Be Played Indoors or Out I Wish to Be a School' (Stein, Gertrude) 202
restaurants 7
Retreat to Pleasure (Shaw, Irwin) 48
Reunion in Vienna (Sherwood, Robert) 55
revolutionary realism 38
Rice, Elmer 34, 35
  American Landscape 35, 55
  Ethiopia 35
  We, the People 238
Rich, Frank 135–6
Richard Boone Show, The (TV show) 212
Rivera, Diego 20, 21
Robbins, Jerome 208
Robbins, Tim 21
  Cradle Will Rock, The 21
Roberts, Kenneth: *Northwest Passage* 17
Robeson, Paul 224
  'Water Boy' 225
Rocket to the Moon (Odets, Clifford) 48, 147, 148, 160, 167–8, 200
Rodgers, Richard 211
Rodgers, Richard/Hart, Lorenz
  'Blue Moon' 23
  I'd Rather Be Right 60–1
Rogers, Ginger 23
Rollyson, Carl: *Lillian Hellman: Her Life and Legend* 234
Roosevelt, Franklin Delano 3
  New Deal 4–6
  radio 26
  social reform 2
Roosevelt and Hopkins: An Intimate History (Sherwood, Robert) 55

Roots of America (Wilson, Charles Morrow) 16
Rose, Billy 209
Rosten, Bevya 219, 220
Rothko, Mark 21
Rothstein, Arthur 21
　Fleeing from a Dust Storm 21
Roughead, William
　Bad Companions 177
　'Closed Doors, or the Great Drumsheugh Case' 177
Rourke, Constance: *American Humor: A Study of the National Character* 16
Rukeyser, Muriel 19
　'Book of the Dead, The' 20
Rushmore, Mount 22
Ruth, Babe 10
Ryan, Katy 125

'S. N. Behrman: The Quandary of the Comic Spirit' (Kaplan, Charles) 67
Sacre du Printemps, Le (Stravinsky, Igor) 90
Safeway 6
Sailors of Catarro (Wolf, Friedrich) 41
St. Louis Woman (Bontemps, Arna/Cullen, Countee)
Salon, The (Bertozzi, Nick) 204
Salon de Fleurs project 119–20
Sanders, Leslie Catherine 140
Santa Fe Opera 202
Sardou, Victorien 179
Saroyan, William 34–5
　My Heart's in the Highlands 48, 77–8
　Time of Your Life, The 35, 56, 78–9
satire 68
Sawyer, Wilbur A. 12
Scarface (film) 26

Scarlet Sister Barry (Hughes, Langston) 142
Schmidman, Jo Ann 195
Schultz, Laura 197
Schultz, Michael 135
science and technology 11–13
Scottsboro Boys case 3, 42, 124
Scottsboro Limited: Four Poems and a Play in Verse (Hughes, Langston) 19–20, 124–5, 205
Scoundrel Time (Hellman, Lillian) 172–3, 217
Scribe, Eugène 179
Seabiscuit 10–11
Searching Wind, The (Hellman, Lillian) 213
Sears, Roebuck 6, 22
Second World War 96–7
Security Administration 15
Selected Poems (Hughes, Langston) 199
Selected Writings of Gertrude Stein, The (Dupree, F. W.) 198
Shadow, The (radio show) 26
Shahn, Ben 21
Shange, Ntozake 196
Shapiro, Hiram 37
Shapiro, Jake 37
Shaw, Irwin 208
　Gentle People, The 48, 54
　Retreat to Pleasure 48
Shearer, Norma 21
Shedd, Sally: 'There is No Keyhole on My Door' 183
Sheeler, Charles 20
Sherwood, Robert E. 34, 55
　Abe Lincoln in Illinois 31, 54, 55, 56–7
　Idiot's Delight 34, 55, 56
　Petrified Forest, The 56
　Playwrights Producing Company Inc. 54–5

Reunion in Vienna 55
Roosevelt and Hopkins: An Intimate History 55
Second World War 57
Shipman, Charles see Gomez, Manuel
Shlaes, Amity: Forgotten Man, The 243 n.8
Sidney, Sylvia 213
Sifton, Claire/Sifton, Paul: 1931–48, 49, 241
signifying 258 n.2
Silent Partner, The (Odets, Clifford) 165
Silver Cord, The (Howard, Sidney) 55
Simple Stakes a Claim (Hughes, Langston) 143
Siqueiros, David 20
SITI Company 195
Six Plays by Clifford Odets (Odets, Clifford) 209
Sklar, George 41
Sklar, George/Maltz, Albert 41
 Merry-Go-Round 41
 Peace on Earth 40, 41–2, 242
Sklar, George/Peters, Paul (Harbor Allen): Stevedore 35–6, 41, 42
Skyloft Players 126
Smalley, Webster 130
Smiley, Sam 32, 33
Smith, Art 153
Smith, Bessie 226
Smith, Clara 224
Snyder, Hartland 13
'So Long, It's Been Good to Know Ya' (Guthrie, Woodie) 23
soap operas 26
social comedies 34
'Social Critiques in Three Prose Plays by Maxwell Anderson: Saturday's Children, Both Your Houses, and The Star-Wagon' (Geary, Fonzie D., II) 59
social drama 33–4
Social History of Indiana, A (Benton, Thomas Hart) 20
social realism 17, 20
social reform 2–3, 8
socialist realism 34
sodium thiopental 12
Sons (Buck, Pearl S.) 18
Soviet Union 125–6
Spaeth, Arthur 141
Spam 7
Spanish Earth, The (film) 27, 174–5
sponsors 25–6
sports and recreation 10–11
Spring Dance (Barry, Philip) 74
Stage Door (Kaufman, George S./Ferber, Edna) 68, 70
'Stage Left: The Struggle of Clifford Odets' (New Yorker article) 209
Staging Gertrude Stein: Absence, Culture, and the Landscape of American Alternative Theatre (Durham, Leslie Atkins) 197
Stand Up and Cheer (film) 27
Stapleton, Jennifer 138
starvation 8
Stein, Gertrude 31, 81, 82–3, 197–8, 201–4
 Adato, Perry Miller 202
 Autobiography of Alice B. Toklas, The 81–2, 90, 95, 220
 Brewsie and Willie 97, 201
 Cage, John 118–19
 Carmines, Al 202, 220
 character construction/deconstruction 115–17

conversation pieces 91–2
Counting Her Dresses. A Play 91
death 204
Doctor Faustus Lights the Lights see *Doctor Faustus Lights the Lights*
Each One As She May 202
early life 83–6
early writing 86–8
Everybody's Autobiography 95, 118
existentialism 117
'Family of Perhaps Three' 203
Faÿ, Bernard 96–7
First World War 91
Four Saints in Three Acts see *Four Saints in Three Acts*
Geographical History of America, Or, The Relation of Human Nature to the Human Mind 95
Geography and Plays 92, 93
Gertrude Stein Symposium 219–21
Gramont, Elisabeth de 97
Hemingway, Ernest 93
history 94
Ida A Novel 96, 108, 111, 201
identity 87, 95–6, 110
Identity A Poem 95–6
'If I Told Him: A Completed Picture of Picasso' 204
impact of 118–19
In Circles 202
In Savoy: or, Yes Is For a Very Young Man 98, 201
Judson Poets' Theater 118
Kornfield, Lawrence 202
Ladies' Voices 91–2
landscape plays 83, 92–3, 105–6

legacy 201–4
Listen To Me 96, 114–18
Living Theatre 112, 118
Making of Americans, The 82, 86–7, 93, 98, 202
Mallorcan plays 91–2
Mexico 91
Mother of Us All, The 98–9, 201, 202
One Carl Van Vechten 90
onstage 119–20
Operas and Plays 94
Orta Or One Dancing 87
Paris France 95, 201
Pétain, Marshal Philippe 97
Play 87
Play, A 91
plays 90, 94, 105–6
'Plays' 90, 101
politics 97, 196–8
portraits 87–8, 90
reception 201–4
'Regular Regularly In Narrative' 103
'Reread Another A Play to Be Played Indoors or Out I Wish to Be a School' 202
saints 92
Saints and Singing 92
Salon de Fleurus project 119–20
Second World War 96–8, 197, 201
Tender Buttons 82, 89–90, 93
Thomson, Virgil 93, 99, 101, 104, 201
Three Lives 86, 93, 198
Three Sisters Who Are Not Sisters 201
Toklas, Alice, B. 81–2, 86, 94
Wars I Have Seen 95, 97–8, 201

What Happened A Five Act Play 89, 99
Wilder, Thornton 106–8, 196
Wooster Group 118
World is Round, The 96, 119
Stein, Leo 84–6
Steinbeck, John 18
  Grapes of Wrath, The 2, 17
  In Dubious Battle 17
  Tortilla Flat 17
Stevedore (Peters, Paul (Harbor Allen)/Sklar, George) 35–6, 41, 42
Stevens, Wallace 19
Stock Market Crash 1–2, 4, 29
  see also Great Depression, the
Stout, Rex 18
'Strange Fruit' (Holliday, Billie) 23
Strasberg, Lee 37, 38, 47,
  Awake and Sing! 158
  Clash by Night 209
  Gentlewoman 52
  Group Theatre 149, 150
  Men in White 52–3
  1931– 49
Stravinsky, Igor: *Sacre du Printemps, Le* 90
stream of consciousness 85
streamline modern 21–2
Strike Up the Band (Gershwin, George/Gershwin, Ira) 68
strikes 14, 43
Stritch, Elaine 217
Styron, William 213
Success Story (Lawson, John Howard) 48, 50–1
sugar 7
Sundquist, Eric 123
supermarkets 6–7
surrealism 77
Sweet Smell of Success (film) 211
swing dance 24

Swortzell, Lowell: *Around the World in 21 Plays: Theatre for Young Audiences* 201
syphilis 12
Szondi, Peter: *Theory of the Modern Drama* 107

table settings 7–8
Target Margin 202–3
Taylor, Elizabeth 200
Teague, Walter Dorwin 22
Teatro Campesino 195
teenagers 8–9
Teflon 13
Temple, Shirley 11, 27
Tender Buttons (Stein, Gertrude) 82, 89–90, 93
Terry, Megan 195, 196
Thalberg, Irving 70
theatre 15, 29–30, 115
  1930s 30–7, 173–4, 195
  agit-prop 36, 38–9, 232
  curtain 182
  financial position 151
  Gorelik, Mordecai 237–42
  labour drama 37–49, 237–42
  lynching dramas 132
  Melodramas 178–9, 181
  national theatre 238–9
  play structure 180
  political drama 33, 36, 39, 59–61
  social drama 33–4
  working class 30, 34, 237–42
Theatre Arts Monthly (magazine) 39
Theatre Collective 37–8, 40, 195, 241
communism 39
Theatre Guild 34, 62
'Theatre is a Weapon' (Gorelik, Mordecai) 39–40, 236–42
Theatre of Action 38

theatre practitioners, overlapping 34
Theatre Union 35–6, 40–5, 195
Their Eyes Were Watching God (Hurston, Zora Neal) 18–19
Theory and Technique of Playwriting (Lawson, John Howard) 50
Theory of the Modern Drama (Szondi, Peter) 107
'There is No Keyhole on My Door' (Shedd, Sally) 183
These Three (film) 177
They Knew What They Wanted (Howard, Sidney) 55
'They Watch Me as They Watch This': Gertrude Stein's Metadrama (Bowers, Jane Palatini) 94, 104–5
They Won't Forget (film) 27
They Shall Not Die (Wexley, John) 242
Thin Man, The (Hammett, Dashiell) 18
Third Parade, The (Peters, Paul/Walker, Charles Rumford) 241
Thomson, Virgil 93, 99, 101, 104, 201
Thompson, Louise 126, 127
Three (Hellman, Lillian) 172, 217
Three Lives (Stein, Gertrude) 86, 93, 198
Three Sisters, The (Chekhov, Anton) 216
Three Sisters Who Are Not Sisters (Stein, Gertrude) 201
Three Songs (Cage, John) 118
thriftiness 6
Thunder Rock (Ardrey, Robert) 48, 53–4
Thurman, Wallace/Rapp, William Jordan: *Harlem* 140

Till the Day I Die (Odets, Clifford) 48
Tillich, Paul 220
Time of Your Life, The (Saroyan, William) 35, 56, 78–9
Timebends: A Life (Miller, Arthur) 196
Titus, Mary 183
To Make My Bread (Lumpkin, Grace) 17, 41, 43
Tobacco Road (Caldwell, Erskine) 17, 75
Tobacco Road (Kirkland, Jack) 75–7
Toklas, Alice B. 81–2, 86, 94, 96–7
Tomorrow and Tomorrow (Barry, Philip) 74
Tone, Franchot 50, 150
Toomer, Jean 226
  Cane 224
Tortilla Flat (Steinbeck, John) 17
Toscanini, Arturo 26
toys 11
Toys in the Attic (Hellman, Lillian) 175, 194, 216
trade unions 13–14
'Tragedy and the Common Man' (Miller, Arthur) 196
Tragic America (Dresier, Theodore) 17
'Triangular Politics: Stein, Bernard Faÿ, and Elisabeth de Gramont' (Van Puymbroeck, Birgit) 97
Triple-A Plowed Under (Living Newspaper play) 46–7
Trumbo, Dalton 16
truth serum 12
Tunc, Tanfer 183
Tuskagee Syphilis Experiment 12
Two by Two (musical) 211
Tyler, Royall: *Contrast, The* 59

Tyrwhitt–Wilson, Gerald Hugh
see Berners, Lord

U. S. News & World Report
(magazine) 24
Understanding Poetry (Brooks,
Cleanth/Warren, Robert
Penn) 19
unemployment 2, 5, 6
unions 13–14
United Action 27
Unfinished Woman, An (Hellman,
Lillian) 172, 217
Unlawful Assembly, Union Square
(Laning, Edward) 21
US Treasury's Section of Painting
and Sculpture 15
utilities 47

vaccination 12
Vallee, Rudy 26
Valley Forge (Anderson, Maxwell)
58
Van Puymbroeck, Birgit:
'Triangular Politics: Stein,
Bernard Faÿ, and Elisabeth
de Gramont' 97
Van Vechten, Carl 21, 90, 139,
198
Vavrek, Royce/Gordon, Ricky
Ian): 27 (opera) 204
veterans 3
Vidal, Gore 208
Vitamin C 12
Vitamin E 12
Vogel, Arthur: Young Go First,
The 38
Volkoff, George 13

Waiting for Lefty (Odets,
Clifford) 6, 32, 147, 153–7,
195–6, 200
House Un-American Activities

Committee testimony
228–30, 232–3
structure 36, 49
success 48
'Waiting on Roosevelt' (Hughes,
Langston) 20
Waldorf-Astoria Hotel 8
Walker, Alice 206
Walker, Charles Rumford 40
Walker, Charles Rumford/Peters,
Paul: Third Parade, The
241
Wall Street Crash 1–2, 4, 29
War of the Worlds 25
Warren, Robert Penn/Brooks,
Cleanth: Understanding
Poetry 19
Wars I Have Seen (Stein,
Gertrude) 95, 97–8, 201
Washington Masquerade (film)
27
Washington Merry-Go-Round
(film) 27
Washington Square Players 30
Watch on the Rhine (Hellman,
Lillian) 172, 182, 192, 213,
235
'Water Boy' (Robeson, Paul) 225
Watson, Steven: Prepare for
Saints – Gertrude Stein,
Virgil Thomson and the
Mainstreaming of American
Modernism 82
Way Down South (Muse,
Clarence/Hughes, Langston)
142–3
We, the People (Rice, Elmer) 238
wealth 8, 11
weddings 8
Weep for the Virgins (Child,
Nellise) 48, 53
Weill, Kurt 48, 53
Weill, Kurt/Anderson, Maxwell:

Knickerbocker Holiday
54–5
Well-Made Plays 178–83
Welles, Orson 25
  Cradle Will Rock, The 47
  Macbeth 47
Wellman, Mac 203, 219, 220
West, Don 43
West, Nathanael 17
western films 27–8
Wexley, John: *They Shall Not Die* 242
Wharton, John: *Life Among the Playwrights* 55, 57–8
What Happened A Five Act Play (Stein, Gertrude) 89, 99
What Price Glory (Anderson, Maxwell) 58
'What the Negro Wants' (Hughes, Langston) 143
Whipple, George H. 12
Whitaker, Forest 206
White Angel Breadline, The (Lange, Dorothea) 21
White Cargo: A Play of the Primitive (Gordon, Leon) 128
Wiggins, Ella Mae 43
Wilder, Laura Ingalls 18
  Little House on the Prairie, The 18
Wilder, Thornton 196
  Long Christmas Dinner, The 107–8
  Our Town 107
  Stein, Gertrude 106–8, 196
Wiles, Timothy J.: 'Lillian Hellman's Political Theater: The Thirties and Beyond' 185
Williams, Tennessee 185, 189
Willinger, Lazlo 21
Wilson, August 206

Piano Lesson, The 179
Wilson, Charles Morrow: *Roots of America* 16
Wilson, Edmund 16, 40
  American Jitters 17
Wilson, Edmund/Cowley, Malcolm/Hughes, Langston: *Culture in Crisis* 3
Wilson, Robert 112, 117, 118
  Doctor Faustus Lights the Lights 112, 113, 202
  Four Saints in Three Acts 113
Winterset (Anderson, Maxwell) 58
Wirth, Andrzej 106, 107, 114–15, 116–17
Wizard of Oz, The (film) 27
WLT *see* Workers Laboratory Theatre
Wolf, Friedrich: *Sailors of Catarro* 41
Wolfson, Victor: *Bitter Stream* 41
Wollcott, Alexander 73
women 36 *see also* feminism
Women, The (Luce, Clare Booth) 213
Wonderbread 7
Woods, Grant: *Daughters of the Revolution* 20
Woolf, George 11
Wooster Group 118, 195
  House/Lights 112–14, 202
Workers Laboratory Theatre (WLT) 37, 38–9, 240, 241
Workers Theatre (periodical) 39
workers' theatre movement 237–42
working class 13–14 *see also* labour drama
  Can You Hear Their Voices? A Play of Our Time (Flanagan, Hallie/Clifford, Margaret) 36
  film 27

theatre 30, 34, 237–42
Works Progress Administration (WPA) 5, 9, 14–15
World is Round, The (Stein, Gertrude) 96, 119
WPA *see* Works Progress Administration
Wright, Frank Lloyd 22
Wright, Richard 19
Native Son 19
Wright, Russel 22
Wright, William 217
Wyler, William 177

yellow fever 12
You Can't Take it With You (Kaufman, George S./Hart, Moss) 32, 35, 68, 71–2
You Have Seen Their Faces (Bourke-White, Margaret) 21
Young, Nancy K./Young, William, A. 22
American Popular Culture through History 8
Young, Robert 213
Young, William A./Young, Nancy K. 22
American Popular Culture through History 8
Young Go First, The (Martin, Peter/Scudder, George [Arthur Vogel]/Friedman, Charles 38
You're Next (Miller, Arthur) 195
youth 8–10

www.ingramcontent.com/pod-product-compliance
Lightning Source LLC
Chambersburg PA
CBHW070014010526
44117CB00011B/1561